PLANNING FACILITIES for ATHLETICS PHYSICAL EDUCATION and RECREATION

REVISED 1985

The Athletic Institute
200 Castlewood Drive
North Palm Beach, FL 33408
and

American Alliance for Health
Physical Education, Recreation, and Dance
1900 Association Drive
Reston, Virginia 22091

Copyright © 1985
The Athletic Institute and
American Alliance for Health, Physical Education,
Recreation, and Dance.

Printed in the United States of America

Library of Congress Catalog Card Number 84-72630
ISBN 0-87670-095-4

790.068
P712

FOREWORD

At the meeting of the Board of Directors of the American Alliance for Health, Physical Education and Recreation in Washington, D.C., in April, 1945, favorable action was taken on a proposal by Caswell M. Miles, AAHPERD Vice-President for Recreation, that a grant be obtained to finance a national conference on facilities. Subsequently, a request for $10,000 to finance the first facilities workshop was placed before Theodore P. Bank, president of The Athletic Institute. At a later meeting of the Board of Directors of The Athletic Institute, the project was approved and the money appropriated to finance the first workshop.

Thirty-eight years have elapsed since the printing of the first **Guide** which resulted from the first workshop at Jackson's Mill, West Virginia, in December, 1946. Since then there have been 14 printings of the **Guide.**

The second workshop was held May 5-12, 1956, at the Kellogg Center for Continuing Education at Michigan State University in East Lansing. The second workshop, like the first, was financed by The Athletic Institute. The 1956 edition of the **Guide,** which resulted from the second workshop, has been widely used in planning and constructing facilities.

The 1963 edition was prepared by the third workshop, which was financed jointly by the AAHPER and The Athletic Institute and was held January 15-24, 1965, at the Biddle Continuing Education Center, Indiana University in Bloomington.

Two years later, April 29-May 8, 1967, another workshop was held at Indiana University. Among those invited were a number of outstanding college and technical personnel engaged in planning and conducting programs of athletics, recreation, outdoor education, and physical and health education. In addition, invitations were extended to a number of specialists responsible for planning and constructing facilities for these programs. These specialists included city planners, architects, landscape architects, engineers and schoolhouse construction consultants.

At the 1974 facilities committee meeting, five members were assigned the task of restructuring the **Guide** in such a way that it would serve as a more practical tool for school administrators, physical education department heads, architects, planning consultants and all others interested in planning new areas and facilities or checking the adequacy of those already in use.

During recent years, there have been many new developments in facility planning and construction. These have been due to a number of factors. The need for improving education, recreation and fitness opportunities for the youth of the nation has been highlighted by many groups. The fine work of the President's Council on Physical Fitness is one illustration of the growing national interest in health, physical education and recreation activities. Much of the research and attention devoted to facility planning and construction during the past three decades has been due to the increased leisure time in our society and a growing realization that recreation and especially physical activity, is a fundamental human need essential to the well-being of all people.

The Athletic Institute and AAHPERD Council on Facilities, Equipment, and Supplies initiated the 1979 revision of the **Guide** following a careful review of the 1974 edition. A blue ribbon Steering Committee was appointed and Edward Coates of Ohio State University, and Richard B. Flynn of the University of Nebraska at Omaha, were selected as co-editors and contributing authors. Professionals well known for their expertise in facility planning and construction were invited to assist in a complete rewrite.

This, the 1984 edition of **Planning Facilities for Athletics, Physical Education, and Recreation** represents a continuing effort on the part of The Athletic Institute and AAHPERD to keep the text current and relevant. Richard B. Flynn of the University of Nebraska at Omaha, was selected to be editor and contributing author. Flynn, recognized as one of the leading authorities in planning facilities for athletics, physical education, and recreation, has contributed to the planning of facilities for schools, colleges, municipalities, industry, military, and private clubs. Chapter input was solicited from carefully chosen leaders in the field as well as from outstanding architects. Efforts were made to incorporate the most recent advances in facility planning and construction. Certain program areas, such as planning for the handicapped, were expanded while outdated or irrelevant materials were deleted.

Since, over the years, so many professionals have contributed to this book, it does not represent any one person's or organization's viewpoint. It does represent the composite knowledge of many experts. AAHPERD and The Athletic Institute are grateful to all who contributed to past editions and especially those who participated in the latest revision (see page iv).

Jack E. Razor, Executive Vice President
American Alliance for Health, Physical Education,
Recreation, and Dance

Dustin Cole, Executive Director
The Athletic Institute

ACKNOWLEDGEMENTS

We are indebted to the following authoritative sources for permission to reproduce material used in this edition of PLANNING FACILITIES FOR ATHLETICS, PHYSICAL EDUCATION, AND RECREATION:

The Council of Educational Facility Planners, International, for permission to reprint material from the "State Requirements Survey for School Construction K-12, 1981", prepared by the Committee on Architecture for Education.

The Department of the Army for permission to use various line drawings in the chapter on "Outdoor Facilities."

The National Swimming Pool Foundation, for permission to reproduce drawings from its **1983 Design Compendium.**

The National Collegiate Athletic Association for permission to reproduce specifications from selected 1984 NCAA rule books. It is understood that these specifications are subject to annual review and change.

The CNGA, for permission to reproduce drawings from **Swimming Pools — A Guide to Their Planning, Design and Operation.**

The Federation Internationale De Natation Amateur, for permission to reprint its swimming rules.

National Spa & Pool Institute, for use of its 1983 Swimming Pool and Spa Industry Survey.

Major Contributors: Margaret Aitken, Western Washington University; Edsel Buchanan, University of Nebraska at Omaha; Gerald P. Carlson, University of Southwest Louisiana; Michael Crawford, University of Nebraska at Omaha; Richard Fleishman, Richard Fleishman Architects, Inc.; Milt Gabrielson, Nova University; Claude E. Rogers, Leisure Concepts and Design.

Special thanks are extended to two of these individuals:
Dr. Milton Gabrielson, for a complete rewrite of Chapter IV: "Indoor and Outdoor Swimming Pools."

Dr. Michael Crawford, for a complete rewrite of Chapter VIII: "Planning for the Handicapped."

Other Contributors: Milton Costello, P.E.; Joe Crookham, Musco Mobile Lighting Co.; Dan E. Gruetter, University of Alabama; Armond H. Seidler, University of New Mexico; Todd Seidler, University of New Mexico.

Contributors of illustrations, charts, and/or facility profiles included in the Appendices and/or used in the text:

Architects: Aquatic Consultants, Inc.; The Architects' Collaborative Inc.; CSHQA Architects/Planners; Curtis and Davis Architects; DAF INDAL Ltd.; Richard Dattner Architects; Davis, Brody and Associates; The Eggers Group P.C.; Fanning/Howey Associates Inc.; Graham/Meus, Inc.; Harry Green Associates Ltd.; Hastings and Chivetta; Heery-Fabrap; Holabird and Root; Hoskins, Scott, Taylor and Partners Inc.; IBG International; Lamp, Rynearson and Associates; The Loaring Group Inc.; Mott, Mobley, McGowan and Griffin, P.A.; Herbert S. Newman Associates, AIA, P.C.; Pfoller Herbst Associates, Inc.; Schaefer and Associates P.A.; Skidmore, Owings, and Merrill; Daniel F. Tully Associates Inc.

Others: Astro-Ice, Skate USA; **Athletic Business** (formerly **Athletic Purchasing and Facilities**); Bowling Green State University; Duragrid Inc.; Emory University; David Griner, The Ohio State University; Hope College; Indiana University-Purdue University at Indianapolis; **The Journal of Physical Education, Recreation, and Dance;** Lake Forest School District; Loyola University of Chicago; Lyon Metal Products Inc.; Monsanto Corp.; National Parks Service; Texas Tech University; U.S. Air Force Academy; U.S. Naval Academy; the University of Arkansas; the University of Florida; the University of Nebraska at Omaha; the University of Rochester; Westroads Racquet Club, Omaha, Nebraska; the YMCA Association of Metropolitan Milwaukee, Inc., North Surburban Branch.

Special appreciation is also extended to the editorial team and contributors who cooperated in the preparation of the 1979 edition. These individuals are noted on page iv. of the 1979 text edition.

Lastly, the editor would like to thank Ray Ciszek of the American Alliance of Health, Physical Education, Recreation, and Dance, and Frank Maradie of The Athletic Institute, for their ongoing encouragement and support during all phases of preparation of the 1985 edition of **Planning Facilities for Athletics, Physical Education and Recreation.**

Richard B. Flynn, Ed. D.
Editor and Contributing Author

TABLE OF CONTENTS

TABLE OF ILLUSTRATIONS

Football Rules
Ice Hockey Rules
LaCrosse Rules
Men's Basketball Rules
Men's Water Polo Rules
Men's and Women's Swimming and Diving Rules
Volleyball Court Rules
Wrestling Rules

Reprinted by permission of the National Collegiate Athletic Association from the 1984 Rules. Specifications subject to annual review and change.

CHAPTER I

The Planning Process

What is Planning?

Planning is the process by which people determine how to proceed from their present situation to a desired future situation. In some fashion, the planning process involves recognizing needs, then searching for and selecting the appropriate means to fulfill those needs. Planners develop detailed understanding of needs based on current conditions and projections of future needs. Searching for and selecting means are conditioned by available technical knowledge, resources, and other limiting factors. Attention to execution of plans is important also. Finally, review of a plan's execution determines whether the plan has succeeded in fulfilling needs or whether it is necessary to plan again.

Planning is an interactive process which recurs at different levels of detail and breadth of scope. For example, one plans the broad characteristics of a facility, down to the exact location of electrical outlets.

Participation of those affected is a key feature of a successful planning process. Participation provides much needed information and a greater acceptance of a plan and its results. Participants in a planning process should include such persons as program specialists, administrators, clientele groups, and representatives from policy-making bodies.

The Need for Planning

Today, we face a rapidly changing environment. The interplay of social, political, economic and technological forces affects all institutions. Scarcity of resources in the face of ever-increasing demands, and spiraling costs, have had a dire effect on institutional budgets. Education has been affected by these trends which have ushered in "the age of accountability," requiring justification of expenditures both for existing and new programs and facilities. Educators and other planners must face this reality.

Education claims a large piece of the tax dollar. Perhaps the costliest of all education services and facilities are those related to physical education, recreation, and athletics. It is not unusual for 25 to 50 percent of the total construction cost of any new high school to be spent on the physical education plant. An Educational Facilities Laboratory report provides a further analysis of costs, indicating that the average enclosed heated area at the high school level devoted 22% to physical education facilities and 15% of the school building dollars are invested in physical education.

Obviously, the need for sound planning and justification of physical education, recreation, and athletic facilities is imperative. Such facilities may limit, enhance, or expand the educational programs they house. The quality of the facilities depends upon the thoroughness and vision of the original planning activities. If facilities for physical education, recreation and athletics are to be justified economically, then time, effort and money must be invested in planning. The end result will be the provision of better facilities at less cost for broader participation by program users.

BASIC CONSIDERATIONS

Before considering the planning of areas and facilities essential for athletics, physical education, and recreation, it is important to understand their basic aims and objectives.

Athletics and Physical Education

The aim of athletics and physical education is to help people live healthy, satisfying, and energetic lives by developing and maintaining optimum physical efficiency, by developing useful knowledge and physical skills, by acting in socially useful ways and by enjoying wholesome physical recreation.

Physical education is the science and skill of movement. All types of sports and activities are used to develop the strength, endurance and coordination essential in both work and play. Through activities, youths and adults are taught the physical skills needed for performing daily work, conditioned through exercise and sports for the maintenance of mental and physical health, and taught the skills that form a part of leisure pursuits.

A school activities program includes participation in appropriate activities for all pupils, a wide variety of intramural activities, and, at the secondary school level, a broad program of interscholastic athletics for those of above average athletic ability and interests.

Recreation

The primary function of recreation is the enrichment of living by enabling individuals to find adventure, fellowship, a sense of accomplishment, the enjoyment of beauty, and the joy of creating, all of which contribute to human happiness. Through recreational programs, people develop interests and skills that enable them to make constructive use of leisure, contributing to proper physical and mental health, safety, good citizenship, confidence and character development.

Recreational activities include games and sports, music, dance, arts and crafts, drama, social activities, nature and outing activities, hobbies, and service projects. The comprehensive recreational program affords people of all ages, backgrounds, and interests the opportunity to engage in a variety of activities. Trained leadership and desirable conditions assure enjoyment and benefits.

GUIDING PRINCIPLES

Overall Principles

All efforts in planning should proceed on the basis of sound guiding principles, as follows:
- Physical education/ recreation/athletic (PERA) facilities should be developed and coordinated as a part of the total school master plan.
- Facility design must take into consideration the long-range future needs for the building and be planned as a functional segment of the total anticipated building.
- Physical education and athletic personnel should be involved in the early planning.
- Educational consultants should be invited to participate in the planning and to evaluate the work of the planning group.
- The facilities should be designed for flexibility in order to provide for a full program of activities.
- Facilities should be located in areas that are easily available to students, but provide isolation from other instruction.
- Safety and healthful environment should be given prime consideration in facility design.
- Planning must be realistic in the light of the financial situation of the community.

The above list is hardly complete. Each institution must determine those guiding principles that best fit its own situation.

It should also be noted that success or failure in the construction of facilities is the direct result of planning. Mistakes in construction are costly, and can handicap programs for which the facility was designed. Because of new and changing programs, the building needs of institutions are often not satisfied in the original construction phase. Long-range planning is imperative to facilitate the expansion of facilities in the

most efficient and economical way in meeting changing needs. Educational and recreational agencies should have *master plans* which are regularly evaluated and reorganized to meet needs of the present and the future.

Many people do not understand the need for large expenditures in physical education. As a result, funds may not be readily approved for expensive facilities and equipment. Physical educators must demonstrate the need through careful planning, and present a well-organized plan for proposed facilities in justifying the needs of the program.

Without long-range planning, buildings become outdated before their 40-50 year life expectancy. Long range planning should include the following considerations:

1. A copy of the master plan for future expansion.
2. Data related to developmental trends in the community (including demographic and other sociological data).
3. The current master plan for future development of the community.
4. A topographical map of the area surrounding the community.
5. Detailed information concerning property adjoining a school that might be available for acquisition.
6. Folders of clippings, pictures and detailed drawings of other facilities that relate to future needs.
7. An annotated bibliography of up-to-date references relating to physical education facilities.
8. A cumulative list of common errors of design and construction with details of where they can be seen and studied.
9. Blueprints of all existing outdoor and indoor facilities.
10. Accurate information related to length of seasons, rainfall, temperature range, winds, soil composition and drainage.
11. Information relative to various means and sources of

raising money.

12. Sources of planning aids for facility development.

Long-range planning requires much time spent in the searching, evaluation, and coordination of information and ideas. Specialists in the field of health, physical education, recreation, and athletics should serve as consultants and be involved in the long-range planning of their programs and facilities. Program specialists must be included on the long-range planning team.

Renovation/Construction Principles

The institutional administration has the responsibility of making the wisest use of existing school buildings. In meeting this obligation, it is necessary to consider the feasibility of renovation and retrofit of existing buildings. Renovation is defined as the rehabilitation of an existing building including the rearrangement of spaces within the building. Retrofit is the addition of new systems, items, features, materials, and equipment to a facility not available at the time of construction.

Four factors must be considered in evaluating the feasibility of renovation and/or retrofit:

1. Adequacy of the site.
2. Architectural and structural adequacy of the building.
3. Meeting present and future educational requirements.
4. The estimated cost compared to the cost of a new facility.

Each of these factors must be evaluated in detail both individually and collectively. A final decision should be based on careful analysis of all the factors rather than on any one or two. Also, it would be helpful if some realistic determination of the expected life of the facility could be determined. Variables affecting this question would include enrollment projections, growth and development patterns of areas surrounding the facility, and the potential reorganization or consolidation of schools in the district. An objective and professional assessment of whether to renovate an existing building is necessary for the school board to make a good decision. The board should obtain the services of an architect and an engineer to determine the structural soundness of the building and to consider the matters of fire, fire safety, planning redesign potential, and probable cost. The Professional School Planner should work closely with the architect in matter of educational adequacy.

The following questions are examples of the kinds of questions to be answered in developing a data base for board considerations:

1. **Site Considerations**
   a. What is the general condition of the grounds and the location in relation to the student population?
   b. Are there sufficient play areas?
   c. Are there provisions for adequate on-site parking?
   d. Are vehicular drives well located for safe ingress and egress?
   e. Are the existing utilities on or near the site adequate to provide the needed services?

2. **Architectural and Structural Considerations**
   a. Are there signs of deterioration of footings, foundations, or piers?
   b. Are structural members adequate and in serviceable condition?
   c. Is exterior masonry sound? Are there structural cracks, water damage, or defective mortar?
   d. What is the condition of the roof and roofing surfaces, roof drains, and skylights?
   e. What is the condition of flashing, gutters, and downspouts?
   f. What is the condition of doors and windows?
   g. What is the condition of door hardware and panic devices?
   h. What are the location, number, type, and condition of plumbing fixtures?
   i. What is the condition and capacity of the present water supply, sewage lines, and drainage systems?
   j. Is the present HVAC system adequate and energy-efficient?
   k. What is the condition and adequacy of lighting and power distribution systems?
   l. Do the existing light fixtures provide adequate illumination in all areas?
   m. Are stairways, circulation patterns and exits adequate?
   n. What is the present condition of fire alarms and intercommunication systems?

3. **Educational Considerations**
   a. Is the building now meeting the needs of the curriculum?
   b. What is the current inventory of rooms and their sizes?
   c. Are laboratories adequately served by required utilities?
   d. Is the library adequate to house the required book collection and to provide media and related services?
   e. Are food service facilities adequate to meet present and projected needs?
   f. Are physical education areas usable or capable of being retrofitted if required?

4. Community Considerations
   a. Will the renovation of the building be consistent with present zoning requirements or policies?
   b. What are the plans for the area served by the school as projected by city or area planning agencies?
   c. Is the school building on or eligible for placement on the register of historic buildings?

5. Estimated Cost
   a. What is the cost of construction needed to bring the facility up to present-day standards?
   b. What is the cost of new construction to provide comparable space?
   c. Will the increased cost of maintaining an older building justify renovation instead of constructing a new facility?
   d. Could the existing facility be sold or leased to a private entity to help defray the cost of new construction?
   e. If the amount of construction time becomes critical, which method could be completed in the least amount of time, renovation or new construction?

PLANNING FACILITIES

Community Involvement and Interagency Cooperation

Traditional methods for planning recreational and physical education facilities have caused agencies to operate independently of one another. This isolation has resulted in public agencies being accused of duplicating facilities and programs, and frittering away community resources.

Traditional planning has often meant statistical planning or hardline planning. Decisions have resulted from taking given sets of data and projecting the program and facility needs. Other types of planning are "political" planning and "grass roots" planning. The former is a decision-making method used to influence certain segments of the population. The latter frequently evolves from negotiations with these segments for certain programs and services. These are giving way to new methods of participatory planning.

Whether elected officials, administrators, representatives from other agencies, community members, students, program participants or taxpayers, all must be concerned with the well-being of the community. Further, each has much to offer to a planning process which can result in the development of programs and facilities which are needed, desired, and supported. Figure 1 identifies the many participants included in planning a school facility.

Whether planning for a university physical education complex or for a rural community center, the needs and desires of those who are to be served, those who serve, and those who must provide financial support for the project, are of utmost importance. The following considerations must be observed:

- Improved coordination and delivery of services.
- Improved opinions toward public institutions.
- Facilities which reflect the needs and desires of the community.
- Accountability-efficiency

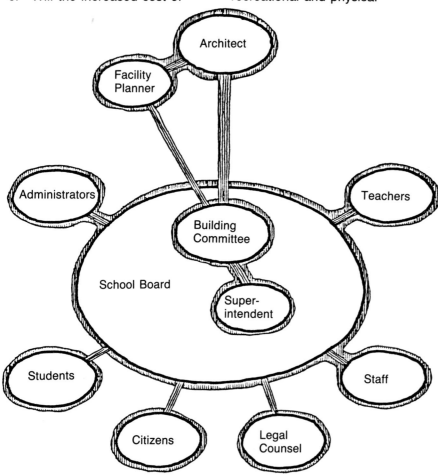

Figure 1-1
Participants included in the Planning Process

The Planning Process

One method in which the above can be accomplished is through participatory planning. The steps in conducting a participatory planning process are listed below:

1. Develop a steering committee that includes inter-agency representatives of elected officials, administrators, community representatives, and other pertinent individuals. This group should be diversified to insure representation of as many segments and opinions of the community as possible.

2. Develop procedures for identifying the needs and desires of the community, as well as what the community is willing to support. Preferably, this is done by the steering committee.

3. Develop a data base of demographic, programmatic, facility, financial, and other related information. Most communities have three or four planning departments from which data can be obtained.

4. Compare survey results and statistical information to determine program and facility priorities.

5. Conduct public hearing(s) to obtain community input to supple-ment needs assessment results.

6. Develop a series of task forces in each of the major priority areas. The task force should be chaired by a community member, and agency representatives should be assigned to the appropriate task force. Each task force is to examine the ramifications of each priority area.

7. The steering committee, after weighing the task force recommendations, should develop alternative solutions for meeting the needs and desires of the community.

8. Each task force reports its findings. The steering committee reports the alternative solutions based on the recommendations of the task force. The meeting concludes with the identification of the preferred alternatives.

9. Preferred alternatives are submitted to policy boards of public agencies for approval. If changes are made, or there are other limiting factors which were not anticipated, repeat the last two steps.

The advantages of participatory planning includes:

• Elected officials, administrators, citizens and others work together for the development of common goals.
• Citizen involvement from beginning to end.
• Hard-line statistical information used to its maximum benefit.
• Input *into* decision-making, rather than reaction *to* decisions made.
• The possibility of duplication of services, programs and facilities is limited.
• Maximum use of community resources and other potential funding sources is provided.
• Communities and agencies work in cooperation rather than in isolation.
• Improved communication is achieved between groups and total community.
• Increased understanding of the needs and desires of the community and increased community understanding of public institutions results.

Figure 1-2

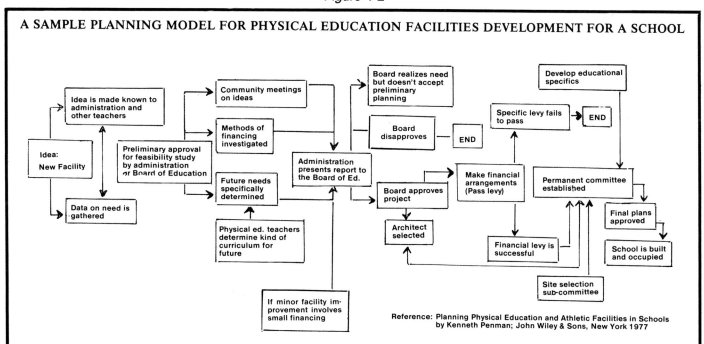

A SAMPLE PLANNING MODEL FOR PHYSICAL EDUCATION FACILITIES DEVELOPMENT FOR A SCHOOL

Reference: Planning Physical Education and Athletic Facilities in Schools by Kenneth Penman; John Wiley & Sons, New York 1977

- Improved support, credibility, and understanding is achieved.

PLANNING STAGES

The planning committee must be able to demonstrate the need for a proposed facility. Much of the preliminary data should already have been gathered by the long-range planning committee.

Figure 1-2 offers one example of an interesting planning model. It includes the various stages required for planning any new facility, such as a public high school. While some appropriate modifications would be necessary for a college or recreation agency, the diagram provides important and useful insights as to the complexities involved in the planning stages. The boxes with heavy lines indicate those stages in which it is particularly important for physical educators to become involved.

Aims and Objectives

A planning committee must realize that it is *curriculum and related programs which dictate the planning of facilities.* Therefore, all facilities should be justified in

relation to the educational objectives. Four specific objectives have been endorsed by the American Alliance for Health, Physical Education, Recreation and Dance for its programs:
- To develop and maintain maximum physical efficiency.
- To develop useful knowledge and physical skills.
- To act in socially useful ways.
- To enjoy wholesome physical recreation.

Specific Factors to be Considered in the Planning Process

A number of specific factors which have significantly influenced and altered concepts of facility planning, development, and construction must be considered in new physical education facilities. These include:
- Enrollment trends.
- District consolidations of schools.
- Present and proposed programs.
- Innovative methods of instruction.
- Soaring construction costs.

- New systems approaches to building.
- Development of new construction materials.
- Health needs of participants.

Steps in the Planning Process

Aside from costs, perhaps the most significant variable in establishing the need for facilities is the philosophy that shapes the form of each community's education. Facilities must be compatible with that philosophy. The planning committee must seek answers to questions such as: Is it a traditional system, or does it encourage experimentation? Are the schools run independently of other public agencies or is cooperation encouraged? Is the community able to pay for quality education? Is there general support for sports programs? Figure 1-3 displays the steps in the planning process.

Answers to these and many other questions can help predetermine what can be expected for a program and facility. A district-wide survey is the initial step for the planning committee, and can serve as an important source of essential data in providing answers (Figure 1-4). It will also provide other important information such as attitudes, interests, desired curriculum, and projected enrollments. Survey committees should include several members of the physical education or recreation staffs. Once the survey is completed, the planning committee can proceed with appropriate action, including assignment of program specialists to specific subcommittees.

Educational Planning

This phase requires the specific, detailed cooperation and contributions of the physical education and athletics staff. Educational planning is characterized by four distinct

Figure 1-3

THE PLANNING PROCESS

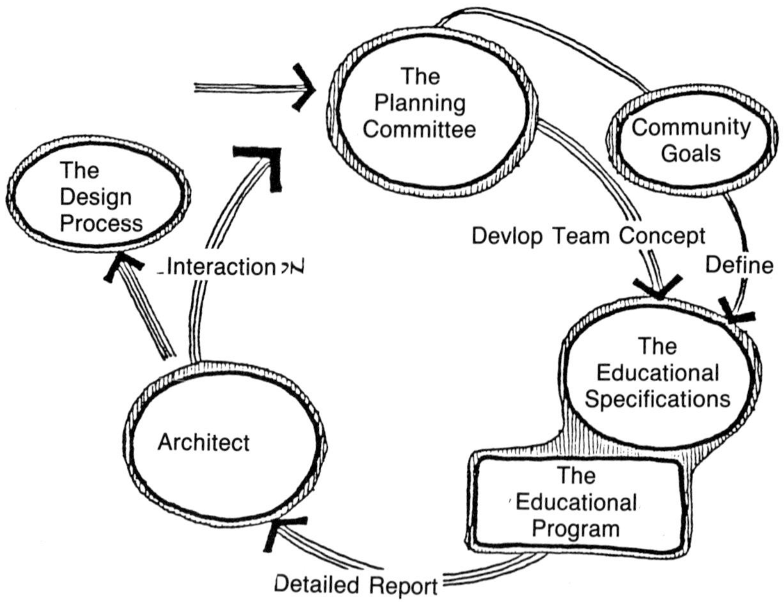

elements of responsibility:

- *Establish the details of the curriculum and specific activities for the various program needs, including instructional areas, clubs, intramurals, and athletics.*
- *Calculate the number of teaching stations needed, considering enrollment, requirements, and other factors.*
- *Develop room and other space specifications (considering such factors as locations, locker facilities, storage, services, size and shapes).*
- *Compile the Educational Specifications (EdSpecs). This is the final phase, and will require the cooperative efforts of all the sub-committee program specialists. EdSpecs are prepared for the architect as a guide. (Figure 1-5) These are essential to describing the learning activities that will occur, the numbers, groupings, and nature of the people involved; the space relationships, the interrelationships of instructional programs; major items of furniture and equipment; minimum and standard dimensions and markings; and any special environmental provisions required for learning and efficiency.*

SURVEY AND EVALUATION OF EXISTING FACILITIES

Educators must ensure that physical education and athletic facilities adequately support the curriculum and the enrollment load of their institutions.

The initial step is to survey existing facility spaces, areas and features concerning their number, size, composition, and location. The data should be compared to accepted standards. This

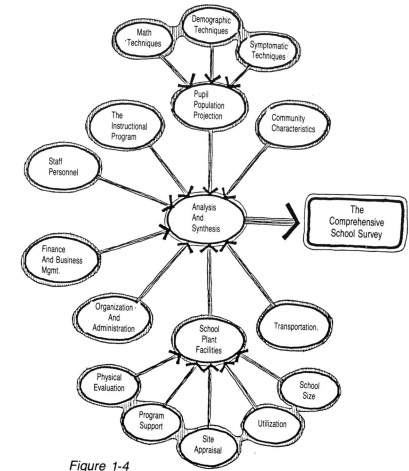

Figure 1-4
Example of a comprehensive school survey.

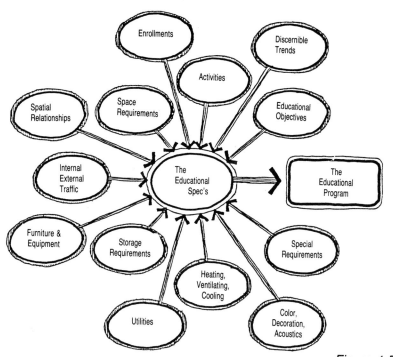

Figure 1-5
Education specifications

The Planning Process

evaluation may reveal inadequacies which need to be rectified. In order for the administration to make a decision to modify existing facilities or to construct new facilities, and to approve the necessary funding, it must be proven conclusively that the improvements are needed. Sound data is required to support and illustrate the case.

The architect, with the assistance of the planning team, should ensure that all planning conforms to state and local requirements and to accepted standards. The standards are meant to be guides, but there may be appropriate deviations due to the local curriculum or situation. The physical education program specialist can be most effective in ensuring that accepted standards are met for both present and projected needs.

The survey and evaluation should be conducted by the most knowledgeable and experienced members of the professional staff, in consultation with the people most directly involved with the use of each space or area. Outside consultants may also be of assistance to ensure the thoroughness of the survey and evaluation. It is recommended that a *Facilities Survey and Evaluation Chart* be used. The sample chart (Figure 1-6) displays the following:

Column (1): List each space or area, with the specific features of that space or area sublisted.

Column (2): Using existing national standards, or in some cases, state standards, compute the size or number which the standard indicates is applicable to the enrollment and curricular situation of the institute being surveyed. List this figure for each corresponding space or area in Column 1. These applied standards should be expressed in two ways in Column 2: for the present program and enrollment, and for the projected program

and enrollment. The standard for walls, ceilings, drains, etc., is usually verbalized (see example). Facility spaces which are recommended by national standards may be listed, even though the institution does not have them. Make notations in subsequent columns to show whether this item is or is not needed. For example, a swimming pool may be recommended but not needed since an adjacent community pool is available. Or a dance room may not exist but the curriculum indicates that a dance room is needed.

Column (3): From the survey, list the data found for each space, area, or feature.

Column (4): Compute the percent of the standard found in the space surveyed. Do this for both the present situation and for the projected future program and enrollment.

Column (5): Compute the percent needed to meet the standard, present and projected.

Column (6): Compute the amount or number needed to meet the standard, both for the present program and enrollment, and for the projected program and enrollment.

Column (7): Conclusions are drawn and marked indicating whether or not the space, area, or sub-feature is adequate now and for future projections:

7.1 Adequate for present program and enrollment.
7.2 Adequate for projected program and enrollment.
7.3 Inadequate for present program and enrollment.
7.4 Inadequate for projected program and enrollment.

Column (8): The Remarks column may be used to record comments concerning the area; to explain

deviations from national standards deemed appropriate due to local situations or curriculum; or to indicate the unacceptability of the national standard if local conditions or experience so warrant.

Space does not permit a complete presentation of a *Facilities Survey and Evaluation Chart* for all areas, spaces, and courts likely to be surveyed, nor to list all the sub-features of them. The example serves as a suitable guide in making up such charts. If a number of schools in a district are to be surveyed and the results compared, a common chart could be developed with code numbers assigned to: (a) each area, space or court; (b) dimensions, square footage or numbers; (c) specific sub-features. Thus the data could be computerized to facilitate handling and comparison.

The *Facilities Survey and Evaluation Chart* may also be used in planning a new facility. The spaces, together with their computed sizes, numbers and features, based on national standards, as applied to the local situation, would be charted in columns (1) and (2). The plans then would be drawn up to incorporate these standards both for the present and for the anticipated programs and enrollment. If the work to be done involves remodeling or adding to an existing facility, a survey and evaluation should be made of the existing facility.

THE TEAM APPROACH TO PLANNING

Depending on the extent and complexity of the project, some form of team planning will be needed at each stage. It is seldom that the best results ever evolve from a one-person planning operation. The various steps outlined below would be appropriate for any facility project.

The Planning Process

Figure 1-6
Facilities Survey and Evaluation Chart

NOW = PRESENT PROGRAM AND ENROLLMENT
FUTURE = PROJECTED PROGRAM AND ENROLLMENT

1	2		3	4		5		6		7				8
SPACE SURVEYED OR SPECIFIC FEATURES WITHIN THE SPACE	NATIONAL STANDARD AS APPLIED TO THE SITUATION SURVEYED		SQ. FT. OR NUMBER WE HAVE	% OF STANDARD WE HAVE		% OF STANDARD WE NEED		AMOUNT OR NUMBER WE NEED TO MEET STANDARD		CONCLUSIONS OUR SPACE IS:				REMARKS
										ADEQUATE		INADEQUATE		
	NOW	FUTURE		NOW	FUTURE	NOW	FUTURE	NOW	FUTURE	NOW	FUT.	NOW	FUT.	
					EXAMPLES									
GIRLS' LOCKER ROOM (1) AREA	a 2400 sq. ft.	3000 sq. ft.	1800 sq. ft.	75%	60%	25%	40%	600 sq. ft.	1200 sq. ft.			✓	✓	
BOYS' SHOWER ROOM (1) SHOWER HEADS	b 33	40	22	67%	55%	33%	45%	11	18			✓	✓	
(2) WALLS	SMOOTH MATERIAL	IMPERVIOUS	TILE	—	—	—	—	—	—	✓				
(3) etc. ADDITIONAL FEATURES														
TENNIS COURTS NUMBER	c 20	25	12	60%	48%	40%	52%	6	13			✓	✓	
(2) FENCING	REAR: 12 FT. HIGH SIDES: 10 FT. HIGH		ALL 12 FT.	—	—	—	—	—	—	✓				
(3) etc. ADDITIONAL FEATURES														
SOFTBALL FIELDS (1) NUMBER	NO PRESENT NATIONAL STANDARD		2	—	—	—	—	—	8	✓			✓	ADDED FUTURE ENROLLMENT
(2) SIZE (EACH)	275' x 275'		EACH 310' x 300'	100%	—	NONE	—	NONE	—	✓				
(3) etc. ADDITIONAL FEATURES														

a NATIONAL STANDARD: 20 SQ. FT. PER STUDENT AT PEAK LOAD
 EXAMPLE: NOW — 120 STUDENTS x 20 SQ. FT. = 2400 SQ. FT.
 FUTURE — 150 STUDENTS x 20 SQ. FT. = 3000 SQ. FT.

b NATIONAL STANDARD: 10 SHOWER HEADS FOR FIRST 30 PEOPLE, ONE
 HEAD FOR EACH ADDITIONAL 4 PEOPLE AT PEAK LOAD
 EXAMPLE: NOW (120 STUDENTS) FOR FIRST 30 = 10 HEADS
 120 − 30 = 90 ÷ 4   = 23 ADDITIONAL HEADS
                       = 33 TOTAL SHOWER HEADS

 FUTURE (150 STUDENTS) FOR FIRST 30 = 10 HEADS
 150 − 30 = 120 ÷ 4   = 30 HEADS
                        = 40 TOTAL SHOWER HEADS

c UNIVERSITY NATIONAL STANDARD: ONE TENNIS COURT PER 400 STUDENTS OF APPLIED STUDENT POPULATION
 EXAMPLE: NOW — 8000 STUDENTS (A.S.P.) = 20 COURTS   FUTURE — 10,000 STUDENTS (A.S.P.) = 25 COURTS
                        400   400

The Planning Process

1. Conceiving the Idea at the Basic Program Level. A particular unit within the whole physical education, recreation, athletics (PERA) area may develop an idea for a new facility or for facility improvement. Before exploring the idea with its parent division, it should first carefully think through the need and feasibility. If the idea is a new swimming pool, unit personnel should be prepared to defend the idea before colleagues, giving the reason for priority over new tennis courts, auxiliary gymnasium, a baseball facility, or other possible facility needs.

Usually, there is a period when a facility need is evident before it actually is planned. During this period, the personnel most directly related to the proposed facility should begin an informal public relations campaign to colleagues who eventually must approve such a proposal.

2. Presenting the Idea to Higher Authority. After the originating personnel have convinced its PERA division that its project should hold the highest priority, a planning team representing the total division should be selected to review the initial proposal and modify, approve, and expand on the various phases of it before presenting it to the higher authority. Quite obviously, representation on the planning team should include personnel from the group that originated the proposal.

In the meantime, long before submitting a finished proposal to a higher authority, an unofficial awareness and enlightening program can begin with higher administrative personnel. This can consist of informal "dropping of ideas," or forwarding copies of related materials. The PERA division should be alert to any higher authority who might be sympathetic to the project.

3. Cooperative Effort to Prepare Proposal to Highest Authority. Some colleges/

universities, school systems, and recreation departments can be quite complex while others are relatively simple. In some situations, Step 2 may be the final step in gaining approval. Often there is an intervening step which requires an overall planning committee or board to evaluate a proposal. If this group looks favorably on a PERA project, one of two actions usually results. It may be that the PERA project committee is allowed to present its facility proposal for final approval.

If, on the other hand, the overall planning committee is expected to make a presentation, this committee needs to include personnel from the PERA committee in order to ensure making the best possible presentation. In the latter case, the presentation needs to be well-integrated, showing the highest priority of the project, not only when compared with other PERA projects, but more importantly, when compared with other projects in the system.

Consulting firms offer special services in educational planning. These services can be comprehensive or of a specific nature, depending on the client. Some institutions employ such firms to assist in their more complicated development plans.

4. Establishing a Public Relations Team. Steps 4 and 5 can be started simultaneously if the project is to be presented to the public for approval. The Steering Committee should have the single responsibility of accomplishing this goal. All the facts should be furnished to conduct a program for the various media and personnel in order to create a favorable public reaction prior to any voting. It should be noted that a last minute publicity campaign to gain approval seldom is successful unless it has been preceded by a conscientious on-going public relations program. If the project is a swimming pool for the school system, the success

of the campaign will depend upon the impression that the school system, the athletic program, and perhaps the recreation program, have made with the public. Any system which can demonstrate a recurrence of successful building projects can also demonstrate a continuous public relations program to its public.

5. Preparing the Program Statement for the Architect. Once a project has been approved for detailed planning by the highest authority in the system, a team needs to be established to accumulate and systemize all information that would be valuable to the architect in designing the facility. The team normally would consist of a representative from the PERA division, a member of the highest planning unit in the system, perhaps one administrator, and a principal from the architectural firm to give direction. Each of these individuals, particularly the PERA representative, will depend on other personnel to furnish desired data, but this smaller committee is responsible for accumulating it and preparing a final coherent and systematic format.

6. Program-Oriented Team to Work With the Architect. The group that ultimately does most of the work, and/or makes most of the crucial decisions, is the planning committee of the PERA division. It is this group that has the responsibility of reacting to the architect's initial concepts and schematic drawings. It will need to coordinate the planning within the various components of the facility (Note Item 7). In addition, the planning committee will need to react to many last minute questions dealing with interpretation, proposal change, and possible deletions. There should be an understanding with the architect that no changes in plans will be made without first having the input of the committee. It is recognized that some decisions take an immediate answer and the chairman of the planning committee will have to make some of these decisions alone, often over the telephone. Crisis decisions should be kept to a minimum.

7. Sub-Unit Teams in More Complex Facilities. It is to the advantage of the builders to have the most knowledgeable people plan with the architect any unique features or areas of a facility. For example, if a physical education complex is being planned that contains gymnasium, pool, wrestling room, dance studio, and total service areas, sub-committees should be established for each. Sub-committees should be encouraged to think ''big.''

The architect's role is to relate these plans with the reality of the Program Statement and plan accordingly. Often, the planning unit will not have the necessary specialists for the sub-committees structure. In such cases, it may become the responsibility of one member of the planning committee to gain the necessary information.

The team approach at any level may be more time-consuming but results in better planned facilities. When using this planning process someone at each level has to be given the ultimate responsibility for communicating suggestions to the next highest level.

In summary, there are a number of different approaches to organizing the planning team. These approaches are often identified as follows:
1. Joint Planning Team (Administration, Faculty, Architects, Consultants, Students, Community).
2. Faculty Planning Team.
3. Outside Consulting Team.
4. Central Staff Planning Team (Large District).
5. Superintendent and Architect.
6. Capital Improvement Planning Division (Recreation).

In the case of PERA projects, the above approaches (1-5) are listed in a descending order of preference. By far the most productive planning team approach is the one identified as the Joint Planning Team. Such an approach best assures the correct defining of the problem before the specific planning is begun. It provides an excellent personnel mix for challenging and extending concepts. In addition, it can provide an opportunity for increased cooperation between the various parties concerned.

WRITING THE PROGRAM

The Program is a written description of concepts and objectives; organizational structure and function; interrelationships of education activities, other institutional activities or functions, or community education functions; and the proposed total future use of the facility. It should be written well in advance of selecting the architect. It is a statement that will be used to communicate the needs of the school program to the architect and the central planning committee. This document has a variety of names. Some architects call it *The Program*. Some educators call it *The Educational Specifications*. Others call it *The Building Program*. By whatever name it is called, this important statement should be written in an organized manner.

Some guidelines for writing *The Program* include:
- Write concisely.
- State the optimal as well as the minimal program needs.
- Make sure the project is rooted in fiscal reality.
- Conduct a critical evaluation of the current programs to determine if new programs should be emphasized, old ones should be eliminated, or

old and new combined.
- Consider all indoor and outdoor facility needs.
- Be aware that the location of facilities will affect the program offered.
- Distribute the initial rough draft of the document to all contributors for review and comment.

The organization for writing *The Program* may vary. An acceptable way of dividing up the work load is to establish a number of sub-committees, or sub-unit teams. Each person serving on a sub-committee presumably is an expert in his area. One suggested sub-committee structure follows:
1. Adapted
2. Administration
3. Aquatics
4. Individual and Dual Sports
5. Dance
6. Games and Outing Activities
7. Science
8. Self-Testing and Combatives
9. Service Areas
10. Team Sports

Sample Outline of the Program

Part I. Objectives of the School Programs:
A. Instructional (Professional and Service)
B. Intramurals
C. Adapted
D. Athletics (Interscholastic and Intercollegiate)
E. Club sports
F. Community-School programs
G. Others

Part II. Basic Assumptions to be Addressed:
A. Facilities will provide for a broad program of instruction, adapted, intramurals, athletics, club sports, and others.
B. Facilities will provide equitable areas for boys and men, and girls and

women.
C. Facilities will provide for use by students, staff faculty, and family of the school community.
D. Existing facilities will be programmed for use.
E. Facility expansion possibilities will be provided for in the planning.
F. Outdoor facilities should be located adjacent to the indoor facilities.
G. Writers of *The Program* will address themselves to the administrative and staff needs.

Part III. *Trends Which Affect Planning:*
A. A re-emphasis of physical education for the handicapped.
B. The club sports movement.
C. The Community Education, or ''Lighted School,'' movement.
D. The surge of new non-competitive activities being added to the curriculum.
E. Expanding intramural and athletic programs.
F. Sharing of certain facilities by boys and men and girls and women (athletic training rooms, and equipment rooms).
G. Coeducational physical education and co-recreation
H. Emphasis on individual exercise programs.
I. The weight training movement.
J. Federal and state legislation (PL 94-142, PL 503)
K. Systems approach in design and construction.
L. New products.

Part IV. *Explanation of Current and Proposed Programming:*
A. Instructional

B. Intramurals
C. Athletics
D. Club
E. Adapted
F. Community-School
G. Others
H. A priority listing of programs

Part V. *Preliminary Data Relative to the Proposed New Facilities:*
A. The existing indoor facilities square footage broken down by area (equipment, storage, training room, etc.)
B. A priority listing for the proposed new indoor facilities.
C. The existing outdoor facilities broken down by area (football field, track, etc.)
D. A priority listing for the proposed new outdoor facilities.
E. The community facilities being used as resource or adjunct facility areas for present programs (golf courses, trap range, rifle range, bowling alleys).

Part VI. *Space Needs and Allocation in the Proposed New Facilities:*
A. Main gymnasium
B. Spectator seating
C. Lobby or concourse
D. Administrative offices
E. Faculty offices
F. Conference rooms
G. Laboratory — classrooms
H. Other considerations (wall clocks, acoustical treatment of certain areas, etc.)
I. Others

VII. *Purposes and Uses of Auxiliary Space Areas:*
A. Exercise — therapy area
B. Multi-purpose gym
C. Golf area

D. Archery area
E. Wrestling gym
F. Main dance studio
G. Street-shoe usage room
H. Handball-racquetball courts
I. Squash courts
J. Others

Part VIII. *Service Facilities:*
A. Locker rooms
B. Shower rooms
C. Toweling areas
D. Toilets for locker area
E. Equipment and supply storage areas
F. Custodial storage areas
G. Athletic training rooms
H. Laundry

Part IX. *Projected Use of Present Facilities*

Part X. *Space Relationship (relationship each has to others.)*

Part XI. *Equipment list (all movable and fixed items identified in the document.)*

THE ROLE OF THE PROGRAM SPECIALIST

The program specialist is an individual actively engaged in a program as a teacher or coach. He is the one who will use the facilities, and consequently, is knowledgeable about the uses and problems of facilities and should be given opportunities for input into facility planning.

The chief contribution of program specialists may well be the written specifications they help develop. These specifications, called *The Program,* serve to communicate ideas to the architect and central planning committee.

Program specialists do not design facilities. This is a function of architects and engineers. However, determining the number of teaching stations needed to serve the instructional, intramural, athletics, club, adapted, and other programs should be a responsibility of program specialists. Selections of materials such as hardwood maple floor and/or synthetic floors, lighting requirements, acoustical treatment, and maintenance problems are all legitimate concerns of program specialists.

The objectives which program specialists should achieve are:
• Communicate the school program purposes, need for facilities and facility plans to all appropriate persons and public whose understanding and support are vital to secure the needed facilities.
• Ascertain the various size of teams, classes, and groups which will use the facilities as well as requirements or official rules for sports and games.
• Explore the multiple-purpose uses which are made possible by the new or expanded facilities.
• Help establish a priority list of program needs. *For example:* A staff agrees that tennis should be taught in the instructional program, introduced as an intramural

activity, and added as an interschool sport. If this is the top program priority, the building of a suitable teaching area would be the top facility priority.
• State trends which are relevant to facilities planning.

Synthetic surfaces, all weather tracks, coed athletic training rooms, coed classes, programs for the handicapped, total community use of school facilities and rapid development of sports clubs are some examples.
• Identify, study, and recommend desired traffic patterns for various individuals and groups, including spectators.
• Identify, study, and recommend proper space relationships for various indoor and outdoor facilities.

Within the locker room complex, the laundry space, equipment storage space (in season and out of season), issue area, athletic training area, and sauna may be so arranged that coed use is feasible. Duplication of personnel and equipment can be avoided by dual usage.
• Point out errors of design, space relationship, traffic patterns, safety, supervision, isolation, accessibility, flexibility, departmentalization, validity, and aesthetics.
• Provide the architect and planning committee with examples of facilities that meet desired needs.

If the sites are too distant for visitation, slides or pictures may be taken as illustrations for the architect and planning committee. Point out areas that represent quality as well as those that represent minimal quantitative standards.
• Point out the special considerations necessary to allow the handicapped full use of the facilities.

THE ROLE OF THE CONSULTANT

Until recently, the profession has given little attention to the area of facilities in the professional preparation of teachers, coaches, and recreational specialists. As a consequence, when a facility project is undertaken, professionals frequently are ill prepared. Time does not permit acquisition of the necessary background. Additionally, the architectural firm assigned to the project may be designing its initial PERA facility. It becomes apparent that competent assistance is needed.

The consultant in physical education and athletic facility design is frequently a professional in the field who teaches a course in facilities planning. This individual is usually familiar with recently constructed facilities in the country and is aware of the latest innovations in design, materials, and concepts.

The consultant can make a valuable contribution. He can suggest to the planning committee the names of successful architects and the location of examples of their work. He can assist the planning committee in developing alternatives and establishing priorities. The role as a knowledgeable expert from the outside enables the consultant to exert considerable influence in favor of the project.

An important contribution is as the liaison between the architect and the planning group, particularly when the architect has difficulty in relating with the professionals. There are times when each has difficulty in understanding the needs of the other. It is important for both parties to realize that the resultant facility must reflect the concerns of the other. The selection of the professional consultant may be one of the most significant steps toward constructing a functional facility.

Another source of consultant assistance is the commercial

agency established specifically to assist school districts, colleges and universities, and recreation departments with the solutions to facility problems. These firms have the capabilities of providing complete consultant services, from program through construction. They will also provide any number of singular services such as broad base data gathering; writing the educational specifications; and assisting with acoustic, lighting, or air handling problems.

SELECTING THE ARCHITECT

A building efficiently and comfortably designed can evolve only from a well-coordinated team effort. The team should consist of individuals well versed in the facts and realistic objectives. The architect is only one member of the team, and the earlier he can begin working with the planning team, the better.

Selecting the right architect is not a simple matter. Important considerations are knowledge, experience, personality and ability to establish rapport. The clients should interview prospective architects, view their work, inspect buildings they have designed, and confer with other clients they have served. Ideally, the entire planning team should participate in the selection of an architect, asking questions to confirm the firm's competency and compatibility with their objectives.

A detailed description of educational specifications should be given to the architect. The specifications are stated in narrative form and include suggested dimensions, spaces needed in the facility, relationships in special features of the facility, and the purposes of the facility that will also be included in the proposed budget. The primary purpose of the educational document is to describe to the architect in clear detail every activity to be conducted in a proposed facility.

Because of training, education, and experience, the architect can be of great assistance to the client in each of the three stages of every building project — decision, design, and delivery. When selecting an architect, the basic considerations are:

1. He should hold membership in the American Institute of Architects.

2. He must be licensed to practice in the state where the facility is to be erected.

3. He should have an excellent reputation in the field, be able to furnish references, and be able to show proof of completion of similar projects.

4. The firm should be in close proximity to the construction site so that no less than weekly visitations could be assured.

5. Superior supervision capabilities should be available through the firm.

The three basic methods of selecting the architect are:

1. If a state-supported institution, the architect may be appointed by the State Building Commission.

2. The architect may be selected by a direct appointment.

3. If a private institution or public school system, the architect may be selected by comparison from a group of prospective architects.

After the selection of the architect, a contractual agreement will be completed and signed. This legally binding contract will be the official AIA document B141 (a standard form of agreement between the client and architect).

STARTING TO WORK

Once the architect is selected, the whole team can be assembled. The team should be representative but not so large as to be unwieldy. It should include the architect, the firm's designated associates, perhaps a consultant expert in the requirements of the problem at hand, and the school or community team.

The first meetings are critical. A constructive pattern of positive accomplishments should be established. The planning team should outline specific and comprehensive program requirements, determine sizes, designate functions, and delineate operational patterns. Meetings should be scheduled regularly, the committee should follow agendas, and notes should be taken, kept, and reviewed.

The architect will develop and revise increasingly detailed drawings as the meetings progress. To ensure steady progress, it is essential that the drawings be developed progressively, each with more detail than the last, without changing the basic concepts. The basic concept developed in preliminary drawings should be evaluated very carefully.

The professional duties the architect is involved in are:
Pre-design planning
Schematic design
Design development
Construction documents
Bidding
Construction

The architect's role during each of these phases is as follows:

Pre-design Planning

Serve as a member of the planning committee in the capacity of a consultant or adviser on the architectural possibilities and limitations.

Schematic Design

With the assistance of the educational planners, translate the written program into a graphic representation of a building plan.

Analyze the relationship of spaces diagrammatically, taking into consideration access of various areas by students and the public.

Study the site, its topography, its relationship to the community and to traffic patterns, and the availability of utilities.

Determine how the site might be developed.

Determine what types of buildings are most appropriate for the site and the program.

Review applicable codes and laws and determine their effect on the design.

Make cost studies of the project.

Provide opportunities for thorough analysis and discussion of strengths and weaknesses of plans, and reach decisions with educational planners on how well the plan satisfies the requirements of the program.

Present the approved schematic design for approval.

Design Development

Develop the basic design.

Prepare sketches of elevations and models to establish the visual character of the project.

Specify building materials and mechanical and electrical systems.

Develop equipment and furniture arrangements to specificiations.

Prepare a detailed cost estimate and final plans for the planning team and proper authorities to review and approve.

Figure 1-7 illustrates the development program in the design process.

Construction Documents

Prepare complete working drawings and construction specifications.

Review and update earlier cost estimates.

Bidding

Assist the client in obtaining bids and awarding contracts.

Determine with the client how the project will be bid and what contractors will be qualified to bid.

Answer questions for bidders and clarify any aspects of the construction documents.

Provide copies of specifications, documents, and drawings for contractors, owners, and others who may need them.

Assist client in preparation of contract.

Construction Phase

Call a meeting with contractor and representative of the client to outline the project and discuss operating procedure.

Issue bulletins and change orders to accomplish changes requested by the client or required by field conditions.

Make periodic visits to site to monitor progress of work.

Issue the client certificates of payment.

Interpret requirements of the contract when questions are raised.

Reject work which fails to meet requirements.

Establish the date of "Substantial Completion" and the date of "Final Completion."

Additional Services

There are a number of additional services the architect may perform as required or as requested by the client. These services require prior authorization from the client, and the architect is paid for them in addition to the basic fee. Some of these services are:

• Make measured drawings of existing construction when required for planning additions or alterations.

• Revise previously approved drawings, specifications, or other documents to accomplish changes not originally initiated by the architect.

• Prepare change orders and supporting data where the change in basic fee is not commensurate with the services required.

• Prepare documents for alternate bids requested by the client.

• Provide detailed estimates of construction costs.

• Provide consultation and professional services concerning replacement of work damaged by fire or other causes during construction.

• Provide interior design work or other services required in connection with selection of furniture or furnishings.

• Provide services as an expert court witness.

It should be added that it is essential that drawings be understood. Often people have great difficulty interpreting drawings and are too embarrassed to ask for aid. Explanations should be thorough, even if they seem agonizingly basic.

Three-dimensional models can help to increase comprehension of the relationship of wall heights to room volumes. Model furniture or miniature figures can contribute to appreciation of room sizes.

As the drawings progress and the total idea of the actual building develops, specific materials and finishes should be chosen. The committee should view either representative samples or actual installations of like materials.

The more each team member knows before actual construction begins, the fewer surprises and less potential for disappointment.

PLANNING FACTORS

The guiding principles associated with creating a master plan are: Every community needs areas and facilities for physical education, athletic, and recreational programs. These programs, which are essential to the well-being of all people, cannot be effective unless a wide variety of indoor and outdoor facilities is provided.

Every community requires a master plan based on a study of its needs. Preparation of this plan is the primary responsibility of established governmental and educational planning agencies. Provisions for a system of properties required for physical education and recreation must be included in the master plan.

The type, location, and size of essential areas and facilities must be related to the total community pattern. These conditions vary in residential areas of different types and densities and are affected by the location of thoroughfares, business and industrial districts, transportation lines, and other

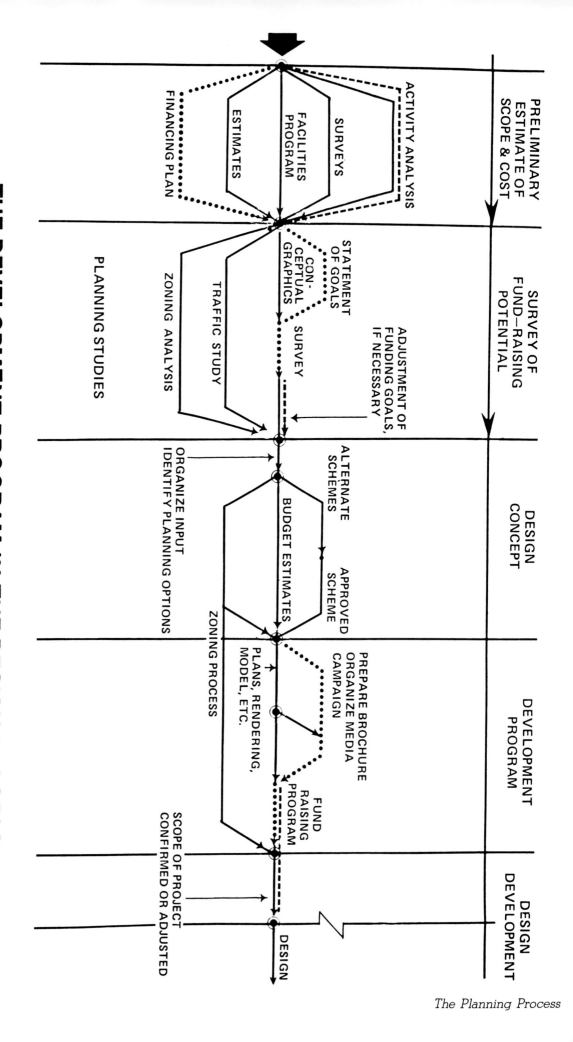

THE DEVELOPMENT PROGRAM IN THE DESIGN PROCESS

Figure 1-7

LEGEND

— OWNER ACTIVITY
--- ARCHITECT/PLANNER & CONSULTANTS
••••• OWNER'S CONSULTANTS

NOT DRAWN TO A TIME–SCALE

The Planning Process

natural barriers.

Areas and facilities should be planned in relation to the social and economic characteristics of the community. The feasibility of providing specific programs in a particular locality is influenced by the interests and financial resources of its total population.

Areas and facilities should be planned with due regard for the full potential use of available physical resources. Plans for acquisition and development can be justified as economically sound only if they are related to an inventory of comparable resources in the community or region. Duplication of facilities and overlapping of services is thereby avoided, and a maximum return from expenditures for areas and facilities can be expected.

Areas and facilities should accommodate programs that serve the interest and needs of all the people. Consideration should be given to the special needs of all ages and both sexes. Resulting programs should comprise a wide range of activities. In view of the increasing proportion of the population in the aged and retired group, special consideration of senior citizens needs is desirable. Facilities should also make it possible for handicapped citizens to participate in most aspects of physical education and recreational program.

Plans for areas and facilities must conform to state and local regulations and, as much as possible, to accepted standards and practice. Planning groups should become familiar with fire, building, electrical, sanitary, and other pertinent codes and make sure their plans conform to them. Unnecessary expense may be incurred in making construction changes required to meet official approval.

Maximum flexibility of design is encouraged to accommodate future needs. There is a danger that this can be practiced to the point where it harms the primary mission of a new facility. For example, an ice facility can be made so flexible that it fails to adequately support a hockey program. Spectators refuse to come because of inferior or inadequate seating, limited security, inadequate ticket area, or poor concession arrangements.

Cost of construction is only one important financial consideration. The operating and maintenance costs of a facility must be considered. It is possible to obtain funds to construct the new facility and then discover that there is no way for the planning unit to obtain the needed funds to operate and maintain the addition.

Close cooperation among all public and private agencies concerned with the development and operation of facilities designed for athletics, physical education, and recreation is of utmost importance. Cooperation involves not only school, park, recreation, and city planning agencies, but also re-development authorities and public and private housing agencies, among others. An interagency planning committee can be an effective means of achieving cooperative action.

All interested organizations, individuals, and groups should have an opportunity to share in the planning of areas and facilities intended for public use. Wide participation in the consideration of proposals requiring the expenditure of public funds for areas and facilities gives people an opportunity to express their desires and needs and helps assure their support of the projects and use of the areas and facilities.

Individuals who are qualified to give expert advice in planning facilities should act as advisors. School, park, and recreation department personnel can contribute materially to the determination of features to be included and can offer valuable suggestions for their design and development. Individuals with professional training and technical competence, such as landscape architects, architects, engineers, sociologists, and professional staff can play major roles in overall planning.

An assigned architect may have a limited background in a specific PERA project. An architect usually feels confident to build any project. However, most PERA projects are unique and background in this area is often lacking. The PERA divisions should provide the architect with sources of information specific to these facilities and the names of specialists that can be used.

Available sources of property and funding should be explored, evaluated, and used when appropriate. Tax funds are a primary source, but large numbers of facilities have been acquired or built with gifts from individuals, or organizations. Localities should take advantage of state and federal funds available for planning and for acquisition and improvement of school and recreation areas.

Widespread publicity, sound interpretation, and public discussion facilitate the implementation of facility plans. Appropriate authorities, community groups, and the public-at-large need to be fully informed if acceptance and support are to be achieved.

AREAS AND JURISDICTIONS FOR PLANNING

Publicly-owned facilities are principally under jurisdiction of two types of local authorities — school districts and departments of parks and recreation. Other public and quasi-public agencies provide such facilities as libraries and museums. Privately-owned facilities, such as churches, settlement houses, health clubs, tennis centers, athletic clubs, and youth clubs also contribute to the public service.

Comprehensive programs and services require that indoor and outdoor areas and facilities of many kinds, shapes, and sizes be available throughout the year. Each area and facility has a special function and serves specific uses. These areas and facilities are classified below according to function, and their sizes are determined by the nature of their services and the number of people to be served. Understanding of this classification is essential to effective planning.

The Neighborhood

The neighborhood is a residential area usually served by an elementary school. A typical neighborhood for planning purposes would be an area three-fourths of a mile to a mile square and containing about 6,000 to 8,000 people.

Population densities of neighborhoods vary from a few thousand to many thousands per square mile. There is also a wide variation in the number of children. Because many residents live within a short distance of the school or playground, they walk to it and tend to use it frequently, often for shorter periods than in the centers planned for a larger geographic unit.

The Community

The community is a section of a city, primarily a residential area. It usually represents the service area of a high school, contains a business center, and commonly constitutes a section of the city measuring two or three miles across. It can be thought of as a "community of neighborhoods" because it is usually composed of three to five neighborhoods.

The City or School District

The area designated as the city, town, borough, or village lends itself to the provision of areas and facilities for use by the entire population of the political subdivision. Major parks, golf courses, camps, museums, and botanical gardens, which cannot be provided in each neighborhood and community, are typical city-wide areas. In small localities comprising one community and a single high school, city-wide planning is comparable to planning for a single community as described above, although some facilities commonly provided in larger city-wide areas are included.

School districts vary widely in size and population, but district-wide school planning involves primarily neighborhoods and communities. Some of the large school districts provide district-wide facilities for an outdoor education-recreation complex, interscholastic activities, consolidated educational programs, and some type of post-high school center or community for day pupils.

Large Units

The county or the region, which is a geographic area that sometimes includes part of more than one county, is increasingly used for recreation planning. Many of these planning units are located close to a metropolitan area and include both the city and the surrounding region. Others are primarily rural in nature and are composed of unincorporated areas. Planning on a regional or district basis lends itself to the provision of extensive properties usable for family outings, winter and water sports, and other activities requiring large land and water areas.

The Park-School Concept

Before the various types of properties that are commonly included in comprehensive plans are described, the current trend toward providing areas that serve both education and public recreation deserve special mention.

The park-school as described is the recommended type of major facility in the neighborhood or community for day-by-day use in organized programs of athletics, recreation, and physical education. It combines the neighborhood recreational area and the elementary school site, and the community recreational area and the secondary school site.

The park-school is an example of cooperative action between school and municipal authorities. It involves a joint agreement as to the location, development, and use of properties to be designed for the school athletic and physical education program and for the recreation of both school and community groups. Since the park-school concept is based on the desirability and economy of dual use, it is important that plans be developed jointly by both school boards and municipal authorities responsible for park and recreational services.

In order to protect the interests of the cooperating authorities and to assure the most effective application of the park-school plan, a formal agreement should be signed by both agencies, specifying respective responsibility for the purchase, development, operation, maintenance, and the use of the facilities.

Although the park-school concept has won wide acceptance in recent years, separate school sites and municipal recreational areas are still being acquired in many communities. While one reason for the continuing separation may be lack of knowledge of the concept, more frequently it is because the school or municipal authorities fail to recognize the advantages and economy of the plan or are unwilling to subordinate their prerogatives under a cooperative program.

1. Community Park-School

The community park-school is an area in which are located a junior or senior high school and a variety of recreational, physical education, and athletic facilities designated for both school and community use. It should be centrally located and provide a parklike environment. If it contains a senior high school, it requires more acreage than if it is associated with an elementary or junior high school, and its service radius is appreciably greater. Many of the people using such centers, especially those with a senior high school, reach them by automobile or public transport.

The function of this area is similar to that of the neighborhood park-school. While the neighborhood park-school contains an elementary school and primarily serves children, the community park-school contains a secondary school and serves primarily young people and adults. The geographic area served by the community school is larger and needs more area to provide for interscholastic athletics, spectator space, and extensive parking.

2. Outdoor Education-Recreation Complex

A land area or a cluster of acreages suitable for more extensive outdoor education-recreation programs, owned by the school district, city, or township, is an important adjunct of the park-school. Such a complex should be located as near the city as possible, yet should include some of the following: a residence camp; extensive nature trails; primitive area for outpost camping and exploration; an outdoor skills and sports center; plots for forestry and wildlife management; and pioneer and modern farms.

3. The Community Room

The community room is probably most representative of the community park-school program in that it is designed specifically to meet community needs. The community room should be at least as large as a regular classroom. Kitchen facilities, including stove, refrigerator, cupboards, tables, and chairs,

help to make it an ideal meeting place for civic and social organizations. The community room may be used during the day for adult club meetings, or casual recreational activities. In the evening, it may be used for adult classes or as a meeting place for community groups. Frequently, the community council, made up of representatives of all groups in the neighborhood, meets in the community room to discuss programs for the area served by the school.

Planning Units for Colleges and Universities

The following includes the various components that may be involved in the planning of any college/university PERA facility. The degree of complexity varies according to the type of institution and scope of the project.

1. *Governing Board.* This body will need to give the final approval for the project. Within the board, there may be two or three individuals responsible for checking on all building proposals. Members of the PERA division are likely to be called before this latter group.

2. *State Planning Division.* If the college or university is state supported, there will usually be a planning division in the state capital which becomes involved. This division normally determines if the facility meets all the state codes. There may be a state appropriation committee that will need to give approval to the project.

3. *Institutional Policy Committee.* In some institutions, this is a standing committee for planning specific educational programs. This often is composed of

key administrators, a member of the governing board, faculty representing the various divisions within the institution, and students. Policy recommendations of this committee give direction to plant development committees, the president, and the governing board.

4. *Institutional Plant Development Committee or Office.* In many institutions of higher learning, such an office may exist. Often it consists of a vice president and one or two in-house architects. They will question ideas as to multiple uses, architectural blending, internal building principles, and campus sources of energy. A person may be designated as project director for a campus-wide facility. The PERA planning committee will need to clear many ideas through this office.

5. *Office of Building and Grounds.* The Superintendent of this office and/or a representative will often sit on or with the planning committee or the architect. It is the responsibility of this office to see that the building codes are followed, maximum use is made of present energy sources, energy conservation is included in new facility plans, and campus beautification is maintained.

6. *Architectural Firm.* If the project is of any magnitude, the architectural firm will have its own team working on the project. This often includes the

principal architect, the principal engineer, and related specialists. The planning committee will meet with the architectural firm as a whole or with individuals from the firm, as the need dictates.

7. *Project Coordinator and Committee.* The coordinator of a PERA project may be a higher administrator, such as the vice president. More likely, it would be the dean or director of PERA, or it could be someone from the office of the physical plant. If it is a higher administrator, the individual would most likely come from the office responsible for institutional facility development, although

conceivably it could be a member of the university's planning committee. Someone from the PERA division would be a member of the committee and serve as chairman of the PERA's planning committee. In many instances, PERA's personnel with a particular interest and expertise, may be asked to be on the committee.

8. *PERA Planning Committee.* The academic discipline has a planning committee which works directly with the architect and is responsible for coordinating all plans, requests, or changes that transpire between the discipline and the

architect. Normally, this committee will be headed by either the dean or director of the division, the athletic director, the physical education director, or the director of campus recreation. There will be a representative on the committee from each of the areas having a direct interest in the project.

9. *Area Specialists.* Much of the detailed planning will be done by sub-committees that report directly to the PERA planning committee. These sub-committees should have one or more meetings with the architect so that he has a clear understanding of their requests. Different

Figure 1-8
WHO IS INVOLVED IN THE PLANNING PROCESS

Planning Unit	College/ University	Elementary/ Secondary	Community/ Recreation
Governing Board	Board of Regents	School Board	City Council
State Planning Division	Coordinating Board	State Board of Education	Outdoor Recreation Planning Department
Institutional Policy Committee	Campus Space Committee	General Planning Committee	City Park & Recreation Board
Institutional Plant Development Committee/Office	Office of New Construction	Office of Facility Planning & Construction	Capital Improvement Planning Division
Office of Buildings and Grounds	Building Maintenance and Utilities	Office of Operation & Maintenance	Parks & Recreation Maintenance Division
Architectural Firm	Same	Same	Various Professional Consultants
Project Coordinator and Committee	Member from Office of New Construction	Member from Office of Facility Planning & Construction & Designated Specialists	Member from Capital Improvement Planning Division
PERA Plannning Committee	Director, College, School, Department; New Construction Committee	Director of Physical Education & Safety	Director, Parks and Recreation
Area Specialists	Sub-Committee Structure	Sub-Committee Structure	Sub-Committee Structure (Staff Planning Specialists)

The Planning Process

facilities will have different emphasis areas which will need special attention.

PLANNING PARTICIPANTS

The accompanying chart (Figure 1-8 suggests appropriate levels of planning units for the public school sector and community recreation commission analogous to college and university planning authority. Referring to the chart, the operational procedures and planning methods for each planning unit for the three areas (college/university, elementary/secondary schools and recreational facility) may differ widely. The basic function of the planning unit, regardless of the area, will be remarkably similar.

Too often the planning committee of the discipline, together with the architect, will do all of the detail planning. They cannot be experts in all areas, and many refinements that a sub-committee can point out get lost.

Students can add a positive dimension to most of the committees through their representation. The same is true of community organizations and agencies that may use the facility after its completion.

Planning facilities for athletics, physical education, and recreation requires attention to a series of complex relationships and involvement of numerous experts. Numerous factors can influence the planning required to design and construct an appropriate facility (Figure 1-9).

Figure 1-9

Factors Influencing The Planning Of Facilities

Factor	Relevance to Planning
Institutional Policy	Relative emphasis on particular programs, current and future: •Intercollegiate, •Intramural, •Physical Education, •Corrective, •Research, •Recreation, •Administrative Organization of above programs.
Interactive Programs	Joint activities with other institutions or community groups may enable sharing of activities.
Attitudes and perception of participants	Increasing awareness of and interest in sports and physical fitness. Growing popularity of specific sports, such as running and tennis.
Activities with similar spatial demands	Opportunity for multi-purpose activity areas.
Participation by women	Increasing participation in a wider range of sports. More co-ed activities. Need to demonstrate parity between men's and women's programs, funding and facilities.
Characteristics of User Population	Need for accurate classification by age, sex, role in institution, in-residence vs. commuting, enrollment in academic programs.
Climatological	Days/year that activities can take place out-of-doors. Increased load on indoor facilities in inclement weather.
Intercollegiate Programs	Traditional strengths in intercollegiate competition. Justification for dedicated space, e.g., arenas, for specific sports.
Intramural Programs	Scope of activities. Probable trend for wider range of sports, more co-ed sports.
Physical Education Programs	Ratio of mandatory to voluntary programs. Curricular trends. Enrollment trends. Instruction in classroom or lecture hall format. Need for corrective programs. Interface with cultural programs, e.g., dance.
Recreation Programs	Existing and projected user groups. Scope of activities. Outreach to community.
Scheduling	Seasonal patterns. Weekly hours available, each facility. Daily schedules. Utilization of available time. Implications of schedule adjustments on staffing and operating costs.
Technology	Opportunities for improved space utilization through new technologies, e.g., multi-purpose synthetic playing surfaces, air-supported structures.
Space criteria for activities and support areas	Floor areas, with overruns and clearances. Minimum vertical clearances. Required adjacencies
Special Events	Design of multi-purpose space for athletics, commencements, concerts, orientation, registration, etc.
Provision for Spectators	Institutional policy. Justification for fixed seating. Implications on physical planning, e.g., code requirements, security, traffic.

Facilities designed for athletics, physical education, and recreation contain many unique areas/features demanding special consideration. Planners must be aware of the human resources and multitude of printed materials necessary to adequately plan a facility that is structurally sound, aesthetically pleasing, technologically updated, energy and cost-efficient, and responsive to program needs. The success of any building project usually can be directly linked to the quantity and quality of planning that occurred at the onset. The desired outcome should then be a facility that successfully facilitates the programs it was designed to accommodate.

SELECTED REFERENCES

A Guide for Planning and Construction of Public School Facilities in Georgia Physical Education Facilities. Atlanta: Georgia State Department of Education, Office of School Administrative Services, 1976.

Architect's Handbook of Professional Practice. Statement of the Architect's Services Volume 2. Washington, D.C.: The American Institute of Architects, 1974.

Aston, Dudley and Irey, Charlotte. **Dance Facilities.** Washington, D.C.: American Association for Health, Physical Education, and Recreation, Council for Facilities, Equipment and Supplies, 1972.

Bass, Alan M. **Physical Education Facilities.** Educational Facilities Review Series Number 14. Eugene, Oregon: Oregon University, February 1973.

Blaicher, John W. "Design Directions: Making Less Into More." **Parks and Recreation** 13 (May 1978): 34-35.

Brewster, Sam F. **Campus Planning and Construction, Physical Facilities for Universities and Colleges.** Washington, D.C.: The Association of Physical Plant Administrators of Universities and Colleges, 1976.

Bronzan, Robert T. **New Concepts in Planning and Funding Athletic, Physical Education and Recreational Facilities.** St. Paul: Phoenix Intermedia, Incorporated, 1974.

Bucher, Charles A. **Administration of Health and Physical Education Programs, Including Athletics.** 8th Edition. St. Louis: The C.V. Mosby Company, 1983.

Christiansen, Monty L. **Park Planning Handbook. Fundamentals of Physical Planning for Parks and Recreation Areas.** New York: John Wiley & Sons, Inc., 1977.

Community School Centers Booklets. New York: Educational Facilities Laboratories, Inc., 1978.

Crompton, John L. "Formulating New Directions with Strategic Marketing Planning." **Parks and Recreation** 18 (July 1983): 56-63, 66.

Curtis, James P. "A Team Approach to Designing the Recreational-Educational Complex." **Council of Educational Facilities Planners Journal** 21 (Jan.-Feb. 1983): 16-19.

Dahnke, Harold L., and Others. **General Support Facilities.** Higher Education Facilities Planning and Management Manual Five, Revised. Boulder, Colorado: Western Interstate Commission for Higher Education, May 1971.

Daughtrey, Greyson and Woods, John B. **Physical Education and Intramurals: Organization and Administration.** 2nd Edition. Philadelphia: W.B. Saunders Company, 1976.

DeChiara, Joseph and Cillender, John, eds. **Timer-Saver Standards for Building Types.** 2nd Edition. New York: McGraw-Hill, 1980.

Ezersky, Eugene M. and Theibert, P. Richard. **Facilities in Sports and Physical Education.** St. Louis: The C.V. Mosby Company, 1976.

Finci, David L. "How to Plan Your New Athletic Facility." **American School and University.** 53 (November 1980): 47-48, 50-52, 54.

Fink, Ira and Body, David. "Developing a Sports and Recreation Master Plan." **Planning for Higher Education.** 11 (Spring 1983): 1-16.

Flynn, Richard B., ed. "Planning Facilities." **Journal of Physical Education, Recreation, and Dance.** 54 (June 1983): 19-38.

_____. "Timely Topics in Facility Planning." **Journal of Physical Education and Recreation.** 51 (June 1980): 25-37.

Flynn, Richard B. "Sequential Planning of Facilities on a Landlocked Campus." **Journal of Physical Education and Recreation.** 45 (April 1975): 23-24.

_____. "The Team Approach to Facility Planning." **Athletic Purchasing and Facilities.** 5 (June 1981): 12-26.

Gans, Marvin. **Sequential Steps in Planning Facilities for Health, Physical Education, Recreation, and Athletics.** Unpublished Dissertation. University of Utah, 1972.

Guide for Planning Educational Facilities. Columbus, Ohio: Council of Education Facility Planners, 1976.

Gwynne, Susan K., Editor. **Guide for Planning Educational Facilities.** Columbus, Ohio: Council of Educational Facility Planner, International, 1976.

Harman, Jerry J. and Hirsekom, Robert. **Administrator's Guide to School Construction, Remodeling and Maintenance.** First Edition. New York: Parker Publishing Company, 1975.

Hawkins, Harold L. **Appraisal Guide for School Facilities.** Midland, Michigan: Pendell Publishing Company, 1973.

Higher Education Facilities Planning and Management Manuals. Boulder, Colorado: Western Interstate Commission for Higher Education, 1971.

Jubenville, A. **Outdoor Recreational Planning.** Philadelphia: W.B. Saunders Company, 1976.

Keller, Roy J. **Modern Management of Facilities for Physical Education.** Champaign, Illinois: Stipes Publishing Company, 1973.

Kombult Esq., Arthur R. "Document A201 Strives to Clarify — Not Change — the Roles of the Architect, Contractor and Owner." **Architectural Record.** (April 1977): 67-68.

"Making Physical Education and Recreation Facilities Accessible to All: Planning, Designing, Adapting." Washington, D.C.: American Alliance for Health, Physical Education, and Recreation (AAHPER), 1977.

Mittelstaedt, Arthur H. "Preparing HPER Professionals to Deal with Facilities and Equipment." **Journal of Health, Physical Education, and Recreation.** 45 (October 1974): 22-23.

Moriarty, R.J. "PERT Planning for Physical Educational Facilities." **CAHPER Journal** (Canadian Association for Health, Physical Education and Recreation). 39 (July-August 1973): 33-37.

Penman, Kenneth. **Planning Physical Education and Athletic Facilities in Schools.** New York: John Wiley and Sons, 1977.

Physical and Health Education Facilities for Secondary Schools. Toronto, Ontario: Department of Education, Toronto, Ontario Ministry of Education, 1975.

Physical Recreation Facilities: A Report. New York: Educational Facilities Labs., Inc., April 1973.

Planning a Site for Physical Education/Athletic/Recreational Programs (Guide No. 2). New York: The Eggers Group, P.C., Architects and Planners, 1980.

Planning a Development Program for Physical Education/Athletic/Recreation Facilities (Guide No. 3). New York: The Eggers Group, P.C., Architects and Planners, 1980.

Planning Educational Facilities. Opelousas, Louisiana: Hamilton and Associates, Architects, 1983.

Schwanke, Dean. "Physical Education, Recreation and Athletic Facilities." **Journal of Physical Education and Recreation.** 51 (June 1980): 62-63.

Theunissen, William. "Planning Facilities — the Role of the Program Specialist." **Journal of Physical Education and Recreation.** 49 (June 1978): 27-29.

U.S. Department of the Army, Navy, and Air Force. **Planning and Design of Outdoor Sports Facilities.** Stock No. 008-020 - 00588-6, October, 1975.

U.S. Department of Housing and Urban Development. "ANSIA 117.1 (1977), Specifications for Making Buildings and Facilities Accessible To and Usable by Physically Handicapped People," 1977.

CHAPTER II
Indoor Facilities

Included in this chapter is information relative to athletic and physical education indoor facilities for elementary school, secondary school, and college/university levels.

Factors common to indoor facilities for all levels are discussed as well as features designed specifically to support programs at the elementary, the secondary, and the collegiate levels. Whereas the planning chapter emphasized that facilities are to facilitate programs, this chapter describes some of these indoor programs. Numerous figures are included which offer detailed specifications required in the planning for selected indoor activities. A checklist relating to general indoor facility features is also included as an aid to those responsible for planning indoor facilities for athletics, physical education, and recreation.

SITE SELECTION

Program specialists, architects, engineers, and others should work together in the selection of a desirable site for any new construction. Some factors that must be considered in selecting a site are:
- Proximity to classrooms
- Pedestrian traffic patterns

CHECKLIST OF FACTORS IN SITE EVALUATION

REGIONAL FACTORS
1. Demographic factors
2. General character of region (rural, industrial, residential)
3. Distance to competitors in sports events
4. Traffic and transportation
5. Potential for recruitment

LOCAL FACTORS
1. Character of environs (urban, suburban)
2. Community acceptance
3. Accommodations for visitors
4. Character and quality of adjacent structures
5. Civic services (fire, police protection, health care)
6. Access
7. Traffic & Transportation
   — Access from major highways and local streets
   — Existing traffic volumes & patterns
   — Public transportation
8. Climate

FEATURES OF THE SITE
1. Acreage
   • Must be adequate for buildings, parking, playing areas, etc.
   • Additional acreage for expansion
2. Shape
   • Generally rectangular usually best shape
   • Acute angles or odd shapes may be wasteful of space
3. Topography
   • Generally level terrain desirable
   • Consider extent of earth-moving in adapting to steep slopes
4. Soil & Subsoil
5. Vegetation
6. Drainage
   • Essential that site be well-drained
   • Possible recharging basin
   • Method of disposing of runoff
   • Environmental regulations
7. Climate

• Precipitation
• Prevailing winds
• Climatic extremes
8. Zoning Regulations
   • Permitted use
   • Parking
   • Setbacks, buffers
   • Height limitations
   • Allowable coverage
   • Procedures
9. Access
   • From principal roads
   • From local streets
   • Traffic capacity of streets
   • Ability to accept additional volume
   • Pedestrian routes and crossings
   • Truck and bus access
   • Emergency access
10. Security Considerations

SITE UTILITIES
1. Sewerage
   • Capacity of municipal system
   • Location of sewage lines
   • Possible on-site plant
2. Electric power
3. Water
   • For buildings
   • For site sprinklers
   • For fire protection
4. Storm drainage
5. Energy sources
6. Telephone
7. Solid waste disposal

ECONOMIC FACTORS
1. Acquisition costs
2. Taxes
3. Financing
4. Development costs

DEVELOPMENTAL CONSTRAINTS
1. Restrictive zoning
2. Easements
3. Covenants
4. Other legal constraints
5. Community resistance

Figure 2-1
The Eggers Group P.C. Architects & Planners

- Motor traffic movement and parking space
- Soil conditions and drainage
- Availability of utilities
- Relationship to other health, physical education, recreation, and athletic facilities
- Proximity to housing

Physical education, athletic, and recreation facilities are often the largest on campus. Space is essential to permit the architect to use creative design ideas. Avoid locating a facility on a site too small to allow for design options or for possible additions. Because of the size of these facilities, attention must be given to making them compatible with surrounding structures.

Ideally, a major indoor facility for physical education, athletics, and recreation should be erected as close as possible to both the student living quarters and the center of the academic teaching area. Probably no other campus facilities will be used as much by as many students. If large spectator activities are to be included in the facilities, the site must allow for auto access and parking.

Figure 2-1 presents a checklist of factors to be considered in site selection.

PEDESTRIAN TRAFFIC CIRCULATION

Building location is a most important consideration in traffic circulation and control. A careful study of the relationship of the proposed structure to student housing, academic buildings, and the community will provide valuable information relative to placement of primary and secondary entrances and exits.

The foremost purposes of planning for traffic circulation and control include: minimizing congestion in corridors, stairwells, locker rooms, and spectator areas; minimizing the disturbance of students and staff in offices,

classrooms, and study rooms; providing for ease of building supervision and separation of various units where necessary; enhancing efficient and safe movement; and providing for future building expansion.

Special circulation problems created by intramural, recreation, and spectator programs should be included in the traffic control study. The placement of service, activity, instructional, and spectator areas should provide for efficient means of supervising those using the facilities.

Space Relationships

The relationship of activity areas, instructional areas, and service areas to the placement and size of corridors, lobbies, stairs, and doors needs careful consideration. Spectator spaces should be separated from the swimming pool and pool deck areas, gymnasium floor, and other activity areas. Entrances to the seating area should be direct from the outdoors or from corridors or foyers without requiring travel through locker rooms or across pool decks or gymnasiums. It is also important that traffic to and from the locker room not cross the gymnasium floor.

The individual components of the locker room areas should permit entrance to, and exit from, each area without cross traffic in wet and dry areas. The location of toilet rooms in relation to the swimming pool and to outside facilities should be given careful consideration, especially with reference to public use.

Units within the building which require truck delivery service should be grouped to reduce the number of delivery points. Delivery of supplies should be planned so there is no traffic or delivery through locker rooms or across gymnasium floors. A loading dock is desirable. In multi-storied structures, elevators should be provided.

Corridors and Foyers

In large buildings, athletic and instructional units should be accessible from at least two passageways leading from the principal classroom areas to prevent traffic congestion during change of periods.

Provision needs to be made for heavy traffic from the dressing room or the locker suite to playfields. The designated corridor widths should be clear of all obstructions, including the swing of locker and room doors. All equipment, such as heating units, drinking fountains, fire extinguishers, and telephones, should be recessed. Each corridor should terminate at an exit or stairway leading directly to a point of exit.

Public rooms, including gymnasiums used for large public groups, should be designed with entrance foyers. The size of the foyer will depend on the seating capacity. The planning of this area should include consideration for ticket sales, public telephones, an information desk, and a cloak-room. The foyer should be accessible to public toilets for men and women. Often, it is advisable to provide cutoff gates so it will not be necessary to supervise the entire building when specific areas are not in use.

Stairways

Buildings of two or more stories should have no fewer than two stairways, located at the extremes. All stairways should be of fire-resistant construction, and all main stairways should lead directly to grade exits. Two-lane stairways are recommended, and they should have a clear width to conform with the local fire code.

Stairways should be divided into runs of not more than sixteen, nor less than three risers. Risers should not exceed 6½ inches, and treads should be at least 10½ inches measured from riser to riser. The rounded nosings of all treads and landings should have

24

Indoor Facilities

nonslip, flush surfaces. Abrupt over-landing nosing should not be used.

Circular or winding stairways should be avoided. Nonslip ramps are desirable to compensate for minor differences in levels in floors and to accommodate the special needs of the handicapped. Adequate stair aisles must be provided for all bleachers of more than three rows, whether movable or fixed.

Exits and Doors

Exits should be located so at least one exit, or stairway leading to an exit, will be within 100 feet of a doorway of every room designed for occupancy. Every floor should have at least two exits, remote from one another, and additional exits as prescribed by the National Fire Protection Association formula in the Building Exits Code. Exits should be located for convenience as well as for safety. It is important that the number of exits and their locations be properly related to the seating capacity and the space in the gymnasium or swimming pool.

All doors should open outward, with the entire door swinging free of the door opening (side-hinges). Double exterior doors should be provided with a removable center mullion so that each door will operate independently; at least one such opening should be a minimum of 36 inches wide. Every room should be provided with exits as prescribed by the Building Exits Code, and all outside doors should be equipped with panic hardware.

The doors to rooms where combustible material is kept should be constructed in accordance with Fire Underwriters' specifications. Exterior doors and all doors in damp areas, such as the swimming pool area, laundry rooms, shower rooms, and dressing locker suites, should be heavy-duty and moisture-resistant.

If exterior doors cannot be recessed, they should be protected against the weather by projections, overhangs, or soffits. Outside entrances should be provided with mud and dirt grates or mats for cleaning the mud and dirt from shoes. One method which has proved satisfactory is the use of a grate-covered recess about six feet long and the width of the door opening, placed so persons entering the building must walk across it with both feet. Consideration should be given to the size of the openings in the grate to prevent accidents to persons wearing high-heeled shoes.

While minimum widths of corridors, stairways, and exits are determined by local codes, these areas should be considered in the light of maximum use of the building's facilities. Stairways and exits are most important in preventing traffic congestion and should, in most cases, be wider than code requirements.

TEACHING STATIONS

The unit of primary importance is the room or space where teaching occurs. All other parts of the school plant are, in a real sense, secondary. In physical education, therefore, the determination of the number and character of the teaching stations is basic to the planning process.

The term "teaching station" is used to identify any room or space where one teacher can instruct or supervise the learning experience of a class or group of students. For instance, a gymnasium would constitute a teaching station and if divided, could provide two or more teaching stations. Swimming pools, auxiliary physical education teaching stations, and dance rooms are examples of other kinds of teaching stations. The number of students accommodated by a teaching station is controlled by the nature of the specific activity as well as the size of the facility.

Institutions will vary as to the timing of peak load and consequently, as to when the re-quired number of teaching stations is needed. Colleges and universities with a large professional preparation program and/or a required program for the general student body will usually have the greatest need during the regular instructional hours. Other schools may find the greatest need for different teaching stations during the after-school hours when athletic teams are practicing or when an extensive intramural program is in operation. Schools in a climate which has a long cold season will have a greater need

Figure 2-2
The number of teaching stations is increased by the use of divider nets at the George Halas, Jr. Sports Center on the campus of Loyola University of Chicago.

for extensive indoor facilities.

The number of teaching stations required is dictated by enrollment, policies pertaining to instructional physical education, average class size, diversity of program, number of periods in the school day, and other uses of the facilities. Folding partitions and dropnets can be effectively used for flexibility and to increase the number of teaching stations.

Planners should be aware that indoor facilities for physical education, athletics, and recreation are difficult and costly to expand at some future date. The ultimate enrollment potential should be researched by school planner. The anticipated enrollment five to ten years after completion of construction should serve as a basis for determining the required number of original teaching stations. Long-range planning is imperative to provide for the logical and most economical expansion. The initial design should make provisions for the anticipated construction.

SURFACE MATERIALS

The selection of indoor surface materials becomes complicated because indoor facilities may be subject to hard usage and/or excessive moisture, and they must meet minimum standards in terms of acoustical and light-reflecting properties. Geographic location and the availability of certain surface materials are factors to be considered.

Figure 2-3 is a guide to suggested indoor surface materials.

Floors

At least three distinct types of floor surfacing are required in facilities described in this chapter. Floors in service areas such as locker rooms, shower rooms, toweling rooms, and toilet rooms require a surface impervious to moisture. In general, gymnasiums and other activity areas require either a hard wood or a resilient synthetic material. Classrooms, corridors, offices, and like areas may be grouped together for common surfacing.

Special activity areas require different treatments. For example, a dance gymnasium that is used for instruction in modern dance should have a finished treatment which will allow the dancers to slide or glide across the floor. In other areas, such as basketball courts, the finish should be of a nonslip nature.

Flexibility, durability, and cost are three criteria that have been instrumental in seeing synthetic surfaces challenge hard wood floors for installation in activity areas. Synthetics take the form of synthetic grass surfaces or as smooth or roughed nongrass surfaces. The most popular synthetic surfacing materials can be classed into two types: plasticized polyvinyl chlorides (PVC's) and polyurethanes. The PVC's are primarily prefabricated while the polyurethanes are either poured in place or produced in factory prefabricated sheets which are adhered down on the site. In general, the polyurethanes possess most of the desirable characteristics sought in a floor surface. The long term differences in the maintenance costs between synthetics and wood seem to be negligible.

In general, classrooms, corridors, and offices have been satisfactorily surfaced with some type of tile, such as asphalt, vinyl, vinyl asbestos, rubber, or linoleum. Consideration should be given to the use of carpeting in offices, golf course locker rooms, and other appropriate areas.

Walls

In addition to segregating

Figure 2-3
SUGGESTED INDOOR SURFACE MATERIALS

ROOMS	FLOORS						LOWER WALLS									UPPER WALLS						CEILINGS			
	Carpeting	Synthetics	Tile, asphalt, rubber, linoleum	Cement, abrasive & nonabrasive	Maple, hard	Terrazzo, abrasive	Tile, ceramic	Brick	Brick, glazed	Cinder Block	Concrete	Plaster	Tile, ceramic	Wood Panel	Moistureproof	Brick	Brick, glazed	Cinder Block	Plaster	Acoustic	Moisture-resistant	Concrete or Structure Tile	Plaster	Tile, acoustic	Moisture-resistant
Apparatus Storage Room			1	2						1		2	1	C											
Classrooms		2			1							2	1			2				2	1		C	C	1
Clubroom		2			1							2	1			2				2	1		C	C	1
Corrective Room	1				2					2	1					2		2	2	1	2				1
Custodial Supply Room			1			2																			
Dance Studio		2			1																		C	C	1
Drying Room (equip.)			1		2	2	1	2	1	1						1		1							1
Gymnasium	1				1					2	1					2	2	2	1	2	*		C	C	1
Health-Service Unit		1			1					2		1			2				2	1					1
Laundry Room			2			1	2	1	2	2		1	C	*							*			*	*
Locker Rooms		3		3		2	1		1	2	2	3	1		*	1		1	2				C		1
Natatorium		2				1	2	1	3	2		1		*	2	2	1		*	*		C	C	1	*
Offices	1		3		2					2		1		1			2	1							1
Recreation Room		2			1			2			2		1		1		2		1	2	*			C	1
Shower Rooms			3		2	1		1			2	1	*	2	1	2	2		*					1	*
Special-activity Room		2			1				2			1		1		1		1	1				C		1
Team Room	1		3		2	1	2	1	2	2	3	1		*	1		1	2					C		1
Toilet Room			3		2	1		1	2	2	2	1		*	1		1	1							1
Toweling-Drying Room			3		2	1		1		2	1	*	2	1	2	2		*					1	*	

Note: The numbers in the Table indicate first, second, and third choices. "C" indicates the material as being contrary to good practice. An * indicates desirable quality.

specific areas, walls should serve as barriers to sound, light, heat, and moisture. In selecting wall surfacing, considerations should be given to the acoustical properties of the material. In general, moisture-resistant walls with good acoustical properties are recommended. Most modern gymnasiums have smooth surfaces on the lower portion of the walls so they may be used as rebound surfaces. Rough-surfaced walls collect dirt easily and are difficult to clean. Recently, there has been a trend to color, murals, and graphics to add aesthetic appeal.

In locker rooms, shower rooms, and toilet rooms, where high humidity is often present, it is important to select wall surfacing that is moisture-resistant and has good acoustical properties. Walls serving as barriers between toilet-rooms, handball courts, squash courts, and other areas where noise is a problem should have a minimum of sound transmission.

Ceilings

Roof design, type of activity, and local building codes should determine the ceiling construction. Ceilings should be insulated to prevent condensation and should be painted to provide pleasing aesthetics and to enhance light reflection. Acoustical ceiling materials are desirable in instructional and activity areas. Dropped ceiling panels susceptible to damage by objects or individuals will require considerable maintenance.

False ceilings with catwalks above them have been effectively designed to permit maintenance and repair of lighting and ventilating systems.

SOUND CONTROL AND ACOUSTICS

The sonic, or audible, environment is the most difficult phase of the total environment to balance and requires the services of an acoustical engineer. In each room, attention must be given to reverberation time. This is influenced by the absorption and reflection qualities of all surfaces within the room. Hard surfaces reflect sound and produce excessive unwanted reflection and reverberations. Thus, the space may be "noisy." Soft or absorbable surfaces turn the sound into another form of energy and can produce areas that are too "dead." Therefore, most areas must have some materials with sound-absorbing qualities in order to balance the sonic environment for good hearing conditions.

Sound Insulation

Unwanted sound, or noise, may be transmitted into the room by means of ventilating ducts, pipes, and spaces around pipe sleeves. The transmission of sound through ducts can be reduced by the use of baffles, or by lining the ducts with sound-absorbent, fire-resistant materials. The ducts may also be connected with canvas to interrupt the transmission through the metal in the ducts. Pipes can be covered with pipe covering, and spaces in the pipe sleeves can be filled.

Sound can also be transmitted through the walls, floors, and ceilings. This can be reduced to a desirable minimum by the proper structural design and materials. In conventional wall construction, alternate studs can support the sides of the wall in such a manner that there is no through connection from one wall surface to another. This is sometimes known as double-wall construction. The space inside the walls can be filled with sound-absorbing material to further decrease the sound transmission. Sometimes three or four inches of sand inside the walls at the baseboard will cut down the transmission appreciably. Likewise, sound absorption blankets laid over the partitions in suspended ceiling construction can frequently reduce the sound from one room to another.

Machinery vibration or impact sounds can be reduced by use of the proper floor covering and/or by installing the machinery on floating or resilient mountings. "Sound locks," such as double walls or doors, are needed between noisy areas and adjoining quiet areas. Improper location of doors and windows can create noise problems.

It is imperative to pay attention to the acoustical treatment of all areas. Gymnasiums, swimming pools, and dressing-locker rooms are frequently neglected.

Materials for Acoustical Treatment

Care must be taken in the maintenance of acoustical materials. Oil paint reduces the sound-absorbent qualities of most materials. Surface treatment for different acoustical materials will vary. The most common treatment of acoustical-fiber tile is a light brush coat of waterbase paint. Most acoustical materials lose their efficiency after several applications of paint.

ELECTRICAL SYSTEMS AND SERVICE

All electrical service, wiring, and connections should be installed in accordance with the requirements of the National Electric Code of the National Board of Fire Underwriters, and of state and local building codes and fire regulations.

The capacity of each individual electrical system should be determined accurately for the obvious reasons of safety and economy. Full consideration should be given to present and future program plans when designing the electrical systems. The increasing use of electrically-operated equipment, higher standards of illumination, and special audiovisual equipment should be anticipated.

Illumination

In addition to the amount of light in any given area, the quality of light is of equal importance. Providing efficient illumination is complicated and challenging, and the services of an illuminating engineer are recommended in order to obtain maximum lighting efficiency. Gymnasiums, classrooms, corridors, and other specific areas have distinct and different lighting requirements. Planning for electric illumination requires that each area be considered relative to specific use.

Measurements of Light

The footcandle is a measurement of light intensity at a given point. Light intensity, measured in footcandles, is one vital factor in eye comfort and seeing efficiency, but intensity must be considered in relation to the brightness balance of all light sources and reflective surfaces within the visual field.

The reflection factor is the percentage of light falling on a surface which is reflected by that surface. In order to maintain a brightness balance with a quantity and quality of light for good seeing, all surfaces within a room should be relatively light, with a

Figure 2-4
Levels of Ilumination Currently Recommended for Specific Indoor Areas

Area	Footcandles on Tasks	Area	Footcandles on Tasks
Adapted physical education gymnasium....	50	Squash	70[2]
Auditorium		Tennis	70[2]
Assembly only	15	Volleyball	50
Exhibitions	30-50	Weight-exercise room	50
Social activities.	5-15	Wrestling and personal-defense room....	50
Classrooms		Games room	70
Laboratories	100	Ice rink.	100[3]
Lecture rooms		Library	
Audience area.	70	Study and notes	70
Demonstration area	150	Ordinary reading	50-70
Study halls.	70	Lounges	
Corridors and stairways	20	General	50
Dance studio.	5-50[3]	Reading books, magazines, newspapers ...	50-70
Field houses	80	Offices	
First-aid rooms		Accounting, auditing, tabulating, bookkeeping, business-machine operation.	150
General	50	Regular Office work, active filing, index references, mail sorting.	100
Examining table	125	Reading and transcribing handwriting in ink or medium pencil on good-quality paper, intermittent filing	70
Gymnasiums		Reading high-contrast or well-printed material not involving critical or prolonged seeing, conferring and interviewing.	50
Exhibitions	50[2]		
General exercise and recreation.	35		
Dances.	5-50[3]		
Locker and shower rooms	30		
Gymnastics	50	Parking areas.	1
Archery		Storerooms	
Shooting tee	50	Inactive	10
Target area	70	Active	
Badminton.	50[2]	Rough bulky	15
Basketball	80[2]	Medium	30
Deck tennis	50	Fine	60
Fencing	70[2]	Swimming pools	
Handball	70[2]	General and overhead	50
Paddle tennis.	70[2]	Underwater[4]	
Rifle range		Toilets and washrooms	30
Point area	50		
Target area	70		
Rowing practice area	50		

These standards have been developed by a panel of experts on facilities for health, physical education, and recreation after careful consideration of the activities involved. In all instances, the standards in this table are equal to, or exceed, the standards which have been recommended by the Illumination Engineering Society, American Institute of Architects, and National Council On Schoolhouse Construction.

[2]Care must be taken to achieve a brightness blance and to eliminate extremes of brightness and glare.
[3]Should be equipped with rheostats.
[4]Must be balanced with overhead lighting and should provide 100 lamp lumens per square foot of pool surface.

Courtesy of Illuminating Engineering Society of North America

Indoor Facilities

Figure 2-5
Illumination Levels for Indoor Tennis Courts

| Class of play | IES current recommended practice—footcandles (lux) maintained in service[a] | Minimum mounting height from floor | | |
| | | Direct See note[b] | Indirect[c] | |
Indoor			Between base lines and outside lines	Behind base lines
Recreational	20 (220)			
Club[d]	30 (320)	23 ft (7 m)	16 ft (4.9 m)	13 ft (4 m)
Professional	50 (540)			
Exhibitions	100 (1100)			

[a]Uniformity ratio of 2.0 to 1.0.
[b]Spacing (spacing-to-mounting height)—2.0 to 1.0 between rows.
[c]Spacing (spacing-to-distance from ceiling)—2.0 to 1.0 between luminaires in a row.
[d]May be increased for commercial considerations.

matte rather than a glossy finish.

The footlambert is the product of the illumination in footcandles and the reflection factor of the surface. For example, forty footcandles striking a surface with a reflection factor of fifty percent would produce a brightness of twenty footlamberts (40 x .50 = 20). These brightnesses are necessary when computing brightness differences in order to achieve a balanced visual field.

Important Lighting Considerations

In addition to the quantity and quality of light from the various kinds of lighting systems available, additional factors to consider in the selection of an electrical illumination system are maintenance, repair, replacement, and cleaning.

The ideal lighting fixture has both an indirect and a direct component, throwing surface light on the ceiling to give it about the same brightness as the lighting unit itself.

There is less need, however, to provide high-ceiling areas with direct-indirect fixtures. In gymnasiums, swimming pools and similar activity areas, an even distribution of light is required to permit the individual to see quickly and distinctly in any part of the room. It is advisable to provide supplementary lighting on such

areas as those containing goals or targets, and to place dimmers on the lighting in spectator areas. Supplementary light sources should be shielded from the eyes of participants and spectators in order to provide the proper brightness balance.

Transparent, nonbreakable, plastic protective covers will protect lighting units in activity areas where balls may be thrown. Vapor-proof lighting units are recommended for damp areas, such as toilets, showers, the dressing-locker suite, and the swimming pool. Locker room lights should be spaced to light the areas between lockers.

Incandescent, fluorescent, mercury-vapor, and sodium-vapor lighting systems are most commonly used in gymnasium buildings. The incandescent light is instantaneous, burns without sound, and is not affected by the number of times the light is turned on or off. Incandescent lights and fixtures are considerably cheaper in initial cost, are easier to change, and the lamp, within limits, may be varied in size within a given fixture.

Incandescent fixtures, however, have excessively high spot brightness and give off considerable heat, a problem when high levels of illumination are necessary.

Fluorescent lamps have the advantage of long life and give at

least two and one-half times the amount of light that incandescent lamps give for the same amount of current used. They are frequently used in old buildings to raise the illumination level without the installation of new wiring.

Mercury-vapor lighting is most expensive in terms of initial installation. The overall cost of mercury-vapor lighting, however, is cheaper than incandescent lighting. The primary objection to mercury-vapor lighting is the bluish color. However, when incandescent lighting is used in addition to mercury-vapor, a highly-satisfactory lighting system results.

Night lights which burn continually are recommended for gymnasiums, swimming pools, handball courts, squash courts, and other indoor activity areas. Lobbies, corridors, and some classrooms should also be equipped with night lights. These lights are extremely important for safety and security purposes and should have separate controls.

Provisions for outside lighting should be considered. Exit lights must follow the prescribed codes of the local community and the state. Electrically illuminated exit lights, clearly indicating the direction of exit to the exterior, should be provided: over all exit doors from gymnasiums, combined auditorium-gymnasiums, multi-purpose rooms, and other rooms used for assembly purposes; over all exit doors from the building; and at the head and foot of exit stairways. All exit lighting should be on special circuits.

Emergency (white) lighting systems should be provided for exits (including exterior open spaces to which the exits lead) in gymnasiums, multi-purpose rooms, and other places of assembly or large group activity. This lighting should be on a special emergency circuit. All controls should be located so as to be under the supervision of authorized persons, and all other aspects of the installation should meet the specifications prescribed by the Underwriters Laboratories, the Building Exits Code, and state and local fire laws and regulations.

A variety of trends in lighting systems have developed in conventional structures. One system utilized primarily skylights and is supplemented with conventional artificial light. In such a system, a light sensor assesses the light level coming through the skylight in the working area just above the floor. At this point, the sensor signals that information to the artificial light system to shine from 0 percent to 100 percent of the wattage capacity, depending upon how much light is coming through the skylights. The sensor in this system can raise or lower the intensity of the artificial light to an acceptable and predetermined candle power dependent on the activity. Installation of skylights plus a light sensor system will add an additional construction cost, but this installation will reward the institution with energy conservation and cost saving. In addition, considering that without the utilization of a light sensor system, a facility's lights would be required to be on full-time whenever the building was occupied. Also, a high percentage of the total kilowatt hours used in a facility are conventionally designed for artificial lighting. A skylight and light sensor system will accrue a

significant saving in energy cost. Artificial lights also generate considerable heat and by reducing the amount of artificial light (heat), a skylight and light sensor system would have a significant impact on saving in air-conditioning cost. Such a system has an approximate theoretical saving projected to reduce air conditioning cost by one-half and lighting costs by one-third.

Fire-Alarm System

Electrical fire-alarm systems should be separate and distinct from all program-signal or other signal systems, and should be designed to permit operation from convenient locations in corridors and from areas of unusual fire hazard. All fire-alarm systems should meet the specifications prescribed by the Underwriters Laboratories and by state and local fire laws and regulations.

Program-Signal System

Gymnasium buildings can be wired for a signal system operated by a master clock or push buttons from the main administrative

offices. Secondary controls may be placed in other administrative units of the facility.

Program signals should be independent of the fire-alarm system and should not be used as a fire-alarm system.

Program signals usually include: buzzers or chimes in the classrooms; bells in corridors, pool, gymnasiums, fields, and dressing-locker suites; and large gongs on the outside of the building. In many instances, signals placed strategically in corridors rather than in individual classrooms are adequate. Electric clocks should be included in all indoor areas in the program-signal system.

Electrical Service Controls

The entrance for electrical service should be installed to ensure the safety of the students and building personnel. When practicable, it should be located at the side or rear of the building, away from heavy traffic or play areas.

Main service panels with main service switches, meters, and main light and power panels

Figure 2-6
In the Student Recreation and Aquatic Center on the Texas Tech University Campus, natural light augments inside lighting.

Indoor Facilities

should be located so as to prevent entrance by anyone except those authorized.

Secondary control panels should be placed for the convenient use of individuals who open or close the facilities during hours of darkness or outside of regular hours. Electric lighting and power should be fully available to all athletic, physical education, and recreation facilities during hours when the main offices and classrooms may be closed.

The main distribution panel, all secondary panels and all circuits should be protected by automatic circuit breakers. A number of spare circuits should be provided in panels for future use. Secondary panels, located in corridors, halls, and similar places, should be of the flush-front type provided with locks.

Wiring for program-signal systems and communications should not be in the regular service conduits. Switches in instructional rooms should be arranged so that lights adjacent to the interior wall may be controlled independently of the lights adjacent to the exterior wall. Consideration should be given for placing light switches at a height convenient for wheelchair users.

Stairway and corridor lighting should be on separate circuits. Three-way switches should be provided at the foot and head of stairs, near each end of corridors, and near doorways of large classrooms, activity rooms, or gymnasiums. This will permit control of the lights from two or more points. Switches should be located on the open side of entrances to all spaces in the building. Switches also should be provided in projection booths to control the lights in the rooms used for spectator activities. Remote control switches should have pilot lights.

Services for Appliances and Other Electrical Equipment

There are many needs for electrical wiring and connections which require careful analysis and planning. The following are illustrative:

- Basic construction: motors to operate folding partitions; blowers for heaters and ventilating ducts; exhaust fans in gymnasium ceilings or walls.
- Custodial and maintenance services: receptacles for floor cleaning equipment and power tools.
- Dressing locker rooms: wiring for hair and hand driers and electric shavers.
- Lounges, kitchenettes, snack bars, and concessions: outlets for refrigerators, water or soft drink coolers, electric stoves, blenders, mixers, coffee urns, and hot plates.
- Office suites: wiring for individual air-conditioners, business machines, floor fans, and other mechanical and electrical equipment.
- Laundry rooms: wiring for washers, driers, and irons.
- Pools: provision for underwater vacuum cleaners, pumps, and special lighting.
- Gymnasiums: provision for special lighting effects, spot lights, and rheostats or controls to lower the illumination for certain activities.
- Health suites: receptacles and provision for audiometers vision-testing equipment, floor fans, and air-conditioning units.

CLIMATE CONTROL

The engineering design of heating, air-conditioning, and ventilating systems should be based on the technical data and procedures of the American Society of Heating and Ventilating Engineers. The selection of the type of heating, air-conditioning, and ventilating systems should be made with special consideration for economy of operation, flexibility of control, quietness of operation, and capacity to provide desirable thermal conditions. The design and location of all climate control equipment should provide for possible future additions.

Since the number of occupants in any given area of the building will vary, special consideration should be given to providing variable controls to supply the proper amount of fresh air and total circulation for maximum occupancy in any one area. Specially designed equipment and controls are necessary to ensure that climate control in some major areas can be regulated and operated independently of the rest of the facility.

All three mechanical systems — heating, ventilating, and air-conditioning — are interrelated and should be planned together. The services of a competent mechanical engineer should be obtained, not only for design, but also for making inspections during construction and for giving operating instructions to the service department.

Some problems involved in the installation of heating, ventilating, and air-conditioning systems include:

- Maintaining a minimum noise level
- Maintaining separate temperature control for laboratory areas
- Insulating all steam, hot water, and cold water pipes and marking them with a color code
- Exhausting dry air through the locker rooms and damp air from the shower room to the outside
- Providing a minimum of four changes of air per hour without drafts
- Installing locking type thermostats in all areas, with guards wherever they may be subject to damage
- Placing the thermostats for highest efficiency

- Zoning the areas for night and recreational use
- Eliminating drafts on spectators and participants

The geographical location of the proposed facility will dictate to some extent the type of climate control equipment selected for installation. Mechanical ventilation is preferred over open windows. Air-conditioning has been strongly recommended for southern climates, but year-round use of facilities makes air-conditioning a desirable building feature in other areas. Special rooms such as locker rooms, shower rooms, swimming pools, and steam rooms need special consideration for moisture and humidity control.

The rising cost of energy also is an important operational consideration.

SECURITY

The athletic and physical education complex presents a unique security problem. The facilities and the programs attract large numbers of individuals who move at all times during the day and week and through many areas in different directions.

It is reasonable to believe that all students and visitors who come to the building have a distinct purpose in coming and should be welcome. This is the type of building which people enter through many outside doors and disperse to offices, classrooms, dressing rooms, activity areas, and spectator galleries. There should be some plan for pedestrian control and for the handling of visitors.

Security is accomplished in two ways:
- Constructing the facilities according to a plan which allows for maximum security
- Adopting an administrative plan for the direction and control of all persons using the building

The physical layout will facilitate security but will not guarantee it. A good administrative plan will help.

However, a good administrative plan cannot completely accomplish effective security if the physical layout does not lend itself to the attainment of such security.

Security Features of Construction

Entrance doors constitute the first barriers against illegal intrusion. Open and descending stairways, walled entries, and deep-set entrances should be avoided. The points of entrance to buildings should be well lighted from dusk until dawn. The corners of the buildings should have floodlights which light the face of the structure. So-called "vandal lights" should be installed and protected to make them vandalproof.

Corridors which are continuous and straight, providing unbroken vision, add qualities of safety and security to the building, its contents, and its users. Corridors are best lined up with entrance doors, providing a commanding view of the doorway from the corridor, and of the corridor from the entrance door. There should be an attempt to avoid angular corridors, and to eliminate niches or cubbyholes.

The use of night lighting within the building and at its entrances will assist in protection against vandalism and other forms of undesirable conduct. Night lighting will require separate wiring and switches in order to maintain a desirable amount of illumination. Switches for such lighting should be key-controlled to prevent their use by unauthorized individuals. A building chart for day and night "on" and "off" lights should be developed. There should be additional directions for "on" and "off" at every switch, and such directions should be changed according to need. A key-station system for night-watch checking is desirable.

Security of the Building

Securing the building and its component rooms against illegal entry is the first and most logical consideration in terms of building protection. Good door framing, substantial doors, and heavy-duty hardware and locks hold up against wear and abuse. In their long life and securing qualities, they constitute a reasonable investment. In reducing replacement costs for materials and labor, the installation of good hardware is economical in the long run.

To reduce loss through breakage and theft, the additional security factor of quality hardware should never be overlooked at any cost.

A lock-and-key system, developed with the help of experts in the field of building administration, will usually result in a plan which considers some of the following features:
- A building master plan, including a lock-and-key system
- Lock-tumbler adjustments so that an area may have its own control and authorization
- Area division (vertical division) by responsibility or usage for key assignment; or "level" division (horizontal division) for key assignment; or a combination of both vertical and horizontal divisions
- A policy of not lending keys is recommended. The person to whom the key is assigned signs a pledge for no lending. The keys for the facilities should be identified by a distinguishing mark, and a policy should be established with key duplicators in the areas that they will refuse to duplicate keys carrying such identifying marks.
- An annunciator system in which outside or other doors of importance, such as swimming pool doors,

may be connected to an electrically controlled system. Any door can be connected in or out of the annunciator by a lock-controlled switch at the door, or a switch at the annunciator. Thus, a door tampered with or illegally opened after the annunciator is set for the "on" position will direct a warning signal. The annunciator may be developed to work by a light on a control box, the sound at a control box, an alarm sound of general broadcast in the building, or an alarm system with signals directed to the campus security office. The nature of the annunciator response should be determined by whether it is wished to quietly apprehend unauthorized persons, or if it is desired to deter them or frighten them away.

Security and Safety of Participants

Security and safety suggestions related to the use of specific facilities ordinarily found in a gymnasium structure include:

• All swimming pool doors are to be locked unless unlocked by a person authorized to do so. When a door is unlocked for a purpose, the individual unlocking the door is responsible for the accomplishment of that purpose. Outdoor and some indoor pools may be connected with a sonar detection system or a sound amplification system which will announce illegal use or entry. The signal can go to one or several strategic control points. Swimming pools should normally be keyed differently than other areas in the structure.

• In a gymnastics gymnasium, or where there are related gymnastic activities, the room, or certain pieces of equipment must

be locked except when an instructor is directly in charge. Providing storage areas sufficiently large to store all equipment for this activity is recommended. If possible, a separate room, secure from students and faculty, is most desirable.

• In viewing balconies, stairs should have handrails and lights at the sides, or luminous reflectorizing material on the edges. Bleacher seats should have aisles and exits to allow rapid clearing other than to the playing floor.

• Activity room floors should be free of objects or floor plates which set up above the floor level.

• Shower room and dressing room floors should be kept free of objects and obstructions which may cause foot injury.

• Shower rooms should be equipped with towel bars to aid in safety of those individuals using the facility. Hot water available through shower heads should have a maximum temperature of 120°F.

• Areas for vigorous activity, where combatives or competitive sports are engaged in should have floor and/or wall covering to protect the participants. No specifications of classifications are given here, but every consideration is urged and every precaution should be taken.

• Doors to steam rooms and dry-heat rooms should be capable of being locked from the outside when the room is unsupervised. The door should have an instruction plate by the door lock, bearing directions to those who have a key to unlock the door. Steam room controls should be set not to exceed a maximum room temperature of 130°F. This control should be tamper-proof. The steam room should have a bar latch of the panic type (noncorrosive hardware) to make exit readily possible under any conditions, even if the door should be locked from the outside.

Dressing room entrances should be away from the main traffic and in the area where only participants

go to change clothes. Toilet rooms should be away from direct view of the lobby, and yet be in service corridors rather than in isolated parts of the building.

Stairs should be well lighted. In some cases, the edges of stairs should be marked. Objects in the building which may need to be identified for safety or position may need to be color coded or marked in some manner. In basement passageways and around motors and equipment, it is important to mark corners, low pipes or beams, and safety zone areas. On main floors, it is desirable to mark fire alarms and extinguishers, some traffic lanes, and first-aid boxes, and to indicate service and toilet areas with their appropriate service designations by door labeling or signs at door top height. Designation of objects can be accomplished by painting the objects or zones according to a color code.

PLANNING FOR SPECIFIC PROGRAMS

The task of the planner is to ascertain the indoor space requirements of the school and the community for athletics, physical education and recreation and to translate their needs into the number, size, type, and location of facilities.

The planner should give attention to the following general concepts:

The locker, shower, and drying room area should be planned for the safety, maximal use of space, comfort, traffic flow, security and the convenience of its users.

The involvement of all men and women staff members who will be using the areas is important. The development of a well-designed priority list should be established to see that the areas needed most will not be eliminated or expensive extras added by a sudden impulse or strong lobby from a special interest group.

To provide adequate variety in

the physical education curriculum, it may be necessary to plan more than a gymnasium. In a school for kindergarten through third grade only, a room smaller than a regular size gymnasium may be used, unless it is also a neighborhood center for adults.

While a single facility may meet the instructional needs of the physical education program, additional space will be necessary if all students are to be given an opportunity to participate in an intramural and/or interscholastic program.

To expand the basic program in physical education, it is desirable to have such additional special facilities as bowling alleys, swimming pools, and archery and rifle ranges. It may be possible for the school to obtain some of these facilities through the cooperative use of existing or proposed facilities owned and administered by some other agency.

As planning for recreation is considered, the entire school plant becomes a potential space resource, and all units should be scrutinized and planned with recreational adaptability in mind.

ELEMENTARY SCHOOL INDOOR ACTIVITY AREAS

The elementary school physical education program centers around the teaching of fundamental movement patterns, rhythmics or dance, games and sports, gymnastic activities, combatives, self-testing activities, and aquatics. The design and scope of physical education facilities should reflect the activities included in the elementary physical education curriculum.

A major consideration fundamental to the planning of an elementary school indoor activity area is the anticipated use by the community. Future years are expected to see more and more community use of these facilities.

Several of the standard planning principles apply particularly to the elementary facility. Such planning principles would include establishing priority use for the facility, giving basic consideration to the primary age group using the facility, allowing for use by physically and mentally impaired children, designing for the participants ahead of the spectators, and remembering considerations for maintenance of the facilities.

Location

Elementary schools are often more compact than other schools and it is desirable to have the activity area apart from the classrooms to reduce noise disturbance. With the increasing use of such facilities by the community, consideration must be given to accessibility from the parking areas. In addition, it should be adjacent to the outdoor play fields. This allows for easier storage of equipment and increases the efficiency of the area to be used as a neighborhood playground in the summer months.

Teaching Stations for Physical Education

Elementary school physical education classes may be organized by a number of methods. The average class size is usually based on the number of pupils in the classroom unit. Because of differences in pupil maturation, physical education periods generally vary from 20 minutes for kindergarten and first grade to 45 minutes for fifth and sixth grades, with the school average (for computation purposes) being 30 minutes per class.

The formula for computing the number of teaching stations needed for physical education in an elementary school is as follows:

$$\begin{array}{c} \text{Minimum} \\ \text{Number of} \\ \text{Teaching} \\ \text{Stations} \end{array} = \begin{array}{c} \text{Number} \\ \text{Classroom} \\ \text{of} \\ \text{Students} \end{array} \times \begin{array}{c} \text{Number of Physical} \\ \text{Education periods} \\ \text{per week per class} \\ \text{(Total number of} \\ \text{Physical Education} \\ \text{Class Periods in a} \\ \text{school week)} \end{array}$$

Example:

• Number of classrooms of students — school contains grades K to 6, three classrooms for each grade level, or a total of 21 classroom units.

• Number of physical education periods per week per class — one period per class for physical education each school day during the week equals five periods per week.

• Total number of physical education class periods in school week. There are five instructional hours in the school day, and the length of physical education period is 30 minutes. Thus, a total of ten 30-minute periods each school day may be scheduled for physical education, or a total of 50 periods for the five-day school week.

The teaching station needs would be calculated as follows:

Minimum number of teaching stations equals 21 classroom units times 5 periods per day, 50 periods per week, equals 105 divided by 50 equals 2.1.

In the above situation, if one classroom section was dropped each week (bringing the total to 20) then the need would be 2.0 teaching stations. Therefore, requiring physical education five periods per week in the school used as example, would necessitate employing two physical education teachers each hour of the day.

In many school systems the above situation would be too idealistic. More likely only one physical education instructor would be available (either a specialist, or the classroom teacher, or a paraprofessional in collaboration with one of the other two). This would then drop the number of sessions per week for each classroom unit from five to an average of 2.5. One teaching station would handle this setup.

If only one teaching station can be provided in the elementary school, then preferably it would be a gymnasium. Despite the fact that some other type of auxiliary station might prove superior for instruction in the lower grades, the elementary gymnasium remains the preferred facility because of its heavy use by both the upper grades and the community. If the school system and the community were in need of an indoor swimming pool, this would be the choice for a second teaching station.

The next choice is an auxiliary teaching station, sometimes called a playroom. Particularly when heavy community use is anticipated, another alternative is to build a larger gymnasium and allow for dividing it by a folding partition or dropdown nets. Such a setup would provide four possible teaching stations, two on each side of the divider. This area would also allow for two basketball intramural courts, one basketball inter-school court, three volleyball courts, six badminton courts, and four multi-purpose game circles.

Multi-purpose rooms and cafeteria-gymnasium combinations have been found to be most impractical for physical education, especially from the standpoint of scheduling. Self-contained classrooms are restrictive in the types of activities that can be offered and have an additional disadvantage. Furniture must be moved whenever activity takes place.

If used, such classrooms must provide an unobstructed area of 450 sq. ft., be of a nonskid surface, have no dangerous projections, and ideally have direct access to an adjoining terrace, part of which should be roofed for protection against rain. These self-contained classrooms would only be used in the lower grades.

The Gymnasium

In planning the elementary school gymnasium, a minimum of 100 square feet per pupil and a total of at least 4,000 square feet is recommended. Spectator seating (if provided) and storage rooms require additional space. Many of the general considerations recommended for secondary school gymnasiums also apply to elementary school facilities. (Figure 2-7)

The specific dimensions of the gymnasium should provide for a basketball court of 42 by 74 feet, with a minimum safety space of six feet around the perimeter. An area of 54 by 90 feet (4,860

Figure 2-7
The North Harrison Elementary School gymnasium was designed to also community recreation programs.

square feet) would be adequate. The ceiling should be at least 22 feet high. This space is adequate for activities normally included in the elementary school program and will serve the community recreational program. The gymnasium will be of a larger size if the decision is made to use it as a multiple teaching facility and include a folding partition or dropnets as part of the design.

Auxiliary Teaching Stations

If a second indoor physical education teaching area is built it should be either a swimming pool or an auxiliary instruction room, sometimes called a playroom. Swimming pools are discussed elsewhere in this text. The auxiliary teaching station is most practical when the main gymnasium cannot fulfill all of the school's needs for teaching stations.

At least 60 square feet per primary pupil, with a total minimum of 1,800 square feet of space, is suggested for this unit. A ceiling height of 18 feet in the clear is preferred, although lower ceilings may be used. One wall should be free of obstruction to be used for target and ball games or throwing practice. A smooth masonry wall will provide an adequate rebounding surface. If included, windows should be of breakproof glass or be protected by a shield or grill and located high enough as not to restrict activities.

The auxiliary unit should be planned to accommodate limited apparatus and tumbling activities, games of low organization, rhythmic activities, movement exploration, and other activities for the primary grades. Often a 25' circle for circle games is located at one end of this room, allowing for permanent or semi-permanent equipment at the other end. The equipment could include such items as climbing ropes and poles, ladders, mats, stall bars, rings, large wooden boxes, horizontal bars, and peg boards. These

should be located so as not to interfere with other activities or so they may be easily moved out of the way. A storage room for equipment and supplies should be included. A section of wall can be equipped with hangers for mat storage.

Electrical outlets are required for the use of sound equipment. This room will, for the most part, be used by the lower grades and should be accessible to those classrooms. If the area is to serve the after-school recreational program for pupils or community groups, toilet facilities should be accessible.

Surfaces

The best floor surface to use may depend upon the number of different teaching areas. The main gymnasium area should have either a hard wood or synthetic surface. Wood, preferably maple, is an excellent all-around surface, although it lacks the durability and flexibility that might be demanded by extensive community use of the facility. Synthetic surfaces have proven excellent for all normal game-type activities and also can better accommodate events that put additional stress on the floor, such as setting up chairs, tables, booths, etc. In an auxiliary teaching station, carpeting is often used. It eliminates the use of certain small wheeled equipment. Tile is not recommended as a play surface.

A special consideration is the structure and material used in the ceilings. Ceilings should be durable and resistant to puncturing.

Storage

Storage rooms are needed for each of the different instructional areas. The room adjoining the gymnasium should be at least 200 to 300 square feet and should be directly accessible from the gymnasium floor through a double door without a threshold. For safety reasons, the doors should

open inward and be provided with locks. Consideration must be given to community use of the facility and the storage of related equipment. Ideally, there would be a separate storage room for each of the programs. The storage areas should have bins, shelves, racks, and hangers for the best utilization of space and the proper care of equipment and supplies. Space to store out-of-season equipment is essential to prevent loss or misplacement between seasons. An outside entrance assists in the handling of equipment that is used outdoors and/or in connection with a summer playground program.

Shower and Dressing Rooms

Although it has been standard practice not to include shower, locker, and dressing room facilities in the elementary school, such facilities are essential if the gymnasium is to be used for intramural-interschool competition and community usage. The size, number of lockers, showers, and toilet facilities will be dependent on the extent of usage. If swimming pools are added as part of the school-community complex, such facilities are a must. Provision for outdoor restrooms is desirable if the general public is involved.

Programming for Construction of a Playroom

Use of Playroom. This area should be suitable for preschool and for grades K-3 for fundamental movement activities, including creative games and rhythms, relays, stunts, and climbing and hanging activities.

Size. The area should be a rectangle measuring approximately 50 by 40 feet, providing 2,000 square feet of space.

Ceiling. The ceiling should be acoustically treated, 14 to 18 feet high (all beams and supports above the minimum height), with suitable fixtures attached to the beams to support hanging equipment.

Walls. Walls below 10 feet should be free from obstruction. A smooth concrete block sealed with epoxy paint works well. Above 10 feet should also be free of obstruction, but made of acoustic or slotted concrete block. A wall free from obstruction will provide practice areas for such activities as kicking, striking and throwing, and a space for the placement of targets and use of visual aids.

Floors. A hardwood maple or synthetic surface of good quality provide the best floor for general activity use. Both have advantages and disadvantages. The decision should be based on how the floor is to be used. Careful consideration should also be given to the location of lines and the installation of equipment.

Lighting. Fluorescent lighting should supply 50 footcandles on the floor, and a switch should be installed at each door. Light fixtures should be guarded to prevent breakage.

Windows. If used at all, windows should be placed on only one side of the room to provide natural light. They should be covered with a protective screen. Window sills should be eight feet above the floor.

Electrical Outlets. Double-service outlets should be installed on each wall.

Equipment Storage Area. At least 200 to 300 square feet should be provided for storage. Cabinets and shelves should be installed. The equipment room should have a double door so wide equipment may be moved in and out easily. A telephone for emergency use should be placed in the equipment room.

Mirrors. Three full-length mirrors should be placed at one end of a wall, side by side, for visual analysis of movement.

Bulletin Board. Cork board should be hung on the wall near the entrance for posting materials and schedules.

Chalkboard. A chalkboard can be wall-mounted to facilitate teaching if this will not interfere with wall-rebounding activities. Otherwise, portable chalkboards can be used.

Drinking Fountain. One should be placed on a wall in the corridor just outside the door to the playroom.

Speakers. Two matched speakers should be placed high on the wall or in the ceiling. Jack plugs should be installed on each wall to use for speaker input.

Paint. Walls should be painted off-white or a very pale color. However, murals, accent colors and designs can be used for aesthetics.

Other Items. If the building is equipped with closed circuit TV, two outlets should be provided for receiver. There should be a separate entrance for recreational use. The teaching station should be isolated from other parts of the building for evening functions.

Adapted Teaching Station

Local philosophy and state/federal laws vary as to the inclusion of physically and mentally impaired students in regular physical education classes. A separate adaptive teaching station would be an ideal setup but any special program for such students often has to be accommodated in the regular facilities (see Chapter 8).

SECONDARY SCHOOL INDOOR ACTIVITY AREAS

Teaching Stations

The type and number of indoor teaching stations for a secondary school depends on the number of students and the specific program of physical education and related activities. In all situations, a gymnasium is required. By determining the number of teaching stations essential for the formal program of instruction, planners will have a basis for calculating other needs. Computation of the minimum numerical requirement is achieved by the following formula:

$$\text{Minimum Number of Teaching Stations} = \frac{700 \text{ Students}}{30 \text{ per Class}} \times \frac{5 \text{ Periods per Wk.}}{30 \text{ Periods per Wk.}}$$

$$= \frac{3500}{900} = 3.9$$

The fraction is rounded to the next highest number, making four teaching stations the minimum requirement. This number would also afford some flexibility of class scheduling.

In computing teaching station requirements for the secondary school, the desired class size must not be set so low as to require an impossible number of teachers and facilities, nor should it be so high that effectiveness is impaired. An average class size of thirty with daily instruction is recommended. However, if the physical education classes meet only two periods per week, the total number of class periods per week in the formula must be adjusted accordingly.

The next step for planners is to determine the degree to which the number of teaching stations for the program of instruction will meet the needs for voluntary recreation, extramural and intramural activities, and interscholastic athletics for girls and boys, as well as the possible use of facilities by the community. The needs must be based upon the season of the year representing the greatest demand for facilities.

The following guide can be used to determine the number of teaching stations needed for activities other than the formal program of instruction in physical education:

Minimum number of teaching stations, or fractions thereof, needed for interscholastic-team practice at peak load
plus
Minimum number of teaching stations, or fractions thereof, needed for intramural and extramural activities
plus
Minimum number of teaching stations, or fractions thereof, needed for student recreation
plus
Minimum number of teaching

stations, or fractions thereof, needed for community recreation

      equals

The total number of teaching stations needed for any specific after-school period

*Physical education facilities for the middle school should follow the standards for secondary schools.

To illustrate, assume a school has two interscholastic squads, an intramural program, a voluntary recreation group, and no community recreational use of facilities immediately after school during a specific season. The total needs are as follows:

Required Teaching Stations

      equals

2 Interscholastic

      plus

1 Intramural

      plus

1 Voluntary Recreation

      equals

4 Stations

The need for four teaching stations for the after-school program must then be compared to the number necessary for the formal program of instruction in physical education. If the after-school needs are in excess of those for the regular periods of instruction, the additional teaching stations should be provided. Careful administrative scheduling results in maximum utilization of facilities.

Variety of Teaching Stations

A wide variety of teaching stations is possible, depending on the number of different activities that would appropriately be included in the physical education program. Among the possible types of indoor teaching stations that might be included are gymnasiums, rhythm rooms, rooms for gymnastics, adapted physical education rooms, wrestling rooms, classrooms, swimming pools, archery ranges, rifle ranges, and racquetball courts.

The problem for some schools is not lack of an adequate number of teaching stations but rather lack of facilities to accommodate the desired variety of activities. For a secondary school with 360 students, a divisible gymnasium will create an adequate number of teaching stations for the program of instruction in physical education but may not meet the peak load requirement for after-school activities. The facility must be planned and designed to serve all program needs as adequately as possible.

Whenever a school's teaching requirements are such that a basic gymnasium is inadequate, planners should consider special purpose stations, such as an auxiliary physical education teaching station, a natatorium, or a dance studio.

Secondary School Gymnasium

The building or portion of the school that houses the gymnasium should be easily accessible from classrooms, parking areas, and the outdoor activity area. This also makes possible use of the facility after school hours or during weekends or holidays without having to open other sections of the school.

Size and Layout

For general purposes, allow a minimum of 125 square feet of usable activity space for each individual in a physical education class at peak load. The space requirements and dimensions of a gymnasium floor are significantly influenced by the official rules governing court games, particularly interscholastic basketball and the extent of spectator seating. The minimum dimensions required of a gymnasium for basketball, however, should be expanded, if necessary, to accommodate other activities. In some instances, an entire gymnasium is not required for an activity. Folding, sound-proof partitions can be used to divide the area and provide two teaching stations.

Walls and Ceilings

The walls of the gymnasium should be of a material that is resistant to hard use, at least to door height. The finish should be non-marking and have a smooth, non-abrasive surface. All corners below door height should be rounded, and there should be no projections into playing areas. Lower portions (10') of the walls should be finished with materials that can be easily cleaned without destroying the finish. An epoxy paint on cement block makes a durable finish.

The ceiling should be 24 feet to the low side of beams or supports, with fixtures attached to the beams to support hanging equipment. High ceilings are expensive, and a natural method for cutting construction costs is to minimize ceiling height. If this is in the area for basketball, volleyball, gymnastics, badminton, or tennis, it can be a critical error. However, in an auxiliary gym used for wrestling, dance, combatives, weight lifting, or table games, a 12-15 foot ceiling is acceptable.

All ceilings should be light in color, and, if support beams are below the ceiling, they normally are painted the same color as the ceiling or background. Contrasting colors have been used effectively, but such color contrast may make it difficult to follow the flight of an object.

Acoustical treatment of ceilings and walls is important where teaching is to take place. To get the best results, at least two adjacent surfaces should be treated. Many types of acoustical treatment are available. However, avoid those which will chip or break when hit with a ball.

Floors

The biggest decision that needs to be made with respect to floors is whether to go with hard wood or synthetic surfaces. The advantages and disadvantages of different surfaces has been discussed previously. Careful consideration should also be given to the location of lines for various activities and floorplates for standards or gymnastic equipment.

Lighting

There are many types of lighting systems which will produce the 50 footcandles needed for a good teaching and spectator area. For television, the footcandles should be closer to 200 fc. and that requires more sophisticated lighting systems. When selecting a lighting system, compare initial costs, annual replacement costs and operational or electrical expenses. Some are less expensive to install but very expensive to maintain or operate.

Windows

Windows should generally be avoided. When located to take advantage of the sun for solar heat, the glare may cause serious problems. When windows are on the north side, there is less glare, but the loss of heat may be significant. Vandalism is another disadvantage.

Folding Partitions

Folding partitions make possible two or more teaching stations in the gymnasium. They should be power-operated, insulated against sound transmission and reverberation, and installed to permit compensation for building settlement. The control should be key-operated. The design and operation must ensure student safety. Partitions should extend from floor to ceiling and may be recessed when folded. Floor tracks should not be used. A pass door should be provided at the end of a partition. When partitions are installed in gymnasiums with open truss construction, the space between the top of the folding doors and the ceiling should be insulated against sound transmission.

Fixed Equipment

If suspended equipment is planned, provision for its attachment should be made before the ceiling is installed.

Basketball backstops will need special care in their installation to ensure rigidity and safety. All basketball backstops should be attached to ceilings or walls, and swing-up or fold-up models should be used where the backstops might interfere with other activities. In addition to the main court basketball backstops, provision should be made for other backstops on clear sidewalls. Hinged rims that collapse when grabbed are recommended for baskets used for recreational basketball play.

In the interest of safety, such suspension apparatus as bars, rings, and climbing poles and ropes should be so placed as to allow sufficient clearance from basketball backstops and walls. If wall apparatus is desired in the gymnasium, a strip of metal or hardwood firmly attached to the wall at the proper height is recommended. Wherever necessary, floor plates should be installed for fastening movable equipment such as horizontal bars and volleyball standards. If mats are to be hung in the gymnasium, appropriate hangers hung above head level to avoid any head injury must be provided. Rubber-tired mat trucks, which may be wheeled into a storage room, are recommended. For safety reasons, padding should be installed on all walls in back of baskets.

Spectator Seating

The extent of the demand for spectator seating depends upon each school and the community it serves. Modern design uses power-driven folding or rollaway bleachers which require little permanent space. If possible, the outer surface of folding bleachers should create a flat, wall-like surface so it may be used for ball rebounding.

The width of each seating space should not be less than 18 inches. Rollaway bleachers most commonly allow 22-inch depths for seats. The number of rows available in rollaway bleachers varies, with 23 rows the maximum for standard equipment. In some instances, bleachers with 30 rows can be obtained by special order. Planners should investigate local and state codes.

Balconies can be used to increase the total seating capacity beyond the maximum permitted at floor level. The space at both levels should be considered as activity areas when the bleachers are closed. It may be desirable, in some instances, to provide less than maximum seating at floor level so a balcony will be wide enough to serve as a teaching station for specific activities. Balcony bleachers can be installed to telescope from the back to the front so that in the closed position they stand erect, creating a divider wall at the edge of the balcony. This arrangement affords partial isolation of the teaching station and enhances the safety of participants.

Traffic Controls

Good traffic control should permit the efficient movement of students to and from the gymnasium, locker rooms, and other related service areas. All traffic arrangements for spectators should provide direct movement to and from bleachers with a minimum of foot traffic on gymnasium floors. Spectators should have access to drinking fountains, refreshment counters, and toilets without crossing the gymnasium floor. Steep, high stairways should be avoided. Ramps with nonslip surfaces might be substituted in appropriate places. Local and state building codes and standards of the National Fire Protection Association should be consulted.

Foyers

Where finances and space will allow, foyers should be placed so they will serve as entries to gymnasiums and will guide spectators as directly as possible to seating areas. Toilet facilities for men and women, ticket-sales windows, ticket-collection arrangements, checkrooms, public telephones, a refreshment-dispensing room with counter, and lockable display case should be provided, opening directly to the foyer.

Lecture Room

The lecture room provides opportunities for formal instruction, conferences, chalkboard drills, staff meetings, movies, and so on. It may serve as a lounge for lettermen, a social center for teams after a game, and other similar uses.

Maintenance-Equipment Storage

Two types of storage rooms are necessary for every physical education facility. The first is for storage of large pieces of equipment needed in the gym, items such as volleyball standards and officials stands, gymnastic equipment, chairs, mats and score tables which, if left around the gym floor, are a safety hazard. This room should have easy access to the gym floor through double doors (with no center post and no threshold). The room should be planned to provide for current equipment and future expansion and should be keyed with safety lights in case of power failure.

The second type of room needed is for the storage and repair of small equipment and supplies. Special bins, racks, hooks and nets, with a work bench for marking and minor repairs, adds greatly to the efficiency of the room. Ideally this room should be located near faculty offices.

Spectator Rest Rooms

All athletic events that attract spectators require rest room facilities. Rest rooms should be designed for proper light, ventilation, and sanitary care. State health codes will influence the number and location of rest rooms.

Concessions

Concessions have come to be considered a necessary service for public gatherings. Appropriate space and distribution as well as adequate fixtures for concession stands within the field should be planned. Since plumbing and electrical services are already available in the field house, the concession stand might be located as a part of or adjacent to the field house.

Other Factors

Provisions should be made for the installation of electric scoreboards, a central sound and public address system, picture projectors, radio and television equipment, high-fidelity equipment, and cleaning machines. Special consideration should be given to locating floor outlets for scoreboards and public address systems adjacent to the scoring table. Wall outlets should be installed near cupped eyes to permit special lighting as needed. Controls for gymnasium lighting should be conveniently located, recessed, and keyed.

Drinking fountains and cuspidors should be accessible without causing a traffic or safety problem. It may be desirable to provide a drained catch-basin, grilled flush with the floor, to care for splash and overflow.

Cupped eyes can be installed in all walls at approximately a 15-foot height and 10-foot intervals for decorating convenience. They may also be used for attaching nets and other equipment to walls at appropriate heights. Bulletin boards and chalkboards should be provided where needed. If wall space is available, such boards may be provided for each teaching station. Three full-length mirrors should be placed at one end of a wall, side by side, for visual analysis of movement.

The Auxiliary Gymnasium

Depending on the demands placed on a facility for classes, after-school athletics, intramurals and student and faculty recreation, more than one gymnasium may be necessary. Careful program scheduling will determine what is best in each situation. However, most schools need at least one auxiliary gym. Room dimensions should be based on the anticipated uses with special attention to the need to accommodate standard-size wrestling mats.

The other type of auxiliary gymnasium closely resembles the main gym except there is little or no need for spectator seating and the floor dimensions may be smaller. A 75 by 90 foot gym will house two volleyball courts, three badminton courts, three one wall handball courts, and space for some gymnastic equipment.

The auxiliary gyms can serve a variety of other activities in the instructional, intramural, recreational, or interscholastic program, which cannot all be accommodated after school in the main gymnasium. Some auxiliary gyms are large enough to be divided into two teaching stations. The characteristics of these facilities are similar to those in the gymnasium. A less expensive type may have a ceiling as low as 12 feet. Such activities as wrestling, tumbling, calisthenics, self-defense, and fencing may be conducted in such a room.

Adapted Area

Federal legislation requires that special considerations be made for the handicapped person. Schools must provide programs which meet their special needs. The adaptive area therefore becomes essential (see Chapter 8).

Gymnastics Area

By planning in detail the equipment layout for gymnastics, attachment hardware for floors, walls, and ceilings can be included in the original design and construction. The manufacturers of gymnastic equipment will supply details for the attachment of their equipment as well as suggestions for floor plans or layout of the apparatus with proper safety areas. Preplanning results not only in proper installation but also in savings on the cost of doing the work at a later date.

Storage of gymnastics equipment requires special attention. A room adjacent to the gym with extra high double doors and no threshold is desirable. Equipment left out or stored around the edge of the gym is a safety hazard and will shorten the life of the equipment. Mat storage requires either a mat truck or hangers. The use of light folding mats will, however, alleviate some of the storage problems.

Climbing ropes are attached to a height of 24 feet and drop to about three feet above the floor. Apparatus may be attached to the exposed beams. If the ceiling is placed below the structural members, the locations of suspended equipment should be planned and eyebolts provided during construction. Ropes should be placed five feet apart, allowing one for each five students in class. The rings should be at least five feet from the walls. End walls at least 35 feet from the point of attachment will afford safety for the participants. Traveling rings are supported from a height of 18 to 26 feet and are located seven feet apart along a continuous line. Lines should be provided for drawing ropes and rings not in use to the overhead so as not to interfere with other activities.

High bars require both floor and wall or ceiling attachments. Adjustable bars for class instruction can be arranged in a linear series. Bars vary from six to seven feet in length and require 12 feet of unobstructed space extending perpendicular to their long axis. Bars for interscholastic competition are commonly located as individual units.

Dance Area

Few secondary schools have specialized facilities for dance. There is some indication, however, that specialized concentrations (dance, sports, aquatics, gymnastics) in teacher preparation is beginning to alter this pattern, particularly in suburban areas and in certain consolidated school districts. As these programs begin to establish their value, obtaining facilities may be easier.

A minimum dance facility will provide 100 square feet per student, one dimension to exceed 60 feet; full length mirrors at a corner for analysis of skill from two directions; a speaker system designed to distribute sound evenly throughout the room; a control system for record players and microphones; and practice barres on one wall at heights of 34 inches and 42 inches. For modern dance, the floor should be of hard northern maple which has been sealed and then buffed with fine abrasive.

Portable percussion racks made in an industrial arts department can solve the problems of storage and efficient class and program use. Portable mirrors, six feet tall and eight feet wide, can be mounted 18 inches from the floor on rollers and moved into the dance area if wall mounted mirrors are not feasible. Portable ballet barres of lightweight aluminum are desirable when unobstructed wall space is at a premium.

Adaptive rooms, gymnastic rooms, weight training rooms, or recreational game rooms may have spaces available for dance. Careful preplanning of new facilities suggests the possibility of combining two or more of these.

Other Indoor Facilities

Some activities require specialized equipment and areas that may be provided in a main or auxiliary gymnasium. Even with careful planning, it is difficult to make adequate provisions without some compromise. In some activities, such as aquatics, the very nature of the activity necessitates a separate facility. The natatorium is considered separately in Chapter 4.

COLLEGE/UNIVERSITY INDOOR ACTIVITY AREAS

Colleges and universities in the United States are facing complex problems related to enrollment and economics. The magnitude of these problems has made the development of a master plan essential to college and university development. Space requirements of various programs of the institutions of higher learning have caused those responsible for master-plan development to request standards for facilities in terms of square feet per student. Standards in these terms are meaningful to campus planners, since relating standards to predicted enrollment results in assured space for all disciplines involved.

The following standards are recommended for consideration by those involved in planning college and university facilities for physical education, intramural sports, intercollegiate athletics, and recreation. It has been estimated by intramural leaders that the extent of participation in physical recreation by graduate students is 25 percent of that of undergraduates. Consequently, it is suggested that planners add 25 percent of the graduate enrollment when computing space needs for recreational areas.

Teaching Stations

The space requirements are 8.5 to 9.5 square feet per student (total undergraduate enrollment). They include: gym floors, mat areas, swimming pools, courts, and the like (adjacent to lockers and showers and within 10-minute walking distance of academic classrooms).

Indoor Space

A breakdown of indoor space would include:

- Large gymnasium areas with relatively high ceilings (minimum 22 feet) for basketball, badminton, gymnastics, apparatus, volleyball and the like (approximately 55 percent of indoor space).
- Activity areas with relatively low ceilings (minimum 12 feet) for combatives, therapeutic exercises, dancing, weight-lifting and the like (approximately 30 percent of indoor space).
- Swimming and diving pools (approximately 15 percent of indoor space).
- Racquetball/handball or squash courts (not included in percent breakdown, however it has been recommended that one such court is needed for 800 undergraduate students).

Also, investigation indicates that a reasonable standard for determining the space needed for lockers, showers, toweling rooms, equipment storage, supply rooms, and offices associated with indoor space is a square footage equaling approximately 40 percent of the play or activity area in a gymnasium facility. As an example of how this figure may be used, assume that a building is being planned to provide 100,000 square feet of activity space. In other words, the square footage of the swimming pool surface and deck and of all gymnasium floors, including high and low ceiling areas, equals 100,000 square feet. The space needed for ancillary

areas would be in the neighborhood of 40,000 square feet.

All other space in a building, including hallways, stairways, wall thicknesses, lobbies, public toilets, bleachers for public use, custodial space, and space needed for service conduits of all types, is spoken of by many architects as "tare." By adding tare, ancillary, and net space, a rough estimate of the gross footage of a building plan can be computed. This figure is helpful in preliminary discussion of costs involved.

Other considerations with regard to indoor space include enrollment relationships and peak load after school hours.

Enrollment Relationships

When standards in terms of square feet per student are used as guides in college or university planning, it is natural to ask where the computation begins. At what point, from ten students up, do the standards become meaningful? Obviously, for a college of 200 students, nine square feet per student of indoor area for sports and athletics would be woefully inadequate. It would not even provide one basketball court.

A university or college meeting the space standards for 1,500 students represents the minimum physical recreation space needs of any collegiate institution. As a college or university increases in size, these standards are applicable regardless of enrollment.

Gymnasiums (Main Area)

The type and size of gymnasium facilities needed for a given college or university will depend upon many factors, including the anticipated enrollment. A gymnasium building planned to serve 2,000 students will, obviously, be considerably smaller than, and different in design and construction from, a facility

planned for a university of 10,000 or more students. If a college or university has a definite enrollment ceiling, the building may be planned for this enrollment. If the enrollment ceiling is indefinite, however, the structure should be planned so additions to the buildings are feasible. Universities of 15,000 or more students may find it desirable to build more than one gymnasium structure, each servicing an area of the campus.

Another factor that will affect the type of building constructed is the philosophy of the administration concerning athletics and physical education. Many questions need to be answered before planning begins:

- What will be the priority for usage, among athletics, physical education, and recreation.
- Will all students be required to take physical education for one, two, three, or four years?
- Will the required program provide the students with a variety of opportunities to develop sport skills?
- Is teacher education in physical education to be part of the program?
- What responsibility does the college or university take for the physical education, recreation, and fitness of its faculty?
- Will research in physical education, health, and recreation be an important aspect of the program?
- What will be done to provide facilities for an expanded program of campus recreation (including intramurals)?

PRINCIPLES OF PLANNING AND CONSTRUCTION

Indoor facilities for sports and athletics should be planned so that all activity areas will be available to both men and women. Good planning will permit easy access to all areas from both men's and women's locker rooms. This type of planning permits the flexibility necessary for efficient utilization and control.

Roll-away or folding bleachers should be used in order to use the available space efficiently. Most colleges and universities can neither afford to invest large sums of money nor give large areas of space to permanent seating that is used only a few times each year.

The traffic patterns for a building should be carefully studied. Lockers, showers, and toweling rooms should be centrally located in the building so they may serve all activity areas. Easy access should be provided from the locker room to the playing fields adjacent to the building.

Storage rooms for equipment and supplies should be carefully planned and functionally located. These rooms should be of three types:

• Central receiving storage rooms, to which all equipment and supplies are delivered and which should be accessible by truck.

• Utility storage rooms adjacent to gymnasiums so bulky equipment may be easily moved to the floor and back to storage.

• Overhead doors or double doors should be large enough to permit free movement of heavy equipment.

• Supply rooms with an attendant's window opening to the locker rooms.

Off-season storage rooms are critically needed. The type of equipment to be moved and stored will define the dimensions of the room and size of the doors needed. Reserve storage should also be provided.

LOCATION

If physical education and athletic facilities are used by all the students, the gymnasium facility should be located conveniently near the academic buildings and student housing. Buildings used only for intramural and intercollegiate activities may be located farther from classrooms and housing. This is especially true if the activities promoted in these buildings are scheduled. If the building is to be used for unscheduled participation of students, however, the amount of use will vary inversely with the distance from housing and other campus buildings.

GUIDELINES FOR DETERMINING NEEDS

The physical education building should include one main gymnasium to be used for general physical education class work, intramurals, and intercollegiate athletic activities. Ideally, the size of the floor for an enrollment of 4,000 students would be approximately 140 by 140 feet. (Use a rectangular dimension if the facility will be heavily used for spectator sports.) This size would provide for one official and three junior-size (35 by 84 feet) basketball courts, with adequate space between the courts and walls. If desirable, folding partitions can be used to provide three practice gymnasiums, each 48 by 140 feet. For the basketball courts, backboards that swing up to the ceiling are needed, since non-folding backboards would interfere with court usage for activities such as volleyball and badminton. In order to increase the number of other instructional units, electrically controlled partitions should be installed.

If the gymnasium is to be used for intercollegiate athletics, seating must be provided for spectators (three square feet per person). Portable folding bleachers, which can be easily moved, are recommended for seating. In larger institutions, it may be necessary to install roll-away bleacher seats in the balcony, which, when combined with the bleachers on the main floor, will provide the required number of seats.

The varsity basketball court should be laid out lengthwise in

NCAA BASKETBALL COURT DIAGRAM

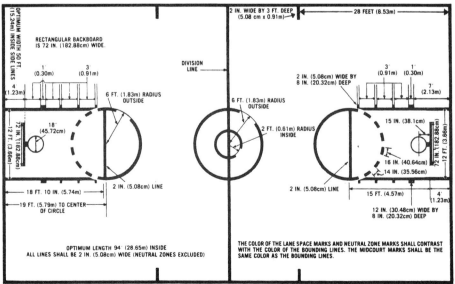

Figures 2-8; 8A

Multi-purpose gymnasium with suspended track at the Ohio State University.

(right) – *NCAA approved basketball court diagram (from 1984 NCAA Basketball Guide).*

MINIMUM of 3 FT (0.9m)
Preferably 10 ft. (3.05m) of unobstructed space outside

SEMICIRCLE BROKEN LINES
For the broken line semicircle in the free throw lane, it is recommended there be 8 marks 16 in. (40.64cm) long and 7 spaces 14 in. (35.56cm) long.

the center of the gymnasium. For the college game, the only acceptable backboard is a rectangle 6 feet (1.83 m) wide by 4 feet (1.23 m) high. The bottom edge of the board must be padded. The upper edge of the basket rings must be 10 feet (3.05 m) above the floor. (Figure 2-8; 8A)

Where intercollegiate basketball is played, there should be adequate provision for sportswriters. A press box is recommended if conditions permit. The placing of tables adjacent to playing courts is not a good practice. Provision should be made for telephone and telegraph connections, for reception and transmission lines for television, for timing and scoring devices, and for the operation of a public address system, including stereophonic music.

Volleyball has been gaining in popularity as an intercollegiate and interscholastic sport. As power volleyball has become the dominant style of play, proficiency has improved markedly. This has created a real concern for perimeter space needs and adequate ceiling height to allow optimum performance levels. Height recommendations for top flight volleyball is thirty feet.

Unless the games are played in an arena which has unlimited ceiling space due to seating needs, it is difficult for an educational institution to justify the cost of a ceiling height in excess of 24 feet from the base of the ceiling support beams. This height will conform to the needs for basketball competition. (If construction design would allow support beams to be placed away from the arena on each side of the floor where the ball is "set," in preparation for spiking, the height problem would be minimized.) (Figure 2-9)

Of greater concern is the need for adequate safety space at the

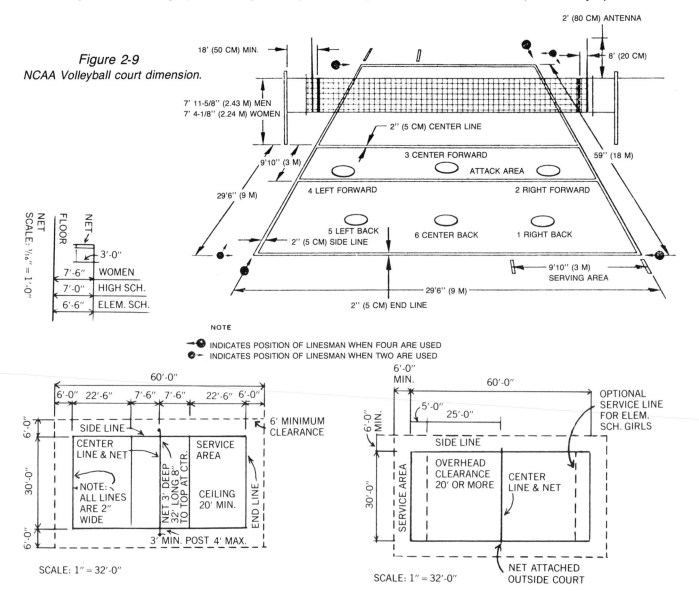

Figure 2-9
NCAA Volleyball court dimension.

sides of the court to give players a chance to save errant hits without fear of colliding with bleachers and walls. A minimum of 12-15 feet for competition-style play is recommended.

Another concern is free space beyond the end lines. Servers in high level competition frequently stand about 12-15 feet behind the base line. Reasonable justification for this extra space must be made by facility planners responsible for overall educational programs. The United States Volleyball Association has adopted the International Volleyball metric system for court dimensions. Planners should be alert to changes in court dimension.

When an area is designed for an activity that will require the use of a piano, phonograph, or tape recorder, a space should be provided for storing this equipment. Electrical outlets to provide current at all times will be needed for such equipment as amplifiers.

Other audiovisual aids can include still and movie projectors, daylight-projection screens, television sets, a scoreboard, a clock, chalkboards, and an intercommunication system.

Concrete is commonly used as a base for constructing the floor of the main gymnasium. Then

sleepers are laid on edge. Maple tongue-and-groove is the most popular type of wood finish, but synthetic flooring is gaining popularity. Synthetic surfaces are either laid in strips over concrete or poured in a liquid state over a concrete base.

It is suggested that a glazed-tile wainscot or a coat of epoxy paint be carried up to a height of seven or eight feet. From that point to the ceiling, the concrete or cinder block should be painted in a light color.

If an elevated jogging track is constructed, it should be at least seven feet wide and 12 feet above the gymnasium floor, providing it does not interfere with activities on the main floor. The surface should provide some cushion and good traction, with consideration given to banking the curves depending on circular length.

Gymnastic Area

In addition to the main gymnasium where gymnastic meets, exhibitions, and other competitions are held before a viewing public, a separate gymnasium should be provided for the permanent installation and storage of apparatus and equipment and for instruction in gymnastics. The dimensions of

this gymnasium should be determined by space requirements needed to accommodate the apparatus and equipment to be installed, by space needs for performance in gymnastics, and by total school enrollment and interest in gymnastics. Ideally, if spectators are to be accommodated the size of this gymnasium should be 120 by 90 feet, with a minimum ceiling height of 23 feet. This height permits a clearance of 22 feet for the rope climb and is ideal for hanging the various mechanical systems used in gymnastics. Some have found it desirable to install tracks on the ceiling supports to make it possible to use trolleys for moving equipment and for attaching safety belts used in the instruction of tumbling and vaulting.

Floor plates for attaching equipment should be recessed and flush with the floor. It may be necessary to reinforce the floor to install floor plates where tension is unusually severe. Wall boards should be securely installed to the wall when equipment is attached to it. Apparatus suspended from the ceiling should be securely attached to metal supports. (Figure 2-10)

The ceiling should be acoustically treated. Lights should be shielded. Doors should be constructed without a threshold and wide enough to accommodate the movement of equipment to other areas. The facility should be air-conditioned in accordance with standard specifications. Wall construction should be of the same materials as recommended for other gymnasiums.

A common failure in planning is to overlook the need for adequately and conveniently placed storage space for gymnastic equipment. If multiple use of this equipment is expected, transportation carts and dollies should be provided. Specifications on size and installation of the various pieces of apparatus and equipment may be obtained from manufacturer. Ideally, the gymnasium for gymnastics should

Figure 2-10
Wall graphics assist in giving color to large areas, such as the gymnastic room painted here.

be equipped with the following types of items: side horse, horizontal bar, long horse, parallel bars, bucks, mats, still rings, uneven parallel bars, balance beam, and other special apparatus.

A gymnastic landing pit, 10 feet wide, 20 feet long, and 30 inches deep, filled with sponge rubber — for use with parallel bars, horizontal bar, still rings, and uneven parallel bars is a desirable feature.

Weight Training/Body Conditioning Room

This room should contain a minimum of 2,500 square feet of floor space. Such space will provide a weight training area and space for the practice of official events in competitive weight lifting. The floor should be covered with a durable, resilient material, making it unnecessary to use weight platforms, which are essential to protect maple or other wood flooring. (Figure 2-11; 11A)

The weight-lifting area should be roped off and approximately 15 by 15 feet for the practice of official lifts. The rest of the room may be used for exercise with barbells, dumbbells, isometric cables, and the like. Several full length mirrors should be installed on the walls. Barbell and weight racks should be attached to the walls so that room may be kept tidy.

The trend is to have a room for weight machines and stretching, open to all students and requiring limited supervision. The use of free weights is then restricted to a separate room used only when supervised due to safety and security concerns.

The recent interest in fitness has caused the general body conditioning room (with exercise machines) to be heavily utilized, thus the size of this room should be adjusted upward depending on total student population.

Wrestling and Martial Arts Area

(Figure 2-11B) This area is

Figure 2-11
Weight training/body conditioning rooms have increased in popularity. The University of Arkansas has provided a variety of exercise options in its new HPER building.

Figure 2-11A
A warm-up/stretching area within the body conditioning room facilitates a complete exercise program at the University of Nebraska, Omaha.

Figure 2-11B
The wrestling area at the U.S. Naval Academy is spacious and well designed.

Indoor Facilities

designed for wrestling and martial arts activities. The room should be rectangular in shape, at least 50 x 100 fet, and should be of sufficient size to accommodate two square mats, each measuring a minimum of 42 x 42 feet. The mats should have 10-foot practice rings consisting of 3 rows of 6 circles to each row for a total of 18 practice rings. A satisfactory standard is 10 by 10 feet or 100 square feet per student during peak usage based on 40-45 students per class. The floor area not covered by the regulation mats should be covered with carpet for classroom instructional type atmosphere. The ceiling should be of acoustic material and should be a minimum of 12 feet high. (Figure 2-12)

The floor of the wrestling room should be constructed of or covered with resilient material to prolong the life of the mats. These materials may be rubberlock products, other new developed resilient materials, or wood. Concrete is not recommended. The wall mats should be covered with resilient materials up to five feet above the floor on all sides. Adequate lighting, heating, and forced ventilation are essential in this room. A wall type water fountain with a cuspidor should be present. A blackboard and bulletin board should be available as well as a scale. An electric scoreboard wall clock should be attached to the wall. A sound system should be present, with a wall pulley machine and a takedown machine included as basic equipment.

Multi-Purpose Activity Area

The size of this room should be approximately 70 by 90 feet. A floor for street shoe usage may be needed in any size college or university with a variety of program offerings. The floor most commonly used is hard maple, tongue and groove, conventional gymnasium flooring. Square dance, folk dance, social dance, physical education for elementary teachers, marching and band practice, and similar activities can be conducted on such a floor. It can meet the demands of such special college and community events as musical and dramatic productions, fairs, and carnivals. The "make-up" room or "warming room" for department and college outdoor programs can be housed in this area and can be served through a door leading to a corridor and immediately to the out-of-doors.

This activity room, when not scheduled in some manner as indicated above, can serve the purpose of any regular gymnasium if so planned in its equipment and floor markings. The floor may need some extra maintenance for the hard use it will receive, but the desirability of the activities that may be scheduled on it will justify the resultant wear.

Multi-Purpose Game Area

The intended use of a multiple-purpose room will determine its dimensions. It should be large enough to accommodate

at least six table tennis tables. A ceiling height of 12 feet is adequate. The room should be equipped with a public address system and record player for instructional and recreational activities, including social and square dancing. This room should be accessible from the lobby or from a building corridor. It should have small kitchen facilities and a floor that can take hard usage. The handicapped should be considered in the planning.

Racquetball/Handball Courts

Suggestions for court construction are the same for both racquetball and handball. The recommended four-wall court is 40 feet long and 20 feet wide, with a front wall and ceiling height of 20 feet, and a back wall at least 12 feet high.

When more than a single battery of racquetball/handball courts is to be constructed, the batteries should be arranged so the back walls of each battery are separated by a corridor approximately 10 feet wide and 8 feet high. A corridor located immediately above and at least 12 feet high may serve an instructor or be used as a spectator galley. Corridors and galleries should be illuminated with indirect light.

The back wall of a single court need not be higher than 12 feet. Shatterproof glass or plexiglass may be used to enclose the remainder of the back wall. Many courts are satisfactorily used with

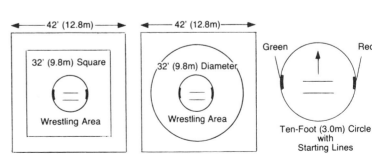

Figure 2-12
At Sinclair Community College in Dayton, the wrestling mat is located in a practice room equipped with padded walls for safety. Official NCAA wrestling mat layout.

Figure 2-13, A, B
Dimensions of a Racquetball Court. Use of glass viewing wall at University of Arkansas. Use of glass back wall and upper observation room at Texas Tech.

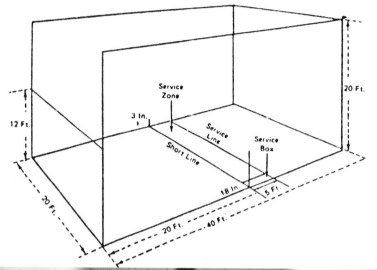

an open upper rear wall.

Racquetball/handball courts may be constructed of hard plaster, fiber board or laminated wood panels, concrete, shatterproof glass, or a nonsplintering durable wood. While plaster is sometimes recommended, maintenance costs may be high. Glass courts provide maximum spectator participation, but the initial cost may be prohibitive. Overall, a reputable panel system is probably the best alternative for selection of front wall, side walls, and ceilings. Floors should be hardwood, as in standard gymnasium construction.

Entrance doors should open toward the corridor and have flush pulls and hinges. A small shatterproof window installed flush with the interior surface of the door should be located at approximately the eye level of an average adult male.

Such fixtures as heat pipes, ventilating ducts, lights, and other mechanical equipment should not project into the playing area. Ventilating ducts and lighting fixtures are best installed flush with the ceiling surface.

A recommended method of turning the lights on and off in handball and squash courts is to install switches that are activated by the opening or closing of the door to the court. When the door is opened, the lights will turn off automatically, leaving only the night light to burn continuously. When the door is closed, lights in the court will turn on. Usually, a two to three minute delay occurs prior to the lights going off after the door has been opened. This prevents a disruption of lighting during the brief time it takes for players to exchange the court. This system eliminates the possibility of the lights being left on when the courts are not in use.

However, the lights, when turned off, will come on instantaneously when new players enter the court and close the door. With this system, warning lights can be located outside each court to indicate when a court is in use. A relatively new concept utilizes

Indoor Facilities

an annunciator (an electrically controlled signal board) to indicate to the building reservation/control center which courts are occupied at any one time. Lights on the signal board are activated by the "trip" switch on each door as it opens or closes.

Air-conditioning, or at least forced ventilation, is desirable for this area. For additional suggestions regarding racquetball club/court construction, refer to Chapter 7.

Squash Courts

Squash is very popular in some localities and the number of courts should be determined by local interest. A singles court is 18.5 feet wide by 32 feet long and 16 feet high. A doubles court is 25 feet wide by 45 feet long and 20 feet high. (Figure 2-14)

It is possible to install movable metal "telltales" across the front of handball/racquetball courts so they can be used for squash instruction purposes. The floors, walls, ceilings, lighting, heating, and ventilation of squash courts are similar to those of four-wall racquetball/handball courts.

Fencing Area

Fencing is often included in the instructional, recreational, and intercollegiate programs for both men and women. The field of play is a piste, or more commonly referred to as a "strip" in the United States.

A room 55' x 90' allows for four fencing strips 40 feet long and 6 feet wide, with 15 feet between strips. These strips may be used for informal competition and instruction. Intercollegiate competition, however, requires a 52 foot length of floor area, with a minimum of 18 feet between the strips. (Figure 2-15)

For instructional purposes, the strip may be painted on a nonslip hardwood floor or synthetic surface, or a rubber runner of correct measurements may be laid on the floor and removed when not in use. For the electric foil and

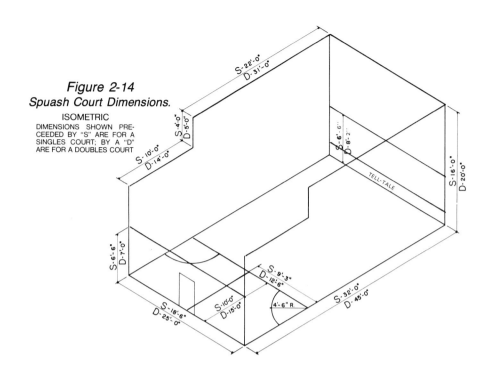

Figure 2-14
Spuash Court Dimensions.

ISOMETRIC
DIMENSIONS SHOWN PRECEEDED BY "S" ARE FOR A SINGLES COURT; BY A "D" ARE FOR A DOUBLES COURT

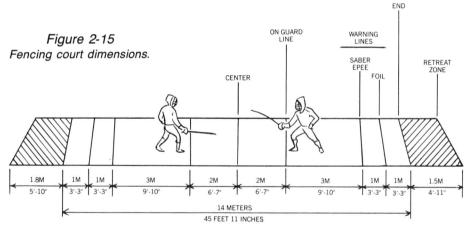

Figure 2-15
Fencing court dimensions.

NOTE: The width of the strip shall be a minimum of 1.8 meters (5'10") and a maximum of 2 meters (6'7"). The length of the retreat zone shall be a minimum of 1.5 meters (4'11") and a maximum of 2 meters (6'7"). For Foil and Epee, the metallic surface of the strip shall cover the entire retreat zone.

epee, a metallic piste must cover the entire length of the strip, including the extensions.

Electrical outlets and jacks should be placed at the rear of the tournament strips to provide power for the electrical equipment. If permanently affixed wall scoreboards are provided, portable score boxes are unnecessary. Brackets or eyebolts for mounting

fencing targets should be either recessed flush with the wall or placed above the seven foot level.

The fencing area should be a well-lighted room with a minimum ceiling height of 12 feet. The installation of roll-away bleachers for spectators may necessitate raising the ceiling height, and it may also require an increased capacity ventilating system.

An equipment room should be located adjacent to the fencing room and should be large enough to store the weapons and protective equipment used by classes. Sixty square feet is the minimal space required for storage and to accommodate a small cabinet work counter for the repair of equipment. Portable strips will require additional space.

Indoor Tennis Facilities

Tennis can be played indoors on any firm surface of sufficient size for a tennis court, especially where court markings and a net are provided. Sometimes tennis court markings are placed on the general use gymnasium floor and provisions are made for temporary placement of net posts, or the net is attached to rings inserted in the wall. Another teaching aid is simply a solid color contrasting line painted net height on a flat wall of the gymnasium which provides a rebound surface for practicing one's strokes. Portable tennis courts might also be used in the gymnasium or field house.

The composition of a synthetic surface can be altered to offset the bounce of the tennis ball. A surface constructed for playing basketball usually proves to be too fast for tennis competition, but will suffice for beginning instruction.

A few colleges have constructed a special indoor facility specifically for tennis. If this is done, the facility should include a minimum of four courts, along with a tennis drill area. Such a facility would enable 16 students to play tennis, while other students use the tennis drill area. This approach would demand frequent rotation of students.

If the courts are in a separate building, it should be conveniently located to locker rooms. Consideration should also be given to a covered passageway between the gymnasium and the tennis building.

Ventilation, lighting, temperature control, and other pertinent considerations are discussed in Chapter 7.

Indoor Archery Range

Instructional and recreational groups need an indoor archery area suitable for practice during inclement weather. (Figure 2-16)

An area 78 feet long is adequate for official ranges of 10, 15, and 20 yards for indoor archery. The 78 feet includes 3 feet for the target, 60 feet for the range, and a 15 foot width is required for 24 students. This area will accommodate six 48-inch targets set 10 feet apart on centers, or twelve 5-foot lanes for indoor targets. A minimum ceiling height of 10 feet should be provided between the shooting line and targets.

The floor in the archery area will receive hard usage from street shoes and flying arrows. A hardwood, tongue-and-groove floor, with the boards running the length of the shooting area, is preferred. A durable synthetic surface may be considered as a viable alternative.

The location of structural features in the archery room should be given careful attention. Obstructions ahead of the shooting line, such as supporting pillars and overhead lights in a low ceiling, should be recessed or otherwise protected from flying arrows. The area behind the target should be covered with a backdrop to protect the wall and prevent arrow breakage. A large heavy run, or a commercially available nylon net which arrows cannot penetrate, may be used. All doors and windows in the area should be located behind the shooting line. The same is true for tackboards and chalkboards.

Targets may be affixed to the backstop or placed on easels in front of it. A variety of targets are available including straw, double-curl excelsior, and styrofoam with composition centers. The target should be constructed and placed so as to allow an arrow to penetrate at least 20 inches without striking any obstruction that would damage the arrow.

A low cost innovative back stop has been designed using flattened cardboard boxes piled from floor to ceiling covering an entire wall. Targets are simply pinned to the cardboard and the arrows penetrate the cardboard 6 to 15 inches.

In a multi-purpose room, target holders should be mounted on wheels or set in floor plates. The plates should be flush with the floor when the target holder is removed. The backdrop behind the targets would be pulled to the side or rolled overhead when not in use.

In a multipurpose room, target holders should be mounted on wheels or set in floor plates. The plates should be flush with the floor when the target holder is removed. The backdrop behind the targets should be pulled to the side or rolled overhead when not in use.

Storage space for targets and other equipment should be adjacent to the range. The size and location of storage areas will be determined by the type of targets used. Racks for hanging bows and shelves for storing arrows should be included in a storage area behind the shooting line. This location enables a student to replace or exchange equipment while other students continue to shoot.

The feasibility of installing automated lanes should be seriously considered. Several types of commercial lanes are available. Automated lanes have lane dividers at the shooting line and an automatic warning system to halt shooting in the event a person steps in front of the shooting line. Electric target returns bring the targets to the shooting line so arrows can be removed, and the targets can be adjusted for different shooting distances without altering the shooting line.

Additional information concerning outdoor archery facilities can be found in Chapters 3 and 7.

Indoor Rifle Range

A rifle range can be used for class instruction, competitive shooting, and recreation for both men and women. On campuses where a range within the athletic and physical education complex is not deemed feasible, the ROTC units might be contacted for possible collaboration in constructing and financing a range.

A room 75' x 42' will accommodate eight firing points, or a class of 24 students. At least eight firing points are recommended on the basis of one point for every three members of a class. The National Rifle Association standard shooting distance for rifles is 50 feet, measured from the firing line to the target. The bulletstop should be 6 to 10 feet beyond the target. This space varies with the type of installation.

A minimum of 15 feet is required behind the firing line for mats, scoring tables, rifle racks, and walking space. The ceiling should be 8 feet high in front of the firing points. This ceiling height reduces the amount of wall space that must be covered behind the backdrop, and facilitates the installation of target carriers. Each firing point should be at least 5½ feet wide.

For specifications on construction of indoor rifle ranges, write to the National Rifle Association of America, 1600 Rhode Island Avenue, N.W., Washington, D.C. 20036.

Indoor Golf Practice Area

Provisions can be made to accommodate golf instruction and practice indoors. Balls may be hit

Figure 2-16
A golf-fencing-archery room was included in the HPER building at the University of Nebraska, Omaha. Archery targets are mounted directly on a flattened cardboard box wall.

Figure 2-17
Commercially produced golf training devices aid players in refining their stroke technique.

Figure 2-17A
Nets are pulled out for easy conversion to golf practice and fencing lanes are painted on the synthetic floor.

into a large durable nylon net or canvas placed several yards in front of the hitting positions. Driving cages may also be used. Hitting positions may be established by placement of practice mats available from golf supply houses. (Figures 2-17, 17A)

In addition, commercial golf systems are now available that compliment any instructional/recreational program. It is usually economical and efficient to consider designing this area to accommodate other activities when not used for golf (i.e. archery, fencing, etc.).

Dance Facilities and Equipment

The essential dance facilities and equipment should be supplied in sufficient quantity and quality to provide for all dance activities in the required and elective curriculum and in the extracurricular program. Particular attention should be given to adequate provisions for the program of professional preparation (both the teaching program and the performance program) and to dance performance and observation.

Provision should be made to include the following units if the dance facility is to be comprehensive:

- Locker-dressing room
- Shower area
- Toilets
- Rest rooms (remote from toilets and showers)
- Public lavatories
- Therapy room
- Storage spaces
- Construction rooms for costumes, props and sets, and music (composing and recording)
- Custodial space
- Office space
- Laundry and cleaning facilities
- Box office
- Parking area

Total facilities should be determined according to the amount of emphasis placed on various aspects of the dance curriculum. Considerations should include classes needed and areas for individual work and for extracurricular and concert practice. Based on the design of the dance curriculum, facilities should be considered in terms of teaching space, practice space and choreography, rehearsal space, performance space, research space, auxiliary space and equipment, and classroom space. At least two distinct areas should be provided, one area for modern dance and ballet and one area for folk and social dance.

Modern Dance and Ballet Area

A minimum of 100 square feet per person is recommended. An area of 3,000 square feet will accommodate 30 students. If an area is to serve as an informal theater and instructional area, it should be between 4,800 and 5,000 square feet to accommodate both the class and the needs of the theater section.

A ceiling height of 24 feet is recommended for all dance areas. Full height is essential for large dance areas (over 2,400 square feet), and 16 feet is the minimum height for small dance areas.

Dance activities require air space between floor and foundation as well as "floating" floors for resiliency. Floors should be of hardwood, such as maple of random lengths, and tongue-and-grooved. They should be laid with the grain going in one direction. The floors should not be slippery and they should be constructed for easy cleaning.

The finish should provide a smooth surface upon which dancers can glide with bare feet or soft sandals. Tung oil is considered by most to be a satisfactory finish; an alternative might be several coats of wood sealer.

Walls should be smooth and easily maintained. Consideration should be given to having one unobstructed wall of neutral background for filming purposes. To support ballet barres, stress factors of the walls should be considered. Thin walls are inadequate.

Incandescent light is preferable to fluorescent light. Lights that also serve as houselights during performances should be controlled from wall switches as well as from the light control board.

Consideration should be given to natural lighting. Large windows contribute to an aesthetically and psychologically desirable atmosphere. To avoid direct sunlight, the best location for windows is the north wall. Windows should be curtained so the studio can be darkened for film showing and studio performances. When total construction necessitates no windows, the aesthetics may be improved by the use of color on the walls. (Figure 2-18)

Storage space for sound equipment should be adjacent to the dance area and locked. Storage rooms should have double doors and a flush threshold for easy movement of such large equipment as a piano. Built-in storage space for records, sound equipment, tapes, and musical instruments should be provided. An area in the storage room where instructors can listen to records and tapes is highly desirable. This area should have adequate acoustics, ventilation, and electrical outlets.

Heavy-duty wiring is essential for all dance facilities. Wiring should be capable of carrying a portable light board as well as phonographs, additional speakers, tape recorders, and projectors. Wall outlets should be convenient to all areas. Television conduits should be installed when the building is constructed.

Temperature should be maintained at 65-68 degrees. The air should be well circulated, and consideration should be given to the use of natural air. Mechanisms for heating and circulating air should be as nearly silent as possible to avoid interfering with the quality of sound and its reception.

Planning for a dance facility should include consideration of accessories. Leaf-fold mirrors, which can be folded for protection or curtained during performances, may be installed along two adjoining walls so that movement can be analyzed from two directions. Wall mirrors should be installed flush with the wall and raised 12 to 18 inches from the floor.

Ballet barres should be smooth in texture and be made of wood, stainless steel, or aluminum. The minimum length to accommodate one dancer is five feet. Barres from 42 to 48 inches in height may be installed permanently; they should extend six to eight inches from the wall. If necessary, barres may be placed in front of mirrors.

In such instances, it may be necessary to use pipes for the barres. The barre supports may be screwed into recessed floor sockets just in front of the mirror, thus facilitating the removal of the barre and supports when not needed. (Figure 2-19)

Custom-made percussion cabinets mounted on rollers are a fine accessory. They may have a carpeted top surface, slide-out drawers lined with felt for small instruments, and larger partitions to accommodate cymbals and drums. Heavy sound equipment should be built in or placed on stands of table height equipped with rollers for ease of transportation. Because moving affects the tuning of a piano, this instrument should be placed on an inside wall where it will not be subjected to extreme heat or cold, and it should be protected by a suitable cover and lock. If it is to be moved frequently, the piano should be placed on a heavy duty dolly.

Chalkboards and bulletin boards are useful accessories. A glass-enclosed exhibit case for photographs, costumes, costume plates, manuscripts, and other items may be installed near the dance area.

Folk and Social Dance Area

An area of 5,400 square feet (54 by 100 feet is suggested) will

Figure 2-18
At the University of Vermont Dance Studio, natural lighting is used attractively.

accommodate a class of approximately 60 students. Dance areas are generally rectangular with a length-width ratio of approximately 3 to 2 (e.g. 90 by 60 feet). Ceiling height should be in proportion to the size of the room but never lower than 12 feet. An outside entrance into a main corridor of the building will provide for traffic flow of the relatively large groups using the area.

Floors as specified for ballet and modern dance are necessary. An epoxy finish will enable the use of street shoes without damage to the floor. Specifications for

Figure 2-19
Mirrors, ballet barres, a smooth floor surface and a 24' high ceiling make this dance area ideal for teaching modern dance and ballet at the University of Nebraska, Omaha.

lighting, ventilation, acoustics, sound equipment, storage space, wiring, and temperature control should follow those for ballet and modern dance facilities. Racks for coats and books should be installed either within the dance area or along the outside corridor wall. Bulletin boards, chalkboards, and display cases are highly desirable.

For additional details concerning the construction of dance facilities (i.e. principles for planning, dance production areas, auxiliary areas, etc.) readers are encouraged to consult the booklet entitled *Dance Facilities* published by and available from American Alliance

of Health, Physical Education and Recreation.

Badminton

Badminton is an individual and dual sport utilizing a shuttlecock and rackets. The activity may be included in programs for class instruction and intramural and recreational competitions. It is an excellent coeducational activity.

The court dimensions are 44 by 20 feet for doubles and 44 by 17 feet for singles.

Posts should be set five feet, one inch high in the center of the sidelines. The net should be five feet high at the center. In indoor or outdoor settings, multi-purpose space may be used for courts. In such instances, the courts should be in batteries of two or more, with 1.5-inch painted or taped lines superimposed on other appropriate areas. All measurements are to the outside of lines. It is recommended that additional space of four or five feet for the sidelines and eight feet for the ends be provided. (Figure 2-20)

Other Indoor Facilities

Information concerning the planning of indoor facilities related primarily to recreation (i.e. bowling

alleys, ice arenas, etc.) is available in Chapter 7.

Research and Testing Laboratories

Research facilities to support physical education, health and recreation are becoming increasingly important in colleges and universities. A majority of the research conducted by physical education professionals requires laboratory settings with special equipment.

It is impossible to list all the tools that any individual investigator will need to use in research. A laboratory (in a sense) takes on the personality of who is in charge of the research being conducted there. Its design often is dictated by the type of equipment to be used in it.

Despite the wide diversity in research tools, there are some facilities and equipment commonly used in laboratories for research in athletics, physical education, and recreation. Some general considerations and some specific types of research facilities now in use or projected for the future follow. (Figure 2-21)

General Considerations

The nature of the educational institution and its objectives and function will determine in large measure the type, number, size, and relative importance of research and teaching laboratories for athletics, physical education, and recreation. In junior colleges, or in four-year institutions in which only service courses are offered, sophisticated research laboratories will seldom, if ever, be required. However, laboratory experience may be desirable as a part of a course, and some testing equipment may be required for use in the gymnasium or on the playing field. Furthermore, there are liberal arts colleges and other research-oriented institutions whose undergraduate curriculums require that the student have research experience. In such institutions, it is not unreasonable to provide limited research facilities and supervision of selected research activities.

A lack of appropriate laboratory space and equipment for teaching/research has hampered many colleges from joining the recent trend toward providing increased professional preparation opportunities in non-teaching areas, i.e. exercise science. (Figure 2-22; 22A)

In colleges and universities offering professional preparation in physical education or recreation, and especially in those with graduate curriculums in these areas, there is a greater need for the development of research and teaching laboratories. Such facilities are required not only to provide experience and training for students but also to attract and retain capable research scholars. Therefore, it is not possible to decide on a "per student" basis what kinds of laboratories or even, in many instances, how many square feet of laboratory space should be provided. The character of the institution and the interest and ability of its faculty must be taken into account.

If health education is also administratively housed in the same unit or building as physical education, then consideration must be given to special teaching/research laboratory needs of health classes and faculty.

Teaching and Research

Years ago, small research laboratories served as teaching laboratories in the conduct of various undergraduate and graduate courses for professional preparation. It is still necessary and desirable to use research laboratories for presenting occasional demonstration experiments in the teaching of classes. However, this cannot be a frequent practice in a productive research laboratory, especially when the classes contain more than just a few students.

Separate teaching laboratories

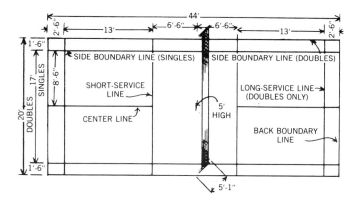

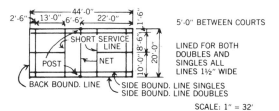

Figure 2-20
Badminton Court Dimensions.

Figure 2-21
Space Needed for Selected Indoor Activities.

Activity	Play Area in Feet	Safety Space in Feet*	Total Area in Feet	Minimum Ceiling Height
Archery	5x60	15e	5x75	12
Badminton	20x44	6s, 8e	32x60	24
Basketball				
Jr. High instructional	42x74	6s, 8e		24
Jr. High interscholastic	50x84	6s, 8e		
Sr. High interscholastic	50x84	6s, 8e	62x100	
Sr. High instructional	45x74	6s, 8e	57x90	
Neighborhood E. Sch.	42x74	6s, 8e	54x90	
Community Junior H.S.	50x84	6s, 8e	62x100	
Community Senior H.S.	50x84	6s, 8e	62x100	
Competitive - College & University	50x94	6s, 8e	62x110	
Boccie	18x62	3s, 9e	24x80	
Fencing, competitive	6x46	9s, 6e	18x52	
instructional	4x30	4s, 6e	12x42	12
Handball	20x40			
Racquetball	20x40			20
Rifle (one pt.)	5x50	6 to 20e	5x70 min.	20
Shuffleboard	6x52	6s,2e	18x56	12
Squash	18.5x32			12
Tennis				16
Deck (doubles	18x40	4s, 5e	26x50	24
Hand	16x40	4½s, 10e	25x60	
Lawn (singles)	27x78	12s, 21e	51x120	
(doubles)	36x78	12s, 21e	60x120	
Paddle (singles)	16x44	6s, 8e	28x60	
(doubles)	20x44	6s, 8e	32x60	
Table (playing area)			9x31	
Volleyball				24
Competitive and adult	30x60	6s, 6e	42x72	
Junior High	30x50	6s, 6e	42x62	
Wrestling (competitive)	24x24	5s, 5e	36x36	

*Safety space at the side of an area is indicated by a number followed by "e" for end and "s" for side.

should be provided to handle laboratory sections of various courses. The same teaching laboratory cannot be used for some of the laboratory sessions in a variety of courses, including tests and measurements, physiology of exercise, and biomechanics. At least one such teaching laboratory should be available, equipped with stationary lab tables containing gas, water, and electricity. Hoods for the Bunsen burner, cabinets for storing small pieces of equipment, and a connecting supply room are also essential. Closed-circuit television receivers are desirable. The laboratory can be designed to accommodate equipment used in conducting experiments with animals and human beings.

Frequently, the teaching laboratory can be equipped with durable, inexpensive, and easily serviced apparatus where students can carry on experiments individually or in small groups. While such equipment may not provide the degree of precision expected of sophisticated research apparatus it is generally accurate enough to present desirable principles. A space of approximately 1,000 square feet, with a 12-foot ceiling, is generally large enough to accommodate a class of 20 students.

A small gymnasium of approximately 2,000 square feet or more, with a ceiling height of 22 feet, may function as another teaching laboratory for conducting other experiments. This facility is useful for instructional purposes and for the student to gain experience in administering tests and taking measurements. Such a facility should be free of obstructions so that fitness or sport tests may be safely administered. Walls should be flat, without ornamentation or equipment, to permit wall-volley tests. Such items as chinning bars, mats, and volleyball standards should be available.

As the fields of physical education and recreation advance in maturity as disciplines, it is probable that laboratory experience will replace some of the course lectures, particularly at the graduate level. This will increase the need for teaching labs as well as research labs. Graduate students should have considerable laboratory experience before they embark on collecting data for a doctoral dissertation.

Individual Laboratories

Several forces are acting to accentuate the role of the research investigator in colleges and universities. The availability of funds, greater specialization, increased research encouragement from the administration, and competition for university faculty have all had a positive influence on the place of research. The recent interest within the fields of physical education and recreation in developing a body of knowledge and the development and expansion of graduate programs in these fields have also created a greater demand for research facilities and trained investigators.

A sizeable proportion of some faculties are now doing research — sometimes several faculty members sharing a common interest or specialty. Provisions must be made for this increased interest and emphasis.

Joint appointments, in which a faculty member holds an appointment in more than one department, are increasing in number in the fields of physical education and recreation. Provisions should be made for some faculty members to do research in other departments, and conversely, members of other departments may be expected to use some of the physical education and recreation research facilities.

A related development is the organization in many large universities of centers or institutes for research that cut across departmental lines. There are a

Figure 2-22, 22A
A variety of classrooms should be planned for the different classes to be accommodated within a comprehensive HPER facility.

Indoor Facilities

number of advantages to such organizational setups, including the cross-fertilization of disciplines and the sharing of elaborate facilities and expensive apparatus. In the planning of research facilities for physical education and recreation, the existing as well as the proposed institutes on the campus should be investigated. (Figure 2-23; 23A; 23B)

Shared Service Facilities

Although there is a need for individual research laboratories, some facilities lend themselves to shared use. A workshop supervised by a capable machinist or other skilled worker is an essential ancillary facility in institutions where considerable research is being conducted. If the research productivity of the physical education and recreation unit is sufficiently great, there is justification for housing and supporting this type of ancillary facility in this unit. If, however, research and laboratory teaching is done on a smaller scale, the facility may be shared by other units in the college or university, or such services may be purchased as needed.

If a workshop is planned, 110v and 220v electric current with good ground connections should be made available. Oversized doors should be provided as well as a good ventilation system so that sawdust and other pollutants will not become a hazard or annoyance. Cupboards with locks should be in ample supply to store hand tools to prevent their being stolen or misplaced. Since considerable noise may be generated, the workshop should be isolated from other facilities where quiet work is being done. There should be a minimum of 80 footcandles of light on the task being performed. The room should be at least 500 to 600 square feet in size, with a ceiling height of 12 feet.

Another unit that lends itself to shared use is a data-processing center. This may be a small room housing a variety of equipment items available for use by various faculty members, graduate or undergraduate students, and nonacademic personnel. It may include card punching and sorting equipment, tabulators, collators, and magnetic or punch-tape equipment. There may also be computer terminals that connect by telephone or other lines to a large centralized computer on the campus or even at other institutions. Computer terminals located in various buildings on the campus will be the most common way of providing computer services at large universities. Punch cards or tapes will not have to be transported across the campus with the use of this arrangement.

The installation of large

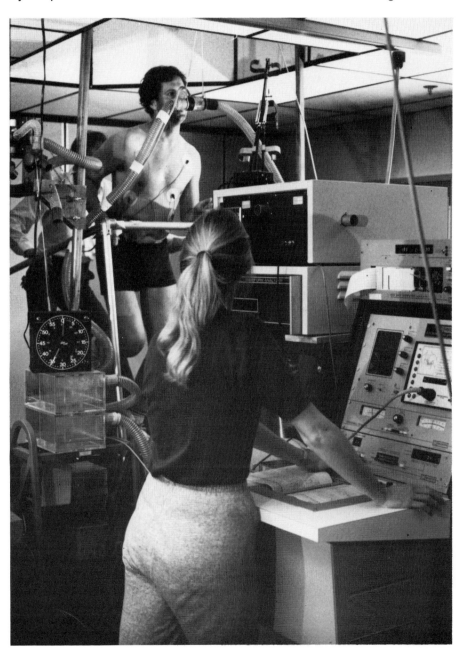

Figure 2-23
Research in HPER has become more popular and sophisticated, thus careful considera-tion must be given to the planning of laboratories. Photos continued on following page.

electronic computer equipment requires the installation of large electrical conduits, good ground connections, and oversized doors. A great deal of heat may be expected to be generated by the electronic equipment, so individually controlled air conditioning equipment is necessary for maintaining the temperature required. Space should be provided to permit direct access to each piece of equipment for servicing. Since considerable noise is developed when data-processing equipment is in operation, acoustic treatment of ceiling and walls is essential. The division of the area into smaller rooms with soundproof wall helps reduce the noise problem.

Regional electronic library services are being planned for various locations in the United States. Provisions should be made for making use of this equipment.

Facilities for Research

The dark room, for obvious reasons, should not have an outside wall with a window. Therefore, good forced ventilation is essential. The room should be provided with running water, sinks, ample wall cupboards, and a generous supply of duplex electrical outlets (110v). The recommended room size is 225

square feet or more, with a 12-foot ceiling.

A number of researchers and teachers have need for graphic services for preparing materials for publication, for presentation at meetings, and for instruction. Camera equipment that can produce a 2 x 2 inch slide and overhead transparencies in a matter of a minute or two at little cost should be provided. Duplicating equipment may also be housed in this facility.

If the needs of the department are sufficiently large, a full-time or part-time employee may be required to prepare graphic materials. A room used for this purpose should be well-lighted — a minimum of 80 footcandles is recommended — and should have large wall cupboards for storing drafting and some camera equipment. A room with a minimum of 400 square feet and a 10-feet ceiling height will provide sufficient space for the usual requirements of this facility.

Suggestions for Purchasing Equipment

The manufacture and sale of research equipment has become a very competitive business. As a result, there is frequently a wide range of the same kind of equipment available under

different brand names. Before purchasing large expensive units, it is worth the time and effort to investigate carefully the various makes. The annual meetings of professional societies generally include exhibits by manufacturers of research equipment appropriate to the particular area of investigation. Consultation with a colleague in the same field who has used the equipment is a good idea before a purchase is made.

In considering particular pieces of equipment, the following determination should be made: (a) if students or trained researchers are to use the equipment; (b) initial and annual servicing cost; (c) if the equipment is electronically compatible with other equipment now in use or contemplated (often it is more economical to purchase units that match others from the same company so that the responsibility for servicing them rests with one company); (d) what power supply is needed; (e) ease with which the instrument may be calibrated, and if other equipment is needed for the calibration; (f) portability of the equipment; (g) what service the company is willing to provide and where the service centers are located; and (h) noise, vibration, and heat generated by the equipment. Unbiased answers to

Figure 23A

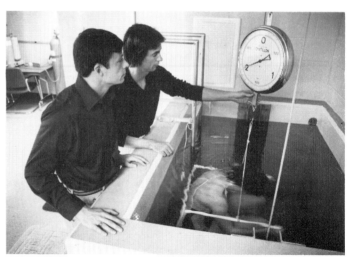

Figure 23B

these and other questions can sometimes best be found by having discussions with other researchers who have used such installations.

Office Space

Individual offices for the various faculty members and graduate students involved in research should be convenient to the various laboratories. The installation of one or more rooms to be used for quiet work (e.g. calculating, reading and writing) is helpful.

Mobile Laboratory

In planning research facilities, serious thought should be given to the development of a mobile laboratory. The trend to eliminate laboratory schools makes the consideration of a mobile laboratory more urgent.

Trailers, campers, trucks, and other vehicles — even railroad cars — have been converted into mobile laboratories. Often the use of a field generator is necessary to provide current for operating mobile-laboratory equipment. It is surprising how much equipment can be compactly installed in a mobile facility.

Specific Laboratory Facilities

The information about laboratories listed in this section comprises only suggestions of how research facilities might be organized. Obviously, the character and organization of the institution itself will be an important factor in determining how facilities are to be organized and administered.

Measurement and Evaluation

Much of the so-called practical or applied research will be conducted in the gymnasium, swimming pool, and other indoor and outdoor activity areas. This means that in order to utilize

measurement and evaluation equipment effectively, the regular activity areas must be planned and constructed in such a manner as to facilitate the conduct of research. For example, many skill tests are administered with the use of some type of wall volley as a part of a battery to measure skill in a certain activity. Therefore, it is important to construct the walls of a gymnasium so that present tests as well as those developed in the future may be utilized.

Consideration should be given to the attachment of special equipment to walls and ceilings, such as jump boards, ropes, and strength-measuring devices. Grids could be painted on the walls of the gymnasium as well as on the wall of a diving well in the swimming pool in order to measure distance and height when analyzing movement.

A great deal of the research equipment needs to be portable so that it can be moved to the action areas. This means that proper electrical outlets and suitable acoustic treatment of these areas must be planned in advance.

These laboratories will contain the equipment that will be used at the elementary, junior high, and senior high school levels. Physical education teachers at these levels should be encouraged to make use of some of this equipment on the job.

Biomechanics (Kinesiology)

There are many areas in the field of biomechanics in which research may be conducted. The type of research may range from cinematography to human engineering. If there is a physiology of exercise laboratory available, experimentation may take place in which the equipment from this laboratory is used either jointly with the exercise physiologist or separately by the kinesiology researcher.

In cinematographic research (especially time lapse and high speed), a room 30 by 30 feet, with a ceiling height of at least 24 feet,

is a necessity. High speed cameras whose frame rates vary from 64 to several thousand frames per second are useful. Special film readers and projectors should be provided in order that accurate measurements may be made. Mirrors may be used to reflect images.

Equipment representative of the type used in this kind of laboratory includes:

- movement developing camera
- 35mm SLR camera
- high speed motion picture camera (motor-driven; 50-500 frames per second)
- stroboscopic equipment (including single and multi-flash units with strobolume and strobotac parts
- force measuring devices (including individual strain gauges and multi-dimensional force plates)
- videotape recorder with two channels and playback capacity
- oscilloscope
- electronic counters
- amplifiers compatible with measuring and recording devices
- metal storage cabinets (approximately 18 inches deep by 36 inches wide) with locks
- computer terminal

Special simulated game areas may be constructed so that a true picture of a performer in action may be studied. A miniature running track may be developed, as well as other similar replicas of playing areas. Nets and other devices may need to be used to catch objects or to prevent them from traversing the customary distance.

Human Performance Laboratory

An area of at least 40 by 40 feet, providing a minimum of 1,600 square feet of space, should be provided for the exercise room for human beings.

The most popular methods of standardizing exercise in human beings are a) by means of a motor-driven treadmill, bicycle, or other ergometer; and b) step tests of various kinds. The exercise room should be large enough to accommodate all the needed equipment. There should be space for several technicians as well as for scientific instruments.

Since some noise and vibration result when the treadmill is operating — and some treadmills are quite heavy — it is well to locate this room on the ground floor, with provisions for reducing noise. The treadmill should be installed in a pit (and even on a pad to help further reduce noise), if possible, with space in the pit for servicing.

The room should be air-conditioned, with control over temperature within a plus or minus 1½ degrees Fahrenheit and control over humidity of plus or minus 5 percent. Electric current (110v and 220v) should be supplied through numerous outlets. A large thermopane observation window should also be installed.

A room 20 by 25 feet with a ceiling height of 12 feet to allow for walking, running, or riding a bicycle up a grade on the treadmill, is generally sufficient. If the treadmill is not installed in a pit, the ceiling may have to be higher. It is usually desirable to have connecting cables, including voice communication, to a space adjoining the exercise room so desirable data can be recorded outside the room. An alternate method of constructing a platform surrounding the treadmill may be more practical. The kinds of equipment found in the exercise room, in addition to exercising apparatus, might include the following:
- multichannel recorder
- tape recorder (multichannel)
- gas meters
- cot
- spirometer

- telemetering apparatus
- electronic gas analyzers
- Douglas or meteorological bags
- barometer
- thermocouples
- submersion tank
- computer terminal

Analytical Rooms. The number of analytical rooms will depend upon the extent of the research being conducted and the number of investigators involved. These rooms should each be a minimum of 20 by 20 feet, with a ceiling height of 10 feet. They should be air-conditioned and contain the benches, cabinets, sinks, fume hoods, and air, gas, and electrical current supplies usually found in laboratories of this type. The typical kinds of equipment used in these rooms include chemical gas analyzer, pH meter, analytical balance, still, spectrophotometer, refrigerator or freezer, titrator, osometer, microscope, autoclave, glassware, Bunsen burner, and desk calculator.

Additional Facilities. In many departments, additional major facilities may be required. Because research in exercise physiology is closely related to research in environmental physiology and nutrition, the following facilities may be needed:
- Barometric chamber (with space for controlled exercise)
- Hot room (with space for controlled exercise)
- Cold room (with space for controlled exercise)
- Diet kitchen
- Flow-through water tank for studying energy metabolism during swimming and rowing
- Isotope storage, handling, and counting equipment

In addition, animal exercise and housing rooms may be considered.

Motor Learning and Psychology of Sports

Much of the research equipment found in psychology, physiology of exercise, and kinesiology

(biomechanics) laboratories can be used in research in motor learning and psychology of sports. However, it is necessary to have a separate room or facility, at least 30 by 30 feet, with a 12-foot ceiling.

The arrangement of the equipment in the room will depend on the research underway at the moment. In any event, the electrical devices used should not be constantly moved or they will become unusable.

Some equipment that might be included in a laboratory for research in motor learning and psychology of sports includes:

Multichannel recorders, standard electric clocks, interval timer, steadiness units, muscle stimulator, electronic counters, variable power supply, electronic kits, audio amplifiers, microphone, audio oscillator, oscilloscope, telemetry transmitter, telemetry receiver, voltage stabilizer, battery charger, seashore test, magnetic tape recorder and storage cabinets (metal with locks).

Check List for Facility Planners Relating to General Indoor Facility Features

As an aid to those responsible for planning facilities for athletics, physical education, and recreation, a check list has been prepared. The application of this check list may prevent unfortunate and costly errors. Note: Information concerning the planning of general recreational buildings such as a community center and specialized recreational buildings (i.e. art center, preschool center, senior citizen center, teen center, etc. is available in Chapter VII.

General

1. A clear-cut statement has been prepared on the nature and scope of the program, and the special requirements for space, equipment, fixtures, and facilities have been dictated by

the activities to be conducted. ☐

2. The facility has been planned to meet the total requirements of the program as well as the special needs of those who are to be served. ☐

3. The plans and specifications have been checked by all governmental agencies (city, county, and state) whose approval is required by law. ☐

4. Plans for areas and facilities conform to state and local regulations and to accepted standards and practices. ☐

5. The areas and facilities planned make possible the programs that serve the interests and needs of all the people. ☐

6. Every available source of property or funds has been explored, evaluated, and utilized whenever appropriate. ☐

7. All interested persons and organizations concerned with the facility have had an opportunity to share in its planning (professional educators, users, consultants, administrators, engineers, architects, program specialists, building managers, and builder) — a team approach. ☐

8. The facility will fulfill the maximum demands of the program. The program has not been curtailed to fit the facility. ☐

9. The facility has been functionally planned to meet the present and anticipated needs of specific programs, situations, and publics. ☐

10. Future additions are included in present plans to permit economy of construction. ☐

11. Lecture classrooms are isolated from distracting noises. ☐

12. Storage areas for indoor and outdoor equipment are of adequate size. They are located adjacent to the gymnasium. ☐

13. Shelves in storage rooms are slanted toward the wall. ☐

14. All passageways are free of obstructions; fixtures are recessed. ☐

15. Facilities for health services and the first-aid and emergency-isolation rooms are suitably interrelated. ☐

16. Buildings, specific areas, and facilities are clearly identified. ☐

17. Locker rooms are arranged for ease of supervision. ☐

18. Offices, teaching stations, and service facilities are properly interrelated. ☐

19. Special needs of the physically handicapped are met, including a ramp into the building at a major entrance. ☐

20. All "dead space" is used. ☐

21. The building is compatible in design and comparable in quality and accommodation to other campus structures. ☐

22. Storage rooms are accessible to the play area. ☐

23. Workrooms, conference rooms, and staff and administrative offices are interrelated. ☐

24. Shower and dressing facilities are provided for professional staff members and are conveniently located. ☐

25. Thought and attention have been given to making facilities and equipment as durable and vandalproof as possible. ☐

26. Low-cost maintenance features have been considered. ☐

27. This facility is a part of a well-integrated master plan. ☐

28. All areas, courts, facilities, equipment, climate control, security, etc., conform rigidly to detailed standards and specifications. ☐

29. Shelves are recessed and mirrors are supplied in appropriate places in rest rooms and dressing rooms. ☐

30. Dressing space between locker rows is adjusted to the size and age of students. ☐

31. Drinking fountains are conveniently placed in locker room areas or immediately adjacent thereto. ☐

32. Special attention is given to provision for locking service windows and counters, supply bins, carts, shelves, and racks. ☐

33. Provision is made for repair, maintenance, replacement, and off season storage of equipment and uniforms. ☐

34. A well-defined program for laundering and cleaning towels, uniforms, and equipment is included in the plan. ☐

35. Noncorrosive metal is used in dressing, drying, and shower areas except for enameled lockers. ☐

36. Antipanic hardware is used where required by fire regulations. ☐

37. Properly placed hose bibbs and drains are sufficient in size and quantity to permit flushing the entire area with a water hose. ☐

38. A water resistant, covered base is used under the locker base and floor mat and where floor and wall join. ☐

39. Chalkboards and/or tackboards with map tracks are located in appropriate places in dressing rooms, hallways, and classrooms. ☐

40. Book shelves are provided in toilet areas. ☐

41. Space and equipment are planned in accordance with the types and number of enrollees. ☐

42. Basement rooms, undesirable for dressing, drying, and showering, are not planned for those purposes. ☐

43. Spectator seating (permanent) in areas that are basically instructional is kept at a minimum. Roll away bleachers are used primarily. Balcony seating is considered as a possibility. ☐

44. Well-lighted and effectively displayed trophy cases enhance the interest and beauty of the lobby. ☐

45. The space under the stairs is used for storage. ☐

46. Department heads' offices are located near the central administrative office which includes a well-planned conference room. ☐

47. Workrooms are located near the central office and serve as a repository for departmental materials and records. ☐

48. Conference area includes a cloak room, lavatory, and toilet. ☐

49. In addition to regular secretarial offices established in the central and department chairmen's offices, a special room to house a secretarial pool for staff members is provided. ☐

50. Staff dressing facilities are provided. These facilities may also serve game officials. ☐

51. The community and/or neighborhood has a "round table" for planning. ☐

52. All those (persons and agencies) who should be a party to planning and development are invited and actively engaged in the planning process. ☐

53. Space and area relationships are important. They have been carefully considered. ☐

54. Both long-range and immediate plans have been made. ☐

55. The body comfort of the child, a major factor in securing maximum learning, has been considered in the plans. ☐

56. Plans for quiet areas have been made. ☐

57. In the planning, consideration has been given to the need for adequate recreational areas and facilities, both near and distant from the homes of people. ☐

58. Plans recognize the primary function of recreation as being enrichment of learning through creative self-expression, self-enhancement, and the achievement of self-potential. ☐

59. Every effort has been exercised to eliminate hazards. ☐

60. The installation of low-hanging door closers, light fixtures, signs, and other objects in traffic areas has been avoided. ☐

61. Warning signals — both visible and audible — are included in the plans. ☐

62. Ramps have a slope equal to or greater than a one-foot rise in 12-feet. ☐

63. Minimum landings for ramps are 5 by 5 feet, extend at least one foot beyond the swinging arc of a door, have at least a six-foot clearance at the bottom, and have level platforms at 30-foot intervals on every turn. ☐

64. Adequate locker and dressing spaces are provided. ☐

65. The design of dressing, drying, and shower areas reduces foot traffic to a minimum and establishes clean, dry aisles for bare feet. ☐

66. Teaching stations are properly related to service facilities. ☐

67. Toilet facilities are adequate in number. They are located to serve all groups for which provisions are made. ☐

68. Mail services, outgoing and incoming, are included in the plans. ☐

69. Hallways, ramps, doorways, and elevators are designed to permit equipment to be moved easily and quickly. ☐

70. A keying design suited to administrative and instructional needs is planned. ☐

71. Toilets used by large groups have circulating (in and out) entrances and exits. ☐

Climate Control

1. Provision is made throughout the building for climate control — heating, ventilating, and refrigerated cooling. ☐

2. Special ventilation is provided for locker, dressing, shower, drying and toilet rooms. ☐

3. Heating plans permit both area and individual room control. ☐

4. Research areas where small animals are kept and where chemicals are used have been provided with special ventilating equipment. ☐

5. The heating and ventilating of the wrestling gymnasium have been given special attention. ☐

Electrical

1. Shielded, vapor-proof lights are used in moisture prevalent areas. ☐

2. Lights in strategic areas are key-controlled. ☐

3. Lighting intensity conforms to approved standards. ☐

4. An adequate number of electrical outlets are strategically placed. ☐

5. Gymnasium and auditorium lights are controlled by dimmer units. ☐

6. Locker room lights are mounted above the space between lockers. ☐

7. Natural light is controlled properly for purposes of visual aids and avoidance of glare. ☐

8. Electrical outlet plates are installed three feet above the floor unless special use dictates other locations. ☐

9. Controls for light switches and projection equipment are suitably located and interrelated. ☐

10. All lights are shielded. Special protection is provided in gymnasium, court areas, and shower rooms. ☐

11. Lights are placed to shine between rows of lockers. ☐

Walls

1. Movable and folding partitions are power-operated and controlled by keyed switches. ☐

2. Wall plates are located where needed and are firmly

attached. ☐

3. Hooks and rings for nets are placed (and recessed in walls) according to court locations and net heights. ☐

4. Materials that clean easily and are impervious to moisture are used where moisture is prevalent. ☐

5. Shower heads are placed at different heights — four feet (elementary) to seven feet (university) for each school level. ☐

6. Protective matting is placed permanently on the walls in the wrestling room at the ends of basketball courts and in other areas where such protection is needed. ☐

7. An adequate number of drinking fountains are provided. They are properly placed (recessed in wall). ☐

8. One wall (at least) of the dance studio has full length mirrors. ☐

9. All corners in locker rooms are rounded. ☐

Ceilings

1. Overhead supported apparatus is secured to beams engineered to withstand stress. ☐

2. The ceiling height is adequate for the activities to be housed. ☐

3. Acoustical materials impervious to moisture are used in moisture prevalent areas. ☐

4. Skylights in gymnasiums, being impractical, are seldom used because of problems in waterproofing roofs and the controlling of sun rays. ☐

5. All ceilings except those in storage areas are acoustically treated with sound-absorbent materials. ☐

Floors

1. Floor plates are placed where needed and are flush-mounted. ☐

2. Floor design and materials conform to recommended standards and specifications. ☐

3. Lines and markings are painted in floors before sealing is completed (when synthetic tape is not used). ☐

4. A coved base (around lockers and where wall and floor meet) of the same water resistant material used on floors is found in all dressing and shower rooms. ☐

5. Abrasive, nonskid, slip-resistant flooring that is impervious to moisture is provided on all areas where water is used — laundry, swimming pools, shower, dressing, and drying rooms. ☐

6. Floor drains are properly located, and the slope of the floor is adequate for rapid drainage. ☐

SELECTED REFERENCES

Ashton, Dudley and Irey, Charlotte. **Dance Facilities.** Washington, D.C.: AAHPER, 1972.

Astrand, Per-Olof and Rodahl, Kaare. **Textbook of Work Physiology.** New York: McGraw-Hill, 1970.

Bronzan, Robert T. **New Concepts in Planning and Funding Athletic, Physical Education and Recreation Facilities.** St. Paul: Phoenix Intermedia, 1974.

Clarke, David H. **Exercise Physiology.** Englewood Cliffs, New Jersey: Prentice-Hall, 1975.

Clarks, H. Harrison. **Application of Measurement to Health and Physical Education.** Englewood Cliffs, New Jersey: Prentice-Hall, 1967.

Crookham, Joe P. "Guidelines for Recreation and Athletic Field Lighting." **Parks and Recreation** 17 (June 1982): 23-26, 28.

Crawford, Wayne H. **A Guide for Planning Indoor Facilities for College Physical Education.** New York: Bureau of Publications, Teachers College, Columbia University, 1963.

deVries, Herbert A. **Physiology of Exercise.** 2nd ed. Dubuque, Iowa: Wm. C. Brown Co., 1974.

Ezersky, E.M. and Theibert, P.R. **Facilities in Sports and Physical Education.** St. Louis: The C.V. Mosby Co., 1976.

Flynn, Richard B., ed. "Focus on Facilities." **Journal of Physical Education and Recreation** 46 (April 1975): 24-36.

_____. "Focus on Facilities in Public Schools." **Journal of Physical Education and Recreation** 47 (September 1976)

_____. "What's Happening in Facilities." **Journal of Physical Education and Recreation** 49 (June 1978): 33-48.

Franks, B. Don and Deutsch, Helga. **Evaluating Performance in Physical Education.** New York: Academic Press, 1973.

Gabrielsen, M.A. and Miles, C.M. **Sports and Recreation Facilities for School and Community.** Englewood Cliffs, New Jersey: Prentice-Hall, 1958.

Hardy, Rex. "Improve Gym Lighting: Save Energy Dollars." **Journal of Physical Education, Recreation and Dance** 54 (June 1983): 27-29.

Larson, Bill and Cundiff, David. "Planning a Fitness Assessment and Teaching Lab." **Journal of Physical Education, Recreation, and Dance** 54 (June 1983): 22-23.

Mathews, Donald K. **Measurement in Physical Education.** Philadelphia: W.B. Saunders, 1973.

National Collegiate Athletic Association. Selected 1984 Rules Guides for Various Sports. Mission, Kansas: NCAA, 1984.

Miller, Doris I. and Nelson, Richard C. **Biomechanics of Sport.** Philadelphia: Lee and Febiger, 1973.

Morehouse, Laurence E. and Miller, Augustus T., Jr. **Physiology of Exercise.** 7th ed. St. Louis: The C.V. Mosby Co., 1976.

Northrip, John; Logan, Gene; and McKinney, Wayne. **Biomechanic Analysis of Sport.** Dubuque, Iowa: Wm. C. Brown, 1974.

Penman, Kenneth A. **Planning Physical Education and Athletic Facilities in Schools.** New York: John Wiley and Sons, 1977.

Research Methods Applied to Health, Physical Education and Recreation. 2nd ed. Washington, D.C.: American Association for Health, Physical Education and Recreation, 1973.

Safrit, Margaret J. **Evaluation in Physical Education.** Englewood Cliffs, New Jersey: Prentice-Hall, 1973.

Scott, Hary A. and Westkaemper, Richard B. **From Program to Facilities in Physical Education.** New York: Harper and Brothers, 1958.

U.S. Department of the Army, Navy, and Air Force. **Planning and Design of Outdoor Sports Facilities.** Stock No. 008 - 020 -00588-6, October, 1975.

U.S. Lawn Tennis Association. **Tennis Courts.** Lynn, Massachusetts: H.O. Zimman, Inc., 1975.

University of Illinois. **Study of Needs and Recommendations for Health, Physical Education, Recreation and Athletics.** Champaign: Stipes, 1961.

CHAPTER III
Outdoor Facilities

The re-awakening of the public to the benefits of exercise and recreation for their general well-being and enhanced quality of life has created an increasing demand on existing facilities and pressures for expanded or new facilities. Combined with a demand for a greater variety of activities in physical education and athletic programs and increased support for women's interscholastic and intercollegiate programs, these developments have created an acute shortage of outdoor facilities for most educational institutions and recreational organizations across the United States.

Outdoor facilities must also compete with the increased demands for indoor facilities which, often through expansion to accommodate their programs, further reduce the available space to provide needed outdoor facilities.

In planning and programming to provide facilities to meet these increased demands, by either redevelopment of existing facilities or the development of new or additional sites, facility planners face the difficult task of developing a program that best addresses the needs and creates the most functional facilities possible.

The intent of this chapter is to provide the facility planner with assistance in this process by defining general criteria for site evaluations, planning guidelines, and specific criteria for various outdoor facilities. This information can be used to re-evaluate existing facilities as well as to plan for new developments.

SITE EVALUATION

General Considerations

Facilities should be planned to accommodate the activity. The activity is determined by the program purposes and upon the interests, needs, and capacities of the participants. The following criteria are important in determining specific activities and the areas necessary for their successful conduct : (1) adaptability (capable of being used appropriately in given situations); (2) seasonableness (relevance to weather and seasons in a geographic area); and (3) progression (a part of the total program and leading sequentially to other skills and activities).

The following factors then must

be considered: (1) the number of participants for any single space and for the total area in a given time span; (2) the number of spectators for any single space and for the total area; (3) the special relationships of each area; (4) the movement patterns of participants, learners, and spectators; (5) the interrelationships of curricular and extra-curricular activities; (6) the priority ranking of each space; (7) the equipment necessary for each space; (8) the environmental conditions for each space; (9) the projected future expansion of the facility; and (10) the predicted changes in programs and activities.

Areas developed for physical education, athletics, and recreation often are the largest on any campus. Space is essential to permit creative design ideas. Whenever possible, care should be taken to avoid locating a facility on a site that restricts design options and, as a consequence, interferes with achieving the ideal program objective. Because of the size and nature of these areas, attention should be given to aesthetic qualities and compatability with surrounding structures and areas.

Specific Considerations

Most outdoor physical education activities require a level play area. Sites that have irregular surfaces, extensive brush and tree growths, and numerous large rocks and other obstructions are difficult and expensive to prepare for athletic fields. Some of these characteristics can be useful in the development of certain kinds of facilities. For example, they are essential for outdoor education activities and/or quiet areas. Trees also act as wind breaks, provide shade, and aid in noise absorption.

Sound planning also takes into account the shape as well as size of site to be developed. Care should be exercised with regard to orientation of the facility or area with the sun. Most outdoor sport areas should have their longitudinal axis approximately north and south. Grading and filling are extremely expensive, but fill from campus building construction can frequently be used to raise sports field to a more appropriate level.

Good drainage is important. Physical activity areas that are temporarily flooded after rains obviously will not afford maximum use, nor will sites that drain slowly. Sandy soils offer excellent drainage; a clay base will require the installation of engineered draining. Rich topsoil will enhance planting and landscaping. Areas with extensive sub-surface rock formations are expensive to grade, and inhibit the growth of other vegetation necessary for the absorption of water.

Listed below are a number of other important factors which merit careful consideration in selecting a site:

Accessibility. The site selected for the development of physical education and athletic fields should be easily accessible.

Isolation. Outdoor physical education and athletic facilities should be isolated from persistent and unnecessary distractions. Conversely, these facilities should be located so their use does not become a distraction for nearby classrooms and living units.

Integration. Outdoor facilities should be located strategically in relation to one another and to other accommodating facilities.

Adaptability. A site for outdoor facilities should combine qualities of permanence with those of flexibility. These facilities should be located and designed in such a way as to permit ease and economy in bringing about the alterations and changes that future requirements may demand.

Expansibility. Plans for long-term efficient use of field areas should anticipate the possiblity of changes in the program through the years. In planning for these eventualities, it is necessary to locate field and court areas on sites which are somewhat larger than minimum requirements demand. It is also important that goal net posts, backstops, and other fixtures be planned in such a way as to permit rearrangement when necessary. In addition, attention should be given to the multipurpose use of facilities.

Another specific factor one must consider in site evaluation is the type of facility being planned. Both the neighborhood park-school and the community park-school are discussed below.

The neighborhood park-school is the primary area in planning for education and recreation. It is a combination of a neighborhood elementary school and playground. It is planned in such a manner that all areas and facilities are used to meet the educational and recreational interests and needs of the people living in a neighborhood. It is essential that areas and facilities be cooperatively planned for the dual purpose of instruction and

Figure 3-1

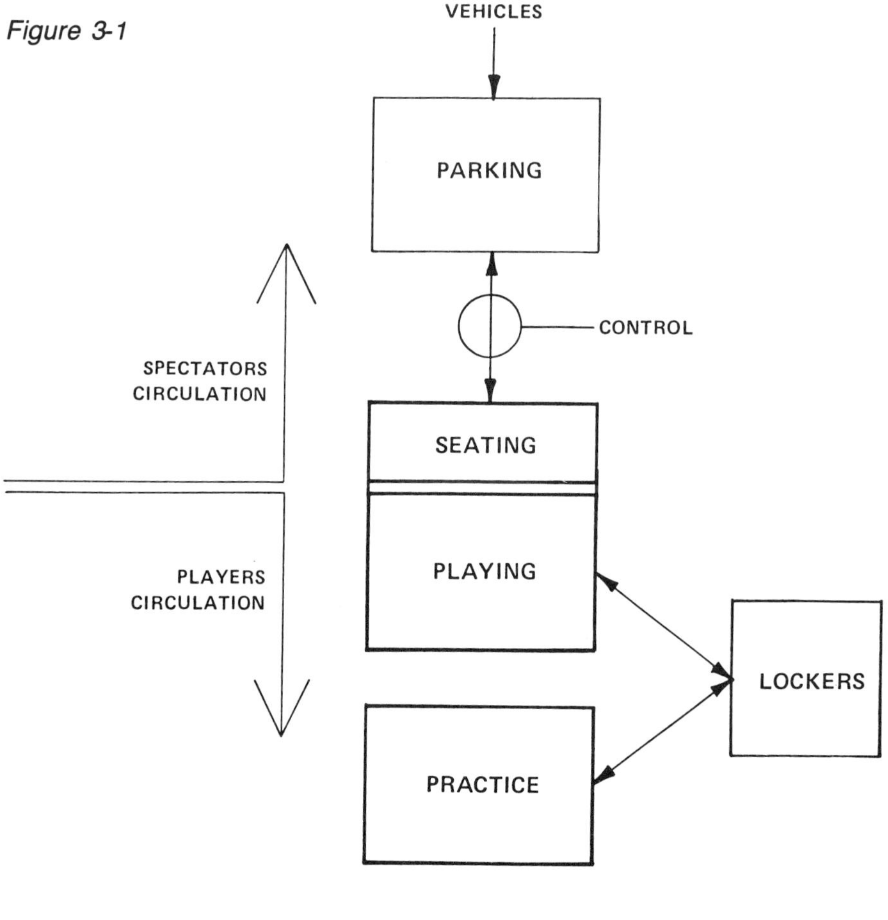

RELATIONSHIP DIAGRAM FOR OUTDOOR ATHLETICS

recreation and that the school and community recreational programs be coordinated for maximum use by the entire neighborhood.

The neighborhood park-school should service an area with a maximum zone of one-half mile and a population of approximately 4,000 to 8,000 people. Any deviation in the population density (larger or smaller communities) may mean a change in needs or interests and thus may alter the service radius and/or acreage required for this installation.

The minimum area recommended for a neighborhood park-school is 10 to 25 acres.

As an illustration, this area might be developed as follows:

	Acres
School Building	1.5-3.0
Parking	0.5-1.5
Playlot and apparatus	0.5-1.5
Hard-surface game courts and multi-use area	0.5-2.5
Turf-games field	3.0-6.0
Park area, including space for drama and quiet activities	2.0-5.5
Buffer zones and circulation	1.5-3.0
Recreation service building	0.2-0.5
Corner for senior citizens	0.3-1.0
Total	10.0-25.0

The community park-school is an area in which are located a junior or senior high school and a variety of recreational and physical education facilities designed for both school and community use. It should be centrally located in the community and provide a parklike environment. If it contains a senior high school, it requires more acreage than if it is associated with an elementary or junior high school, and its service radius is appreciably greater. (Figure 3-2)

Many people using such centers reach them by automobile or public transport. Relatively few live close enough to walk to them. A portion of the area is usually developed as a playground for the children living in the immediate neighborhood, while another portion serves as a landscaped park.

The function of this area is similar to that of the neighborhood park-school. While the neighborhood park-school contains an elementary school and serves primarily children, the community park-school contains a secondary school and serves primarily young people and adults. The geographic area served by the community school is larger (usually consisting of three or more residential neighborhoods). Its space

requirements are much greater, and it provides facilities not feasible in the neighborhood unit because of the cost and needed space. The community park-school with a senior high school needs more area in order to provide for scholastic athletics, spectator space, and extensive parking.

In communities where the park-school plan cannot be put into effect, separate sites are required for the secondary schools — the junior and senior high schools. A smaller site will serve the needs of the school physical education, recreation, and outdoor education programs better than if the area were also expected to provide the recreational service for the entire community.

The senior high school needs a larger site than the junior high school because the enrollment is usually higher and because of the greater space requirements of the interscholastic athletic program. Even though separate public indoor and outdoor recreational facilities are provided elsewhere in the community, the junior and senior high school plants should be designed to facilitate community use when they are not required for school purposes.

One example of close cooperation between a

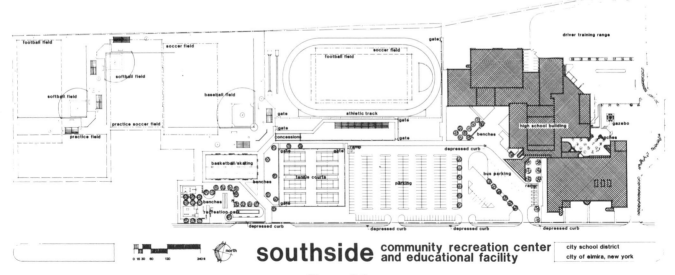

Figure 3-2

The Southside Community Recreation Center and Educational Facility in Elmire, New York is a good example of a comprehensive athletic complex to serve both the high school and the community.

Outdoor Facilities

municipality and the public school system is the installation of municipal tennis courts on school property. The municipality's recreation budget supports the cost of court installation while the school provides the land. The school retains priority for use during school hours and courts are available for community use after school hours and on week-ends.

PLANNING GUIDELINES

Safety Factors in Site

The first aspect of safety in selecting sites for physical education is to have adequate acreage to provide for safety in locating areas of activity. A planner should never increase the risk of potential injury to students by using all available space for activity areas and sacrificing area for safety. Before thinking quantity, think safety.

Traffic safety around activity areas is the most important factor to be considered in selecting sites. Outdoor play areas should be located so there is no interference with the traffic of pedestrians, buses, automobiles, service vehicles and bicycles. Driveways should be planned to give direct access to parking areas, and should normally not bisect or parrallel play areas. If the condition demands that areas be bisected or parralled, fencing should be installed to separate the play areas from the traffic pathway. This will prevent loose balls from entering the pathway and prevent students from wandering into the traffic. Adequate driveways within the school area also provide easy access to areas for emergency vehicles.

Walkways should provide direct access between areas and facilities. However, care should be taken to prevent interference with activities or the creation of a safety hazard. This restriction will protect both pedestrians and participants from injury.

Different play areas used by different age groups should be isolated. Shrubbery hedges, trees, fences, concrete walls, or even buildings have proven to be effective barriers. It is important that these areas be separated because different age groups play different games at different levels of intensity. With a high school soccer field located next to an elementary playground, an errantly kicked ball chased by a student into the playground area full of elementary children could result in serious injury. This possibility could be easily prevented if the field and playground has some type of divider to isolate the areas.

Due to the obvious danger, no play areas should be placed alongside railroads or open water. However, a high chain link fence can be installed to separate the play area if such location cannot be avoided.

Present and future environment conditions should be taken into consideration when selecting sites for areas of activity. Locating outdoor activity areas adjacent to an industrial site is not desirable. Being close to such an environment causes unnecessary distractions during class periods. Another hazard of industry close to activity areas is the factor of prevailing winds blowing pollutants over the fields.

Activity areas should never be placed near utility wires or poles of any kind. There should not be excessive trenching for water drainage without protective barriers. Sewage areas should be placed well away from activity areas and gas lines should not run under areas of play. Utilities of any kind are potentially dangerous around activity areas and never should be close to or encroach upon a play area.

All play fields (not varsity fields) should be located well away from driveways, roads, or parking lots. School play areas should be close to the school, directly accessible from both the boys' and girls' locker rooms. Areas involving varsity sports can be placed on

the outer edges of the school property and along driveways and parking lots provided there is adequate fencing surrounding the areas. Being placed along the driveway or next to the parking lot provides easy accessability for proper entrance and exit of spectator vehicles. If an athletic event takes place during school hours, the event will not disrupt other classes.

Another important consideration is security. It would be advantageous to place facilities and storage areas in places that are well lighted and easily observed. This can be effective in deterring vandalism and theft.

Orientation

Courts and fields should be oriented to give protection to both players and spectators. It may not be possible to get the best orientation of a particular court or field because such factors as topography, shape of the area, and location of other facilities may dictate variations.

Outdoor courts and fields should be oriented so players will not have to face into the late-afternoon or early-morning sun. In rectangular fields and court, the long axis should generally be at right angles to the late-afternoon sun's rays. Locate the sunset position at midseason of the sport and orient the field or court accordingly.

On baseball, softball, and similar fields, the general pattern of the ball's flight covers an arc of more than 90 degrees. Since the field cannot be oriented to give equal protection to all players and spectators, a choice must be made. Because the batter, pitcher and catcher are in the most hazardous positions, they should be given first consideration. A line through these positions should be the axis for orienting the field.

Site Development

Problems which are commonly present in site-development

projects are concerned with grading, drainage, landscape design, fencing, and accessibility to water and electricity.

Grading

Outdoor physical education and sports activities are best promoted on field and court areas that are relatively level. However, the topography of available sites and the cost of filling and cutting often make some terracing necessary.

Drainage

It is always necessary to provide for a gradual slope of all playing sites to assure the efficient removal of excess surface water. A one-percent slope is recommended as maximum for turf areas. For a stadium football field, a 12-inch crown down the longitudinal axis on the middle of the field is recommended.

For baseball, the pitcher's box should be elevated 10 inches above the base lines and home plate. The slope from the pitcher's box to home plate and to all base lines should be gradual. A one-percent drainage grade for the outfield is recommended.

Large, hard-surface, multipurpose areas are generally sloped so that surface water is directed toward specific collection points. It is recommended that for tennis, volleyball, badminton, and other net games the slope be from one side of the court to the other.

A widely accepted standard for the finished grade for hard-surfaced court areas calls for a slope of one inch in eight feet, as a means of providing adequate surface drainage. A few experienced tennis court contractors can flatten this somewhat to one inch in ten feet.

Attention should be given to the problem of subsurface drainage in the development of playing fields. This problem is generally peculiar to local conditions, and consultation with a competent soils engineer is recommended. Due to the hazards of damage from freezing, subsurface drainage is also an important consideration in the construction of hard-surface court areas.

Fencing

Fencing is frequently required for many physical education and sports areas for security, safety, isolation, enclosure, separation, noise abatement, wind screening, sun screening, traffic control (pedestrian and vehicular), and for the protection of participants, the general public, spectators, and property.

In the case of baseball, field hockey, softball, soccer, rugby, lacrosse, and tennis, fences are used to confine the ball to the playing area, and thus enhance the play of the game and the enjoyment of spectators. Unfenced baseball and softball fields reduce the home-run potential.

In lacrosse, field hockey, soccer, and rugby, a fence three feet beyond the end line of the playing field confines most out-of-bounds balls and reduces time lost in retrieving the ball. A 10 to 12-foot fence on all sides of tennis courts is recommended to confine balls and speed up play.

Some characteristics of good fencing are stability, durability, economy of maintenance, attractiveness, and effectiveness. Among the many types of suitable fencing available, woven wire fencing of the chain-link type (minimum thickness—11 gauge), using H type or circular line posts, meets requirements. Chain-link fencing is available in the standard galvanized steel and also in aluminum-coated steel, plastic-coated steel and aluminum alloy mesh. The new plastic coatings are smoother to the touch and come in a variety of colors. Forest green is the most common color since it blends well with grass and shrubs. The appearance, security and isolation qualities of the chain-link fence can be enhanced with the insertion of wood, metal or plastic strips into the fencing. The most commonly used insertion is redwood strips woven vertically.

All chain-link fencing should be installed with the smooth edges at the top. In special cases, however, it may be desirable to have smooth edges at both top and bottom. A hard-surface mowing strip about 12 inches wide may be placed under the fence to facilitate maintenance. To prevent balls from rolling under the fence (such as in a baseball facility) redwood or pressure-treated boards may be attached to the bottom of the fence if it does not reach to the mowing strip.

The most common material used for fencing of tennis courts is chain-link fabric. This fencing should have a minimum height of 12 feet along the rear lines of the courts and a minimum of 10 feet on the sides. The courts should be entirely enclosed. Where cost is a major factor, the fencing may be placed along the rear of the courts, with a 20-foot wing return on the sides. The fence fabric should be placed on the inside of the fence posts. Canvas or plastic wind screens, or redwood, plastic or metal inserts should be installed on the windward side.

Rebound walls are recommended. They should be 12 feet in height topped by 3 feet of light fencing to reduce the number of lost balls. These walls should be located on the north end of the courts so the players are not facing the sun and so the wall's shadow does not fall on the court where it would delay the drying of overnight moisture. Entrance gates should be located at the ends of the courts to reduce cross-court traffic. A gate at each end between each pair of courts is recommended.

Where admission is charged, a fence with a minimum height of seven feet surrounding the spectator structure and the enclosed field is essential. Landscape architects often use vines, shrubs or other plantings along fences to create an attractive appearance. Gates are necessary for spectator and service entrances and exits. Admission gates should be located near the parking lots and other main approaches to the structure including public transportation stops. The number and size of entrances depend on anticipated attendance. Exits should permit the crowd to vacate the enclosure within ten minutes. Twenty-two inches of linear exit space should be provided for each 500 spectators. At least one gate 14 feet high and 14 feet wide should be provided to accommodate trucks and buses.

Walkways

All-weather walks should be confined to a minimum in open play areas and should be provided only where the foot traffic is heavy enough to warrant. Circulation walks serve as guideways to interesting features and may be of many kinds of surfacing material such as concrete, asphalt, brick, adobe, exposed aggregate concrete, loose aggregate, tile, stone or wood. Basic considerations in the choice of surface type include: intended use, cost, ease of installation, durability, appearance and maintenance. Portland cement and asphalt best meet the requirements of heavily trafficked areas.

The walks should vary in width in consonance with the traffic density and should not cross through game courts or areas. To accomplish the desired circulation of traffic, it may be necessary to use signs, pavement lines and fixed or planted barriers. The degree of slope, and subsurface drainage should be given careful consideration. Drainage tiles may be used if necessary.

In developments where it is impractical to service features and facilities with drives, or from adjacent street pavements, selected walks should be of heavier construction and of sufficient width to accommodate service-truck loads.

Landscape Design

Landscaping should be planned so as to improve the playing conditions. Shrubs, hedges, trees, and vines can be used as windbreaks, background barriers, spectator screens and ground cover. They also enhance the value of adjacent property and provide a better environment for the enjoyment of the activity.

An important duty of the landscape architect is to provide proper and well-designed entrance and exit walks, drives, and parking areas for all playing areas.

Plans and specifications for landscaping plantings should be prepared at the same time as those for the original site development. This will ensure that the plantings will be in keeping with the total development.

Utilities and Electricity

No turf playing area can be properly developed or maintained without an adequate water supply. Therefore, in designing a field area, it is recommended that an automatic sprinkler system be installed to reduce field maintenance.

Electrical outlets should be available at all field and court areas. The number, size, and voltage should be determined by the requirements of field lights, public-address systems, concession facilities, scoreboards, and maintenance equipment.

Consideration should always be given to the location of a telephone at all field and court areas. This is a safety precaution for emergencies, an aid and important time-saver for maintenance help, and a convenience for players and spectators.

Parking

The need to provide off-street parking for automobiles is a major consideration in the design of facilities. Each parking space should be marked. It is often more desirable to construct parking

areas in several locations, near the facilities which have the highest concentration of users. This will also make it easier to blend the parking areas into the landscape. Where possible, parking areas should be located near the perimeter and should be designed to not interfere with normal pedestrian traffic. In the case of large parking areas, it is necessary to make a study of the traffic pattern in the surrounding area to facilitate the movement of traffic to and from the parking area.

The off-street parking areas should be hard-surfaced, and may be used also for sports, free-play activities, driver education, marching band maneuvers, and other activities. Either post sleeves flush with the surface, or portable standards will make it relatively easy to conduct a variety of net games in these areas.

Surfacing

There is no one surface which will satisfactorily meet the needs of all outdoor activities. Each activity has its own surface requirements, which will dictate what type or types, of material can be used.

In the selection of surfacing material for any outdoor area, certain qualities should be sought, including multiplicity of use, durability, dustless and stainless, reasonable initial cost and economy, ease of maintenance, pleasing appearance, nonabrasiveness, resiliency and year-round usage.

Obtaining the proper surface for outdoor areas continues to be a perplexing problem. Over the years, however, there have been significant developments in surfacing. The various types of surfacing materials are shown in the accompanying table.

Turf

The advantages of using grass as a surface are its attractiveness, resiliency, and nonabrasiveness, and the fact that it is relatively dust-free. Such a surface lends itself very well to activities that require relatively large areas, as most field games do.

Turf is difficult to maintain in areas where there is intensive usage. In some parts of the country where watering is essential, maintenance costs are high. Turf surfaces are not practical for most activities when the ground is frozen or wet, and in addition, must be given time and care to recuperate after heavy use. It is now possible, however to have a complete turf installed with built-in moisture and temperature control. (Materials Table and Figures 3-3 and 3-A)

Soils

Among the difficulties encountered in the use of earth as a surfacing material are dust and the tendency to become rutted, which, in turn, create drainage problems and relatively high maintenance costs. These difficulties can be partially overcome by mixing the earth with sand. When this is done, the resulting surface is often less resilient and somewhat abrasive.

Natural soils can also be stabilized by the addition of asphalt, calcium chloride, resin, or cement, which are the most commonly used stabilizers. The use of stabilized soils is a possibility in many areas where turf is impractical or cannot be grown.

Masonry

Natural-stone slabs, or blocks, and manufactured brick can be used for such installations as walks and terraces, where interesting and attractive patterns, colors, and textures are designed.

Concrete

Portland cement concrete surface provide year-round and multiple usage. Installation costs are high, but maintenance costs are low and the surface is extremely durable.

Types of Surfacing Materials

Group	Type
Earth	Loams, sand, sand-clay, clay-gravel, fuller's earth, stabilized earth, soil-cement.
Turf	Bluegrass mixtures, bent, fescue, Bermuda.
Aggregates	Gravel, graded stone, graded slag, shell, cinders.
Asphalt	Penetration-macadam, asphaltic concrete, (cold and hot-laid), sheet asphalt , natural asphalt, sawdust asphalt, vermiculite asphalt, rubber asphalt, cork asphalt, other patented asphalt mixes.
Synthetics	Rubber, synthetic resins, rubber asphalt, chlorinated butyl-rubber, mineral fiber, plastics, vinyls.
Concrete	Monolithic, terrazzo, precast.
Masonry	Flagstone (sandstone, limestone, granite, etc), brick, etc.
Miscellaneous	Tanbark, sawdust, shavings, cottonseed hulls.

Figures 3-3, 3A

With the installation of turf (below), weather and maintenance problems no longer limit the use of this field at Susan Wagner High School on Staten Island.

Asphalt

The common asphaltic concrete surface has many of the advantages which are sought in any surfacing material. It provides a durable surface which can be used on a year-round schedule. Maintenance is easy and inexpensive. Such a surface can also be used for many different activities. When properly installed, the surface is dust-free and drains quickly. Asphalt surfaces can be marked easily and with a relatively high degree of permanence. Asphalt also provides a neat appearing, non-glare surface that will blend well with the landscape.

Asphalt can be combined with a variety of other materials to provide a resilient or extremely hard surface. The use of such materials as cork or rubber in combination with asphalt will yield a quite resilient surface. Aggregates such as slag or granite will produce a firmer surface when combined with asphalt.

Synthetics

The past 15 years has seen a proliferation of synthetic surfaces both for indoor and outdoor use. Various names (synthetic, all-weather, artificial) have been applied to these surfaces. Originally, the synthetic surfaces were developed to provide all-purpose, all-weather surface for a variety of activities. More recently, however, although many of the surfaces may have a multi-purpose use, most are specifically designed for a particular type activity. The prospective facility planner should recognize that there are wide differences between the various types of surfaces as well as production differences between surfaces of the same "brand" name to be used for different purposes.

Considerations

Synthetic surfaces have several exceptional benefits. They provide a consistently smooth and uniform surface; greatly expand the use of the area, not only for multi-use, but for all students rather than exclusive use by athletic teams; provide the opportunity for use under all but the most adverse weather conditions; are generally regarded as safe as many of the natural surfaces (the controversy over this aspect of synthetic turf has not been fully resolved); increase the effective use of an allotted area; provide economic benefits through reduced acreage requirements; increased use and decreased maintenance costs. Finally, many of the top regional, state, national and international events in some sports are conducted on synthetic surfaces, providing for greater uniformity in performance.

Outdoor synthetic surfaces do have major disadvantages, some types more so that others. In general the following should receive attention and consideration.

• Initial costs are high, some types double or triple others, depending upon grading, sub-surface, installation process, and selected material.

• Maintenance, although minimal in some cases, is necessary. When required, it is both costly and time-consuming. Maintenance is reduced if measures are taken to reduce or eliminate vehicular and pedestrian traffic and security measures are taken to reduce the possibility of vandalism and misuse.

• Aspects of the weather do affect the outdoor synthetic surfaces. Extreme temperatures may alter the resiliency of the surface. The character of the composition may also alter over a short period of time either from temperature extremes or ultra-violet exposure. Asphaltic compounds may become brittle due to oxidation of the asphalt cement.

• Limited research studies have indicated a heat build-up on the surface which may affect the performer.

Types

There are three basic types of synthetic surfaces in widespread use today under a variety of trade names: synthetic turf, asphalt composition and plastic surfaces. Synthetic turf (grass) is used on those playing areas for games (baseball, football, soccer, field hockey, lacrosse, etc.) traditionally played on natural grass surfaces. The various asphaltic surfaces and the newer plastic surfaces (polyvinylchloride or polyurethane) have found their greatest use on tennis courts, tracks, and multi-purpose play areas.

Synthetic grass is a turfed carpet made from polyvinyl chloride or urethane plastic. It may be applied on a variety of subsurfaces, but asphaltic concrete is the more common. The composition of the subcarpet base varies in thickness and resiliency, depending upon anticipated use of the surface. Embedded in, or bonded to, the subcarpet base are plastic fibers resembling grass. The density and height of the blades vary with anticipated use. Installation of the combined fibers and subcarpet base is generally accomplished from rolls five yards wide of appropriate length. It may be bonded to the base or stretched and anchored in place.

Asphalt Composition — the numerous varieties of asphalt mixes, often in combination with cork, fiber, rubber, or plastic, are classified into two types — those with a cushioned surface and those with a non-cushioned surface. These surfaces require a base course (compacted stone, gravel, or rough aggregate asphalt), a leveling course (hot asphalt mix, emulsified mix or cold asphalt mix), and a surface course (non-cushioned) or a cushion course (hot or cold mix). A color finish coat made from synthetics (epoxies, neoprene, acrylic vinyls or latex) is often applied to the non-cushioned surface to smooth it and give it color. The cushioned materials are color impregnated.

Lines are applied by use of a synthetic paint, appropriate for that type of surface.

Plastic Surfaces — the two plastic surfaces used in outdoor setting include polyvinyl chloride (PVC) and an elastomeric polyurethane. PVC has not proven totally satisfactory at this time for outdoor use due to its reaction to the sun's rays and resiliency fluctuations caused by temperature changes. The plasticizer used in the PVC setting process also tends to exude through the top surface.

A two-part polyurethane, laid in prefabricated sheets or monolithically applied on a suitable base, provides a durable, color-fast, and wear resistant surface with consistent resiliency. The surface may be smooth or embossed, depending upon projected use. Lines are painted with a synthetic paint as recommended by the manufacturer.

Evaluation Criteria

Criteria used to evaluate any of the outdoor synthetic surfaces include initial cost, maintenance and repair, durability, color, traction, impact absorption, resiliency and consistency of resiliency, effects of temperatures and sun, tensile strength, texture, color stability and utilization.

Communications

A simple public address system would be adequate for all events other than a football game. A good press box is needed at the football stadium. Each newspaper should have its own working space, while television and radio personnel need separate booths. A duplicating and processing area, telephones, a distribution and storage area for food, and a deck for photography should be included in the press box plans. The main controls need to be located in or adjacent to the public address system. Microphone jacks should be installed at strategic

locations at field level, and a direct telephone connection should exist between the field level and the press box.

Service Facilities

Facilities for the dispensing and storage of playing equipment should be on or readily accessible to the site. These facilities should include space for maintenance equipment, and for benches, tables, and chairs, and rest rooms for men and women spectators.

Plans for such areas should include consideration of the accessibility of dressing and shower facilities for home and visiting teams, game officials, and coaches. In many situations, it has been found more economical to provide transportation to and from the playing site than to construct these facilities.

SPECIAL CONSIDERATION IN OUTDOOR LIGHTING

Lighting of the outdoor athletic and recreational facility presents three areas of specialized problems. They are distance, weather elements, and safety. The first two elements, distance and weather, impact on and affect the quality and therefore the dollar value of the system that is being purchased. The third element, safety, deals with a specialized concern for participants and spectators due to their direct access to the electrical system and the specialized structures of the outdoor lighting system.

Distance

In the outdoor facility, the light sources must be placed outside the perimeter of the area to be lighted. That means that light must be produced at a location sometimes several hundred feet from the area where the light is needed. Transmission of the light efficiently and effectively over that distance becomes a critical element in the success of the

lighting system. The nature of light is such that it dissipates by the square of the distance it travels. In other words, at a distance of 100 feet from the light source, the light intensity is reduced to 1/10,000 of its source intensity at a distance of 200 feet, the intensity will have dropped to 1/40,000 of its source intensity. Figure 3-4 lists illumination levels recommended for outdoor facilities. The purpose of the reflector around the lens is to take the light output and concentrate it into an appropriate intensity and direct that intensity to a designated distant point.

Weather Elements

Wind and air contaminants work against the reflector in achieving its purpose. The reflector is exposed to the winds 24 hours a day every day of the year. Misalignment of the reflector by as little as ten degrees through buffeting by the wind could reduce the light level of an average high school football field by as much as two thirds. That is, ten degrees of misalignment of the reflector could reduce the light intensity on the field from 30 footcandles to 10 footcandles. Even more important, movement of reflectors of even smaller amounts could dramatically affect the quality or uniformity of the light, creating bright and dark spots on the field.

Once a desired lighting level has been selected for a facility, careful attention should be given to the design of the luminaire assembly (the lights and crossarms mounted on the pole) to determine that it has been designed and installed with components that will not shift and misalign with wind changes.

Figure 3-4
Levels of Illumination
Currently Recommended
For Outdoor Sports Areas

Sports Area	Footcandles on Task
Archery	*10*
Badminton	*10*

Baseball . . . . 20 outfield
                          30 infield
Basketball 30
Corkball 30
Field Handball 30
Field Hockey 30
Football 30
Golf Driving Range 10
Handball 10
Horseshoes 10
Ice Hockey 20
Lacrosse 30
Rifle and Pistol Range 10,
                       Firing Line 20
Rugby 30
Skating 30
Soccer 30
Softball . . . . . 20 Outfield, 30 Infield
Speedball 30
Tennis 30
Volleyball 20

Air contaminants can cause the reflector surface to change by increasing diffusion and decreasing total reflection. More diffusion decreases the intensity causing a reduced projection over a distance. Decreased reflection means more light energy is absorbed and less total light energy leaves the face of the light. Accordingly, luminaires should be selected which are air and water-tight except for a filtered pressure release port.

Safety

In the outdoor system for athletic and recreational facilities, electrical power must be distributed from the service entrance to the various structures around the perimeter of the field. The electrical system should be underground wherever possible for safety. Out of necessity, the wires come out of the ground at each structure and must pass through various connecting boxes and switching devices.

Because it is usually impractical to make these structures inaccessible to participants and spectators, it is important to use all reasonable cautions to protect against people coming in contact with the electrical power. Minimum guidelines of Underwriter

Laboratory standards for equipment to be used at these facilities, and the National Electrical Code should never be compromised.

Furthermore, consideration should be given to the fact that these are minimum standards frequently established for more generalized electrical applications of residential, commercial, and industrial uses. Special safety considerations may be necessary due to the distances, multiplicity of the structures, and exposure to the public, particularly children.

It is important to remember that safety is an overhead expense and an effort that those involved in the installation may try to avoid. Short cuts frequently will not show up in the operation of the system until someone is injured. Accordingly, special care must be given to ensure that proper safety is designed into the system and that the system is installed as designed.

Housing for Electrical Controls

A vital part of any outdoor lighting system is the protective and control equipment necessary to make it function. The very nature of this equipment represents a real hazard to anyone not familiar with its operation and the characteristics of electricity.

The development of new light sources has resulted in more frequent use of high voltage for larger outdoor lighting systems. Distribution systems of 240 and 480 volts are common, and, in some instances, a primary distribution system using 2,400 or 4,160 volts to strategically-placed distribution transformers can be justified.

Wherever such equipment is located, the controls must be adequately housed and padlocked. Where buildings or bleacher complexes are adjacent to the lighted area, consideration should be given to locating the controls inside a control room where they can be protected from unauthorized persons.

FIELD SPORTS

General

Sports fields in general require the greatest quantities of space in the outdoor facilities area. The activities are conducted on large playing areas, and additional acreage is required for spectators and circulation among activities.

The usability of the areas, in particular after inclement weather, often requires substantial support utilities such as draining and irrigation, along with appropriate grading of the surface to provide a good and consistent facility.

The surface material, generally turf, is critical to the use and success of the facilities to support the intense use that the sport activities demand.

Baseball Field

The area required for a baseball field should be 400 feet by 400 feet, an area of approximately three acres. This will allow for dugouts and bleachers as well as the playing area.

Its orientation may vary a little, depending on where the field will be located and the time the games will be played — afternoon or twilight. However, if possible, the back point of home plate should be set to point due south to southwest. Another check is to have the baseline from home plate to first base run easterly.

The official diamond is 90 feet on a side, with the dimensions across the diamond 127 feet 3-3/8 inches. There should be a minimum of 60 feet from home plate to the backstop. From home plate, down the foul lines to the outfield fence, the distance varies. However, 320 feet should be a minimum. The shortest part of the ball park is usually down the foul lines with the fence gradually going out to reach its deepest point in centerfield.

A large frame backstop with a sturdy wire fence should be located 60 feet behind home plate. This backstop should be a minimum of 20 feet high to help keep the ball in the field of play. Attached to each end of the backstop should be a fence at least four feet high, 60 feet from the nearer foul line, and extending to the outfield fence where they join in foul territory at least 45 feet from the foul line. The outfield fence should be eight feet high for maximum safety. If a shorter fence is used, be certain that no points or other sharp obstructions extend up above the top rail. All fence posts should be on the outside of the playing area.

Dugouts, warning track, scoreboard, press box, auxiliary mounds, and other accessories should be taken into consideration. Dugouts are too often built too small, with not enough head room. It is recommended that the end of one dugout be used for storage. The traditional dugout, sunk into the ground to allow for spectator clearance, is costly because of drainage problems.

Figure 3-5

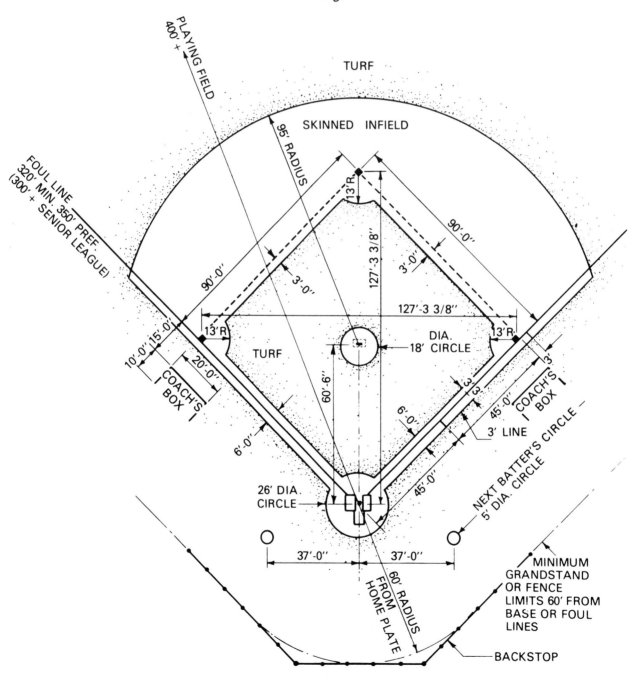

BASEBALL DIAMOND LAYOUT

Outdoor Facilities

Figure 3-6

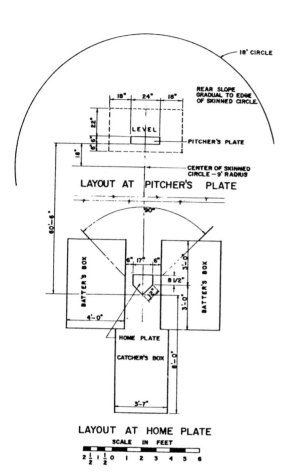

18' CIRCLE

REAR SLOPE
GRADUAL TO EDGE
OF SKINNED CIRCLE.

18" 24" 18"

22" LEVEL

6'6" PITCHER'S PLATE

18" CENTER OF SKINNED
CIRCLE - 9' RADIUS

LAYOUT AT PITCHER'S PLATE

60'-6"

90°

6" 17" 6" 3'-0"

BATTER'S BOX 8 1/2" BATTER'S BOX

4'-0" 3'-0"

HOME PLATE

CATCHER'S BOX 8'-0"

3'-7"

LAYOUT AT HOME PLATE

SCALE IN FEET
2 1/2 1 1/2 0 1 2 3 4 5 6

Junior baseball facilities are similar to regular baseball, except that the playing area may be reduced, depending on the age of the participants. Some national organizations that sponsor junior baseball programs have modified the official rules to fit the needs of the players. For example, the distance between bases is shortened as are the distance from home plate to the outfield fences and from home to the pitcher's plate. For recommended dimensions of Little League, Pony League, and Babe Ruth League see Figures 5, 6, 7, 8 and 9.

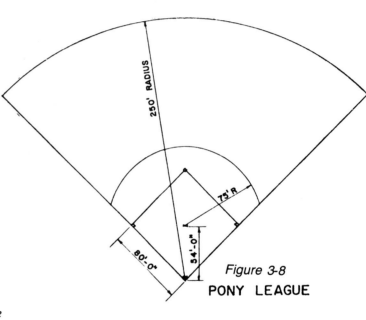

250' RADIUS

75' R

54'-0"

80'-0"

Figure 3-8
PONY LEAGUE

The degree of slope from a point 6" in front of the pitcher's plate to a point 6' toward home plate shall be 1" to 1', and such degree of slope shall be uniform.

Figure 3-7
Boy's Baseball Field Diagrams

180' RADIUS

50' R

46'-0"

60'-0"

LITTLE LEAGUE

Figure 3-9

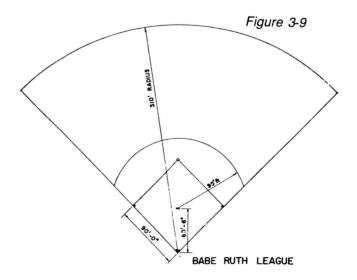

310' RADIUS

95' R

60'-0"

90'-0"

BABE RUTH LEAGUE

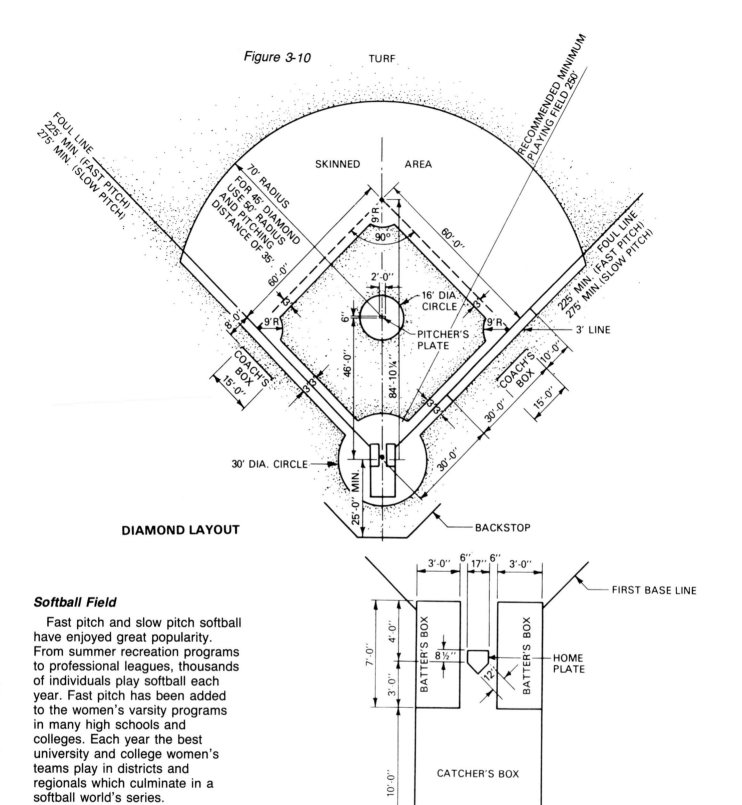

Figure 3-10

TURF

FOUL LINE
225' MIN. (FAST PITCH)
275' MIN. (SLOW PITCH)

RECOMMENDED MINIMUM
PLAYING FIELD 250'

SKINNED   AREA

70' RADIUS

FOR 45' DIAMOND
USE 50' RADIUS
AND PITCHING
DISTANCE OF 35'

60'-0"

90°

9'R

60'-0"

16' DIA.
CIRCLE

2'-0"

6"

PITCHER'S
PLATE

9'R

3' LINE

8'-0"

9'R

46'-0"

84'-10¼"

9'R

COACH'S
BOX

15'-0"

30' DIA. CIRCLE

25'-0" MIN.

COACH'S
BOX

30'-0"

30'-0"

10'-0"

15'-0"

FOUL LINE
(FAST PITCH)
225' MIN. (FAST PITCH)
275' MIN. (SLOW PITCH)

BACKSTOP

DIAMOND LAYOUT

3'-0"   6" 17" 6"   3'-0"

FIRST BASE LINE

BATTER'S BOX

7'-0"

4'-0"

3'-0"

8½"

12"

BATTER'S BOX

HOME
PLATE

10'-0"

CATCHER'S BOX

8'-5"

LAYOUT AT HOME PLATE

Softball Field

Fast pitch and slow pitch softball
have enjoyed great popularity.
From summer recreation programs
to professional leagues, thousands
of individuals play softball each
year. Fast pitch has been added
to the women's varsity programs
in many high schools and
colleges. Each year the best
university and college women's
teams play in districts and
regionals which culminate in a
softball world's series.

Softball fields vary in types from
"cow pasture" variety to well-kept
diamonds. The best fields have
skinned diamonds with all grass,
weeds and rocks eliminated. Three
features which are common to all
"class" playing areas are: good
construction, proper soil structure,
and careful maintenance. All three
must be present for a quality field,
A well-kept diamond and outfield
give each player a chance to

perform at the best of her or his ability. A good facility can be used earlier in the spring and made playable sooner after a rain storm.

For elimination of complicated ground rules, it is recommended that the field be enclosed with a fence approximately 8 feet in height. The rule book states that the playing field shall have a clear and unobstructed area within a radius of 225 feet for males and female fast pitch, 250 feet for female slow pitch and 275 feet for male slow pitch from home plate between the foul lines. Outside the foul lines and between home plate and the backstop, there should be an unobstructed area of not less than 25 feet in width.

The official diamond should have 60 foot base lines with pitching distances as follows: Fast pitch, male — 46 feet, female — 40 feet; slow pitch, male — 46 feet, female — 46 feet. Layout of the diamond is shown in Figure For best all around orientation in the northern hemisphere, the line from home plate through second base should point north-northeast.

The field must also have a backstop erected not less than 25 feet behind home plate. The backstop should consist of three panels 12 feet wide, one panel centered on home plate, with the other two panels on each end flaring out at an angle of 30 degrees with the center panel. Each panel should be 18-20 feet in height. The upright and cross pieces of each panel can be made from steel or wood. One and one half inch galvanized wire mesh is stretched and fastened between the uprights on each panel. (Figure 3-11)

Softball fields must have adequate seating for spectators if interest in the sport is to be maintained. The bleacher area should be separated from the playing field by a fence or rope. If possible, position bleachers so that spectators are not looking into the sun. Players' benches with back rests should be provided for each team and positioned at least 25 feet from each foul line.

Figure 3-11
This softball complex in Montgomery, Alabama is an example of the many such parks that have been constructed in communities to save a growing number of softball teams.

A scoreboard adds interest for both spectators and players. It need not be elaborate but should show results by innings.

Field Hockey

The dimensions of the field are 300 feet long and from 150 to 180 feet wide. A smaller field of 255 feet by 135 feet can be used for younger players.

The field should be marked with two-inch white lines. There should be four lines across the width of the field that divide the length of the field into four equal parts 25 yards apart. The lines at each end are called goal lines. The line that bisects the field is called the center line. The other two lines between the goal and center line are the 25-yard lines. When the field is smaller, the 25-yard lines should be 25 yards from the goals lines. Parallel to, and five yards from each side line, is a broken 5-yard line. The space between the 5-yard and side lines is called the alley. At each end of the field is a striking circle. The striking circle should be marked regulation size, which is 45 feet from each goal post out to the side. The "circle" part should have a 45 foot radius from each goal post. The penalty corners are marked 30 feet to the side of each goal post on the goal line. These penalty

lines run 12 inches from the goal line into the field. At the center of each goal line is a goal 12 feet wide.

The playing surface should be a multipurpose turf or loam. This turf should be crowned down the center, sloping one-fourth inch per foot toward the sidelines for better drainage. The field should be oriented so that play is in a north and south direction. (Figure 3-12)

The goals also have certain specifications. The goal posts should be two-by-three inches and painted white. The goal posts are seven feet high, twelve feet apart, and joined by a crossbar seven feet above the ground. Six feet behind the goal line are two six-foot post. The sides, back, and top are enclosed by netting or wire mesh.

Flicker Ball

The outdoor flicker ball field shall be rectangular in shape, its length being 53⅓ yards, its width 30 yards. Each goal shall be set 5 yards back of the end line, equidistant between the side lines, and parallel to the end line. The bottom of the hole in the flicker ball board shall be eight feet above the ground. A free throw line, 6 feet long, will be placed 30 feet in front of each end line, directly in front of the goal. It is

Figure 3-12 - Field Hockey Layout

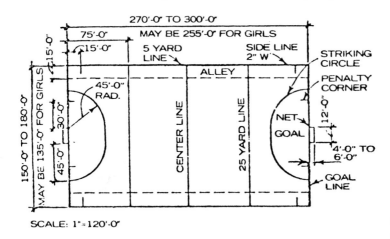

SCALE: 1" = 120'-0"

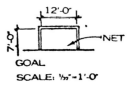

GOAL
SCALE: 1/2"=1'-0"

Figure 3-13
Flicker Ball Field

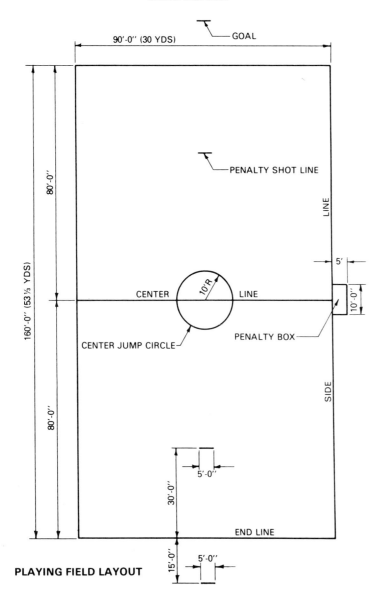

PLAYING FIELD LAYOUT

suggested that game fields be laid out across the width of a practice football field — as many as three flicker ball fields may be laid across a regulation football field. (Figure 3-13)

Football Field

Dimensions and Descriptions

The football field is a level area, 360 feet long and 160 feet wide. If games are played during daylight hours or the field is used for practices, it should be oriented so that play is in a north and south direction to insure that the sun does not shine directly into the eyes of the contestants.

White lines, called yard lines, run across the width of the field every five yards, and lines called sidelines, run down the length of each side. The goal lines run at each end of the width of the field at 100 yards apart, with the end zones extending 10 yards beyond each goal line. The yard lines are numbered at 10-yard intervals from the goal lines to midfield. Two broken lines, called inbounds lines, or hash marks, run parallel to the sidelines. For college, hash marks are 53'4'' from each sideline, and for professional games, they are 70'9'' from each sideline.

In high school and college football, two goals posts, each 20 feet high, stand 10 yards behind each goal line. A crossbar connects them 10 feet from above the ground. The posts are 18'6'' apart in high school games, and

Outdoor Facilities

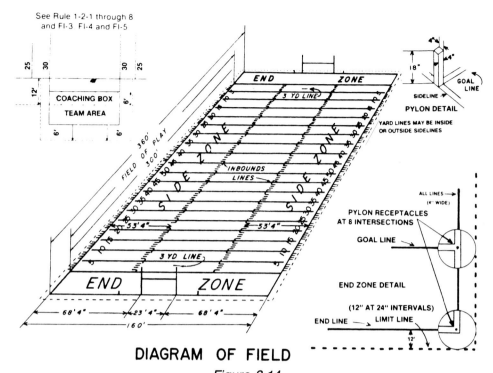

See Rule 1-2-1 through 8
and FI-3 FI-4 and FI-5

DIAGRAM OF FIELD

Figure 3-14
NCAA approved intercollegiate football field (from 1984 NCAA Football Rules Book).

23'4'' apart in college.

Facilities should be provided for the press, radio and motion picture groups along with the public address system, scoreboard operators, spotters, scouts and other officials or dignitaries. The press box should be located opposite the 50-yard line, high in the west stand to eliminate direct sun glare.

The scoreboard should be designed as an integral part of the structure. For activities attracting a smaller number of spectators, mechanical or movable scoreboards may be more practical. (Figure 3-14)

Lacrosse

The inside dimensions of the lacrosse field for men are 330 by 180 feet. There are no definite boundaries, but goals must be placed not less than 270 nor more than 330 feet apart. The minimum width is 159 feet.

The goals lie on the 15-yard lines at each end of the field.

The Lacrosse Field of Play

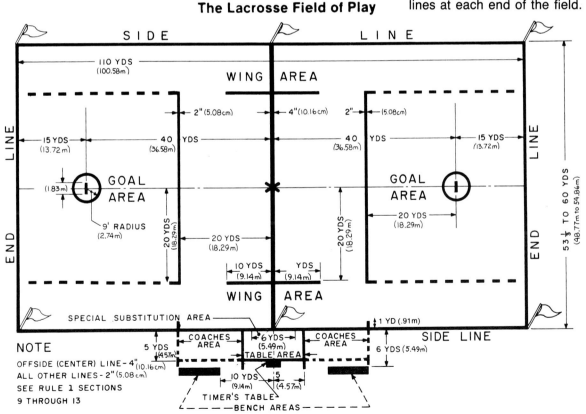

Figure 3-15
NCAA approved lacrosse field (from 1984 NCAA Lacrosse Rules Book).

These goals consist of two square posts six feet apart and joined at the top by a rigid crossbar six feet above the ground (all inside dimensions). The wooden posts are two by two inches, painted white. Netting of not more than 1.5-inch mesh must be attached to the posts and crossbar and to a point seven feet behind the center of the goal. The net is firmly pegged to the ground. A line, called the goal line, is drawn from post to post.

Orientation, surface, and grading are the same as for football. A five or six foot barrier fence at least 10 feet outside the end and sidelines is recommended. (Figure 3-15)

Rugby

A rugby field differs in some respects from a football field; however, the game can be played without the addition or deletion of any football field markings. It is more desirable to have a properly marked rugby field.

Soccer

Soccer fields should be laid out on the most level area of land available. In many high schools and colleges, the football field is also used for soccer games. When this is done, portable goals are used and if possible, the width of the field is increased 10-15 yards. Preferably, the field should be grass and free of rocks, holes and other debris, with no obstacles on the playing area. The orientation of the field should be in a north-south direction. (Figure 3-16)

The same consideration should be given to the soccer field as to all outdoor fields. The fields should have subsoil tiling for proper drainage and a top soil composition which enhances a good growth of grass. Rubber-capped water outlets, and at ground level, should be spaced at convenient locations throughout the playing area. By using these water outlets and a few lengths of hose, the grass can be kept in good condition during the dry

months. Be sure to allow for a drinking fountain when positioning your pipes for field irrigation.

The rules state that the field of play must be rectangular and not more than 120 yards in length or less than 100 yards. The width not more than 75 yards or less than 65 yards. The recommended size for high school and college fields is 120 yards by 75 yards. Fields for elementary school age players should be smaller in size.

The longer boundary lines are called touch lines, and the shorter, the goal lines.

The goal lines will be placed on the center of each goal line with

two wooden or metal posts, equidistant from the corner flag and eight yards apart. A horizontal crossbar of the same material will join the uprights with the lower edge eight feet from the ground. The width of the uprights and crossbar will not exceed five inches or less than four inches. The goal will be painted white and goal nets should be attached to the back of the goal posts.

Each end of the playing area has a penalty area of 18 yards by 44 yards and a penalty kick line 12 feet from the goal line and centered between the uprights of the goal. Using the center of this

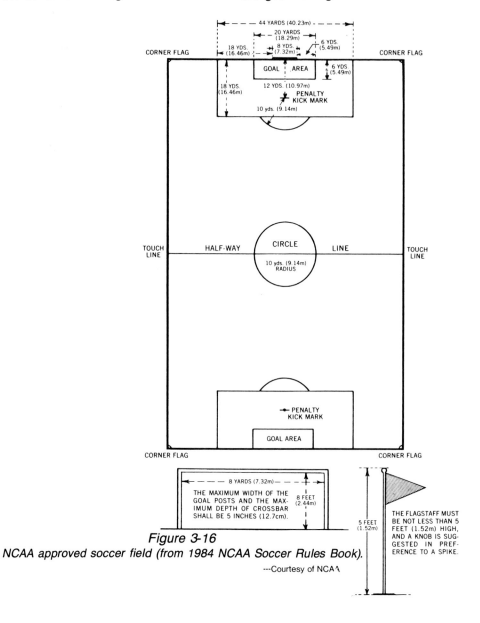

Figure 3-16
NCAA approved soccer field (from 1984 NCAA Soccer Rules Book).

---Courtesy of NCAA

Outdoor Facilities

penalty kick line, mark a 10 yard area arc outside the penalty area and closing on the penalty area line. This is the restraining line for penalty kicks. Also at each end of the field of play, two lines shall be drawn at right angles to the goal line, six yards from each goal post. These lines shall be joined by a line drawn parallel with the goal line. The space enclosed by these lines on each end of the field is called the goal area.

In each corner of the field a quarter circle having a radius of one yard shall be marked inside the field of play. Where the touch line and goal lines intersect, a metal sleeve should be installed in the ground to hold the corner flags.

A half line will be marked out across the field of play. The center of the field will be indicated by a suitable mark and a circle with a 10-yard radius will be marked around it.

If portable bleachers are selected, they can be moved each season and used by different sports. Spectator seating should be no closer than 15 feet from the touch lines. Players' benches, and a timer's table should be provided and placed on the same side of the field. These also should be at least 15 feet from the touch line.

Speedball

Speedball is a vigorous team sport played on an area 180 by 300 feet. The game combines the skills of soccer and basketball. It requires goal posts, end zones, and a soccer ball. There are 7 to 9 players to a team. (Figure 3-17)

The size of the field should be reduced for young players and/or intramural activities. A multipurpose field or soccer field can be adapted to the game.

Team Handball

Team handball is played in both indoor and outdoor facilities. Official games, however, such as the Olympic games and European or international championships, are played only in indoor facilities. The

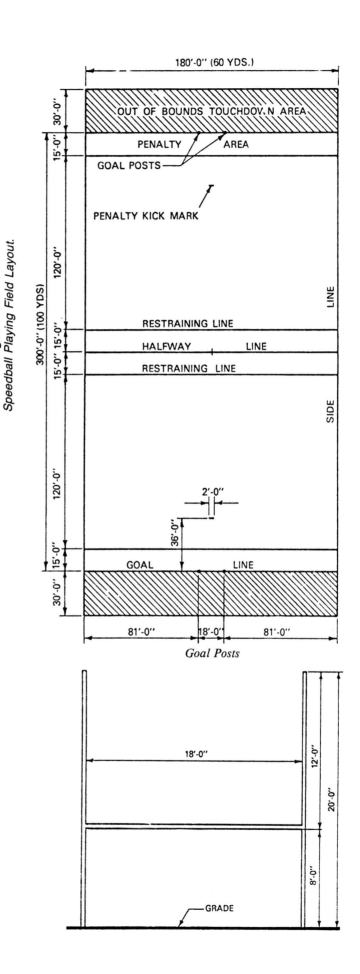

Figure 3-17
Speedball Playing Field Layout.

recommended floor is hardwood (similar to basketball). The ceiling height is a minimum of 18 feet or 5.5 meters (m).

The court is a rectangle. The length ranges from a minimum of 124'8-1/8'' (38m), to a maximum 144'4½'' (44m). The width ranges from a minimum of 59'⅔' (18mm), to a maximum of 72'1¼'' (22m). Courts are often made 20m by 40m; however, if meters are being used, 21m by 42m is most convenient for getting all measurements correct.

The goal is in the center and behind the goal line and is fixed and stable. It is 6'6¾'' (2m) high, and 9'10-1/8'' (3m) wide. Behind the goal there is a net made of cotton or nylon. The goal posts and crossbar are made of squared wood 3.14'' (8cm) thick. The goal is painted with two contrasting colors. The corners are painted with two rectangles of 11.2'' (28 cm) each. Each contrasting colored block on the goal post and crossbar is 7-7/8'' (20cm) long. There are ten of these on each goal post and 15 on the crossbar.

The goal area is created by marking a line 9'10-1/8'' (3m) long, 19'8¼'' (6m) from the goal. To each end of this line, a quarter circle is added, with a radius of 19'8¼'' (6m) which has as its center the front legs of the goal (the inner back edge).

The free throw line (9m line) is a dotted line 9'10-1/8'' (3m) from the goal area line and parallel to it. The line is made of paint or 2'' (5m) plastic tape, i.e.,
15cm   15cm   (5¾'').
15cm   15cm   15cm
The penalty mark is 23' (7m) from the center of the goal and is 3'3⅓'' (1m) long and 2'' (5cm) thick.

Metric conversion factor: 1cm= .394''; 1 m = 3.281' (3'3-3/8'').
(Figures 3-18 and 3-19)

COURT SPORTS
General

The development of outdoor court areas represents a substantial financial commitment to the use of space. Therefore, location, orientation, and determination of need are essential before construction begins.

As a further savings, courts are usually constructed in groups or batteries of two or more. This consolidates some of the safety

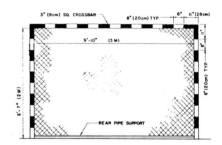

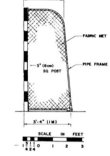

Goal line between goal posts. Posts and crossbar are metal or wood, painted all sides in two contrasting colors. Goals will be firmly fixed in ground with hooked stakes. Field lines are 2'' (5 cm) wide and form part of the area they enclose.

Figure 3-19
Team Handboom Goal Details.

Figure 3-18
Team Handball Field.

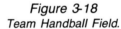

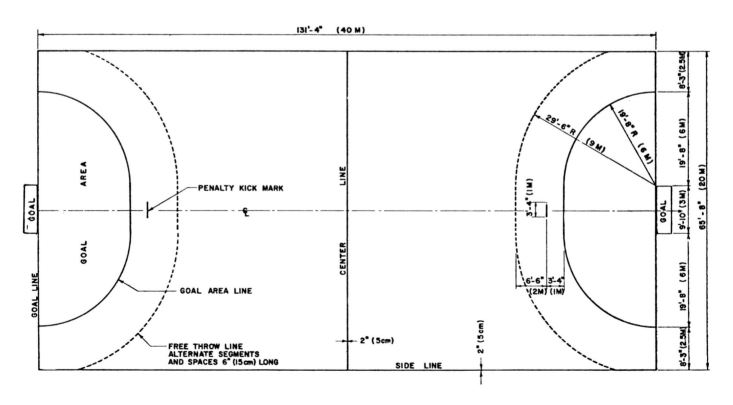

Outdoor Facilities

areas required around courts.

Multiple use of courts may also be developed, but care must be taken to avoid conflicts in uses.

Orientation

Basketball courts should be oriented so the baskets face one another at approximately a north-south direction.

Surface

A smooth, hard surface is essential for playing the game of basketball, particularly the dribbling aspect.

The recommended surface is asphaltic concrete. It provides a durable surface which can be used on a year-round schedule. When properly installed, the surface is dust-free and drains quickly. Asphalt surfaces can be marked easily and with a relatively high degree of permanence. The asphalt surface also gives a neat-appearing surface that will blend well with the surroundings. The surface can also be colored and maintained inexpensively.

Portland cement concrete and synthetic surfaces have also been used, but they are much more expensive to install. The concrete surface may crack when constructed in a cold climate, due to frost heave.

Drainage

Drainage can be done many different ways, but it is recommended that the court be slanted from one side to the other. One inch of slant should be allowed for every ten feet of court. It would also be helpful if the court is elevated from the surrounding area for drainage purposes.

Court Markings

Lines should be permanently painted on the surface in contrasting color. These lines should be two inches in width. There should be line markings for the boundaries for the court, the mid-court line, the center circle, the foul lane area, and the three second line.

Dimensions

The dimensions for a basketball court are usually determined by the age group which is to use the facility. Recommendations for each age group are as follows:

Age Group	Court Size	Basket Height	Foul Lane Width	Foul Line To Basket
Elementary	74'x42'	8'	5'	10'
Jr./Sr. High	84'x50'	10'	12'	10'
College	94'x50'	10'	12'	10'

When constructing a court for a recreational area, it is recommended that the 84'x50' court be built. If the court is less than 74 feet in length, it should be divided by two lines, each parallel to and 40 feet from the further end lines. These lines would be used as the ten second lines.

Safety Areas

When devising an outdoor basketball court, the following safety areas should be accounted for.

- Allow ten feet on all sides of the court, including the area between two courts.
- Poles used to hold the baskets should be off the playing court, and extended out at least four feet onto the court and padded.
- If possible, there should be some absorbent material around the basketball pole and the bottom of the backboard.

Backboards and Baskets

There are two popular types of basketball backboards, rectangular and fan-shaped. The size of the rectangular backboard should be six feet by four feet and the size of the fan-shaped backboard is fifty-four inches wide and thirty-five inches high.

It is recommended that an official iron basketball rim with an eighteen inch diameter be used. Chain nets may be used outdoors because they are more durable than the nylon or rope nets.

Fencing

Although fencing is not absolutely necessary, it can be a helpful addition. If finances allow the purchase of a fence, the recommended type of fencing is an anodized aluminum chain-link fabric. The desired height would be ten feet. The fence fabric should be located on the inside of the fence poles and the poles placed six inches to a foot onto the hard surface. Posts should be in concrete 25% to 40% of the length of the pole above the surface. Doors should be provided which are large enough to allow maintenance equipment into the court area.

Handball

Indoor handball (4-wall) is discussed in Chapter 2.

Outdoor handball is either

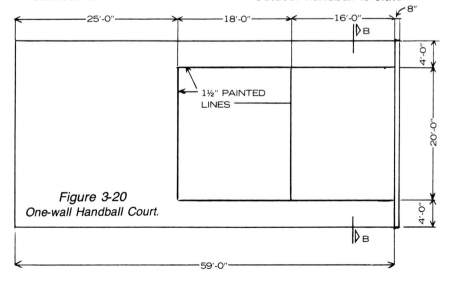

Figure 3-20
One-wall Handball Court.

one-wall or three-wall. Both can be played by two to four players on a smooth portland cement concrete or asphaltic surface. Courts may be constructed so as to allow one court on each side of the wall. It is often desirable to locate the courts near soccer fields or tennis courts to permit soccer and tennis players to use the walls for practice

Dimensions for the one-wall handball court are: 16' high, 20' wide by 34' long with 8'6" width on each side and 11' surfaced area to the rear. (Figure 3-20)

Dimensions for three-wall handball are: 20' high, 21'8" wide by 40' long with 10' to the rear.

The courts should be pitched away from the wall with a grade of 1" to 10'. The wall should be 8 to 12 inches thick and constructed of reinforced concrete. (Figure 3-21)

Shuffleboard

The shuffleboard court shall measure 52 feet long and 10 feet wide. The actual playing area shall be 39 feet long and 6 feet wide, or that area of the court from base line and from inside rise to both adjacent gutters. (Figure 3-21)

Shuffleboard courts should be oriented north and south. A level, smooth surface is essential.

The courts are marked off by painting lines with a black dye, white road paint, or white acrylic stain. Lines will have a maximum width of one inch with a minimum width of ¾ inch. The base lines shall be extended to adjoining courts, or to 24 inches beyond sides of the court. The separation triangle in the 10-off area is 3 inches at the base, running to a point in the direction of the scoring area. The outline of the legs of this triangle shall be ¼ inch in width, with a clearance of ½ inch at both the point and base. The base of the separation triangle is not marked.

It is highly important that the area beneath the court be well-drained and the court properly reinforced. A depressed alley must be constructed between and at the

sides of all courts. The alley should be at least 24 inches wide and not less than 4 inches deep at mid-court, where a suitable drain shall be installed. The alley, from both extensions of the base lines, should slope down toward the center of the court. The downward fall shall begin with a one inch drop in the first six inches, and then gradually slope down to mid-court.

Shuffleboard courts are commonly lighted from poles erected outside the courts. A 20 inch hinged pole with a 1500 watt

quartzlit floodlight would be installed at the base of the court next to the scoreboard or benches at the base of the court. Overhead lights can also be used, especially in recreational areas.

Other equipment frequently used are wood 2"x2" backstops installed (loosely) to prevent discs from rebounding back onto the court and thereby eliminate the half-round being played over. The end of the court with a scoreboard shall be designated the Head and the opposite end shall be known as the Foot of the Court. (Figure 3-22)

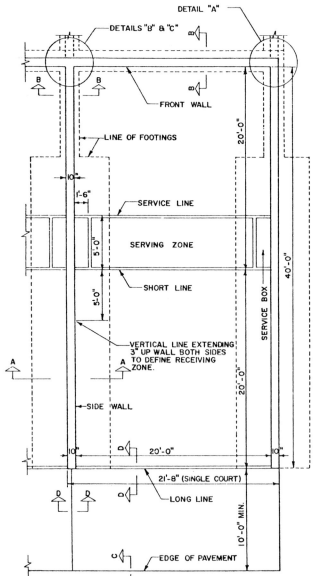

Figure 3-21
Three-wall Handball Court.

Figure 3-22
Shuffleboard Court.

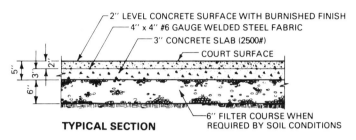

TYPICAL SECTION

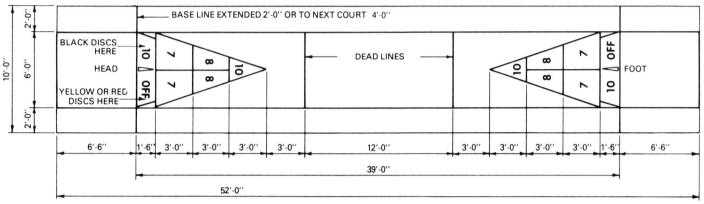

COURT LAYOUT

Tennis

Space

A single, double court is 36 feet by 78 feet. There should be 12 feet of clearance on each side of the court and 21 feet of clearance between the baseline and the fence. This would mean that there will be an area of 60 feet by 120 feet for each court. The baseline fence distance remains constant regardless of the number of courts. If several courts are placed side-by-side, the courts may be placed so that there are 12 feet between adjacent sidelines. Considering a bank of eight tennis courts, an area of 47,520 square feet would be required (120 x 396).

For ease of construction and economy, courts are generally laid out in two rows of four courts each or in a single line. When the courts are laid out in one line, the area of 47,960 square feet and its perimeter is 1092 (including a center fence between the two rows of courts). Surface area and fencing is greater with the arrangement of two rows of four courts.

A group or bank of eight courts was used merely as an example. In most private club installations, two courts for each battery is preferred because of aesthetics, reduced drainage problems, and reduced traffic.

The number of courts planned should depend on the specific needs of the school. If all courts were in use, the eight-court facility would serve 32 students. Large classes could be accommodated by having wall rebound areas and/or scheduling systems so that half of the class would be taught the tennis unit at one time.

It is recommended that courts drain from side to side. The U.S. Lawn Tennis Association suggests the slope for porous courts to be 1" in 20' to 30'; and 1" in 10' for non-porous courts. (Figure 3-23)

Surfaces

The court surface can be selected from more than 100 available finishes suitable (in varying degrees) for tennis courts. The following classification of surfaces by type and characteristics is reprinted by permission of the United States Tennis Association (USTA). More detailed information regarding

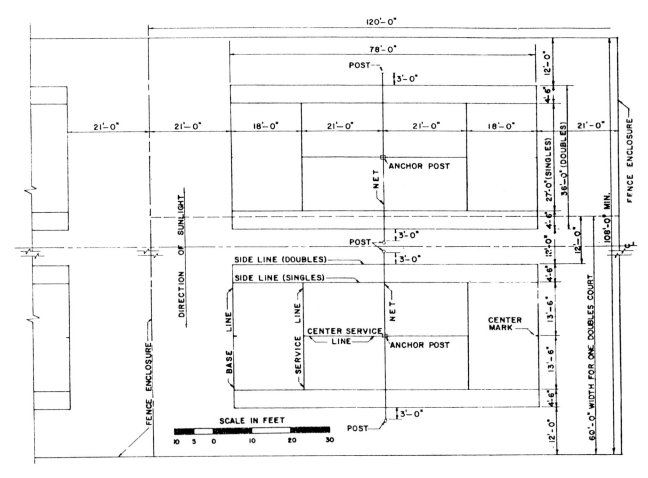

Figure 3-23
Tennis Court Layout.

tennis court construction is available in the booklet, *Tennis Courts,* published by the USTA and available from USTA Education and Research Center, 729 Alexander Road, Princeton, N.J. 08540.

Factors To Consider In Selecting A Tennis Court Surface

1. Player preference.
2. Maintenance Cost and Amount of Maintenance required.
3. Initial Construction Cost.
4. Surface on which Player can Slide or Not Slide.
5. Length of time until resurfacing is required.
6. Resurfacing Cost.
7. Softness of surface desired for Player Comfort.
8. Surface adaptability for possible Other Uses.
9. Fast or Slow surface (see glossary).
10. Uniformity of Ball Bounce.
11. Effect of Color on Glare and Heat Absorption.
12. Drying Time after rain.
13. Availability of Service from Court Builder.
14. Color-Fastness of Surface and its effect on Ball Discoloration.
15. Effect of Abrasive surfaces on balls, rackets, shoes and falling players.
16. Effect of Lines on Ball Bounce, Tripping Hazards, Maintenance of Lines.

Classification of Tennis Court Surfaces (as established by the U.S. Tennis Court and Track Builders Association)

A. Pervious Construction (one which permits water to filter through the surface)
   1. Fast Dry (Fine crushed aggregate)
   2. Clay
   3. Grass
   4. Others (Dirt, Grit, etc.)
B. Impervious Construction (one on which water does not penetrate, but runs off the surface)
   1. Non-Cushioned
      a. Concrete
      b. Asphalt
         (1) Hot Plant Mix
         (2) Emulsified Asphalt Mix
         (3) Combination of Hot Plant and Emulsified Mix
         (4) Penetration Macadam
         (5) Asphalt Job Mix
      c. Others (Wood, etc.)
   2. Cushioned Construction
      a. Asphalt Bound Systems
         (1) Hot Leveling Course and Hot Cushion Course

Figure 23A
Chart Comparing Various Tennis Court Surfaces

Court Type	Repairs May Be Costly	Glare	Av. Time Before Resurfacing	Other Uses	Surface Hardness	Ball Skid Length	Ball Spin Effective	Colors	Drying Time After Rain	Is Ball Bounce Uniform	Stains Ball	Abrasive Surface (hard on balls, shoes & rackets)	Humidity Problem Indoors	Slide Surface	Lines Affect Ball Bounce
POROUS															
Fast Dry	no	no	10 yrs.	yes	soft	short if damp court	yes	green	fast	some (if maintained)	do	no	yes	yes	yes
Clay	no	generally	5 yrs.	yes	soft		yes	red varies	slow	Yes (if maintained)	yes	no	yes	yes	yes if tapes
Dirt	no	yes	3 yrs.	yes	soft	long dry court	yes	varies	slow	yes (if maintained)	yes	no	yes	yes	yes if tapes
Grit	no	yes	3 yrs.	yes	soft		yes	varies	slow	yes (if maintained)	yes	no	yes	yes	yes if tapes
Grass	no	no	indefinite	yes	soft	moderately long	yes	green	slow	irregular	yes	no	won't grow	yes	no
Special (Porous concrete)	yes	no	3 yrs. (if colored)	yes	hard	medium	yes	wide variety	fast	yes	no	no	yes	no	no
NON-POROUS NON-CUSHIONED															
Concrete	yes	no (if colored)	3 yrs. (if colored)	yes	hard	long if glossy court finish; medium if gritty court finish	no if glossy finish; yes if gritty finish	wide variety	fast	depends on installation	no	varies	no	no	no
Asphalt Plant Mix *(Colored)	no	no	5 yrs.	yes	hard			wide variety	fast	yes	no if colored	no if colored	no	no	no
Asphalt Job Mix (Colored)	no	no	5 yrs.	yes	hard			wide variety	fast	yes	no if colored	no if colored	no	no	no
Asphalt Penetrated Macadam	no	no	5 yrs.	yes	hard	short	yes	wide variety	fast	yes	no if colored	*no	no	*no	no
Wooden	no	no	indefinite	yes	hard	long	no	wide variety	fast	yes	no	no	no	no	no
NON-POROUS CUSHIONED															
Asphalt Bound System (Colored)	no	no	5 yrs.	no	soft	long if glossy finish, short if gritty finish	no if glossy finish; yes if gritty finish	wide variety	fast	yes	no	no	no	yes	no
Synthetic	no	no	varies	yes	soft	medium to short	yes	green	fast	yes	no	no	no	slight	no
Synthetic Carpet	no	no	varies	yes	soft	short	yes	green	fast	yes	no	no	no	no	no
Removable	no	no	varies	yes	soft	varies, shortest to longest	yes	variety	fast	yes	no	no	no	slight	no

Maintenance of all Non-porous surface types is very minor. Porous types, with the exception of porous concrete (very minor) require daily and annual care

(2) Hot Leveling Course and Cold Cushion Course
(3) Cold Leveling Course and Cold Cushion Course
b. Synthetic
(1) Elastomer
(2) Textile
c. Others

Platform Tennis
Construction Suggestions

In staking out the space for the 60' by 30' surface, an extra 4 feet should be allowed on each side and end for the foundation beams at the corners and at the locations of the uprights. This is to enable them to project far enough to furnish a base for the outer support of the uprights. Thus, the total area needed for the foundation beams is 68' by 38'. Commonly used specifications call for 4-inch by 6-inch foundation beams across the base of the platform, resting on concrete blocks, set to allow a distance between the beams of 4 feet from center to center. Four concrete blocks, evenly spaced, are required for each beam. Beams of wood should be waterproofed with creosote. The planking for the deck surface should be 2 feet x 6 feet Douglas fir and should be spaced from 1/8 inch to 1/4 inch apart to allow for drainage between planks. The corner uprights are of 4 inch by 4 inch, and the intermediate uprights of 2 inch by 4 inch, all projecting 12 feet above the surface of the court, as previously indicated.

The Backstop

Around the platform are horizontal bars known as top rails connecting the tops of the uprights and bolted to the insides of each. These rails are of 2 inches by 4 inches along the sides. Thus, the rails to which the wire is fastened project inside of the uprights, by 4 inches at the ends and 2 inches at the sides. The wiring covers all of the space around the platform except 12-foot openings in the center of each side, at least one of which is closed with either netting or light gauge wiring. This center closure is intended to contain errant balls.

All wiring should be attached inside the uprights, running vertically and stretched in 6-foot widths from the top down to the tension rail below.

Track and Field

The planning and design of most track and field facilities include a multiple use sharing of spectator facilities. Many smaller schools include the track in the football stadium with the field events located where space and orientation will permit.

Track Layout

The planning of a new track and field facility or the remodeling of an existing one should begin with a study of the International Amateur Athletic Federation rules on track and field facilities. National Collegiate Athletic Association and National Federation of State High School Athletic Association rules on track and field facilities generally conform to IAAF rules but should be consulted for possible deviation. (Figure 3-24)

Marking

An all-weather track should only be marked with a paint compatible to the surfacing. The best means of insuring this compatibility is to use the paint recommended by the track surface manufacturer. A non-compatible paint can cause, among other things, peeling and cracking.

Relay zones and staggers should be located by survey. The engineering firm responsible for installation of the track and their surveyor should certify, in writing, that measurements are exactly as required in the track and field rules. Various colors may be used for each set of markings.

The start and finish line for all races run around the track should be located approximately 15 meters from the bend of the first curve. A curve starting line for all races not run in lanes must be included in the markings.

Drainage

The track should shed water to the inside. Small curb openings permit the water to drain from the track. Since the area just inside lane one is usually used for warm-up and jogging, the drain field ditch should be located about 6 to 8 feet inside the track.

FIELD EVENTS

The Steeplechase

The steeplechase water jump will be located on the inside edge or outside edge of the track. Running surface off the track and back again must be provided. If the water jump is on the inside of the track, a removal curb will be necessary. Plan for drainage and locate water connection near the water jump pit.

The High Jump

The high jump approach area should provide 22 meters of level surface (21.3 meters required by rule) from any angle within an arc of 150 degrees. The arc should be of synthetic material, usually the same as the track. The high jump pit must be a minimum of 4.88 x 2.44 meters and of a composition to provide a safe landing (no bottom out).

The Pole Vault

The vaulting box must meet the IAAF specifications and be immovable. The pit shall be a minimum of 4.88 meters wide and 3.66 meters deep. The pit should be made of sponge rubber and have a height of 91.44 centimeters (36 inches). The vaulting runway must be at least 38.1 meters in length (45 meters is a desirable length). Locate the pole vault so that the prevailing wind will be at the vaulters' backs.

The Long Jump and Triple Jump

The minimum length of the runway of long jump and triple jump is 39.62 meters, but 52 meters is desirable if the triple jumpers are to have sufficient runway. If possible, the location should place the prevailing wind at the jumpers' backs, or to the side, but not head-on.

The landing pit shall be sand. It is not less than 2.74 meters in width and usually 10 meters long. The pit elevation must be identical with the take-off board.

The take-off board for the long jump must be at least one meter (four meters recommended) from the near edge of the pit and ten meters from the far end of the pit.

The take-off shall be from a board 20 centimeters wide and at least 1.22 meters long. The board must be immovable (Note: painting a take-off area on the runway does not satisfy this rule).

In the triple jump, the nearer edge of the landing pit to the take-off board shall be 10 meters for high schoolers and 12.5 for collegiates. A 10.97 meter scratch line could be used by the better high school athletes and the younger collegians.

Throwing Circles

Portland cement concrete is the recommended material for throwing circles. Brushing the concrete while it is setting produces small ridges which aid in preventing slipping. A band of angle iron or steel is to be set flush with the concrete outside the circle.

The inside diameter of the shot put and hammer circles is 2.135

meters. The diameter of the discus circle is 2.5 meters. The metal circle shall be six millimeters in thickness and two centimeters in height. The metal circle must be firmly secured and flush with the throwing surface.

The discus circle should be located so the athletes throw into the prevailing wind.

If the hammer is to be thrown, a cage must be set up around the ring to ensure safety (the rule books contain a recommended design).

The Javelin

Figure 31 illustrates the javelin throw layout and detail of the javelin throw scratch board.

Archery

Today, the teaching of archery and competitive archery takes place both indoors and outdoors. Indoor archery is discussed in Chapter 2. Factors such as weather, type of program, terrain, space, and costs are considerations to be taken into account when developing an outdoor archery range.

While the emphasis in this section is on outdoor instructional archery, additional information on indoor archery (Chapter 2) and recreational archery (Chapter 7) should be consulted. An outdoor archery range layout is included in Chapter 7. For added breadth to an archery program, consideration should be given to the competitive rounds of various organizations. Those archery activities that would require special areas are:

- Field archery range — According to the National Field Archery Association, a field course is designed in units of 14 targets each, requiring from 50 to 10 acres per unit, depending on the terrain. Two units or 28 targets, compose a Round, the shooting distance ranges from 20 feet to 80 yards.
- Clout shooting requires approximately 300 yards with the regulation distance for women at 120 and 140 yards, and for men 180 yards.

- Archery-golf can be set up on a golf course or on existing large intramural fields. Dimensions can be established according to available space, keeping in mind the importance of providing sufficient space to insure the safety of participants and passersby.
- Competitive archery rounds. The variety of rounds varies greatly in distance, targets, and scoring. Consideration should be given to providing a range large enough to accommodate the FITA round. The longest shooting distance for the FITA is 90 meters for the men's round.

To insure a safe range, space should be provided beyond the target line, free from stones and other substances that cause the breakage of arrows falling beyond the target.

If a backstop is used, it should be of a "see-through" type (i.e. a

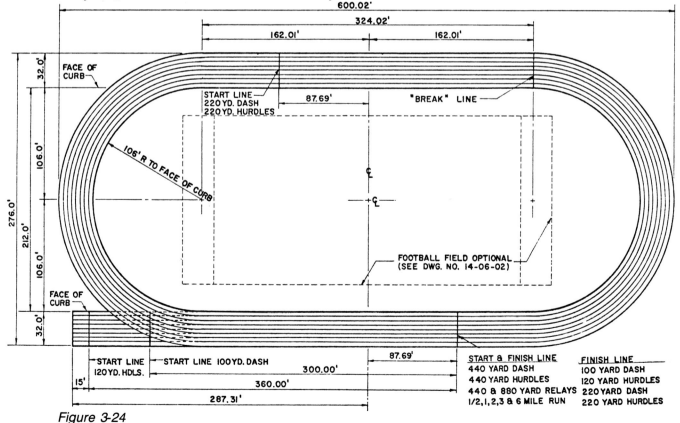

Figure 3-24
Layout of 440-yard Running Track.
Outdoor Facilities

Figures 3-25, 3-26, 3-27, 3-28

Layout details for weight events, including shot put, hammer and discus throw. (All detail drawings for track and field events provided by U.S. Army Corps of Engineers.)

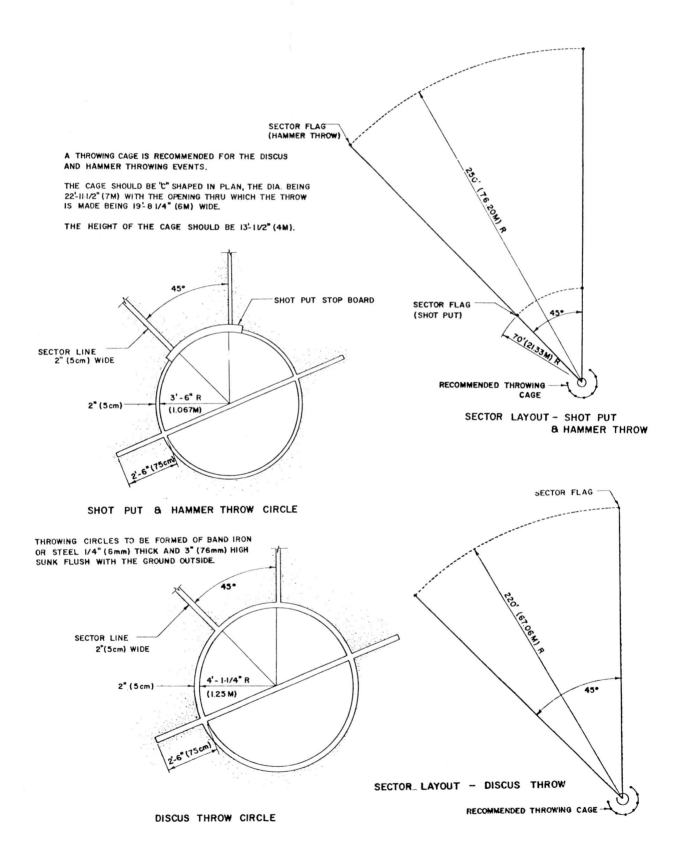

A THROWING CAGE IS RECOMMENDED FOR THE DISCUS AND HAMMER THROWING EVENTS.

THE CAGE SHOULD BE "C" SHAPED IN PLAN, THE DIA. BEING 22'-11.1/2" (7M) WITH THE OPENING THRU WHICH THE THROW IS MADE BEING 19'-8.1/4" (6M) WIDE.

THE HEIGHT OF THE CAGE SHOULD BE 13'-11/2" (4M).

SECTOR FLAG (HAMMER THROW)

250' (76.20M) R

SECTOR FLAG (SHOT PUT)

45°

70' (21.33M) R

RECOMMENDED THROWING CAGE

SECTOR LAYOUT - SHOT PUT & HAMMER THROW

45°

SHOT PUT STOP BOARD

SECTOR LINE 2" (5cm) WIDE

2" (5cm)

3'-6" R (1.067M)

2'-6" (75cm)

SHOT PUT & HAMMER THROW CIRCLE

THROWING CIRCLES TO BE FORMED OF BAND IRON OR STEEL 1/4" (6mm) THICK AND 3" (76mm) HIGH SUNK FLUSH WITH THE GROUND OUTSIDE.

45°

SECTOR LINE 2" (5cm) WIDE

2" (5cm)

4'-1-1/4" R (1.25 M)

2'-6" (75cm)

DISCUS THROW CIRCLE

SECTOR FLAG

220' (67.06M) R

45°

SECTOR LAYOUT - DISCUS THROW

RECOMMENDED THROWING CAGE

Figures 3-29, 3-30, 3-31, 3-32
Layout details for high jump (and long jump and triple jump), pole vault and javelin throw.

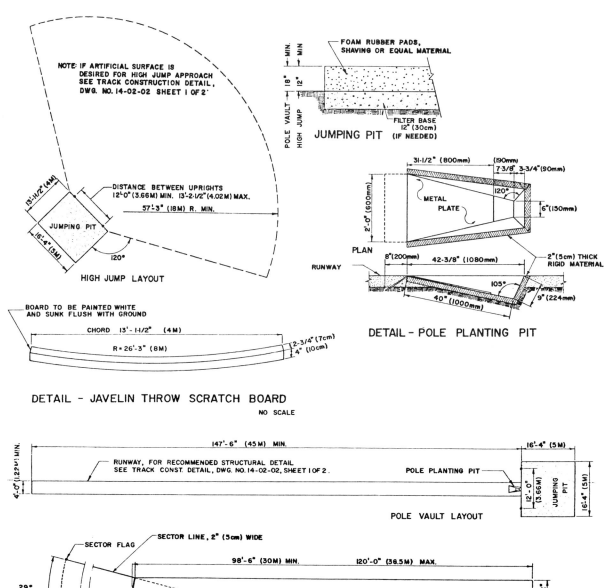

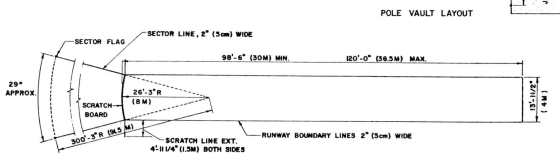

JAVELIN THROW LAYOUT

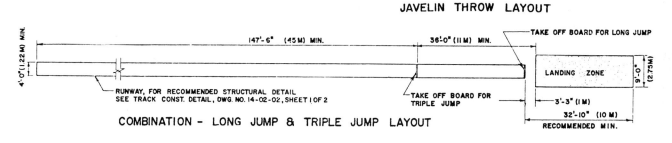

COMBINATION - LONG JUMP & TRIPLE JUMP LAYOUT

nylon net) to enable the instructor to have complete visibility behind the target line. Posts on which the net is hung should be approximately 25 feet apart. The net should be hung from a heavy wire (No. 8 clothesline). The recommended net height is 10 feet.

When shooting from beginning distance (20 feet to 20 yards), there should be a minimum of 30 yards clear behind the target if no backstop is used. A hill is a natural backstop, but care should be taken to prevent anyone from wandering over the hill while class is in session.

When existing outdoor areas serve several activities, an archery range can be placed on one of several school sites: football field, practice field, hockey field, playground, or tennis court.

The overriding concern when an area of multiple use is used should be safety. To this end, grass or dirt surfaces are preferable to hard surface areas.

The type of target used is determined by the range and the round to be shot. Often the targets need to be taken in at the end of the day, requiring portable targets.

When targets must be installed and removed for each archery class, the movable kind is recommended. They can be set up in the following manner:

Pipes that are two feet long and 1½ inches in diameter should be spaced 38 inches apart and driven into the ground until the top end of each pipe is slightly below the surface of the ground.

Prior to each class, the instructor and/or students can insert a pipe or stake that is 5 feet long and 1 inch in diameter into each of the recessed pipes and secure the target matts to the pipes or stakes by attaching two wire loops on each side of the matt and sliding the loops onto the pipes or stakes.

If desired, the recessed pipes can have a threaded end so that a cap can be placed over the pipe opening. This will prevent rain and debris from falling into the pipes when the range is not in use.

Commercial movable target stands can also be used. Tripods can be used, although they are more cumbersome to transport and set up. In an outdoor range, the tripods should be anchored. Another idea for target stands is to use track hurdles upside down and wire the matts to the legs.

Permanent targets can be installed in the following manner:

Each target will require two supports. The supports should be approximately 6 feet long and can be of the following materials: 1-inch pipes, 2½-inch cedar posts, 2- by 4-inch wooden stakes, or steel fence posts. Stakes should be driven into the ground 38 inches apart and to a depth of at least 2 feet. An old rubber tire or 2 by 4s should be placed on the ground between the two supports.

The bottom bale of excelsior or straw should be placed on top of the tire or 2 by 4s so that it does not rest on the ground. This preserves the bales and eliminates arrows from sliding underneath. Two more bales should be stacked on top of the first, and all three bales should be banded together by using a banding tool or two straps of No. 8 wire. This is done by completely encircling the bales and tightening the wire. If four or five bales are desired, the target supports should be within 6 inches of the top. Supports should never extend higher than the tops of the bales.

When using the metal supports, it is best to cover the surface of the supports with heavy rubber, such as old car tires, bicycle tires, or rubber hose cut in half lengthwise. To protect excelsior or straw bales from too much water, the top bale should be capped with a protective covering of plastic or roofing paper.

A shooting line can be indicated by marking compound or with a rope or measuring tape stretched between stakes. The stakes should be placed directly in front of each target. For a permanent range, cement or patio blocks, bricks, or similar blocks can be recessed into the ground to indicate shooting positions. The distance from the target face to the shooting position may be painted on the face of the block.

The Archery Manufacturers Organization has designed a sheltered archery range that provides the maximum safety for a cost comparable to a doubles tennis court.

SELECTED REFERENCES

Adra, Tom. "Inadequate Lighting — How to Triple Illumination and Save Money." **Athletic Purchasing and Facilities** 2 (April 1978): 38.

Bureau of Outdoor Recreation. **Outdoor Recreation Space Standards.** Washington, D.C.: United States Government Printing Office, 1967.

Crookham, Joe P. "Guidelines for Recreation and Athletic Field Lighting." **Parks and Recreation** 17 (June 1982): 23-26, 28.

Delameter, James. **Design of Outdoor Physical Education Facilities for School and Community.** New York: Columbia University, 1963.

Graves, Charles M. "Siting Sports Facilities." **Parks and Recreation** 11 (August 1976): 21-22, 49.

Hulvershorn, J. Kip. "Recreation Complexes." **Journal of Physical Education and Recreation** 48 (November-December 1977): 45-47.

IES Lighting Handbook. Fifth edition. New York: Illuminating Engineering Society of North America, 1981.

Lafferty, Robert E., III. "How to Apply Metric Principles to Track Conversion." **Athletic Purchasing and Facilities** 2 (April 1978): 40-43.

National Collegiate Athletic Association. Selected 1984 Rules Guides for Various Sports. Mission, Kansas: NCAA, 1984.

"Tender Loving Care for Athletic Fields." **American School and University** 49 (June 1977), 8-10.

"Track and Field Layouts." **American School University** 44 (November 1971): 26.

Whalen, Joe. "Construction Today." **Tennis Industry** 1 (May 1973): 5.

Wilkens, Vern. "How to Buy or Build a Running Track." **Athletic Purchasing and Facilities** 2 (December 1978): 25-27.

U.S. Departments of Army, Navy, Air Force. **Planning and Design of Outdoor Sports Facilities.** Washington, D.C.: United States Government Printing Office, 1967.

(Refer to REFERENCES section in Chapter II, INDOOR FACILITIES and Chapter VII, RECREATION AND PARK AREAS AND FACILITIES.)

CHAPTER IV
Swimming Pools

The purpose of this chapter is to discuss the current state-of-the-art with respect to swimming pools. This will encompass innovations in pool design and equipment, various operating procedures, and safety aspects related to both design and operation of pools.

The development and growth of swimming pools in the United States since the end of World War II has been nothing short of phenomenal. The most significant aspect of this growth has been the introduction of low-cost pools for homes and such other living units as motels, hotels, and apartments.

As of 1984, residential-type pools represented about 80 percent of the pool market. However, the rush to buy pools appears to be subsiding. This is particularly true of pools for schools, colleges, municipalities, clubs, the Y's and Boys' Clubs. These pools are typically referred to as public pools. A recent trend is to refer to the motel, hotel, and apartment pools as "semi-public." In the calendar year 1984, it is expected that between 1,000 and 1,200 public pools will be built in the United States, and this number will gradually decrease with an expected leveling off number of between 500 and 600 pools annually. On the other hand, the number of residential pools constructed or sold annually is expected to remain at its present (1984) level of 85,000 pools a year. (Figures 4-1; 4-2)

A major need which has become increasingly evident is the renovation or replacement of pools that were built thirty or forty years ago. Some of the need for modernization may be attributed to poor planning during the initial phase of development and more often than not the desire to reduce the cost of the pools by going the minimum cost route. Many older pools do not meet current safety standards or program needs.

It is impossible to detail all the information that goes into pool planning. Readers are advised to use the list of references at the end of the chapter for additional information regarding specific design and operating features of pools.

THE PROCESS INVOLVED IN PLANNING AND CONSTRUCTION

The process of planning a pool involves all the activities and steps which must be taken before construction can begin. Once the contractor commences to dig the hole for the pool, changes in design become difficult and often costly. How the planning process is managed will differ according to the agency. The Y's and Boys' Clubs have excellent planning personnel at their national headquarters to assist local planners. On the other hand, schools and municipalities rely heavily on the architect they select to design the pool. If an architect has never designed a pool he will need considerable help. Even in situations where the architect has designed pools, he still needs advice from those who will be the users. Seven essential steps, in the order in which they should be taken, are outlined below:

1. The Planning Committee

A committee or some individual must be charged with the responsibility for the preliminary planning of the pool. The following items should be covered by the committee:
  a) Determine the need.
  b) Visit other recently constructed pools to see what they have done and to learn their annual operating budget.
  c) Determine what activities are to be accommodated in the pool and establish which have priority. Then

Figure 4-1

Inground Swimming Pools by Region: Historical Perspective

	Dec. 31, 1983	Dec. 31, 1982★	Dec. 31, 1981★	Dec. 31, 1980★	Dec. 31, 1979★	Dec. 31, 1978★	Dec. 31, 1977★	Dec. 31, 1976★	Dec. 31, 1975★	Dec. 31, 1971★	Dec. 31, 1967★	Dec. 31, 1957★	Dec. 31, 1947†★
West	**15,300***	**13,000**	**16,400**	**21,810**	**35,400**	**31,700**	**28,020**	**24,600**	**19,400**	**18,700**	**16,900**	—	—
	609,280‡	593,980	580,980	564,580	542,770	507,370	475,670	447,650	423,050	335,500	261,100	62,400	—
Southwest/ Mountain	**22,400**	**15,800**	**25,800**	**22,690**	**26,500**	**25,250**	**19,635**	**16,800**	**14,100**	**11,500**	**8,900**	—	—
	358,425	336,025	320,225	294,425	271,735	245,235	219,985	200,350	183,550	122,150	80,550	5,900	—
Midwest	**11,100**	**7,700**	**11,000**	**12,730**	**12,750**	**11,150**	**12,050**	**11,900**	**9,800**	**18,700**	**17,200**	—	—
	341,580	330,480	322,780	311,780	299,050	286,300	275,150	263,100	251,200	196,000	120,900	15,000	—
South	**20,000**	**15,800**	**13,600**	**11,880**	**10,350**	**10,600**	**9,800**	**6,900**	**6,900**	**7,600**	**5,500**	—	—
	261,330	241,330	225,530	211,930	200,050	189,700	179,100	169,300	162,400	130,200	102,100	21,900	—
Florida	**20,700**	**19,000**	**20,100**	**19,400**	**16,000**	**13,000**	**11,300**	**9,800**	**10,000**	**10,700**	**8,700**	—	—
	304,000	283,300	264,300	244,200	224,800	208,800	195,800	184,500	174,700	123,950	83,200	10,100	—
Northeast	**20,500**	**16,200**	**18,500**	**20,030**	**13,300**	**12,400**	**13,195**	**14,200**	**16,900**	**22,700**	**21,400**	—	—
	463,825	443,325	427,125	408,625	388,595	375,295	362,895	349,700	335,500	247,500	156,350	17,700	—
TOTAL	**110,000**	**87,500**	**105,400**	**108,540**	**114,300**	**104,100**	**94,000**	**84,200**	**77,100**	**89,900**	**78,600**	—	—
	2,338,440	2,228,440	2,140,940	2,035,540	1,927,000	1,812,700	1,708,600	1,614,600	1,530,400	1,155,300	804,200	133,000	10,800

* = Top numbers are pools built during given years. ‡ = Bottom numbers are cumulative totals. ★ = CCI Data. † = Regional breakdowns unavailable for 1947.

Inground Swimming Pools by Type: Historical Perspective

	Dec. 31, 1983	Dec. 31, 1982★	Dec. 31, 1981★	Dec. 31, 1980★	Dec. 31, 1979★	Dec. 31, 1978★	Dec. 31, 1977★	Dec. 31, 1976★	Dec. 31, 1975★	Dec. 31, 1971★	Dec. 31, 1967★	Dec. 31, 1957★	Dec. 31, 1947★
Hotel, Motel, Apartment, Condominium	**3,590***	**3,000**	**4,095**	**3,570**	**4,350**	**3,800**	**2,825**	**3,665**	**4,850**	**9,000**	**9,550**	—	—
	222,045‡	218,455	215,455	211,360	207,790	203,440	199,640	196,815	193,150	158,000	112,800	14,200	600
Club, Community, Institutional, Other	**2,310**	**1,700**	**3,865**	**3,560**	**4,450**	**4,000**	**3,775**	**2,835**	**5,850**	**7,300**	**7,450**	—	—
	200,245	197,935	196,235	192,370	188,810	184,360	180,360	176,585	173,750	146,000	115,700	31,300	7,700
Residential	**104,100**	**82,800**	**97,440**	**101,410**	**105,500**	**96,300**	**87,400**	**77,700**	**66,400**	**73,600**	**61,600**	—	—
	1,916,150	1,812,050	1,729,250	1,631,810	1,530,400	1,424,900	1,328,600	1,241,200	1,163,500	851,300	575,700	87,500	2,500
TOTAL	**110,000**	**87,500**	**105,400**	**108,540**	**114,300**	**104,100**	**94,000**	**84,200**	**77,100**	**89,900**	**78,600**	—	—
	2,338,440	2,228,440	2,140,940	2,035,540	1,927,000	1,812,700	1,708,600	1,614,600	1,530,400	1,155,300	804,200	133,000	10,800

* = Top numbers are pools built during given years. ‡ = Bottom numbers are cumulative totals. ★ = CCI Data.

SOURCE:
NATIONAL SPA AND POOL INSTITUTE 1983 SWIMMING POOL AND SPA INDUSTRY SURVEY

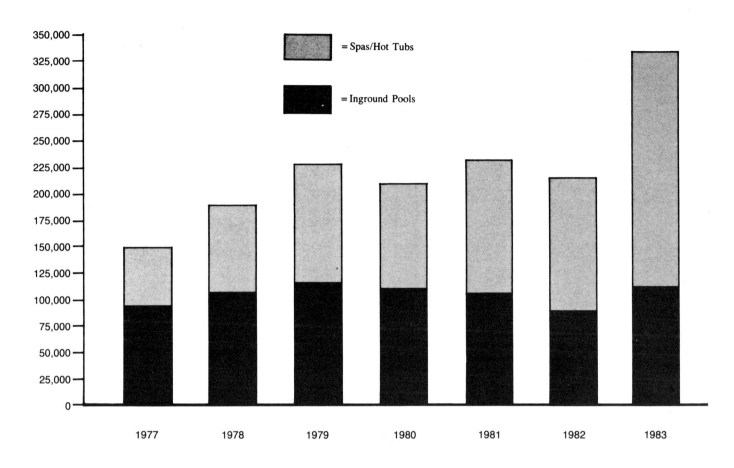

Figure 4-2

Total Combined Unit Sales:
Inground Pools and Spas/Hot Tubs: 1977-1983

	Inground Pools	Spas/Hot Tubs	Total Combined Unit Sales
1977 :	94,000	54,000	148,000
1978 :	104,100	85,000	189,100
1979 :	114,300	110,000	224,300
1980 :	108,540	100,000	208,540
1981 :	105,400	125,000	230,400
1982 :	87,500	125,000	212,500
1983 :	110,000	220,000	330,000

SOURCE:
NATIONAL SPA AND POOL INSTITUTE 1983 SWIMMING POOL AND SPA INDUSTRY SURVEY

Swimming Pools

prepare a statement of the requirements for each activity.

d) Study alternate sites for the pool with a view toward existing physical and utility conditions that will affect construction costs.

e) Obtain and study all state and local laws, regulations, and ordinances that apply to the pool.

f) Review the standards and guidelines for pool design and operation promulgated by the pool industry and professional organizations. A list of the agencies which have published standards or guidelines for either design or operation of pools is listed at the end of the chapter.

g) Outline all safety features to be incorporated into the pool's design.

h) Suggest to the proper authority what the committee considers to be the qualifications needed by the person who will direct the operation of the pool.

i) Be prepared to work with the architect/engineer.

2. Selection of the Architect/ Engineer

It is desirable to interview several architects/engineers before making a selection. The candidates should be advised during the interview that they will be working with the Planning Committee or an individual assigned to the project. The program requirements and other information developed by the committee should be transmitted in report form to the architect/engineer.

3. Preparation of Preliminary Plans and Cost Estimates

It is the responsibility of the architect/engineer to prepare the preliminary plans along with estimates of the cost of

construction and equipment. These plans should be carefully reviewed by all concerned. Suggested changes are best made at this junction in the planning process. The planner's checklist located at the end of the chapter should be used during the review of the plans.

4. Preparation of Construction Document (or Project Manual)

These include the working plans which the contractor will use to build the pool. The Project Manual will include a set of "Specifications" in addition to the legal and administrative provisions for the construction. These should be carefully checked by the committee.

5. Bid Request

Once the construction plans have been approved, a request goes out in various forms and methods inviting contractors to bid on the project. A bid time of not less than one month should be established. The lowest bidder usually (although not always) is awarded the contract to construct the pool.

6. Supervision of the Project

Supervision of the construction is a responsibility of both the architect and the contractor. However, the owner (school or agency) should have someone designated to check the progress of construction from time to time. The idea, of course, is to assure that the construction is done in strict accordance with the plan and specifications previously approved by the owner.

7. Acceptance of the Project

When construction in every detail has been completed, the owner along with the architect and the contractor make a final inspection of the pool. If satisfied that the pool meets all specifications, the owner officially accepts the pool. Written

guarantees directly to the owner of at least two years guaranteeing the water-tight integrity (no leakage) of the pool tanks including appurtenances should be obtained.

POOL DESIGN AND PLANNING FEATURES

There are a number of decisions which must be made during the planning process which will directly affect the design of the pool. An attempt is made to indicate not only trends in design but what is considered to be the owner's optimum project design program.

Program Requirements

It is imperative that every conceivable activity that will be conducted in the pool be anticipated in order that the pool requirements of each be incorporated into the pool's design. In addition, some consideration as to possible future pool activities should receive attention. For example, at the initial stage it may not be considered desirable or necessary to include a ten-meter diving tower. If such a tower is ever to be constructed, a water depth of 17 feet must be incorporated into the initial design — otherwise no tower can ever be added. Establishing the program requirements is a function of the Planning Committee with the help of a program specialist.

For the guidance of planners, the typical activities conducted in pools are listed on next page (Figure 4-3) with their recommended specifications. They are not listed in any order of priority.

Establishing Priorities

Following the identification of activities a discussion of relative priorities must take place. That is, which activity or activities have the highest priority? The requirements of these activities must then receive the greatest attention.

FIGURE 4-3

ACTIVITY	RECOMMENDED POOL SPECIFICATIONS
INSTRUCTION for pre-school children	*Water 6″ to 30″ deep and ability to raise water temperature to 86°F.*
SWIMMING INSTRUCTION for various age groups and swimming abilities	*Water 3'6″ to 6'0″ deep with water temperature of 82° to 84°F.*
RECREATIONAL SWIMMING for all ages and abilities	*Should have a minimum of 50-80 percent of pool water under 6'0″.*
COMPETITIVE SWIMMING for organized swimming teams	*See rule books for competitive swimming by appropriate ruling body: USS, NCAA, FHSAA, and FINA.*
SPRINGBOARD AND PLATFORM DIVING for competition and recreation	*See rule books of governing bodies USD, NCAA, FHSAA, and FINA.*
SYNCHRONIZED SWIMMING for clubs and team competition	*See rules for synchronized swimming.*
SCUBA INSTRUCTION for individual and club members	*Any portion of pool for preliminary instruction and water at least 12' for advanced instruction.*
LIFE SAVING AND WATER SAFETY for groups and individuals	*Must have both shallow and deep water for instruction.*
WATER POLO for competition	*See rules governing water polo competition.*
SPECIAL GROUPS such as elderly, scouts, police, etc.	*No specific requirements. One or more sets of large, recessed built-in steps with handrails is preferred.*
HANDICAPPED instruction and recreational swimming	*Need to provide means for handicapped people to get into the pool. Ramps and hoists are the most common methods. Deck-level pool construction is an increasingly favored design idiom.*
RESEARCH	*Most important is need for underwater observation room with electric outlets. Ideal is one room located in deep well pool, and another in shallow competitive pool on the side 10 feet from the end of the pool.*
CANOE AND BOAT INSTRUCTIONS and for demonstrations	*Large 50 meter pools are preferred.*
POOL PARTIES	*Areas for dancing, lounging, and eating. A small band shell is a very desirable addition.*

Inevitably, there will be need for compromise. It is because of this dilemma that the multiple pool concept has emerged as the best solution. However, the multiple pool complex costs more, occupies greater space, and is more expensive to operate. It is usually a safer facility. It is far easier to achieve this concept in outdoor pools than indoor natatoriums.

Shape and Dimensions of the Pool

It is here where the decision must be made whether to build one pool or a complex. The trend in community outdoor pools where space is seldom a problem is towards construction of an aquatic complex with a minimum of three pools and preferably four. These pools would be:

a) **Main Pool** — used for general recreational and instruction in swimming and competition.

b) **Deep Water Well** — for springboard and tower diving and other activities requiring deep water such as scuba diving, synchronized swimming and life saving.

c) **Familiarization Pool** — often referred to as the "kiddie pool" or "wading pool" where children below the age of six become introduced to water.

d) **Training Pool** — where children as well as adults learn to swim.

The separation of pools is strongly recommended as opposed to combining all activities in one pool, which inevitably leads to a conflict in scheduling. (Figure 4-4; 4-5)

Depth of Water and Bottom Contours

Recommended depths and bottom slopes for each of the pools listed above are:

a) **Main Pool:** *3'10'' to 6'0''
deep*
b) **Deep Water Well:** *13'0''
constant depth when
diving stands up to 3
meters are to be installed.
17'0'' constant depth when
a 10 meter tower is
desired.*
c) **Familiarization Pool:** *6''
to 30'' deep*
d) **Training Pool:** *2'6'' to
4'0'' deep*

The listed depths satisfy the
requirements and specifications
held forth by the ruling bodies for
swimming and diving. When a
single pool is to be constructed,
further details apply and program
requirements should be consulted.
A number of swimming coaches
have come out in favor of all deep
pools (8'0'' and deeper) for
competitive swimming. They
believe it makes for a "faster
pool." This is questionable, and
one must consider the effect such
greater than usual depths have on
other aspects of the overall
aquatic program. Appendix
includes several official layouts for
pool designs.

Bottoms of pools should always
be uniform in their slope. The
"hopper bottom" concept in the
diving portion of the pool is not
recommended because it is

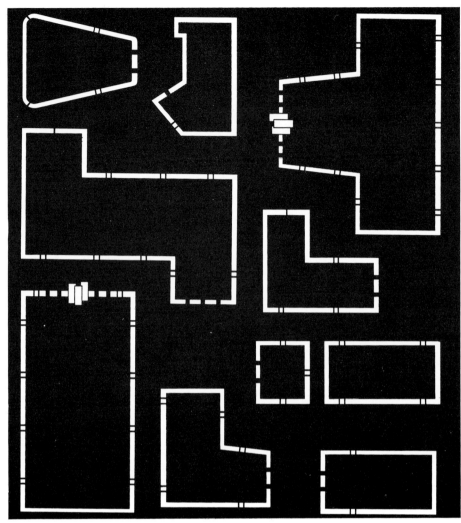

*Figure 4-4
Some typical pool shapes.*

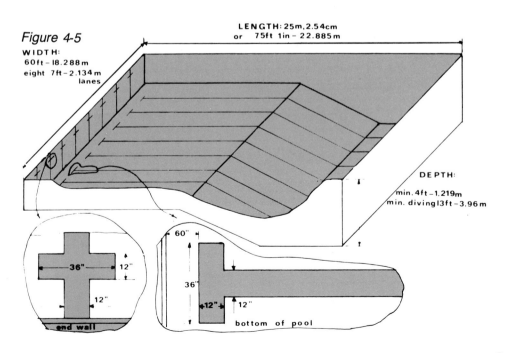

Figure 4-5

WIDTH:
60ft – 18.288 m
eight 7ft – 2.134 m
lanes

LENGTH: 25m, 2.54cm
or 75ft 1in – 22.885 m

DEPTH:
min. 4ft – 1.219m
min. diving 13ft – 3.96 m

36''
12''
12''
end wall

60''
36''
12''
12''
bottom of pool

deceptive to the diver. Similarly, the "spoon-shaped bottom" in the deep end has been determined to be unsafe because recreational divers seldom enter the water at the pool's deepest point. (Figure 4-6)

Construction Material

Most shells of public pools are constructed with reinforced concrete, either poured or applied by pneumatic pressure (referred to as "gunite"). Steel and aluminum have also been employed in pool basin construction. Fiberglass molded pools have been manufactured for use in small pools, primarily for homes and motels. The most prevalent material used in residential pools is vinyl, both for above-ground and in-ground pools. With vinyl, however, unless extreme care is exercised, a useful life of only five years should be expected. Well-laid concrete pool shells containing a well-designed number of steel reinforcing rods has a life of at least 40 to 50 years, and is considered to be the best type of construction.

Interior Basin Finishes

Pool basin finishes are classified as: coatings (paint), tile, plaster, and natural. Thick-set ceramic tile which is slip resistant is the best. A carefully approved and applied trueing (or "scratch") coat should be first applied to the roughened and clean concrete shell. Next comes white marbledust-cement plaster finish placed over trued, cleaned, and roughened concrete surfaces. Troweled raw (natural) concrete is used in many outdoor pools to reduce cost. The "plaster" finish, which is made from white cement with a granular component such as marbledust, will have to be resurfaced about every eight to ten years depending on the care it is given, and the pool water chemistry balance. Ordinary "plaster lime" *is never* used in a pool plaster finish. Painting of pools should be done only as a last resort. Once

painting is started the pool will have to be re-painted at least every three years depending again on the quality of paint used and its application. The epoxy coatings appear to be more successful than paint. All indoor pools should be finished with white ceramic tile, preferably "square edge" with flush struck joints, which to this date remains the classical permanent swimming pool finish. Pools which were constructed 50 to 60 years ago still have the tile which was installed when the pool was built. There have been a few pools that have used black or dark blue tile, particularly in diving pools. Divers claim that it gives them better visibility of the water's

surface. This is a questionable practice since in water depths of 16 to 17 feet it is difficult to see anyone lying on the bottom. Tank acuity, the ability to adequately and safely see the tank interior is unreasonably compromised unless a highly definitive (150-200 f-c) underwater lighting design is employed. All interior pool walls and bottoms should have bottom lines and wall targets preferably in black. All outdoor pools which have a plaster finish should be covered during the off-season to protect the finish.

Overflow Systems

There are a variety of overflow systems incorrectly referred to as

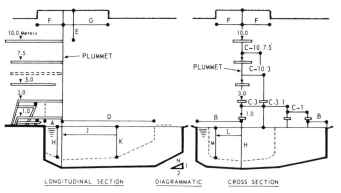

MINIMUM STANDARD DIVING FACILITY DIMENSIONS Adoption by NCAA in 1969		1-METER SPRINGB'D 16'x1'-8" (4.88m x 50.8cm)		3-METER SPRINGB'D 16'x1'-8" (4.88m x 50.8cm)		INTER-MED. PLATFORM 16'x5' (4.88m x 1.52m)		7½-METER PLATFORM 18'x 6' (5.49m x 1.83m)		10-METER PLATFORM 20'x6'6" (6.10m x 1.98m)	
		DIST	DEPTH	DIST	DEPTH	DIST	DEPTH	DIST	DEPTH	DIST	DEPTH
A	FROM PLUMMET BACK TO POOL WALL	6' (1.83m)		6' (1.83m)		5' (1.52m)		5' (1.52m)		6' (1.83m)	
	BACK TO PLATFORM DIRECTLY BELOW							5' (1.52m)		5' (1.52m)	
B	FROM PLUMMET TO POOL WALL AT SIDE	10' (3.05m)		12' (3.66m)		14' (4.27m)		15' (4.57m)		17' (5.18m)	
C	FROM PLUMMET TO ADJACENT PLUMMET	8' (2.44m)		8' (2.44m)		10' (3.05m)				12' (3.66m)	
D	FROM PLUMMET TO POOL WALL AHEAD	29' (8.84m)		34' (10.36m)		34' (10.36m)		36' (10.97m)		45' (13.72m)	
E	ON PLUMMET, FROM BOARD TO CEILING OVERHEAD	16' (4.88m)		16' (4.88m)		10' (3.05m)		10'6" (3.20m)		11' (3.35m)	
F E	CLEAR OVERHEAD, BEHIND AND EACH SIDE OF PLUMMET	8' (2.44m)	16' (4.88m)	8' (2.44m)	16' (4.88m)	9' (2.74m)	12' (3.66m)	9' (2.74m)	12' (3.66m)	16' (4.88m)	12' (3.66m)
G	CLEAR OVERHEAD AHEAD OF PLUMMET	16' (4.88m)	16' (4.88m)	16' (4.88m)	16' (4.88m)	16' (4.88m)	12' (3.66m)	16' (4.88m)	12' (3.66m)	20' (6.10m)	12' (3.66m)
H	DEPTH OF WATER AT PLUMMET		12' (3.66m)		13' (3.96m)		14' (4.27m)		15' (4.57m)		17' (5.18m)
J-K	DISTANCE, AND DEPTH OF WATER, AHEAD OF PLUMMET	20' (6.10m)	10'9" (3.28m)	20' (6.10m)	11'9" (3.58m)	20' (6.10m)	11'9" (3.58m)	26' (7.92m)	13' (3.96m)	40' (12.19m)	14' (4.27m)
L-M	DISTANCE, AND DEPTH OF WATER, EACH SIDE OF PLUMMET	8' (2.44m)	12' (3.66m)	10' (3.05m)	11'9" (3.58m)	12' (3.66m)	11'9" (3.58m)	13' (3.96m)	11'9" (3.58m)	14' (4.27m)	14' (4.27m)
N	MAXIMUM RATIO, VERTICAL TO HORIZONTAL, OF SLOPE TO REDUCE DEPTH 1:2	1:2		1:2		1:2		1:2		1:2	

LONGITUDINAL SECTION   DIAGRAMMATIC   CROSS SECTION

Figure 4-6

gutters. They are the:

a) Perimeter overflow system often termed the "Rimflow" or deck-level pool.

b) Roll-out overflow sometimes referred to as "open gutter," first introduced by the YMCA in the early 1930's.

c) Recessed gutters of which there are a great number of different designs.

Any overflow system must serve the primary function of an absolutely level skimming rim for the pool surface water.

The next essential feature of any overflow system is the necessity for storage of water that is displaced by swimmers. This is accomplished in one of the following ways:

a) A surge trench located in the deck of the pool usually integral with the overflow coping.

b) Deep recessed gutter with a capacity to accommodate the displaced water in conjunction with a separate surge tank.

c) A preformed steel compartment system which in place of a larger (fully adequate) surge trench employs an overload pump to remove excess water from the flooded gutter and return it directly to the pool.

d) A balancing tank system where a tank is located below the deck or in the filter room to hold displaced water. Water is then withdrawn from the tank as needed to maintain the proper water level in the pool.

The basic requirement of any overflow system is to accept water displaced by swimmers. The returning of the water is a function of the filter pumps. Any other pumps increase the operating energy costs. The pool itself should never be used for surge storage since the rim should overflow constantly at all times.

Skimming of the water surface must be uniformly level and continuous during operation.

The Hydraulic System

All pools must be equipped with a recirculation and filtration system. Filters fall into three general classes: sand, diatomaceous earth (D.E.), and cartridge-type filters. Rapid-flow and high-rate sand filters and cartridge filters are of the pressure system variety. Diatomaceous earth filters can be of either the pressure or vacuum system type.

Each system includes a pump for moving the water and piping to take the water from the pool and pass it through the filter and treatment units before returning it to the pool. Local and state sanitary codes must be consulted for requirements.

In the sand filter systems, water impurities are held on top or within the media bed. A coagulant floc may be used to remove extremely small particles. The system is cleaned by reversing the flow and backwashing the bed.

Cartridge type filters are composed of permeable cylinders of fibrous material which traps particulate matter as the water passes through. They may be cleaned by backwashing, or by removing and cleaning the cartridge.

Diatomaceous earth (D.E.) filters remove particular matter as the flow passes through a thin layer of D.E. which is held by water pressure against a woven cloth or metal mesh element. When the layer of media becomes clogged, the filter is cleaned by sluicing the elements with water until the media is washed away. A fresh layer (precoat) of D.E. is then placed on the elements and the filter is returned to service. During the filter cycle, the element coating is kept porous longer by the addition of small amounts of diatomite slurry to mix with the dirt from the pool.

In all cases, flow rates and filter sizes should be calculated to produce a minimum turnover rate of six hours. Exceptionally heavy use may require a turnover rate of four or five hours to insure

Cambridge, Ontario, Canada City Swimming Pool

maximum water clarity in main pools. Wading pools are usually designed for a one hour turnover.

The most innovative filter system is the "regenerative cycle D.E. pressure filter" which has stainless steel flexible mesh elements. No backwashing is needed. This is accomplished by flexing the steel element, thereby knocking off the D.E. which is then reformed onto the element. Another term to describe this process is the word "bumping." It is accomplished by merely pushing a button.

The automation of the filter system and chemical treatment of water is readily accomplished and is expected to be greatly perfected in the future. Planning of new pools should seriously consider automation.

Chemical Treatment of Water

Swimming pools would not be able to operate if the water were not chemically treated in order to make it safe for human use. Two elements must be controlled — first is the pH (hydrogen ion concentration) or the acidity of the water; second is the bacteria count. Boards of Health have established rigid standards for pools along with specific requirements for testing and recording data. The most common agents used in the disinfection of water are chlorine, bromine, and iodine. Chlorine comes in a variety of forms and compounds, namely gas, liquid, powder, and tablets. For larger pools chlorine in the form of a gas is the least expensive and liquid the most expensive. Other disinfecting agents which have been tried with varying degrees of success are ultraviolet radiation and silver salts.

The equipment or apparatus used to feed the chemicals into the pool water must be of high quality. The trend in water treatment is towards automation where it is unnecessary for an individual to do anything but check gauges. Readings are automatically taken and chemicals added as needed.

Water Temperature

Water of 80°F is most desirable for comfortable swimming. Even in warm climates a heater is necessary for maintaining a proper temperature. Pool heaters are manufactured by several companies. They employ either gas, oil, or electricity for the heating. Solar collectors for pool heating are cost-effective and can be successfully employed in many locations. The use of so-called "solar blankets" has helped reduce the cost of heating water because the blanket placed on the surface of the water at night reduces heat loss. It is strongly recommended for use with outdoor pools, although a more efficient system for removal of the blanket is needed. The actual heating of pool water by the sun has proven to be successful. Employing solar energy to heat pool water appears to be the direction to go in the future. Even though the initial cost may seem high, the equipment will likely be amortized in 3 to 4 years.

Diving Facilities

The most efficient way to provide diving facilities is the construction of a separate diving pool often referred to as the "deep water well." It is so-called because it also accommodates other activities which require deep water. Most major pools today have separate diving pools. Planners should refer to rule books of the various governing bodies for detailed specifications for diving facilities and equipment, the depth of water, springboards, diving stands, towers, separation between equipment, and pool dimensions for safe diving. It is strongly recommended that at least one low springboard (one-half meter from the water) 10 to 12 feet long be provided along with the competitive types and length boards. This will give young children a facility in which to

Pool at Texas Tech University can be covered in cooler months for non-interrupted year-round swimming.

acquire the basic skills of diving before being placed on the one- and three-meter high boards.

Planners should remember that when a diving tower (5 to 10 meters high) is contemplated, the depth of the pool must be increased to 17 feet.

Pool Lighting

Any pool which is to be used at night must have adequate lighting both in and around the pool. Very few pools today have good underwater lighting systems. The major source planners should refer to in determining requirements are:

    a) The Illuminating

space varies greatly between indoor and outdoor pools. Outdoor pools require much more space around them than indoor pools. The main reason is obviously that people add sun bathing to their swimming activities at outdoor pools. Studies have shown that in a well-planned pool only 20 to 25 percent of the patrons will be in the pool at any one time. The rest are lounging or eating. The most recent trend in outdoor pool planning is to provide grassed areas for lounging which reduces the amount of concrete deck needed around the pool to accommodate the traffic of swimmers. Furthermore, grass is considerably cooler than concrete.

machines, along with an area for eating, is desirable, if not essential, to the success of outdoor pools. This trend is being extended to more and more indoor pools.

Safety Features

Safety is no accident. It must receive careful consideration by planners, architects, and operators of pools. Many people have been confronted with litigation as a result of an accident in their pools. Lawyers inevitably look for areas of negligence both in the operation of the pool or any defect in the pool's design. Listed below are some essential safety principles, procedures, and policies which should be adhered to in the process of designing the pool and in its operation:

- Rules governing pool use must be conspicuously posted at all points of entry to the pool.
- Special rules should be developed and posted for use of such facilities as diving boards, slides, towers, and the use of toys — particularly flotation devices in the pool.
- Water slides should only be located at the deep end of the pool (minimum 9'0" deep).
- A lifeguard should be on duty at all times that the pool is open even in situations where the only people using the pool is an organized class with an instructor.
- In areas of the pool which contain less than 5'0" of water, signs and warnings should be placed at the edge (coping) of the pool which state "SHALLOW WATER — NO DIVING." In shallow water, training pools with depths of water 4'0" and less, signs should be painted on the edge of the pool stating "DANGER — SHALLOW WATER — NO DIVING."

University of Nebraska, Omaha has 50 meter pool with two movable bulkheads, acoustic treated walls, wet classroom, generous storage areas, plus many other functional features.

    Engineering Society (Underwater and Pool Area)
    b) Article 680 of the National Electric Code (for safety)
    c) The ruling bodies for competitive swimming and diving.

A minimum of 60 footcandles of illumination is recommended for area lighting around outdoor pools, while 100 footcandles is suggested for indoor pools.

Deck and Lounging Areas

The requirements for deck

Locker Rooms and Bathhouses

The details of planning locker rooms and bathhouses are discussed in another chapter in the book. One fact that should be kept in mind is that people using outdoor pools in the summer seem to prefer to come to the pool in their bathing suits. Therefore, less dressing area is needed. Other facilities, such as toilets, should be planned to accommodate peak pool loads.

Refreshments

A snack bar or vending

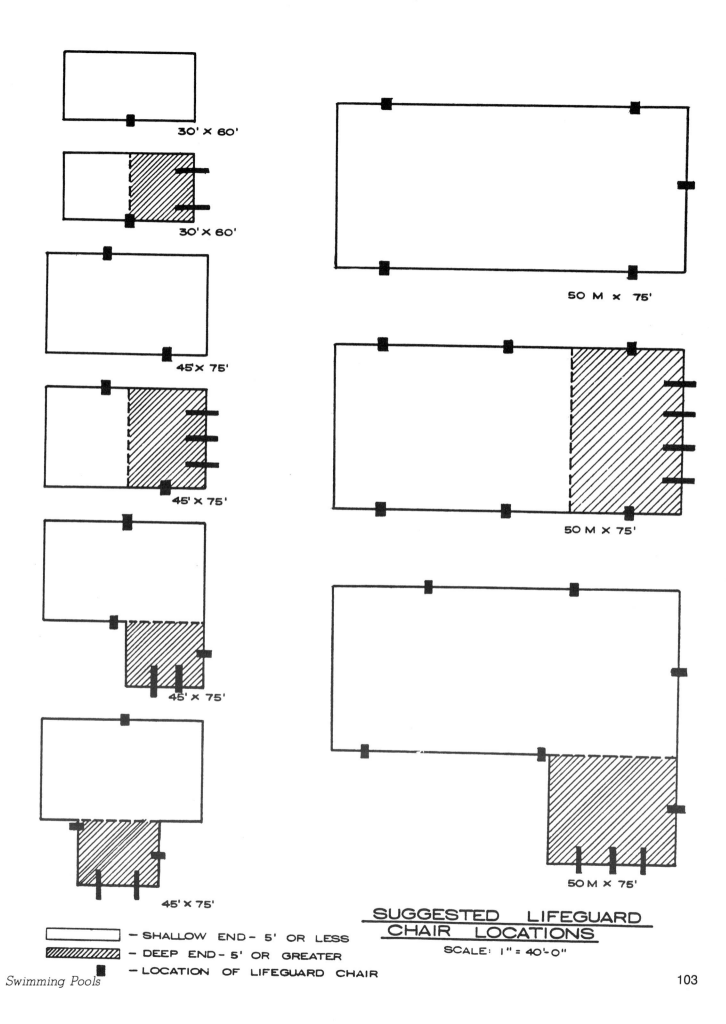

30' X 60'

30' X 60'

45' X 75'

45' X 75'

45' X 75'

45' X 75'

50 M X 75'

50 M X 75'

50 M X 75'

SUGGESTED LIFEGUARD
CHAIR LOCATIONS
SCALE: 1" = 40'-0"

☐ — SHALLOW END- 5' OR LESS
▨ — DEEP END- 5' OR GREATER
■ — LOCATION OF LIFEGUARD CHAIR

Swimming Pools

- Where springboards and platform diving is provided, the depth of water and other related measurements must conform to the rules of the USS, NCAA, or the NFHSAA.
- The "hopper-type" bottom should never be constructed in the diving well of a pool. Similarly, the "spoon-shaped" bottom which has only one deep point should not be constructed where springboards are to be installed.
- Starting blocks for competitive swimming should be installed in the deep end of pools unless the shallow end of the pool is at least 6'0" deep.
- Adequate lighting, both underwater and in the pool area, must be provided to assure the safety of users.
- Clarity of pool water is essential. People have drowned in pools where their bodies were not visible from the deck of the pool because of the water's turbidity.
- Depth markers at least 6" high must be placed both on the interior wall of the pool and on the edge or coping of the pool at every variation in depth of one foot.
- Never consider the minimum standards for pools promulgated by state governments or the pool industry to be the proper level to achieve in planning a pool. Minimums often become obsolete very quickly.
- Ladders which hang on the edge of a pool and extend into the water represent hazards to swimmers. All ladders should be recessed into the pool wall.
- No safety ledge should

ever extend into the pool. Instead they should be recessed into the wall at a depth of 4'0".
- Springboards should be mounted onto a concrete bed at least 4'0" wide so that if a person should

accidentally step off the board he will not fall to the pool deck.
- Spacing between horizontal guard rails of diving stands should not exceed 12", and the guard rails should extend at least

The new pool at the University of Arkansas includes towers for diving and a bulkhead for diving well separation.

The D.C. Kaufman Family Y.M.C.A. in Kitchener, Ontario has many outstanding features including a slide and a jacuzzi.

Swimming Pools

12" over the edge of the pool, with 24" preferred.
- Steps leading up to a 3-meter board or tower are safer than vertical ladders.
- All metal springboards should have some kind of protective material on the end to reduce or prevent serious injury if a diver strikes the board.
- All equipment used in and around the pool should be inspected daily or on some regular basis to assure that the equipment is usable. Any equipment found to be defective should be secured until repaired or replaced.
- An emergency plan should be developed and understood by all who have any responsibility for the pool so that no time is lost when an accident occurs. Everyone must know what his function is during an emergency.
- Proper daily maintenance of the pool's water and circulation system is essential to the health and safety of patrons. Daily operating records must be maintained.
- The most hazardous areas of any pool are the deep portion, or diving well, and decks of pools if they are permitted to become slippery.
- The most dangerous activities and conditions associated with pool use are:
  — diving into shallow water (less than 4'0")
  — swimming underwater particularly after hyperventilating
  — horseplay
  — unsupervised use of scuba equipment
  — head first descents down water slides
  — young children using 3-meter springboards
  — playing follow-the-leader off springboards
  — games such as tag and sharks and minnows
  — over-crowding of pool
  — over-exposure to the sun
  — unsupervised use of flotation devices by children
- No public pool should ever place responsibility on parents for the supervision of their children. Parents may not be qualified to assume this responsibility.

POOLS FOR SCHOOLS AND COLLEGES

Pools for schools and colleges are invariably different from typical community pools. They will vary according to the educational level to be served and the school's enrollment. Here are some considerations for planners:

Elementary School Pools

Two types of pools may be planned for elementary schools. The first is a training pool which is primarily for teaching young children to swim. It can be, and usually is, an all-shallow pool ranging in depth from 2'6" to 4'6" to 5'0". The minimum recommended size is 20' x 50', while the preferred size is 25' x 60'. The second type is the "school-community pool" which is larger and deeper to accommodate teenagers and adults in evening and weekend swim programs. Minimum recommended size is 20' x 60'. The preferred size is 30' x 75'.

With many communities confronted with vacant classrooms because of decreasing enrollments, the possible conversion of some of these empty classroom spaces for swimming pools should be considered. Portable above-ground pools, which may be purchased for as little as two to three thousand dollars are available and offer elementary schools a real potential. A note of caution: these portable pools should only be placed in areas located on the

Natural light and a removable roof highlights this aquatic facility at the North Coast Y.M.C.A. in Encinitas, California.

ground floor. Because of the weight of the water they must rest on a concrete slab. On the other hand, it is possible to also place in-ground pools in vacant classrooms that are on the ground floor. The floor will have to be removed and the ground excavated. This plan is more costly but far more permanent, since the portable pool cannot be expected to last more than ten years. The minimum recommended size for in-ground pools is 16' x 24', and the preferred size is 20' x 40'.

Junior High and Senior High School Pools

There is little difference between the junior and senior high pools. Both should be designed to permit a comprehensive aquatic program, including use of the pool by the public. However, in many cases it is not possible to construct the size pool desired because of cost. Obviously, even a small pool is better than none. Suggested pool sizes are:

Feature	Minimum	Desirable
Size	30' x 75'	45' x 75'
Shallow Water	3'0"	3'6"
Deep Water	5'0"	12'0"
Ceiling Height	16'0"	18'0"

If possible, the high school pool that is to serve the total aquatic needs of the community should provide a separate "well" or pool for diving and other deep water activities. This deep water well may also be provided by designing the pool in an "L" or "T" shape.

Some provision for spectators should be included either by construction of a balcony, through use of roll-a-way bleachers placed at deck level, or by constructing permanent stands on one or two sides of the pool.

An approach to obtaining pools for schools which has merit is the joint planning and financing of the pool by both the school board and the local city council. The one arrangement which has proven successful is where the schools

have exclusive use of the pool during the school week and the city takes over its operation on weekends and summer months. Sometimes the use by the public is extended to evenings during the school week.

College and University Pools

The swimming pool is emerging on many campuses as the focal point of the college's recreation program. A recent trend is the partial or complete financing of the college pool from student activity fees.

Without a doubt the most important development in college and university pools has been the move towards the construction of 50-meter pools and often multiple pools, with facilities for diving and training provided separately from the main pool. The pools at the University of Texas, Indiana University at Indianapolis, the U.S. Naval Academy, and the University of Florida are excellent examples.

The question of whether it is more desirable to construct a

single, large, centrally located pool or several small pools strategically placed throughout the campus has confronted colleges and universities for some time. The answer appears to be increasingly in favor of the large complex.

Factors that support the trend towards single large pool complexes are:

- Students seem to enjoy being a part of a large group in a recreation setting involving swimming.
- Larger facilities provide the opportunity to include supplemental facilities such as lounge areas, sunning decks, tables for eating or socializing, sauna baths, and other recreational facilities.
- The use of the university's outdoor pool by summer school graduate students and their families.
- It provides the faculty and their dependents with an enjoyable aquatic facility.
- The large pool complex provides opportunities for holding major swimming championships, water shows, demonstrations, and pageants.
- The large pool permits the aquatic director to

A fish design on the pool bottom of this pool at the Century Gardens Community Centre in Brampton, Ontario.

Natatorium at the U.S. Air Force Academy uses wall graphics to highlight large wall space.

schedule several different activities or classes in the pool at the same time. At least three or four separate teaching stations may easily be accommodated in a 50-meter pool.

RECENT INNOVATIONS IN POOL DESIGN AND EQUIPMENT

There are a number of new developments in the design of pools and in the equipment used in them. Some have been around for a few years but have failed to achieve the level of acceptance that they deserve. Limited space does not permit a full discussion of each item. Architects and planners are urged to give careful study of them to determine which, if any, they should incorporate in the proposed pool.

• **Bottom inlets** as opposed to conventional wall inlets for the return of water into the pool.

• **Tile tube** is an innovation which employs a PVC flat tube with hundreds of small holes as the bottom racing line in competitive pools. The idea is to distribute the water as it enters the pool on a much greater scale.

• **Low and short springboards** (10 to 12' long) installed 1/2 meter above the water in the diving wells of pools as a training device for young children and other beginning divers.

• **Bottom targets** in front of each springboard to provide divers with an underwater reference point.

• **Black or dark blue bottoms** in diving wells for the purpose of providing divers with greater visibility of the water's surface. This is a questionable move since it also reduces visibility of the bottom and what might be down there.

• **Solar heating** of pool water to help reduce or eliminate high fuel cost (oil, gas, electricity).

• **Solar blankets** for use with outdoor pools to reduce the heat loss during periods the pool is not operating. It also prevents people from using the pool when it is closed.

• **Color and murals** on walls to decorate indoor natatoriums.

• **Rimflow gutter systems** (level-deck pools) with accompanying surge trench located in deck.

• **The Paddock SCRS-ASR gutter system** made of stainless steel.

• **Regenerative cycle filter system** which practically eliminates the need for diatomaceous earth,

The U.S. Naval Academy incorporates many of the latest features in its recently completed natatorium.

lowers labor cost, and eliminates conventional manual backwashing of filters.

- **High rate sand filters** speed up the filtering process. Some people have raised questions relative to their effectiveness.
- **Variable depth bottoms** created by use of hydraulic lift systems provides opportunity to have shallow water for teaching of young children.
- **Movable bulkheads** which permit a large rectangular pool to be divided into several different length pools to accommodate diving, 25 meter and 25 yard pools, and, if needed, a shallow water instruction area.
- **Carpeting of decks** is used mostly with outdoor pools. Must get approval of State Health Departments. Many will not approve because of the difficulty of keeping carpet in sanitary condition.
- **Covers** to prevent pool use when the facility is not open. Made of nylon or other plastic material.
- **Skylights** rather than side windows in indoor pools. Eliminates glare on water surface usually caused by windows on the side walls.
- **Automation of filter room** is now available with technology to provide complete automation of filters and chemical treatment of water. Cost is high for good systems, but will save money in the long run.
- **Steps** placed along the entire wall of diving pools under the boards. This facilitates the diver's exit from the pool.
- **Doubling surface lines** to reduce wave action during swimming meets.

- **Ramps and hoists** in pools provided to permit handicapped people entrance and exit from the pool.
- **Saunas, whirlpools, and steam rooms** included as supplemental facilities adjacent to the pool for use by swimmers.

There have been some interesting pool innovations in the past which for one reason or another never caught on. Some of the major ones are:

- **Natatorium structure constructed on a track** which enabled this complete building to be removed, thereby creating an outdoor pool.
- **Diving stands placed on hydraulic lift,** thereby permitting the board's height to be adjusted from one to three meters.
- **Sliding glass doors** constructed as one wall of the pool building which when opened provides an indoor-outdoor concept.
- **Joining an indoor and outdoor pool** to permit swimmers to have access from one to the other. It is a novelty and costly to heat the outdoor pool in the winter.

SUMMARY

Although swimming is the number one recreation activity in America, the United States lags far behind Europe and Japan in the development of comprehensive aquatic facilities at the community level. It is not uncommon to find a pool in a city in Germany, France, England, or Holland which is not only self-supporting but, through a plan of memberships and fees, is amortized in three to five years. The main difference is that the pool is located in a center which offers patrons a wide variety of activities. While the pool is the focal point of the complex, other recreational opportunities are available to members of the family who do not care to swim. Co-generation facilities are the hallmark of these forward designs which include restaurants, snack bars, bowling alleys, handball/racquetball courts, exercise rooms, and gyms. The recreation complex provides a cafeteria of opportunities for the passive recreator integrated into lifestyle and living essentials such as shopping and banking.

Innovative in terms of technology as well as philosophy, heat rejected for the ice-making equipment of an ice rink may be used to heat the swimming pool. Solar intake from the passive features on the south side is transferred to cooler offices on the north side.

It is interesting to note that some of the major hotel and motel chains in this country are beginning to incorporate these concepts, such as the Holidome, a development by Holiday Inns.

Thoughtful and thorough planning of new aquatic facilities into exciting and lifestyle-oriented recreation complexes and leisure centers can continue to provide safe and satisfying recreational opportunities for swimmers of all ages, abilities, and interests.

Check List for Use by Planning Committee and Owner

Planning Factors

1. A clear-cut statement has been prepared on the nature and scope of the program and the special requirements for space, equipment, and facilities dictated by the activities to be conducted. ☐

2. The swimming pool has been planned to meet the requirements of the intended program to be conducted as well as special need. ☐

3. There are other recreational facilities nearby for the convenience and enjoyment of swimmers. ☐

4. An experienced pool consultant, architect, or

engineer has been called in to advise on design and equipment. ☐

5. The design of the pool reflects the most correct knowledge and experience regarding the technical aspects of swimming pools. ☐

6. The pool plans reflect the needs of handicapped persons. ☐

7. All plans and specifications meet the regulations of both state and local boards of health. ☐

8. Provision for accommodating young children has been considered. ☐

9. Consideration has been given to provide a room or area near the pool suitable for movies and lectures. ☐

10. The site for the outdoor pool is in the best possible location (away from railroad tracks, heavy industry, trees, and dusty open fields). ☐

11. Adequate parking space has been provided. ☐

Design Factors

1. The bathhouse is properly located, with entrance to the pool leading to the shallow end. ☐

2. The locker rooms or bathhouse are large enough to accommodate peak loads. ☐

3. The area for spectators has been separated from the pool area. ☐

4. There is adequate deck space around the pool. More space has been provided than indicated by the minimum recommended deck/pool ratio. ☐

5. The swimming pool manager's or director's office faces the pool and contains a window through which provides a view of the entire pool area. ☐

6. There is a toilet-shower-dressing area next to the office for instructors. ☐

7. The specifications for competitive swimming set forth by ruling groups have been met. ☐

8. If the pool shell contains concrete finish, the length of the pool has been increased by three inches over the "official" size in order to permit eventual tiling of the basin without making the pool become too short. ☐

9. The width of any moveable bulkhead has been considered in calculating total pool length. ☐

10. Consideration has been given to an easy method of moving the bulkhead. ☐

11. Provision has been made for the switch to metric distances. ☐

12. All diving standards and lifeguard chairs have been properly anchored. ☐

13. Separate storage spaces have been allocated for maintenance and instructional equipment. ☐

14. A properly constructed overflow gutter extends around the pool perimeter. ☐

15. The gutter waste water has been piped and valved to return water to the filters or waste. ☐

16. Where skimmers are used, they are located so that they are not on walls where competitive swimming is to be conducted. ☐

17. The proper pitch to drains has been allowed in the pool, on the pool deck, in the overflow gutter, and on the floor of shower and dressing rooms. ☐

18. Inlets and outlets are adequate in number and located to ensure effective circulation of water in the pool. ☐

19. There is easy access to the filter room to permit the transport of chemicals and other supplies. ☐

20. The recirculation pump is located below the water level. ☐

21. The recirculation-filtration system has been designed to meet anticipated future pool loads. ☐

22. Underwater lights in end racing walls have been located deep enough and directly below surface land anchors, and they are on a separate circuit. ☐

23. There is direct access from deck to the underwater observation room. ☐

24. There is a tunnel around the outside of the pool or a trench on the deck permitting ready access to pipes. ☐

25. There is adequate acoustic treatment of walls and ceilings of the indoor pool. ☐

26. There is adequate overhead clearance for diving (16 feet above one and three meter boards, 11 feet above 10 meter platforms). ☐

27. Reflection of light from the outside has been kept to a minimum by proper location of windows or skylights. ☐

28. All wall bases are coved to facilitate cleaning. ☐

29. The wall and ceiling insulation are adequate to prevent "sweating." ☐

30. Proper subsurface drainage has been provided. ☐

31. An area for sunbathing has been provided for the outdoor pool. ☐

32. The lights are placed far enough from the outdoor pool to prevent insects from dropping into the pool. ☐

33. Diving boards or platforms are oriented so that they face north or east. ☐

34. The pool is oriented correctly in relation to the sun. ☐

35. Wind shields or breakers have been provided in situations where heavy winds prevail. ☐

36. Lounging for swimmers has been provided. ☐

Safety and Health

1. The pool layout provides the most efficient control of swimmers from showers and locker rooms to the pool. ☐

2. Toilet facilities are provided for wet swimmers separate from the dry area. ☐

3. There is an area set aside for eating, apart from the pool deck. ☐

4. There is adequate deep water for diving (minimum of 12 feet for one meter, 13 feet for 3-meter boards, and 17 feet for 10 meter towers). ☐

5. Adequate space has been provided between diving boards and between the diving boards and sidewalls. ☐

6. Recessed steps or removable ladders are located on the walls so as not to interfere with competitive swimming turns. ☐

7. There is adequate provision for life-saving equipment and pool cleaning equipment. ☐

8. The proper number of lifeguard stands have been provided and properly located. ☐

9. All metal fittings are of non-corrosive material. ☐

10. Underwater lights are the 12-volt type , and all metal in the pool area is grounded to a ground-fault interrupter. ☐

11. Provision has been made for underwater lights. ☐

12. The gas chlorinator (if used) has been placed in a separate room accessible from and vented to the outside. ☐

13. A pool heater has been included if pool is in northern climates. ☐

14. Automatic controls for water chemistry have been considered. ☐

15. Proper ventilation has been provided in indoor pool. ☐

16. There is adequate underwater and area lighting. ☐

17. There is provision for proper temperature control in the pool room for both water and air. ☐

18. The humidity of the pool room can be controlled. ☐

19. Sand and grass have been kept the proper distance away from the pool to prevent cuttings and dirt from being transmitted to the pool. ☐

20. A fence has been placed around the outdoor pool to prevent its use when the pool is closed. ☐

21. Rules for use of the pool have been developed and prominently displayed. ☐

22. Warning signs are placed where needed and on such equipment as diving boards and slides. ☐

23. Starting blocks are placed in the deep end of pool (Min. depth 6 ft.). ☐

24. There is a telephone in the pool area with numbers of rescue and emergency agencies. ☐

25. Emergency equipment including a spineboard has been provided. ☐

26. The steps leading into the pool have a black edge to make them visible to underwater swimmers. ☐

27. Bottom drain covers are securely fastened to prevent their removal by children. ☐

28. The diving stands are equipped with guard rails which extend at least one foot over the water. ☐

29. Water slide is located in water at least 8 feet deep. ☐

30. The deck is made of non-slip material. ☐

RULING BODIES OF COMPETITIVE SWIMMING AND DIVING

USS (United States
Swimming, Inc.)
1750 East Boulder St.
Colorado Springs, CO 80909

USD (United States Diving, Inc.)
901 West New York Street
Indianapolis, IN 46202

NCAA (National Collegiate
Athletic Association)
P.O. Box 1906
Shawnee Mission, KS 66201

NFHSAA (National Federation of
State High School Athletic
Associations)
11724 Plaza Circle
Box 20626
Kansas City, MO 64195

FINA (Federation International De
Natation Amateur)
2000 Financial Center
Des Moines, IA 50309

SELECTED REFERENCES

Batterman, CHarles. **The Techniques of Springboard Diving.** Cambridge, Massachusetts: MIT Press, 1968.

Coates, Edward and Flynn, Richard B., eds. **Planning Facilities for Athletics, Physical Education and Recreation.** Washington, D.C.: AAHPERD and The Athletic Institute, 1979.

Conferences for National Cooperation in Aquatics. **Lifeguard Training Manual.** New York: Association Press, 1964.

Dawes, John. **Design and Planning of Swimming Pools.** Boston: CBI Pub., 1979.

Gabrielsen, M. Alexander, ed. **Swimming Pools: A Guide to Their Planning, Design and Operation.** 3rd Edition. A project of the Council for National Cooperation in Aquatics. Fort Lauderdale: Hoffman Publications, 1975.

Gabrielsen, Spears, and Gabrielsen. **Aquatics Handbook.** 2nd Edition. Englewood Cliffs, New Jersey: Prentice-Hall, 1968.

Graves, Charles M. "Making Community Swimming Pools Profitable." **Parks and Recreation** 17 (April 1982): 30-34.

Hunsaker, D.J. "Designing a Natatorium." **Journal of Physical Education, Recreation, and Dance** 54 (June 1983): 20, 21, 38.

IES Lighting Handbook. 5th Edition. New York: Illuminating Engineering Society of North America, 1981.

Lee, Dr. Sammy. **Diving.** New York: Atheneum, 1979.

Lifeguard Training. Washington, D.C.: American National Red Cross, 1983.

Minimum Standards for Public Swimming Pools. Washington: National Swimming Pool Institute, 1977.

1984 NCAA Men's Water Polo Rules. Mission, Kansas: National Collegiate Athletic Association (NCAA), 1984.

1984 NCAA Men's and Women's Swimming and Diving Rules. Mission, Kansas: National Collegiate Athletic Association (NCAA), 1984.

Perkins, Philip H. **Swimming Pools.** London: Elsevier Publishing Co., Ltd., 1971.

Rachman, George. **Diving Complete.** London: Faber and Faber, Ltd., 1975.

Safety in Aquatic Activities. Monograph #6. Washington, D.C.: American Alliance for Health, Physical Education and Recreation, 1980.

Suggested Ordinances and Regulations Covering Public Swimming Pools. New York: American Public Health Association, 1981.

Swimming and Water Safety. Washington, D.C.: American National Red Cross, 1968.

Thomas, David G. **Swimming Pool Operators Handbook.** Washington, D.C.: National Swimming Pool Foundation, 1972.

Torney, John and Clayton, Robert. **Aquatic Organization and Management.** Minneapolis: Burgess Publishing Co., 1982.

U.S. Department of Health, Education, and Welfare. **Swimming Pools: Safety and Disease Control through Proper Design and Operation.** Atlanta: HEW Publication No. (CDC) 76-8319, Public Health Service, Center for Disease Control, 1976.

U.S. Lifesaving Association. **Lifesaving and Marine Safety.** New York: Association Press, 1981.

CHAPTER V
Encapsulated Spaces and Stadiums

The term "encapsulated space" by definition refers to surrounded, encased, or protected space. In common usage, the term has come to refer to any sport building or relatively large enclosed space, including fieldhouses, domed stadiums, natatoriums, ice rinks, arenas, tennis centers, auditoriums, and warehouses. This chapter will be limited primarily to analysis of the fieldhouse and stadium, with a brief review of the large physical education/recreation center.

Fieldhouses were first constructed in the United States to meet storage needs near outdoor sports fields. In inclement weather, it was a natural step to move practice periods for outdoor sports under the roof and onto the dirt floors of the fieldhouse. As the structures became more sophisticated, dirt floors became unacceptable, and flooring surfaces were added which included wood, asphalt, urethane, and artificial turfs. Designers began to include locker and team rooms, full plumbing facilities, offices, and spectator accommodations providing wider indoor recreational and instructional usage.

Stadiums are built more specifically for exhibition purposes with mass seating. In addition to competitive athletic events, these structures are often used for such

purposes as convocations, concerts, mass meetings and rallies. If located near educational facilities, they are also used for instructional purposes.

Too often, single purpose facilities are not cost efficient and they become liabilities rather than assets. Many large spaces, constructed primarily to serve an athletic team, become financially self-supporting only by serving a variety of other events. The continual emergence of new synthetic materials, improved building techniques, and changing program needs complicates the selection of an appropriate athletic/physical education/recreation facility. Certainly the trend is to construct multi-purpose buildings with the flexibility to adapt to a number of diverse needs. More than ever before, facility planners are exploring a multitude of avenues to respond to the need served by the traditional fieldhouse.

GENERAL PLANNING CONSIDERATIONS

To ensure that the facility will meet the intended needs of users, whether students, faculty, professionals, or the general public, a preliminary study should include a survey of existing facilities and resources; present

and projected physical education, athletic, club or recreational programs; maintenance requirements; tournament and mass meeting requirements; and landscaping and parking needs. Ultimately, architectural design should take into account the survey findings as well as general terrain, regional building styles, practicality, diverse materials, and aesthetics.

The plans and specifications must conform both to state and local regulations and to accepted standards and practices. The building committee must understand its role; to coordinate, approve, recommend, support, challenge, advocate and deny. It is a task with many ramifications. When an institution has determined that more space is needed for current or projected programs, exploratory meetings are essential for determining what to build and how to build it. Remember that the technology is available to build whatever can be envisioned, and, in the early stages, all ideas are valuable.

LOCATION

The location of the facility must take into consideration accessibility, drainage, aesthetics, landscape and topography, property lines and easements, utilities, ecological and biological conditions, parking, and security.

The facility should be accessible to those who use it most frequently. Therefore, it usually should be located near dormitories and physical education buildings. The facilities open to spectators should be easily accessible to the public and, at the same time, separated from other buildings. An analysis of the anticipated pedestrian traffic flow in the building will pay enormous dividends In terms of efficient supervision and lower maintenance costs.

Facilities should be located to permit expansion. Attention should also be given to the slope of the land outside the buildings to assure surface drainage. Engineering features for foundations, reinforcement, drainage, pumps, and valves should be carefully assessed.

The facility should be located in attractive surroundings and should be pleasing in design. The design should be functional rather than traditional. It is possible for an architect to plan a building that will be modern and functional but still blend in with the existing architecture of an area. An effort should be made to locate the structure away from industrial and congested areas.

Adequate parking areas adjacent to the facility, with a paved access roadway leading to the building, are necessary. When admission is charged for parking, a fence with a minimum height of seven feet surrounding the spectator structure and the enclosed field is essential. Gates are necessary for spectator and service entrances and exits. Admission gates should be located near the parking lots and other main approaches to the structure. The number and size of the entrances depends on the projected and potential attendance. Exits should permit the crowd to vacate the enclosure within 10 minutes. Twenty-two inches of linear exit space should be permitted for each 500 spectators or as specified by local building code. At least one gate 14 feet high and 14 feet wide should be provided to accommodate trucks and buses.

FIELDHOUSES

Today, the building most commonly known as the "fieldhouse" is a structure that encloses a large sports area for physical activities that do not warrant an expensive, monumental school structure. Instead, the activity area is enclosed by low-cost construction. The structure, a competitive necessity in cold weather climates, is common in the northern latitudes.

Time and acceptance of low-cost construction has made it difficult to differentiate between the gymnasiums built in recent years and the fieldhouse of earlier decades. Historically, the gymnasium was a small enclosed area for indoor sports surrounded by the main school structure. Today it is a large expanse located in a wing of the building or in a separate building. In many cases, the gymnasium and fieldhouse have become synonymous.

Typical education functions performed in the fieldhouse include instruction in the physical education program; practice for intercollegiate athletics; intramural, interscholastic or intercollegiate competition; informal play; horseback riding; exhibitions; commencement exercises; registration; and final examinations. Community uses may include concerts, exhibits and mass meetings. (Figures 5-1; 1A)

Location and Size

Some institutions may wish to plan a fieldhouse in connection with a stadium or arena. In this case, consideration should be given to combining the two structures in such a manner that the back wall of the stadium may

Figure 5-1, 1A
The multi-purpose pavilion at Boston State University supports a variety of events.

Encapsulated Spaces and Stadiums

Figure 5-2, 2A
Exterior and interior views of satellite recreation building at Ohio State University.

serve as one of the sidewalls of the fieldhouse. Such a plan may have interesting possibilities, both from the standpoint of economy and effective development of the areas under the stadium.

If the fieldhouse is needed for class instruction on a campus, the preferable location is adjacent to the main gymnasium building and natatorium. If space is not available in proximity to the gymnasium, the fieldhouse will effectively service the intramural activities and intercollegiate sports, even though it is constructed in a peripheral area of the campus. It should, however, be placed in an area contiguous to athletic fields and free from critical parking problems.

A recent innovation on some large university campuses are satellite fieldhouses, developed at several locations on campus contiguous to the dormitories or living quarters. This makes recreational areas immediately available to the students and eliminates the need for locker room facilities at the site. Locating facilities "where the students are" promotes recreational participation and reduces parking problems at the central area facility. (Figures 5-2; 2A)

The size of the fieldhouse should be determined by careful study of the present and future needs of programs in athletics, physical education, and recreation; climatic conditions of the area; existing facilities; and available funds. Consideration should be given to the size and make-up of

the population likely to use the facility simultaneously.

The minimum length of the fieldhouse should accommodate at least a 60-meter straightaway for track, plus sufficient distance for starting and stopping. A wide door at the end of the straightaway, to permit competitors to run outside the fieldhouse, will prevent injuries and eliminate a psychological hazard where space is limited. Six lanes are desirable. Field level entrances for the public should be sharply limited to prevent collisions between runners and other individuals. The track size should be compatible with the demands of competitive running events.

The area surrounded by a one-eighth meter track can include the following facilities: a regulation basketball court (or several basketball cross-courts), tennis courts, long jump, high-jump and pole-vault runways and pits, and a shot-put area. It is preferable to isolate the shot-put area at one end of the building. Portable pit boxes can be brought within the track oval for shot-put, high-jumping and pole-vaulting during meets attracting spectators. The minimum width required to house a baseball infield is 125 feet.

If the facility serves a variety of activities, it may be desirable to locate the long jump/triple jump pit in one corner. If a synthetic floor surface is used, space efficiency can be increased by cutting out a portion with a sand pit beneath it. The cut out portion, which needs

to fit tightly, can be replaced when indoor track meets are not in session.

Thus, the size of the facility depends in large part on the kinds of activities it will house and the number of participants. Dimensions of the activity area should not be less than 150 by 250 feet. The practical number of square feet per person is determined on a sliding scale. Under normal circumstances, a college of 1,000 students requires 18 to 20 square feet per student, while for a large institution the figure decreases to 12 to 15 square feet per student.

The height of the structure will be determined by the number and location of the balconies to be provided. The fieldhouse must be able to accommodate crowds effectively and safely, particularly when many different types of activities are scheduled.

Fieldhouse Encapsulation

The encapsulation of vast surface areas to accommodate multipurpose field layouts has created the opportunity to develop a variety of construction techniques. Tensile structures, systems engineered buildings with modular capabilities, geodesic domes, and air-supported membranes are examples of building designs that have been successfully used in fieldhouse development.

Systems Construction

The term "systems

construction" commonly refers to buildings consisting of pre-designed, pre-engineered, factory-constructed units shipped to the site for installation. The layman usually refers to these buildings as prefabricated or modular buildings. These buildings offer a wide range of possibilities for exterior and interior design. Systems building was introduced in the United States in 1962, and, interestingly enough, schools were major clients. The one-level sprawling schools that dot so much of the American landscape are testimony to the systems approach. More sophisticated designs and technology now enable facilities to be built in this fashion while escaping sameness of appearance.

The prolonged construction time of many projects renders buildings obsolete the day they are completed. A viable school building program, therefore, depends in large measure on effecting economies in both time and money. Systems construction has managed to control the length of building time and subsequently the cost of construction.

Ideally, systems building comprises four stages:

1. Study of user requirements.
2. Establishment of performance standards for the building subsystems or the entire system.

3. Integration of individual building subsystems into a coordinated building system.
4. Testing of components (or subsystems) to assure that they satisfy performance standards.

One begins, always, by describing the way in which a facility must work. Then portions of the project are isolated for open, competitive bidding, creating a series of solutions, or subsystems. It is a condition of each solution that it must integrate with all the others, a requirement that fosters cooperative efforts on the part of many subcontractors.

Construction systems are erected quickly, enabling inside work to proceed uninterrupted by unfavorable weather. Site construction depends on a builder's ability to apply the modular systems to a particular type of structure. The full value in systems construction depends on the builder's performance in fitting the pieces together.

One advantage of systems building is "fast track scheduling." This technique saves time and thereby reduces construction money. The system permits several construction steps that normally follow one another to proceed simultaneously, resulting in significant time savings. The theory behind fast tracking holds that any phase of a project can be

begun on a foundation of generalized knowledge. The specific needs can be determined at a later date without sacrificing efficiency in either the design or construction processes. The necessary beginning drawings for the systems portion of the project can be issued as soon as basic design decisions are reached. This enables the architect to apply fast track scheduling. Consequently, those parts of the building which require the most time, such as foundations may be begun immediately.

The modular concept is employed in the construction of the popular fieldhouse/arena activities center with the hyperbolic paraboloid architectural style. Any number of modules are developed, and the activities spaces are placed inside the building. Additional modules can be added as needed at a future date. (Figures 5-3; 3A)

Geodesic Dome

A geodesic dome offers another option in encapsulation. Basically, a geodesic dome is a "framework to enclose space." In this context it is encapsulating space. In technical language a geodesic dome is the result of a series of physical and complex mathematical properties that create a lightweight, strong,

Figure 5-3, 3A
A hyperbolic paraboloid design for the Lifesport Center at Albright College in Reading, Pennsylvania.

Encapsulated Spaces and Stadiums

transportable and economical structure that can be used in a multitude of ways. It is made by precisely interlocking triangles which appear as a series of hexagons on a completed building. Enormous spans and heights can be achieved, including a complete sphere, without the need of inside support walls. The familiar half-sphere shape has given way to many complicated shapes as engineering knowledge and confidence has progressed.

Fabric Structures

A fairly recent development in the area of physical education, recreation, and athletic facilities is the concept of fabric structures. The fabric used most commonly is a Teflon coated fiberglass material. The fiberglass yarn is pound for pound stronger than steel and is less expensive. It can withstand temperatures of 1300 to 1500 degrees Fahrenheit and is not affected by cold or the ultraviolet rays of the sun. Fabric structures offer a number of advantages over other types of construction:

- Lower Initial Cost — Initial costs are usually less than with conventional construction. Several factors contribute to this, the main one being weight.

A fabric roof is about 1/30 the weight of a conventional steel truss roof. This reduced weight means that the walls, footings, and foundations are not required to be nearly so strong as in a conventional building.

- Less Construction Time — The amount of construction time is directly related to the initial cost of the structure. The total time necessary to build a fabric roof is usually less than for a conventional roof.
- Natural Lighting — Since the fiberglass fabric material which is used is translucent, it results in a high quality of interior natural lighting. Without using artificial lights during the day, the light intensity inside can vary anywhere from 100 to 1000 footcandles, depending on weather conditions. The interior light is considered of high quality because it is non-glare and shadow-free.
- Lower Energy Costs — In some climates or regions, energy costs may be substantially reduced by

the fabric's translucency which may eliminate the need for artificial daytime lighting. The energy costs required for air conditioning to overcome the heat generated by the artificial lights also are reduced.

- Less Maintenance — The non-stick characteristics of Teflon allows the fabric to be washed clean each time it rains.
- Full Utilization of Space — Depending on the fabric structure's configuration and support, the area that can be encapsulated is almost limitless.

There are two basic types of fabric structures being utilized today. These two types are tension structures and air-supported structures. Tension structures are made by stretching the fabric across between rigid supports. Air structures are sealed buildings which maintain a positive internal air pressure for support. They are actually inflated like a balloon and must maintain the positive air pressure to remain inflated.

Tension Structures

Some projects lend themselves more naturally to tension structures than to air-supported

Figure 5-4, 4A
Interior and exterior views of LaVerne College Student Center and Drama Center.

structures. Some of the conditions in which a tension structure may be preferable are as follows:

- Free and open access from the sides is desirable or required.
- A unique design or aesthetics are of importance.
- The facility will be largely unattended or not monitored.
- Possible deflation of an air-supported structure would constitute a severe operational or safety problem.
- A retrofit to an existing conventional building structure such as a swimming pool or an outdoor stadium is desired.

Examples

La Verne College — La Verne College in La Verne, California, contains the first permanent enclosed fiberglass structure in the United States. The tent-like structure covers 1.4 acres with the fabric roof having been erected in just three days. Called the Campus Center, it contains a gym seating 900 people. Men's and women's locker rooms, offices, the campus bookstore, and a lecture area are also located inside. A smaller separate structure houses

the drama center. Completed in 1973.

Hanover Park — This city-owned community and recreation center is located in Hanover Park, Illinois. The center houses six tennis courts and a gymnasium. Completed in 1976.

Lindsay Park — The Lindsay Park Sports Centre in Calgary, Alberta, Canada, houses a 50-meter pool, diving pool, a fully equipped 30,000 square foot gymnasium, and a 200-meter running track. It incorporates an insulation with the fabric roof which gives it an R-value of 16 compared with the R-value of 2 common in most fabric roofs. Despite the great improvement in insulating qualities, the fabric roof is still transparent enough to allow for an interior illumination of 200 footcandles. Completed in 1983.

Air-Supported Structures

There are two basic types of air-supported structures. These are the large permanent air structures and smaller, more portable, air structures. This section will discuss the large air structures.

Air-supported fabric structures are supported by a positive air pressure within a totally enclosed structure. This positive air pressure is produced by a group of large fans. In conventional

structures the internal columns, walls, and foundations must support a roof weight of from 10 to 40 pounds per square foot. On the other hand, in air-supported structures, a roof weight of about one pound per square foot is transmitted directly to the ground by columns of air. This increased air pressure of about 4 or 5 pounds per square foot greater than ambient pressure is usually unnoticed by the building's occupants. Some of the instances when an air structure may be preferable to a tension structure are:

- When column-free spans of greater than 150 feet are desired.
- When large, column-free spans are desired at a cost which is greatly reduced compared to conventional structures. In fact, cost-per-unit area usually decreases as the size of the span increases.
- When a low silhouette is desired.

Examples

The U.S. Pavilion — The first large air-supported fabric structure in the world was the U.S. Pavilion at Expo '70 in Osaka, Japan. This pioneering low-profile, cable-restrained, air-supported roof

Figure 5-5, 5A
University of Northern Iowa Unit Dome has fiberglass membrane covering with Teflon coating. It has a cable suspension system combined with an air support system.

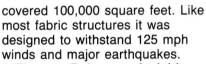

Figure 5-6, 6A
The Hubert H. Humphrey Metrodome has brought indoor professional baseball and football to fans in Minneapolis, Minnesota.

covered 100,000 square feet. Like most fabric structures it was designed to withstand 125 mph winds and major earthquakes.

Thomas E. Leavey Activities Center — This physical education and athletic complex is at the University of Santa Clara in Santa Clara, California. It contains a 5,000 seat arena for basketball and volleyball along with racquetball courts, wrestling, gymnastics, weight training and conditioning areas, conference rooms, staff offices, and a 25-meter swimming pool. The pool is covered by a separate fabric roof which can be removed in the summertime, converting the structure into an outdoor pool. Completed in 1974.

DakotaDome — Located at the University of South Dakota in Vermillion, South Dakota, the DakotaDome contains five basketball courts, volleyball courts, two tennis courts, an eight-lane 200-meter track, four racquetball courts, a six-lane 25-meter pool, locker rooms, athletic department offices, and classrooms. The main floor is a synthetic surface which is used for most court activities, and has an artificial turf football field which can be rolled out on top for football, soccer, and other field events. When the facility is set up for football, there is seating for 12,000 spectators. The entire facility was built for about $51 per

square foot. Completed in 1978.

Carrier Dome — The Carrier Dome in Syracuse, New York, is the home of Syracuse University athletics. This stadium seats 50,000 for football and 25,000 for basketball. Also a great bargain, the total construction cost was $27,715,000, which figures out to $554 per seat. This is very inexpensive when compared to conventional covered stadiums. Completed in 1980.

Others:
Uni-Dome — University of Northern Iowa, 1975.

Steve Lacy Field House — Milligan College, Milligan, Tennessee, 1974.

Sun Dome — University of South Florida, Tampa, Florida, 1981.

Silverdome — Pontiac, Michigan, 1975.

Metrodome — Minneapolis, Minnesota, 1982.

B.C. Place Amphitheater — Vancouver, B.C., Canada, 1983.

Hoosier Dome — Indianapolis, Indiana, 1984.

Small Air-Structures

This section will discuss the merits of the smaller and more portable air structures. Air structures work well as environmental covers placed over existing recreational areas and, for many institutions, the "bubble" is

the answer to an increasing need for large activity areas at a nominal cost. Cost savings are in proportion to the size of the space to be covered. Spaces over 300 square feet usually bring a cost savings when compared to conventional roofing. Because of heat gain, which seems to present a more severe problem than heat loss, the northern areas of the United States seem better suited for environmental covers. There are numerous playing fields around schools and colleges which lend themselves easily to air fabric encapsulation.

Canadian Architecture listed the following advantages and disadvantages of air structure technology:

Advantages

• *Low initial cost.* Air shelters allow a client with a small capital budget to acquire a facility that could not be obtained if conventional construction techniques were employed.

• *Speed of erection.* The actual erection of the envelope takes only one or two days. However, additional time is required for the ground work, site services, foundation, anchorage, flooring, and installation of mechanical and electrical equipment. Only minimal field labor is needed.

• *Ease of deflation, inflation, and repair.* Deflation and inflation of the fabric envelope does not require skilled labor. Many existing structures come supplied with repair kits. (The repair of a major fault requires skill and special equipment such as that needed for electronic fabric welding.)

• *Portability.* When deflated and packed, the fabric envelope can be stored in a small space or easily transported elsewhere for storage or use. Depending on the size of the envelope, deflation and packing usually requires one or two days.

• *Adaptability for temporary functions.* For temporary use, the air-supported structure has definite physical and financial advantages over a conventional building. A number of manufacturers are now preparing to lease their air-supported structures, which will increase their attractiveness for short-term use.

• *Long-span and high-ceiling features.* Clear and unobstructed spaces is an inherent feature of the structure. Conventional long-span and high-ceiling structures are much more expensive. When the intended function demands these structure attributes, the air-supported structure may have a definite economic advantage.

• *Integrated heating, ventilation, and air-pressure system.* The integrated system is also an inherent principle. Lengthy duct works and pipe works are not required. The warm-up time of the space is a matter of minutes.

• *Maximum use of daylight illumination.* Translucency is characteristic of some kinds of envelope fabrics. Artificial lighting is minimized during daytime use.

Disadvantages

• *Limited portability in certain applications.* The degree of portability depends on the type of construction (concrete foundations and most conventional flooring), and site services such as gas and electricity are not portable.

• *Life span.* The fabric envelope in use today has a life expectancy

of up to 25 years, with longer-life materials being tested. All other items such as the foundation, flooring, and mechanical equipment have the life span of a conventional building.

• *Poor thermal insulation.* The cost of heating is a significant factor and should be evaluated against that for a conventional building over time. During winter months when the heat is required to melt the snow or to cause it to slide off, a safe level of temperature will have to be maintained at all times at the expense of heating costs. If the bubble is not to be heated during the inactive hours, it will have to be supervised constantly for the dangers of unexpected snowfall. In the summertime the heat gain of the air-supported structure poses a cooling problem.

• *Acoustic problem.* The curved shape of the air-supported structure produces a peculiar acoustic environment. This poses limitations on its use for large gatherings and open-plan arrangements for different groups.

• *Pressure.* Although the air pressure in the structure is only one inch of water column, some sensitive people feel a slight effect on their eardrums, particularly at the moment of entering the structure.

• *Uncertain performance over a long-term period.* Although the structure has undergone numerous tests by recognized laboratories, many long-term predictions are extrapolated from short-time tests. Some regard this kind of "accelerated test" as of little use, whereas others place great faith in it. Because of the short history of this type of structure, it is not yet possible to demonstrate performance value over time.

• *Restriction due to wind.* In winds of hurricane velocity, most codes require that the structure be evacuated.

The true capabilities of encapsulated space have barely been uncovered. With today's advanced technology, and with

creative minds in the architecture, engineering and physical education professions, future facilities for sports can reasonably be expected to be technically sound, programmatically utilitarian and aesthetically pleasing.

New Ideas

A recent development in the construction of fabric structures is the idea of combining both an air-supported roof and a tension roof in the same building. An example of this concept is the **Stephen C. O'Connell Center.** This physical education, recreation, and athletic complex is located at the University of Florida at Gainesville. This was the first structure to combine both air-supported and tension roofs in one building. The center or main arena is covered by a large air-inflated dome while the outer areas of the building are the tension-covered spaces. The main arena has an indoor track and can seat 10,400 spectators for basketball. Located under the tension-supported areas are a gymnastics studio, dance studio, weight room, locker rooms, offices, and a 3000-seat, 50-meter natatorium. Like most fabric structures, this facility was a bargain. The total construction cost was $11,954,418 which comes out to about $49 per square foot. Completed in 1980.

Since the concept of fabric structures is still quite new, not all the problems have been resolved. However, each new fabric structure appears to have fewer problems and to be an improvement over those built previously.

Wooden Domes

Another recent development in the area of encapsulated spaces are wooden domes. These spherical wooden structures have several advantages over conventional structures. Column-free spans of up to 800 feet are possible, and they are

Encapsulated Spaces and Stadiums

generally easier to build. There are several wooden dome structures around the country ranging from high school gymnasiums to very large arenas.

Examples

J. Lawrence Walkup Skydome — This laminated wood dome is located at Northern Arizona University in Flagstaff, Arizona. Opened in 1977, the Skydome is 502 feet across and covers 6.2 acres. It contains a full size, roll-up, synthetic football/soccer field, a professional sized ice hockey rink, a 1/5 mile running track, a portable wood basketball court, and has seating for more than 15,000 people. The total construction cost was $8.3 million, or about $620 per seat.

Tacoma Dome — The Tacoma Dome in Tacoma, Washington, was opened in 1983. This $44 million multi-purpose complex is 530 feet across and is presently the largest wooden dome in the world. It can seat 20,722 for football, 25,138 for basketball, and contains a permanent ice hockey rink.

Conventional Design

Although building to encompass large areas in the fieldhouse concept will satisfy many of the activities which meet the needs of individuals, there is still the necessity to house other teaching areas in smaller sectors or isolated teaching stations. Thus, the conventional design still remains popular when program needs dictate.

The architectural style is generally designed to conform with the municipal or campus surroundings. Function, rather than appearance, should determine the building style ultimately accepted.

Many of the larger complexes have been built to incorporate the fieldhouse as a segment of the total building.

Figure 5-7
Recently remodeled, the Munster High School Fieldhouse in Munster, Indiana incorporates wooden arches.

Fieldhouse Floors

The floor of the fieldhouse should be resistant to weather and heavy usage. Dirt floors are not recommended. Rubber asphalt, urethane, and poly vinyl chloride synthetics are most commonly used in multipurpose areas. Wood, still a popular flooring, is sometimes used in combination with synthetics when basketball and volleyball are located in the fieldhouse.

Lighting, Heating and Ventilation

Windows should be located to prevent the interference of sunlight with player performance at any time during the day. Walls and ceilings should be light in color. Catwalks are necessary for servicing the ceiling lights, spotlights and drop nets for partitioning.

Condensation problems should be given major consideration, particularly where extreme temperatures require sprinkling of surface or dirt areas, or when large crowds witness events in the fieldhouse. To promote reabsorption of excess condensation, the building should be heated by the circulation of warm air in addition to radiant heat. Adequate means should be provided to supply and exhaust air. The walls inside and outside should be impervious to vapor pressure. Technical heating, ventilating, and lighting problems should be referred to a specialist. In the typical fieldhouse, which includes a tunnel vault roof, there should be no parapets.

Bleachers and Balconies

Permanent seating facilities may be provided in a balcony and on the level of the playing floor. Because permanent seats restrict the use of a floor space, they should not be used at the level of the playing floor in such a facility.

The height of the last row of seats is determined by the number of rows and the increased elevation of each. The height of the seating surface of the first row should be 22 inches from the floor, and each successive row should be 8.5 to 11.5 inches higher than the preceding one.

The width of each seating space should not be less than 18 inches. The required space per person will vary from 2.7 to 3 square feet. Sight lines should be considered in relation to the increase in elevation between successive rows. Spectators should have focal points of vision at the court boundary line nearest the seats. Focal points more than three feet above those boundary lines are unsatisfactory.

When bleachers are extended, the first row should be at least 10 feet away from the court sidelines and end lines. The depth of closed bleachers varies from 3 feet for 10 rows to 4.5 to 7.5 feet for 23 rows.

The elevated seating deck or platform can be used to supplement the number of seats provided at floor level. Removable bleachers for the deck should be the same as those used at floor level. By adopting this design, planners provide additional activity space on the deck and in the area under it. The depth of the deck depends upon the number of bleacher rows. Temporary bleachers should be thoroughly inspected before they are used, and their capacity should never be taxed.

Balconies may be constructed to provide seats to supplement retractable bleachers at court level and on the elevated deck. They can be either a continuation of retractable bleachers or elevated above them and extended partially over the seating at a lower level. Balcony seats may have backs or be similar to those for stadiums.

When permanent balconies are planned, they should be constructed without supporting pillars that would interfere in any way with the playing or visual area. They should be served by ramps connecting directly, or by means of wide corridors with convenient entrances and exits. Ramps have a slope of at least one-foot rise in 12 feet. Minimum landings are 5 by 5 feet and extend at least one foot beyond

the swinging area of a door. The ramps should have at least a 6-foot clearance at the bottom and level platforms at 30-foot intervals on every turn.

The fieldhouse should be so designed that the normal flow of traffic will not encroach upon the activity areas, to avoid interference with instruction and participation and to decrease maintenance costs. Permanent seating should be kept to a minimum in areas used primarily for instruction. Roll-away bleachers are preferable.

In areas designed primarily for basketball, spectators should enter and exit at a single level at various points around the circumference, from an exterior perimeter walkway. Designers may decide on the use of a continuous cross aisle connected through the exit tunnel to the concourse. In such a design, all seats above this cross aisle are accessible only by means of stairs at each exit tunnel, while the lower seats can be reached from the vertical aisles connecting the main cross aisle. This system simplifies the flow of spectators to and from an event and allows for efficient management and control at one level. A portion of the lower seats are attached to telescopic platforms, which roll back into wall pockets when a larger arena floor is desired.

To determine requirements for ramps, stairs, exits, doors,

corridors, and fire-alarm systems, planners should consult local and state laws and the local safety and fire codes.

Accommodations for Public Events

Scoreboard and timing devices should be of sufficient number and so placed as to be readily seen by players and all spectators. They should be easy to operate and readily accessible for maintenance purposes. Provision should be made for installation of a public address system. Acoustical treatment of the building is desirable.

Accommodations for reporters, sports broadcasters, and talent scouts should be planned in the original design. Sound-proof broadcasting and television booths should be provided for these services if the fieldhouse will be used for attractions of considerable public interest. At basketball games, however, the working press prefers to be as close to the action as possible, and space should be provided at courtside.

When the fieldhouse is designed to accommodate large crowds, concession booths should be constructed. They should be equipped with electric or gas stoves, sinks, running water, and sewer connections and should be located where they do not interfere with the normal flow of traffic. The

Figure 5-8
The Welsh-Ryan Arena at Northwestern University utilizes long spinning steel arches.

Encapsulated Spaces and Stadiums

booths should be accessible from all seats. Approximately 100 square feet per 1,000 spectators should be allowed for permanent concession booths.

Entrances and Exits

Entrances to the fieldhouse should be located with reference to parking and traffic approaches. Provisions should be made for a paved access roadway and at least one entrance large enough to accommodate trucks. The main body should be of sufficient size to accommodate anticipated crowds checking tickets and admission, particularly in northern climates.

The lobby should be designed for ticket selling and collecting so that the traffic will flow in a straight line, or nearly so, from the entrances to the box office to the ticket collectors. To avoid congestion, approximately two-thirds of the lobby should be planned for accommodating box offices and ticket purchasers. The remainder should be reserved for ticket holders, who should have direct access to admission gates.

The seating capacity and the number of seats in each section will determine the number of entrances and exits required. It is important that spectators be dispersed speedily. It is highly desirable to have exit ramps leading from stepped aisles. Ramps, stairs, and passageways

should be as wide as the deck aisles served. Stairs or ramps not opening directly into a street or open space should have lanes at least 20 feet wide leading out of the area.

Service and Auxiliary Units

If the fieldhouse is adjacent to the main gymnasium building and the natatorium, the requirements for lockers, showers, and toilets can, in some instances, be reduced. An underpass from the gymnasium to the fieldhouse may be desirable to make the gymnasium service units available to some participants in the fieldhouse. If the fieldhouse is not adjacent to the gymnasium, consideration should be given to the erection of a small building or basement, simple in design, with dressing, shower and toilet facilities, rather than use space for such purposes that might be used more advantageously for sports activities.

Convenient and accessible dressing units (for men **and** women) equipped with chalk and tack boards for the home and visiting teams should be provided. When the fieldhouse is to be used for interscholastic basketball tournaments and indoor track meets, consideration should be given to providing separate locker rooms with adjoining shower and toilet facilities. These units could

be used regularly throughout the year by intramural participants and intercollegiate squads. It is desirable to provide passageways from dressing rooms directly to the basketball floor to avoid crowd interference.

Dressing rooms with adjoining shower and toilet facilities should be provided for male and female staff members. These accommodations can also be used by game officials.

Separate toilet facilities in sufficient number for men and women spectators should be provided close to the seating areas. Toilets should be provided near traffic lanes. Where large crowds attend games, it is advisable to place supplementary toilet facilities off the main lobby. The number of authorized building users, the capacity of spectator seating, and the local building codes will dictate the number of toilet facilities required.

A room for first-aid treatment should be provided if the fieldhouse program is planned to attract spectators. This room may also serve the purpose of a training room for emergency treatment of injuries.

Provision for a lounge room may be advisable after consideration of such factors as available space and funds as well as the functions of such a room for clubs, members of athletic squads, letter

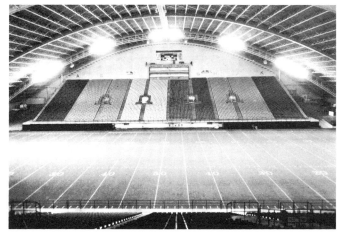 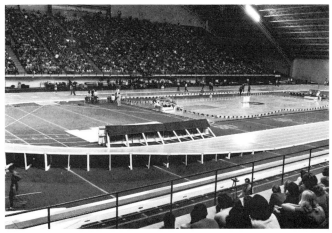

Figure 5-9, 9A
Two interior views of Idaho State Mini Dome shows flexibility of dome design.

men, officials and coaches, and visitors. An adjoining kitchenette is desirable.

Storage Space

Many fieldhouses are constructed with insufficient storage space. It is essential to have adequate and conveniently placed storage space if the facilities are to be fully usable.

Space should be provided for equipment and supplies for the physical education, athletic, and recreational programs. Supply rooms should be large enough so that supplies and equipment can be cared for and issued from them. Shelves in storage rooms should be slanted toward the wall.

After a building is completed, it is impossible to add storage space unless that space is taken from areas designed for other uses. Thoughtful planning of storage space should be done when setting forth total space needs. Adequate maintenance and control over supplies and equipment is possible only when proper storage space is available.

A major consideration in connection with storage is the provision of adequate entrances to storage areas. A loading dock and elevator may also be required, depending on the type of supplies and equipment to be used.

STADIUMS

This consideration of stadiums is primarily concerned with the type of structure frequently needed for school and community use, with a capacity of 10,000 or less and with limited spectator accommodations. It should be obvious, however, that the basic considerations for such structures will also apply to larger units. Those responsible for planning stadiums should keep in mind that their creation is an integral part of the physical education, recreational, and athletic programs of the school and community.

For the purposes of this section, the terms "spectator structure"
and "seating structure" include both permanent and temporary outdoor seating facilities, while the word stadium refers only to permanent accommodations. Spectator structures provide seating from which people can satisfactorily view athletic events without inhibiting the activities of the participants. Seating structures can be justified more readily if they have multiple uses. In addition to serving athletic contests, these facilities can be used for concerts, conventions, patriotic observances, plays and pageants, lectures, commencement exercises, and other mass gatherings.

The space underneath a stadium may provide physical education and activity areas. These facilities should supplement rather than duplicate existing units.

Seating Capacity

If possible, the seating capacity of a stadium should be sufficient to meet present needs, with plans for expansion to satisfy predicted needs for a period of at least 20 years. The number of seats required will be influenced by the sports served: enrollment of the school or college; population and socioeconomic status of the town, city and region; and planned expansion of the program. The provision of an excessive number of seats should be avoided because construction and maintenance costs make it impractical to provide accommodations that are seldom used.

Design

Rectangular spectator structures provide the most practical seating accommodations for field games, tennis, outdoor basketball, volleyball, and other outdoor sports, and special events or demonstrations. For baseball, a structure can be located parallel to either the first-base or third-base lines. The most favorable view of
tennis is from behind the ends of the courts. Seating facilities for other outdoor events should be adjacent to the activity area and as near as possible to the probable center of action consistent with the rules governing the activity.

Track-and-field spectator seating is generally parallel to the straightaway for the dashes. Some planners, however, have located spectator seating so that the structure angles gradually toward the straightaway end of the track. The front end of the structure nearest the starting line should be farther away from the track than the front end nearest the finish. This arrangement faces the spectators toward the most common center of continuing action.

The multiple use of a stadium for softball, baseball, and football often results from the desire to use existing floodlighting. In most cases, sufficient seating facilities can be provided with a small permanent structure or by relocating mobile bleachers used for football.

The combination baseball-football field should be avoided if possible, and especially if planners do not intend to use artificial turf. Superimposing an infield upon a portion of the gridiron makes undesirable viewing and playing conditions for football and soccer. A baseball area that overlaps a track-and-field site presents safety problems. Competitors have had serious collisions on such combined facilities.

Site and Location

A primary requisite for a satisfactory site is adequacy of size. The site must be large enough to accommodate the play and safety areas for the sport or sports to be conducted, the proposed present and future seating, and service areas. The site should be flat or easily leveled. However, natural inclines of the topography can be used for support or partial support of a structure. Surface drainage of a site and adjacent areas as well as the subsurface soils and geological formations should be considered.

Cities with two or more secondary schools should consider the construction of one stadium for their combined use. Teams from each school may practice on local fields and play their regular games at the stadium. If possible, the structure should be located on or adjacent to one of the schools' sites for reasons of greater accessibility, maximum use, and more efficient maintenance, operation, and supervision.

Seating Decks and Supports

The main considerations in planning spectator structures involve seating decks, deck supports, seats, and means of ingress and egress. Several factors should govern the selection of materials used for seating decks and deck supports, including expected capacity, intended use of the structure, availability of funds, climatic conditions, and desired aesthetic qualities.

Wood, stone, brick, steel, and reinforced concrete are the materials most frequently used. The inclusion of service and other facilities under the stadium makes mandatory a solid, continuous, and waterproof deck of either concrete or metal. Wooden treads and risers may be used if the underneath area will not be developed. Appearance, tensile strength, adaptability, exhaustability, durability, and cost of construction and maintenance are items that should guide the buyer in the selection of building materials.

Concrete, structural steel, wooden columns, and natural or artificial embankments serve as supports for decks of spectator structures. Reinforced concrete columns are generally used to support most wooden decks. The supporting structure of the stadium should rest upon foundations of concrete. The design of deck support should meet structural strength requirements of state and local building codes, and the supports should be so located that they provide unobstructed spaces of the appropriate dimensions to accommodate proposed uses of the underneath portion of the stadium.

Stress standards should be considered at all times in stadium construction. Regardless of the materials used, all spectator structures should be designed to meet the following specifications: to support, in addition to their own weight, a uniform distributed line load of not less than 100 pounds per square foot of gross horizontal projection; to resist a horizontal wind load of 30 pounds per square foot of all vertical projections; and to withstand a seat load of 24 pounds per linear foot of seats and a force of 10 pounds per linear foot applied in a direction perpendicular to the seats' length. Seating standards require that all seats and footboards carry line loads of not less than 120 pounds per linear foot.

Bent steel plates may be used in the construction of steel decks (prefabricated sections of treads and risers). This type of deck affords flexibility in expansion. A facility of this kind may be salvaged and moved to a new site, and it is a sturdy, durable, and watertight (if welded) structure. However, steel plates do tend to deteriorate if not painted regularly.

A structure with a seating capacity of less than 5,000 persons might be constructed of wooden treads and risers mounted on concrete, steel, or wooden substructures. The advantages of this type of construction are lower cost and portability. Deterioration of the wood and the almost constant maintenance problems are disadvantages.

Treads and Risers

In the seating deck of a spectator structure, the treads form the horizontal surface while vertical surfaces form the risers. To minimize expense, treads and risers should be as small as possible but sufficient in size for comfort and good view. The height of the first riser should be kept to a minimum because it affects the ultimate height of the entire structure and, therefore, the cost. The width of the treads is governed by factors of economy and comfort. A minimum depth of 24 inches is recommended for treads with backless seats. For structures without continuous seating decks, this measurement should be taken between the front edges of the seating surface of successive tiers. The minimum depth for tread supporting seats with backs is 30 inches. Tread widths remain constant except for the first tier, unless there is a railing, low wall, or fence in front; in which case, additional space is required for spectator movement.

Drainage must also be considered in the design of treads for solid decks. A forward slope of one-half to one inch per tread will permit water to drain off rapidly, in addition to facilitating hosing the deck for cleaning purposes. Gutters and drains should be included for large structures. The standards for the size of the drain are based on the minimum ratio of one square inch to each 300 square feet of deck surface served.

State and local building codes set standards for aisles, entrances, and portals for spectator structures. Planners should be cognizant of such codes. Aisles may not be necessary in small seating structures. For structures with many rows and larger capacities, aisles are necessary. Sections between aisles should contain tiers with 21-32 seats.

The first aisles should be located 11 to 16 seats from the ends of the structure. Horizontal walks are generally undesirable because persons using them will obstruct the sight lines of others. If such walks are used, the next tread above should be high enough to permit the spectators to look over those persons walking in front of them. In addition, the first tier of seats should be high enough to allow its occupants an unobstructed view.

Aisles should have a minimum width of 36 inches, and if divided by a portal or obstruction, each side should be at least 21 inches wide. Whenever the riser exceeds nine inches, an intermediate step is necessary.

The seating capacity and the number of seats in each section will determine the number of entrances and exits required. It is important that spectators be dispersed in a minimum amount of time. It is highly desirable to have exit ramps leading from stepped aisles. Ramps, stairs, and passageways should be as wide as the deck aisles served. Stairs or ramps not opening directly into a street or open space should have lanes of at least 20 feet in width leading out of the area.

Deck Walls and Railings

The ends, backs, and in some instances the fronts of the seating structures should be bordered by walls or a railing. These walls or railings should extend at least 12 inches above the treads and be designed to prevent spectators from sitting on them.

Sight Lines

Seating facilities should be constructed to provide spectators with a good view of the performance. Nearness and an unobstructed sight line to the desired points affect the quality of the accommodations. A sight line is a straight line from the eyes of the seated spectator, over the heads of others below, to a point on the field that represents the spot nearest the structure that should be in his field of vision.

Recommended focal points for sight lines are as follows: for football, the nearest side boundary lines; for baseball, several feet behind the catcher; for track, about knee-height of the runner in

the nearest lane; for side seating tennis, four feet in toward the seats from the doubles boundary line; and for end seating for tennis, 10 feet behind the base line.

Seating Arrangements

Considerations involved in the design of seating facilities include the nature of the contest, the comfort and convenience of spectators, proper balance of cost and comfort, stadium cleaning, and maintenance expenses.

Back supports are generally unnecessary in stadiums because of the nature of the activity and the added cost of such supports. For planning purposes, an area of two by two feet, or four square feet per seat, should be allowed for bench seats. The height of the seats above the foot-support treads should be between 16 and 18 inches. Some designers make no allowance for seating other than directly on the treads. However, elevated bench seats are more satisfactory.

Douglas fir, redwood, and southern cypress are the woods most used for bench construction. Such factors as decay resistance, bleeding, strength, silvering, and cross-section of grain warrant consideration in selecting the kind and quality of wood. Types of commercial covering that protect and aid in the maintenance of wooden seats should be investigated. Synthetic materials of plaster, Fiberglass, and the like, molded into seating structures, are now past the experimental stage. Extruded aluminum, natural in color, is fabricated into seats and may be found in many modern stadiums. The natural type is neither hot nor cold, withstands weather, defies insect destruction, and drains and dries quickly and cleanly.

Lighting and Electrical Facilities

General lighting and electrical outlets should be planned to satisfy the requirements of the

specific spectator structure. If night games are to played, illumination is necessary for all areas to be used by spectators. The playing areas should receive extra illumination in situations where the last row of seats is several hundred feet away from the action on the field. Uniform illumination is necessary for proper player judgment of the ball and its trajectory. Lighting must now be provided in terms of footcandles required for filming and television. Standards for the design and location of lights are published by the Illuminating Engineering Society.

Manufacturers have a wide variety of lighting systems, direct and indirect. Some of the most popularly used systems are mercury vapor, fluorescent, incandescent, luminaries, quartz-flood, filament, Lucalox, and multi-vapor.

Communication Facilities

A press box to accommodate reporters, sports broadcasters, television and motion-picture cameramen, and scouts should be planned in the original design. It should be sturdy, permanent construction and should be high enough to permit the occupants to see over the spectators standing in the row immediately in front. It should be heated and enclosed, with a glass front.

In cold climates, consideration should be given to providing an area for sports photographers at either end of the press box. A protected and heated structure providing overhead cover, with an open area in front from which pictures could be taken, might be constructed for a nominal sum.

Stairs and/or an elevator should provide access to the press box, and the latter is recommended if the press-box floor is more than 30 feet above ground level. Public toilet facilities should be immediately adjacent, with a minimum of two water closets, or one for every 10 occupants.

The football press box should be

located opposite the 50-yard line, preferably on the west side of the stadium. Baseball press boxes usually occupy some portion of the stand behind home plate, and tennis matches can best be served by a press box behind the end of the courts. A means of communication between the press box and the field is necessary.

Developing Space Beneath Stadium

The space underneath stadium seating can serve a variety of purposes. Planners should not consider service units in this section of the stadium if no more than 15 rows of seats are contemplated. Under-stadium development is economically advisable only if the cost of construction of needed facilities is less than it would be at other available sites. Many colleges and universities may find it more feasible to develop the area underneath the stadium than to have the various functions that might be served there dispersed to more remote areas.

A variety of uses can be made of this space. The most common facilities to be located in this area are public toilet rooms, storage rooms, concession booths, and dressing rooms for competitors. Activity areas, a weight training room, classrooms, and offices might also be included in this area. In larger stadiums one or more lounge rooms for pregame meetings and/or luncheons with the press or other similar purposes might be provided. Other possibilities include auditoriums and band rooms, dormitories and dining halls, instructional areas, a rifle range, an archery range, maintenance shops, housing for the caretaker, basketball courts, auxiliary gymnasiums, practice facilities for baseball and track, and squash and handball courts.

Steps in planning the area under the stadium include a determination of the capacity and type of the proposed structure, a study of other present and probable future facility needs, and a determination of which needs can best be satisfied through development of the space. Three important questions should be answered in determining the feasibility of developing this portion of the stadium. Is it possible to construct the facilities in keeping with previously determined requirements? Will these facilities permit the intended use? Is it economically practical? If the space under the stadium is to be developed, other important factors that should be considered are whether the structure is above ground and/or of permanent construction; whether the seating deck is watertight; the space requirements of the various facilities, which will indicate the location and design of columns, trusses, beams and other supports; and whether the substructure is designed to support the seating deck and, at the same time, provide a framework for the construction under the stadium.

Ramps, stairs, walks and other stadium service facilities should be located to satisfy the intended purpose, but also with consideration of facilities under the stadium. Common errors made in the development of this area are the failure to provide a watertight seating deck — with the necessary inclusion of expansion joints — and insufficient windows and ventilation.

Field Surface

Every consideration should be given to the latest developments in surfacing. The basic functions to be served by the stadium in the particular institution will determine the final selection. With the exception of cost, there is no longer any reason to have dirt areas that become mud areas on playgrounds or fields. With artificial turf, the use of an outdoor field can be increased 300 to 600 percent in a normal year. Football stadiums can be designed to serve baseball and track. They may also be designed to use the same lights. Artificial turf can be used all day, everyday, by everyone.

Artificial grass is feasible since it causes no allergies, or baldheaded fields, and it is good for all grass sports — football, baseball, soccer, golf, tennis and lawn bowling. There are other synthetic surfaces that service smooth surface sports such as basketball.

Additional Accommodations for Public Events

Scoreboards are essential for football, softball, and baseball fields. Time clocks are also desirable for football.

It is advisable to have the scoreboard designed as an integral part of the structure, especially in the case of larger stadiums. For activities attracting a small number of spectators, mechanical or movable scoreboards may be practical.

One public telephone should be provided for every 1,000 spectators, with a minimum of two for the stadium regardless of the seating capacity. Booths should be enclosed to eliminate noise and should be placed in accessible locations.

For suggestions on concession booths and dressing units for participants and staff, see the discussions in the section of this chapter on fieldhouses.

The availability of electricity, gas, water, and sewer connections significantly affects the use and validity of a spectator structure. The concession center, press-box area, rest rooms, scoreboard operations, field illuminations and watering, and many other functions depend on one or more of these utilities.

Public toilet units should be located in an area that is easily reached from the seating area. Because the stadium structure is ordinarily not heated, all plumbing should be constructed so that it can be completely drained of water, and water lines should be buried beneath the frost line of the locality. Toilets used by large groups should have circulating (in and out) entrances and exits.

Stadium cleaning can be expedited by providing the recommended deck slope and drains with hose bibbs located not more than 100 feet apart. Paving the surface under the stadium seats and installing drains and hose bibbs designed to prevent freezing facilitates stadium cleaning.

Provisions For Future Expansion

If there is a possibility that the size of the stadium will need to be increased in the foreseeable future, the method of expansion should be determined and the necessary details incorporated in the original footings and other construction. Insofar as possible, the requirements for future expansion should be built into the initial structure.

THE ICE ARENA

The ice rink is a highly specialized area and should be planned with the help of experienced ice rink people. The planning committee should visit as many rinks in operation as possible and talk to the owners and managers. Many worthwhile construction and operation pointers can be gathered from these experienced people.

Planners should first define the objectives and purposes of the skating facility:
- To solve a community need?
- To be revenue-producing?
- Single-purpose or multi-purpose?
- Spectator or non-spectator?
- Types of skating to be accommodated? Public skating? Youth skating programs? College and/or high school hockey? Amateur hockey? Semi-pro hockey? Pro-hockey? Hockey tournaments? Figure skating? Instruction? Ice shows?

From the above, you should be able to establish the requirements of location and size, accessibility, parking area, etc.
- Spectator seating needed
- Inside service areas required (skate sharpening and rental, pro-shop, locker-rooms, etc.)
- Skater and public entrances and exits
- Estimated cost of land, building, rink equipment and its installation
- Length of year rink will be operable

An estimate of the cost of the structure can be determined when these requirements are defined. If the project is financially feasible, an architect can be selected and planning can begin.

Building Size

The building size will depend on the types of events to be accommodated. However, the recommended size for the ice surface is 85 feet by 200 feet. The rink should also include at least 4 dressing rooms, refrigeration room, ice resurfacer storage room, which is accessible to the ice surface. The clear span portion of the building need only cover the rink plus seating.

The number of seats desired will depend on the planned programs, but remember that the width of the building will determine to a great extent the number of seats. It will cost more to increase the width of the structure than the length. The minimum width needed for 1,000 seats plus ice width, dasher boards, walkway in front of seats, players, seat width at 2½ feet per row, benches, penalty bench, scoring tables is approximately 120 feet.

Length of the building will depend on whether all facilities will be included under one roof or if a block building is added for dressing rooms, refrigeration room, offices, etc.

Refrigeration

It is very important to choose the right type of refrigeration system along with a competent and reliable installation company. In selecting an ice rink installer, the following qualifications should be weighed: education and experience of company directors, age of the firm, qualifications of its personnel, list of rinks designed and volume of business during last four years.

Before a final contractor is selected, the committee should visit numerous rinks constructed by each potential installer and talk to their owners, managers and engineers. Determine if there was

Figure 5-10
An exterior view of the fieldhouse and hockey rink at Massachusetts Institute of Technology.

satisfaction with the installation, training of personnel to run the system and follow-up to problems that developed. Study the records of operation of the refrigeration system with respect to expense for energy and operating personnel.

Producing and maintaining a good ice sheet is imperative to any rink operation. If there is a breakdown in refrigeration and you lose your ice, your programs are lost for that time. In privately-owned rinks, money is lost which will never be recovered. It should be noted that in refrigeration there is no such thing as "cold." Cold is the absence of heat. With this in mind, it will be much easier to understand and evaluate ice rink refrigerator systems. Heat is absorbed from a material when it comes in contact with a material having a lower temperature. In the case of refrigerants, this heat-absorbing quality is increased by the ability of the refrigerant to change to a gas which produces a greater cooling or freezing effect.

Basically there are two types of refrigeration systems: the indirect brine system and the direct system with two variations (Direct Liquid Refrigeration "DLR" and Direct Expansion "DX").

The indirect method is the oldest system used in ice rink refrigeration. Rapid progress in ice rink refrigeration started in the 1930's and 1940's when Dupont developed Freon refrigerants. Before that time, because of high installation, maintenance and operating costs, only wealthy municipalities could afford ice rinks. Also ethylene-glycol was developed as a possible replacement for calcium chloride (salt) for use with water as the brine in indirect systems. Ethylene glycol is non-corrosive and made possible substantial reductions in refrigeration equipment size. The calcium chloride unit must be monitored regularly to prevent chemical imbalance which can produce unwanted scale within the distribution network or acidify

sufficiently to accelerate deterioration not only of its own components, but those of adjunct equipment as well.

Both systems use compressors and condensers. The compressor is that part of the system that compresses gaseous refrigerant. During the compression process the gas becomes hot and is pumped under high pressure by the compressor to the condenser. The condenser is a heat exchanger that liquifies compressed refrigerant gas.

The indirect system uses a brine pump and if the pump fails, the system is inoperative. Two of these centrifugal pumps should be built into the system to eliminate this possibility. One would be used as a standby in case the other fails.

The indirect brine system is a two-step system. First a refrigerant, either ammonia or Freon 22, is pumped through a series of pipes in a brine chiller, where the brine is chilled to a temperature considerably below the freezing temperature of water. The chilled brine is then pumped from the brine chiller through the pipes in the rink floor which in turn absorbs heat from the water and freezes the rink floor. Because the refrigerant does not go through the piping in the rink floor, the system is called indirect. "Brine" is only used in this system and not in the direct system.

In the direct system, refrigerant is used throughout the entire network. It is supplied directly through the rink floor pipes. Freon 22 is both the refrigerant and chilling agent. It is highly dependable, stable and has excellent safety features. With this method the brine chiller and pumps are eliminated. There are two variations of this system. The direct liquid refrigeration "DLR" and the direct expansion "DX."

The "DLR" system is pumpless with no moving parts; only float valves which open and close automatically. Discharge pressure from the compressor is used to

mildly pressure the transfer tank which feeds "cold" liquid Freon under low pressure to the rink floor pipes. There are no restrictions in the rink floor perimeter feed pipes. As the Freon 22 flows through the rink floor piping, it draws heat from the water or ice causing the water to freeze or the ice to freeze harder. Skaters generate heat in the area where there is skating activity. Any change in the ice temperature at any place in the rink causes an immediate pressure equalization throughout the entire rink field system. An in-ice thermostat is used to signal changes in temperature and works automatically.

The direct expansion system "DX" differs from the "DLR" in the following manner: Freon 22 refrigerant is pumped under high pressure from the compressor-condenser into a holding tank which feeds the perimeter feeder pipes around the rink floor. The refrigerant is then forced under high pressure through a series of expansion orifices at the head of each run of pipe in the rink floor. There are approximately 255 runs of pipe in a rink floor, so it has 255 individual orifices.

Until a few years ago the refrigeration unit was assembled on the job, but now installation time and costs have been reduced by the development of the "packaged" ready-for-hookup refrigeration unit. It is shipped to the job site ready to hook up to the rink floor. The unit has been pre-assembled, pre-wired, pre-insulated and pre-tested for immediate use at the new arena.

The planning committee should ask representatives of each type of system to give a presentation. One system will not satisfy every need. However, in choosing the rink installer it is recommended that the company chosen assume total responsibility for all the equipment, installation and satisfactory operation of the rink, along with training rink personnel.

Insist that the installer of the refrigerator system be responsible for the entire rink portion of the facility. In this way, only one company need be consulted.

Energy Conservation

Conservation of energy is a critical consideration and promises to become more important. Three things determine the energy requirement for an ice rink system:

1. Horsepower needed to operate the refrigeration equipment, compressors, condenser, pumps, etc. The size and number of the operating components of the refrigeration system determines the horsepower needed to operate the unit. The higher the horsepower the more in cost per month for operation.

2. The more efficiency that is designed and built into this unit, the less the refrigeration equipment will need to be running.

3. Rate of efficiency loss of the refrigeration unit and system over a long period of time. Causes of efficiency loss are corrosion, mineral deposits and oil accumulation in the entire rink network.

The direct refrigeration unit uses less power to operate than the indirect. The direct unit uses smaller compressors, no brine chiller, and does not need two brine circulating pumps. In the brine system, the refrigerant has to be chilled to a temperature of 10°F to 15°F colder than the brine temperature.

With direct liquid refrigeration the refrigerant in the rink field need only to be cooled to the temperature of the rink floor. This means that the indirect system must be in operation longer and at a less efficient, lower compressor pressure. It stands to reason that if a system operates longer at a less efficient manner, the cost rises. It has been learned by comparison of the two systems operating at peak efficiency that there is a savings in electrical power of approximately 30% with direct refrigeration.

Ice Hardness

All ice for skating is not the same. The best temperature for each type of ice activity is as follows:

Hockey: 15°-17°F (Hard Ice)
Pleasure Skating: 17°-20°F (Softer than for hockey)
Figure Skating: 20°-22°F (Reasonably fast ice, but skates cut into ice)
Curling: (Soft ice without melting)

Rink Floor

After selection of the refrigeration unit, the next key portion of the project is construction of the rink floor. The rink floor can be constructed in different ways — steel pipes in concrete, steel pipes in sand, plastic pipes over a hard surface covered with sand. Steel pipes in concrete is preferred. This is the most expensive, but over the long haul will prove to be the most practical.

If the rink is to be a single purpose rink for skating only, a sand floor will give satisfactory service and is lower in initial cost. However, a sand floor is more costly to operate because sand is inferior to concrete for heat conduction.

The use of plastic pipe is not recommended except for use in small portable rinks. The efficiency of the refrigeration, using plastic tubing, is less than using steel pipes. Plastic tubing does not conduct heat as well as steel pipes. The only advantage to plastic piping is lower initial cost. Also, plastic pipes cannot be used with the direct system.

Before the rink floor can be poured, the sub-soil must be tested to establish the water table. The presence of water in the sub-soil within four feet of the rink floor can cause heaving of the floor due to freezing and expansion of the soil under the rink.

If there is a possibility of water at a depth of less than four feet

under the rink, one or all three of the following things can be done: (1) a drainage system in the sub-soil, (2) removal of the moisture-holding soil and replacement with a non-wicking type fill and/or (3) installation of sub-soil heating. Sub-soil heating is inexpensive to operate because waste heat from the condenser is used to heat the antifreeze which flows through the pipes embedded in the sub-soil. This weak solution of glycol is maintained at a temperature of 40°F by a thermostat. This means that during the operation of the rink, the temperature of the sub-soil never drops below 40°F and never freezes.

Most rinks built today are insulated by using two layers of 2-inch thick polystyrene foam directly under the rink floor. This insulation prevents the transfer of heat from the sub-soil to the rink floor. A vapor barrier of polyethylene film separates the insulation from the concrete or sand floor.

In a full-size 85' x 200' rink there are approximately 51,000 running feet of pipe. This pipe covers the total rink floor and is spaced 4" on center. The concrete floor must be poured in one continuous pour at a depth of 5-6 inches and be separated from the surrounding concrete floor of the building. The grid piping is only one inch below the surface of the rink floor to assure dependable and efficient freezing of the ice surface.

There are approximately 2805 pipe connections in the standard size rink. This means that leaks in the rink floor are a possibility unless a professional job of coupling or welding is accomplished at each connection. Welding is the best choice if there is good quality control. One recent development is the use of steel tubing which has no welded connections from one end of the rink to the other. Using this tubing the possibility of leaks in the rink floor is minimal.

Double Rinks

There is a trend in some metropolitan areas to construct a double rink. The typical double rink has a full-sized rink for hockey and public skating and a smaller rink (at least 5000 sq. ft.) for instructional and figure skating.

Dehumidification

Dehumidification in ice rinks is a low cost way of removing fog and condensation problems that occur in a rink area during the hot humid months of the summer. Air conditioning the rink area is seldom necessary. However, in southern climates it may be desirable to air condition other parts of the rink, especially the spectator area, locker-rooms, offices, etc. Remember that dehumidification just removes moisture from the air and is by no means a substitute for ventilation.

Heating

It is recommended that the building be maintained at around 50°-55°F at all times. If a crowd is expected, a lower temperature should be maintained because body heat from the crowd will

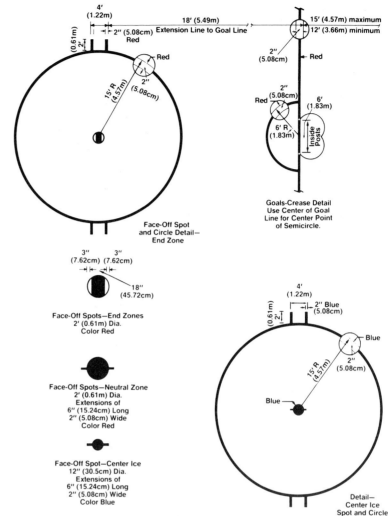

Figure 5-11, 11A
Official NCAA approved Ice Hockey layout.

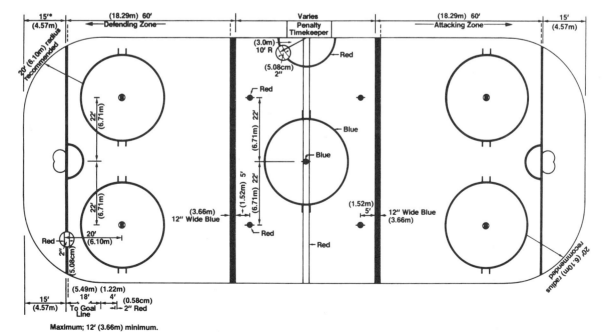

raise the building temperature 10°-15°F. Office space along with locker-rooms and showers should be maintained at around 65°-70°F. The heating fixtures should never circulate warm air directly over the ice surface, because of the added load this puts on the ice making equipment.

Since all types of heating methods are used, a heating and ventilation contractor should be consulted for the best system. One recently developed heating factor is using the waste heat from the compressors to help supplement other heating apparatus in the building.

Dasher Boards and Protective Screening

Every ice rink which is built for a full schedule of ice activities needs dasher boards and protective screening. Dasher boards can be made of marine plywood or the newer high density polyethelene material. Plywood is serviceable, but almost impossible to remove the black puck marks on the white boards and must be painted often. The synthetic polyethelene dashers are about the same in price, clean up well and give the rink an attractive appearance. A 6-inch to 8-inch kick board around the bottom of the dasher should be made of the same synthetic and in a contrasting color.

The frame for the dasher boards and protective screen should be solidly built to withstand the constant impact from the hockey pucks and the shock of body checks. The dasher boards should also have entrance and exit doors for player benches, doors for penalty boxes and public skating sessions, and a 10-foot-wide door for the ice resurfacer to enter and exit. Doors should never swing towards the skating surface.

The protective screening around the rink can be made of plastic netting, wire mesh or of clear acrylic glass. The height must be at least 4 feet and preferably a few feet higher. Plastic netting is easily torn; wire mesh can be dangerous because of sharp edges. Acrylic glass is more expensive, but easier to see through for spectators.

Locker-Rooms

At least four locker-rooms are a "must" in any arena which plans to have hockey as a money maker. The rooms should be at least 12 by 20 feet to accommodate the normal team. Four locker-rooms are suggested so two teams may be on the ice and two teams dressing or undressing at the same time. Showers with the proper number of shower heads should be in close proximity to each

locker-room. Thievery is a problem in any locker-room and special attention should be given to security measures.

Floor Covering

In all areas of the rink where individuals will be walking with skates, it's imperative to have a floor covering which will not be injurious to the skater or skate blades. Indoor-outdoor carpeting, rubberized matting, or poured-in-place synthetic materials are available. Carpeting is the least expensive but creates a cleaning problem, and skaters can cut the surface. Rubberized interlocking skate tile can be purchased at an intermediate price and is easily cleaned, and comes in many colors. The poured-in-place synthetic is very good quality but quite expensive when compared to the other two coverings.

Scoreboard

For competitive play, a scoreboard should be installed. It gives the arena a professional appearance and the spectators and players can easily follow the game. Many arenas sell advertising on the scoreboard to offset the expense of the purchase.

Figure 5-12, 12A
Exterior and interior views of the Ice Arena at Bowling Green State University.

Encapsulated Spaces and Stadiums

Combined Skate Shop and Pro Shop

The skate shop and pro shop, if run efficiently, can help defray cost of ice arena maintenance. The rooms do not have to be especially large, but the skate shop should have enough space for skate rentals and a skate sharpening operation. Proper ventilation must be provided for the skate sharpener, so that the residue will be eliminated from the air. The pro shop would retail skates, hockey sticks, pucks, friction tape, skate laces, and other paraphernalia that will be used for arena programs.

Lighting and Sound System

Knowledgeable lighting and acoustical engineers should be consulted about the systems to be installed in the arena. Incandescent, fluorescent and high-intensity discharge lights may be used separately or in combination. Banks of lights should be wired to separate switches, since there are times when a minimum of light is necessary and desired. When planning other electrical outlets, proper wiring for scoreboard and goal lights needs to be provided.

Sound systems are important in every arena because public skating requires taped or recorded music. Also regular day-to-day activities and hockey games will require announcements. Acoustics over ice presents special problems, so experienced personnel should install the sound system and speakers.

The following items should also be remembered when planning your ice arena:

- Ice resurfacer storage room, with pit and drain for dumping ice shavings
- Hot water outlet adjacent to ice resurfacer
- Adequate public rest rooms and drinking fountains
- Offices
- Rental lockers
- First Aid room and training room
- Public phones
- Concession areas
- Workshop
- Adequate parking around arena
- If arena is used for collegiate or professional hockey, provisions for radio and television, press box, and ticket booths need to be provided. The most recent edition of the NCAA Ice Hockey Guide also should be consulted.

Check List for Encapsulated Spaces

1. Provide ample space for the activities desired. ☐
2. Include adequate administrative, recreational, and service facilities. ☐
3. Design for future needs. ☐
4. Provide accommodations for men and women. ☐
5. Provide drainage around the exterior of the building. ☐
6. Provide adequate storage space. ☐
7. Install proper lighting. ☐
8. Provide for maintenance of light fixtures. ☐
9. Provide adequate wiring with provision for high-voltage current. ☐
10. Provide windows and skylights with minimum glare intensity. ☐
11. Install sufficient and well-placed heating vents. ☐
12. Provide for sufficient natural ventilation. ☐
13. Include adequate exhaust fans and vents. ☐
14. Provide well-placed ticket-sale and ticket-taking facilities. ☐
15. Provide for telephone, television, radio, and telegraph facilities in the press area. ☐
16. Provide an adequate sound system. ☐
17. Provide an entrance large enough for the delivery of equipment. ☐
18. Provide waterproof insulation for the ceiling. ☐
19. Place pipelines an adequate distance from the floor. ☐
20. Provide sufficient shower and locker facilities. ☐
21. Install an adequate public-address system. ☐
22. Include adequate facilities for cleaning and maintenance. ☐
23. Include sufficient water outlets. ☐
24. Provide for expansion or change. ☐
25. Provide for portable facilities. ☐
26. Plan for accommodation of spectators in areas where needed. ☐
27. Provide well-designed spectator exits. ☐
28. Include an adequate lobby and vestibule. ☐
29. Provide a sufficient number of electrical outlets, and place them for easy access. ☐
30. Select good paint colors for the interior of the buildilng. ☐
31. Place windows away from goals and goal lines. ☐
32. Provide filters in the air-circulation system. ☐
33. Include movable and folding partitions, power-operated and controlled by key switches. ☐
34. Include wall plates located where needed and firmly attached. ☐
35. Include hooks and rings for nets placed (and recessed in walls) according to court locations and net heights. ☐

SELECTED REFERENCES

"A Dome Amidst the Hexagons." **American School and University** 48 (August 1976), 33-34.

Brozan, Robert T. **New Concepts in Planning and Funding Athletic, Physical Education and Recreation Facilities.** St. Paul: The Phoenix Intermedia, Inc., 1974.

Cleary, William J., ed. **1984 NCAA Men's Ice Hockey Rules and Interpretations.** Shawnee Mission, Kansas: NCAA, 1984.

Davis, William E. "A Stadium For All Seasons." **College Management** 7 (February 1972): 21-24.

"Domes over Canada." **Athletic Business** 8 (April 1984), 28-30.

"Domes Provides Beauty and Low Cost Space." **American School and University** 48 (January 1976), 60.

"Energy Savings Expected from Fabric Dome." **Athletic Purchasing and Facilities.** 5 (November 1981), 90.

Ezersky, Eugene M. and Thiebert, Richard P. **Facilities in Sports and Physical Education.** St. Louis: The C.V. Mosby Company, 1976.

"Lightweight Column-Free Membranous Field House." **Scholastic Coach** 44 (January 1975): 22.

"Multi-Purpose Mammoth." **College Management** 5 (August 1970): 18-21.

"Notre Dame's Twin Domed Wonderland." **Scholastic Coach** 39 (January 1970): 20.

Penman, Kenneth. **Planning Physical Education and Athletic Facilities in Schools.** New York: Wiley and Sons, 1977.

Peterson, Alex. **Guide for Planning The Fieldhouse at a College or School Physical Education Facility.** New York: Columbia University, 1969.

Physical Recreational Facilities. New York: Educational Facilities Laboratory, Inc., 1973.

Schmidt, Lawrence W. "'New Athletic Programs Fill Three Domes." **Athletic Purchasing and Facilities** 1 (April-May 1977): 42-46.

"Special Report: Sport Surfaces." **Athletic Purchasing and Facilities.** 6 (November 1982), 44-81.

"Sports Dome Offers Something for Everybody." **American School and University** 49 (December 1976): 30-31.

"A Spreading Idea: Domed Stadiums." **U.S. News and World Report** (September 1975), 45.

"Superdome's Seating." **Architectural Record** 159 (April 1976), 143-144.

CHAPTER VI
Service Areas

The recommendations in this chapter are predicated on the provision of equal opportunities for men and women. Space to provide equal opportunities for men and women has created a significant increase in the size of service facilities to support new and changing programs — particularly competitive athletics. Planners need to project service facility requirements carefully for both men's and women's sport teams. Failure to include space needs for immediate as well as future expansion can be very costly because of the unique problems and the great expense associated with locker area construction.

Planning can include joint use by men and women when possible. Storage rooms, equipment issue, conditioning and athletic training rooms, and laundry facilities should be planned for such use.

Understanding the various service areas in activity centers is vital to the efficient use of the building. The location of the respective facilities should result in easy, direct traffic patterns for participants, instructors, and custodial employees. Ideal space utilization and operational systems can result in efficient administration at minimal expense.

THE DRESSING LOCKER ROOM

Location

Accessibility is the most important aspect. The locker room should be located to serve the indoor and outdoor teaching stations and other service facilities requiring dressing space. The dressing room should be immediately accessible from corridors. Planning for several corridors leading to these areas will reduce overcrowding during class changes.

Whenever possible, the dressing room should be on the same floor as the gymnasium and the swimming pool when a common level is used for both stations. This will alleviate traffic congestion and possible injuries resulting from movement up and down stairways. However, architectural problems may make this location impractical.

The dressing room should have direct access to outdoor recreational areas and indoor teaching stations without requiring individuals to cross main corridors. As students return from outside activities they should have access to an area equipped with special drains for cleaning purposes.

When the swimming pool adjoins the locker room, participants, for hygienic reasons, should be required to pass from the dressing area through the shower to the pool. In some designs, it is desirable that a second dressing room be located at the pool area. This is particularly true if a pool is used extensively by community and after-hour groups. (Figure 6-1)

Locker Room Size

The size of the dressing/locker room usually is based on the number of individuals using the area. If there is an overlap of classes or simultaneous use by athletics, physical education, and intramurals, the room must be large enough to accommodate this traffic flow without confusion. The locker system and the method of distributing towels, uniforms, and equipment affect size demands. A general rule of thumb recommends a minimum of 20 square feet per person. A preliminary scaled plan drawn to include the locker placement, visual barriers, and accessories is the ideal way to provide sufficient space allocation. Additional space should be allowed if faculty, graduate assistants, and intramural and sports groups also will use this facility.

Placement of doors for dressing rooms should facilitate a logical traffic flow. In locker rooms that have many participants arriving and departing simultaneously, it is wise to provide an entrance and a separate exit to a common passageway to eliminate a hazardous condition. All doors should be of heavy-duty moisture-resistant material and, when open, form a natural sight barrier. Doors should be in such a position as to offer protection to individuals who move through a main adjoining corridor. Locker rooms' outside doors should be equipped with panic bars of non-corrosive metal.

Wall materials should be moisture-resistant, easy to maintain, and finished in a pleasing, light color. All corners in rooms should be rounded, and the junction of the wall locker door should be coved for ease of cleaning. There are many

materials, including synthetics, which are durable and easy to clean.

Floors should be of non-skid, impervious materials with a carborundum impregnated surface such as ceramic or quarry tile. Concrete floors with non-skid surfaces should be treated with a hardener to prevent penetration of moisture and odors. Terrazzo can be slippery for the average locker room; the same holds true for vinyl or asphalt tile. Floors should slope toward drains. Recessed bibbs provide for easy cleaning.

Synthetic carpeting, laid directly over concrete, is becoming very popular for locker room use. It is aesthetically pleasing, affords excellent footing, and reduces noise to a minimum. Other advantages are that the floor need not slope since it is not hosed down for cleaning and repairs can be made easily. The maintenance cost for carpeting is greater since regular vacuuming and periodic shampooing are required.

However, in well supervised areas, the carpeted locker room offers unique advantages. One disadvantage of carpeting is that moisture remains in the carpet and odors may persist. Keeping carpet away from wet areas will alleviate this problem. Other synthetics may also be used for the same reasons that carpet may be desired.

Locker bases, 8 inches to 16 inches high, should be of the same material as the floor and coved at the base.

Ceilings and Lights

Ceilings of a light color should be acoustically treated with a material impervious to moisture. The lights should have vapor proof fixtures and be centered directly over the locker aisles for maximum efficiency. Electric outlets (including 3-prong units) should be approximately 3 feet above floor level. Emergency lighting should be available at all times.

Sidewall windows, if desired,

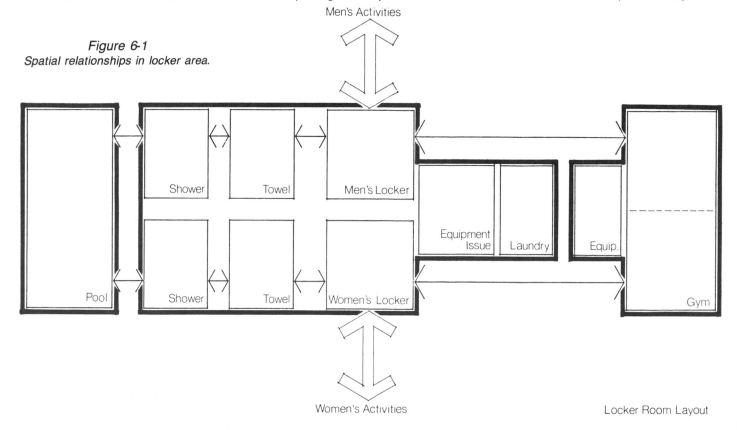

Figure 6-1
Spatial relationships in locker area.

Men's Activities

Shower   Towel   Men's Locker

Equipment Issue   Laundry   Equip.

Pool   Shower   Towel   Women's Locker   Gym

Women's Activities

Locker Room Layout

should be strategically located and provide maximum privacy. The lower portion of the walls should be used for other services or for an additional bank of lockers. If windows are designed for opening and closing, they should be controlled easily from the floor. In most instances, the ventilation system should eliminate the necessity of opening and closing windows. Windows of frosted, translucent material should be used to allow natural lighting to pass down locker aisles rather than against a bank of lockers. Placement and size of windows should be planned in conjunction with the entire locker arrangement and should not dictate or limit locker placement. It is recommended that glass not be used but rather one of the newer acrylic synthetics. These new,

unbreakable materials reduce vandalism and provide increased safety in the locker rooms. They can be purchased in a variety of finishes, thicknesses and colors.

Vented sky domes serve as an effective source of natural light.

Accessories

Mirrors should be placed at strategic locations in the dressing room and vanity areas. Full length mirrors should be placed at least 12 inches from the floor and be available for individuals as they leave the room. They also can be placed over the sink area and in other locations as well.

Refrigerated drinking fountains of stainless steel or non-corrosive material should be located near traffic flow. They should be recessed or placed to protect the

user from traffic movement.

Hair-drying facilities are encouraged. Wall blowers — preferably with separate hoods, mounted at varying heights, and spaced at three to four foot intervals — are recommended. If the dressing room services are used by swimmers, one dryer for four or five men is sufficient. A ratio of 1 to 3 is recommended for women.

Color

Attention should be given to planning a total color scheme for the dressing facility. Locker rooms no longer need to be planned with an antiseptic appearance. A variety of locker colors, coordinated with decorated walls and carpeting, create a pleasing environment. Renovation or new construction should plan for the use of color to improve locker room aesthetics.

Saunas/Steam Rooms

In many colleges and universities, as well as in private membership clubs, saunas and/or steam rooms have become common amenities. Whereas saunas can often be purchased as pre-assembled units, steam rooms require more careful consideration. Both areas should be contiguous to shower rooms or drying areas.

It is important to publicize instructions/precautions in the use of saunas and steam rooms; to centrally regulate temperature controls (locked box); to include inside lights and timers; and to make certain regular, thorough cleaning occurs to curtail bacterial growth and transference. Redwood is most often used for the dry heat saunas while tile is recommended for steam room finishes due to the constant moisture and high temperatures. A see-through portion of the door is recommended for safety.

Utility and/or electrical requirements to support these functions will need to be added if they will be a part of a new facility. (Figure 6-2)

Figure 6-2
Sauna provides relaxation opportunities for users of the George Halas Jr. Sports Center at Loyola University of Chicago. Window in door is for safety.

FACILITIES FOR LOCKERS AND SHOWERS

Supervision

Supervision is of constant concern. Strategic placement of offices or service areas can facilitate administrative control. In a public school, the teaching personnel office is best located adjacent to the locker room. Direct access from the office permits efficient performance of routine chores and consistent surveillance. A glass partition, or side window facing the locker room, provides for supervision. The office floor could be elevated to improve sight lines.

Supervision can also be provided by placing the equipment issue room adjacent to the locker rooms. Lockers should be placed perpendicular to the supervisory staff spaces for ease in observing locker aisles. Towel distribution areas within the locker rooms for use during peak periods can assist with security.

Security is important and must be considered in planning. Double security systems on main storage areas can aid in preventing vandalism. Electrical systems monitored in a central security office could be used at large facilities. (Figure 6-3)

Shower Rooms

Location

Shower rooms should be centrally located in relation to the dressing rooms. When possible, provide a shower room that can service more than one area, sized to accommodate peak loads in all areas. The nature of the groups using the facility is an important consideration. For example, if a swimming pool will be used extensively by community groups, it may be advisable to build separate service facilities for the pool. Such excluded facilities offer greater flexibility of programs along with improved supervision and security.

In general, lavatory, toilet, and

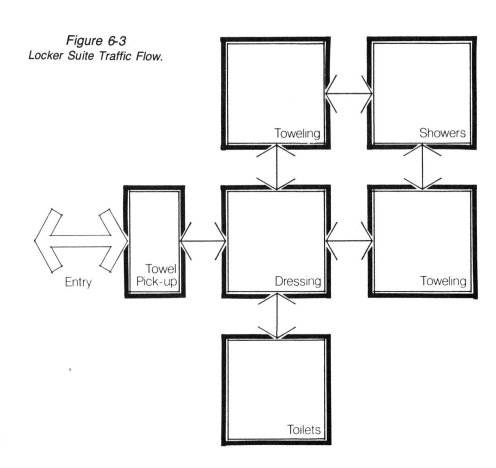

Figure 6-3
Locker Suite Traffic Flow.

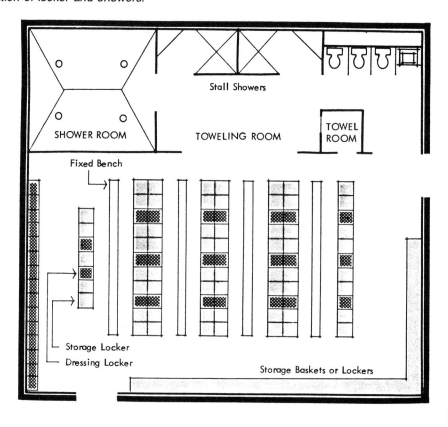

Figure 6-4
Location of locker and showers.

shower facilities should be grouped in close proximity. Cost of installation is reduced since the amount of piping will be considerably lessened. (Figure 6-4)

Size

The size of the shower room is determined by the type of shower arrangement and the number of people served at a peak time. Since time for showering is usually limited, a sufficient number of shower heads must be planned. Ten shower heads are recommended for the first 30 people and an additional shower head is recommended for every additional four persons. (Figure 6-5)

Installation

All types of shower installations should be studied and the selection made according to the advantages of a particular system for the situation at the individual institution. The center post system provides for a grouping of shower heads on a single pole. This arrangement allows for the use of splash barriers rather than solid walls around the room and thus affords easy supervision. In this system all hardware and piping attached to the post should be of a non-corrosive material. (Figure 6-5A)

Installations along the outside walls are the most economical in terms of space, since at least three full walls can be used for shower heads. It is absolutely necessary that provision be made to repair plumbing defects by putting plumbing in pipe spaces and providing access from the back of the shower wall, unless exposed systems are utilized.

Allow areas for special alcoves designed for handicapped use, including ramps, grab bars, possible hand shower and seat. Overhead showering (the progressive walkthrough) installations are adequate for showering before swimming. However, longer hair styles makes this system unpopular except for swimming pools. Without close supervision it doesn't ensure proper cleansing.

Shower Heads

The head should be self-cleaning, water-conserving, and adjusted for fine spray. It is recommended that the angle of spray should not be adjustable. Spacing between heads should be two and one half feet for colleges; the height should allow the spray to be directed at shoulder height, making it possible to keep the hair relatively dry if desired. Most shower rooms are used by varying age groups and community programs, and thus it may be desirable to vary the height of a few of the shower heads. A master temperature control should prevent excessive water temperatures. Each shower head should have an individual control consisting of one hand control rather than separate hot and cold water controls. Handicapped units may require

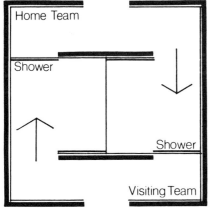

A. ATHLETICS (use both showers during games).

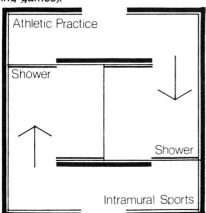

C. AFTER SCHOOL (athletic practice and intramurals each use one shower).

Figure 6-5
Various arrangements for flexible showers.

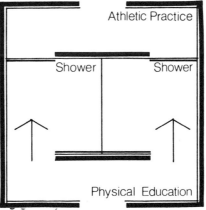

B. PHYSICAL EDUCATION CLASSES (uses both showers during day).

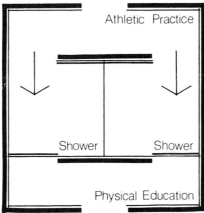

D. ATHLETIC PRACTICE (can use physical education showers after school).

Figure 6-5A
Individual lockers and showers at Methuen (Mass.) High School.

hand-held shower heads on armored hose. Gang showers are most economical, though some booth showers should be provided for privacy. At least 10 percent of the shower heads for women should be of individual booths. (Figure 6-6)

A liquid soap dispensing system, if used, should be designed so that all piping is behind the shower room walls. This system should allow the custodial staff to refill the reservoir at a source away from the wet area. These systems, however, require extensive maintenance to remain operative. (Figure 6-7) Recessed soap dishes are still required since many individuals prefer to use a particular bar soap or shampoo. Consideration must be given to the dangers of bar soap on wet floors and the use of any glass bottles for shampoo, etc. (Figure 6-8; 8A)

Doors

Access to the shower room should be as wide as possible to allow freedom of movement and facilitate supervision, with half walls or splash barriers used as

Figure 6-6
Example of center post shower system.

much as possible. A sloped surface may separate the shower and dressing room, depending upon the locker room drainage system. A curb should not be employed since this creates a safety hazard.

Walls

The shower room walls should

consist of a smooth and impervious material that can be cleaned easily. Structural glazed tile, ceramic tile, or glazed concrete block may all be used. Certain Epoxy coatings may be painted on masonry for an economical finish. All corners should be rounded.

Figure 6-7
Shower head types and arrangements.

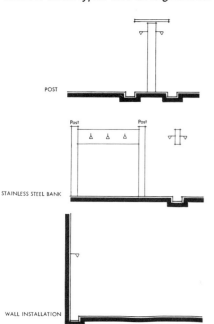

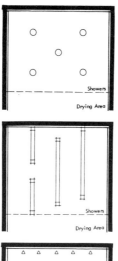

SHOWER HEAD ARRANGEMENTS

Figures 6-8, 8A
Shower room at the University of Windsor, Ontario, with tiled floor and wall, perimeter gutter, recessed single control spigots and moveable shower heads.

Service Areas

Ceilings

Ceilings should be moisture-resistant, hard finished, painted, and a minimum of nine feet in height. All lights must be vapor-proof, with switches located in dry areas. Acoustical materials may be used in locker areas of moisture and abuse-resistant types.

Floors

Non-skid, ceramic tile or equal material should be used as the floor surface. The floor should be pitched away from the dressing room area and toward adequately-sized drains. The most desirable drainage system for shower rooms consists of tiled perimeter gutters directly beneath the shower heads leading to appropriately spaced drains. However, correctly designed floor drains may be used for economy reasons. Post showers usually contain drainage connections within the unit. All edges and floor and wall joints should be coved. Hose bibbs, for cleaning purposes, should be located outside the shower room for safety.

Ventilation

A ventilation system is required to eliminate condensation and odors. This should be ducted to the exterior. Whole room exhaust is preferred over locker bank systems. Tempered air should be introduced into all areas, directed to prevent drafts.

Toweling Room

In general, the drying or toweling room should be comparable in size to the shower room in order to encourage complete drying in this area rather than in the locker area. This is particularly important when carpeting is planned for the dressing room. (Figure 6-9)

The walls, floor, and ceiling should be of the same material and quality as the shower room.

Provisions should be made for drainage. A bull-nosed, non-skid curb should separate the drying room from the locker room to protect against flooding. Non-corrosive towel racks should be attached securely to the walls. The towel-issue room, if used, should be adjacent to, or near, the drying room. For sanitary and safety reasons, benches should not be installed in the toweling area.

Toilet and Lavatory

Rest room facilities must be located in all locker rooms, sized to the expected usage. Locate in a supervised area near the exit pattern. Strategic placement of toilet and lavatory areas facilitates traffic pattern controls. All restrooms should have forced exhaust systems at a rate of 30 changes per hour or as required by local code. Water closets, lavatories and urinals should be wall mounted to facilitate cleaning. Special consideration must be given to the handicapped. Individual stalls should be securely anchored to floors, ceilings, and walls. In locations of heavy use, it may be more economical to use glazed brick or tile partitions. When soap dispensers are provided above lavatories they should be mounted in such ways

Figure 6-9
Drying areas with tile floor and walls, and wall mounted hair dryer at University of Arkansas.

Figure 6-10, 10A

Shower and lavatory facilities for the handicapped at the University of Illinois, Urbana, Ill.

that soap will not fall on the floor or on chromed fixtures. Paper towel dispensers are provided most frequently for hand drying and require disposal cans, though electric hand dryers are effective and more economical than paper. Dispensers and electric hand dryers should be located away from the lavatories to improve traffic flow. Back-up towel dispensers should be provided even when electric dryers are installed. (Figures 6-10; 10A)

Mirrors should also be located away from the lavatories. A good location for mirrors in the locker room is at the ends of locker banks. Tilted mirrors will be required for handicapped users. A shelf should be installed in school restrooms, outside the locker area, where students' books may be placed. In toilet areas for women, dispensers and disposers should be built in. Wall mounted electric dryers can be provided for hair drying near the locker area. For the required number and type of plumbing fixtures, planners must review state standards, regulations, and building codes.

Lockers

The administrative and teaching personnel should be active participants in the selection of the locker system, since they are familiar with the problems of locker room administration.

Locker and locker units are available in many sizes and combinations. They should be chosen after careful consideration of the needs. Typical combined storage-dressing room locker arrangements are usually selected according to the number of instructional periods available in a day. Frequent variations in lengths of periods, and therefore changes in the number of periods per day, will upset a carefully planned locker system. Modular scheduling, split sessions, and independent course study also tend to disrupt the operation of a well-planned system.

The locker system and locker dimensions must be established prior to the determination of the room size. These, coupled with plans for future expansion, should be the criteria in determining a functional layout and overall size

for the locker room. It is recommended that the number of lockers should be equal to the peak load plus 10 to 15 percent with adequate allowance for overlapping classes, variations in class size, scheduling and anticipated use by intramural, recreation and athletic participants. Projected enrollment must be considered. (Figure 6-11)

Basic Locker Room Systems

The basic locker room system concerns the physical layout, placement of the dressing and storage lockers, and their relation to the various service facilities. In selecting the desired size of specific lockers and determining the most appropriate locker system, a number of questions need to be considered:
- What equipment must the user store in storage lockers?
- What athletic equipment is provided and stored by the school?
- Are other lockers available to store needed equipment?

PERIODS PER DAY	STUDENTS PER DAY	UNIT ARRANGEMENT	UNIT LOCKER CONTENTS	UNIT HEIGHT W/ 8" BASE	TOTAL UNITS & LINEAR FT. REQ'D
6	240		6 STORAGE 9" x 12" x 24" 1 DRESSING 12" x 12" x 48"	56"	40 UNITS 130 LIN. FT.
6	240		6 STORAGE 9" x 12" x 20"/24" 1 DRESSING 12" x 12" x 60"/72"	68"/80"	40 UNITS 100 LIN. FT.
6	240		6 STORAGE 12" x 12" x 12" 1 DRESSING 12" x 12" x 48"	68"	40 UNITS 80 LIN. FT.
6	240		12 STORAGE 12" x 12" x 12" 2 DRESSING 12" x 12" x 36"	80"	20 UNITS 60 LIN. FT.
7-8	320		8 STORAGE 9" x 12" x 24" 1 DRESSING 12" x 12" x 48"	56"	40 UNITS 160 LIN. FT.
7-8	320		8 STORAGE 12" x 12" x 12" 1 DRESSING 12" x 12" x 48"	56"	40 UNITS 120 LIN. FT.

Figure 6-11
Various combined storage-dressing locker arrangements.

- Does the program require sweat suits and jackets for outside participation in cool seasons?
- Will the same locker be used for physical education and for an athletic team?
- Who provides the gym suit?
- Who provides the towel?
- Is a laundry system available or planned?
- Will other groups — such as community recreation — be using the same locker facility?
- Are personnel available to administer a basket system?
- What is the financial feasibility?

There are several locker systems, and selection should be made after carefully considering the following requirements:

- Security of street clothing and physical education equipment
- Efficient use of space and facilities
- Control of odors
- Efficient administration for student
- Administrative feasibility, including supervision and maintenance
- Economy of operation
- Flexibility for use by different groups

(Figure 6-12; 6-13)

Individual Dressing Lockers

Individual dressing lockers best fit all needs. Cost in terms of the space required usually makes it impossible to provide this convenience for all users. Usually, such lockers are installed for athletes, coaches, teachers, game officials, and/or professional major students. In schools where all equipment is carried by the student, this system has also been used.

The individual locker should be large enough to handle the equipment for the sport requiring the maximum space; for example, football. If an equipment drying

Figure 6-12

Dressing locker and box storage arrangement separating the clothing storage and dressing areas.

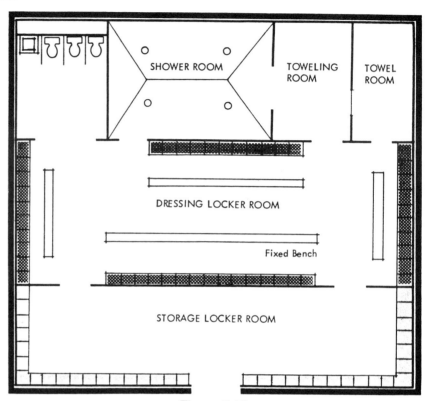

Figure 6-13

Dressing locker and box storage equipment combining the clothing storage and dressing areas.

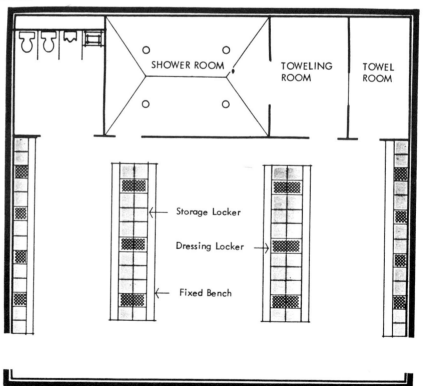

Service Areas

room is available in which bulky equipment can be stored conveniently, the size of the lockers can be reduced.

Lockers with mesh sides and doors offer the best visual inspection and maximum control of odors. The locker should contain an upper shelf for such items as books, a low shelf for shoes, and adequate hangers.

Dressing Locker and Box Storage System

A dressing locker and box storage system is the most common for institutional use. Figures 6-14 and 14A show various arrangements. A series of smaller lockers to hold equipment is located near a large dressing locker. Therefore, during any given class, each member has the use of one large dressing locker. In some cases, storage lockers are located in a separate area. This system is more cumbersome, although it does allow for special ventilation of the storage area. If the latter system is used, the uniform and towel issue rooms should be located between the two areas for convenience.

Maximum security requires that the padlock of the box locker be transported to the dressing locker when in use and all contents of the box locker be placed in the dressing locker. Adequate supervision and operating instructions must accompany this system. Permanent combination locks on box lockers are not recommended. (Figures 6-15A, B, C)

Color coding of lockers is a popular means of assigning lockers. It not only affords easy recognition but assists in overall supervision and makes the locker room attractive.

The size of the box locker is important. Do not purchase lockers in sizes too small for efficient use. Order box lockers in sizes to coordinate with the dressing lockers.

Increased shelf space rather

Figure 6-14
Single ties lockers at Washington State University.

Figure 6-14A
Rectangular box lockers at West High School in Aurora, Illinois.

than height, has been found to provide more efficient storage in lockers. However, the program dictates the need. If raquets for tennis, squash, or racquetball are not furnished, for example, the institution has an obligation to provide adequate storage space somewhere in the building. Similarly, programmers offering outside instruction in cool weather should reasonably expect to offer facilities that properly care for additional clothing.

Box Locker System

For institutions that offer laundering of uniforms, the box locker plan, which can be serviced from the issue room by an attendant, has distinct advantages. This plan saves student time because uniforms can be laundered and replaced systematically by the staff. The system also utilizes space more economically. Daily changes of uniform reduce odors in the building. However, the operational costs of this system are high because of labor costs for attendants.

Tote Basket System

The tote basket system has been used most frequently in elementary school or municipal swimming pool areas. It is administered in several different ways. In some operations, the basket is stored inside a storage room and issued through windows. The basket is then carried to the locker room area. This system requires attendants and breaks down when a large number of users arrive and depart simultaneously.

In another arrangement, baskets are stored on special racks in the locker room itself. A student is issued a padlock and has ready access to his equipment. This plan often results in pilfering, since it is very difficult to construct baskets and supporting racks that withstand deliberate damage attempts. When overnight storage is needed in the locker room, storage lockers are preferred over baskets.

Another system allows for the storage of baskets on wheeled dollies for each class in a special security area. When the class arrives, the attendant rolls out the dolly and returns the baskets from

Figure 6-15, 15A, 15B, 15C
In its new HPER facility, the University of Nebraska at Omaha has four different styles (and colors) of lockers to accommodate different users. The benches allow for easy maintenance and maximum space utilization.

the previous class to the secured area. In many situations, it is not necessary to put locks on individual lockers as long as adequate supervisory controls can be maintained.

The main advantages of the tote basket system are:
- A need for fewer standing lockers (wall hooks around the locker room perimeter may offer sufficient space for street clothes)
- Relatively good ventilation
- The economy of space

The disadvantages of this system are:
- Fragility of baskets
- Possibility of misplacing baskets
- Need for greater supervision

Locker Construction

The proper selection of lockers is imperative. Equipment of this kind should be chosen according to the nature of the program and the usage it will receive. Failure to install sturdy materials can be costly. Lockers usually receive extensive use and must serve for many years. Specifications should be followed after a thorough study of locker construction.

Heavy gauge metals should be used. Steel sheets are manufactured in thicknesses varying from .1196 to .0239 inches. Normally, the doors are of greater thickness than the sides and back. Special materials are used as needed at ends or exposed areas. Heavy duty latches should be furnished, which are removable for future repair or replacement.

In most cases, it is advantageous to purchase all-welded factory assembled units, which are more sturdy than units delivered ready for assembling at the site with nuts and bolts. Although initial costs and charges are higher for a pre-assembled unit, savings are frequently realized by avoiding assembly costs and errors at the construction site.

A second consideration in locker selection is ventilation. Lockers with expanded mesh construction assure adequate circulation of air and speed drying, and reduce the growth of bacteria by the admission of light. A total room ventilation system is preferred to a system internally installed in lockers. A third consideration is the need for visual inspection. This is an item of local concern, but it can be an important function of administration.

Sloping tops have the advantages in that dust cannot accumulate and that they can be cleaned easily. Ventilation systems may be affected by the additional height necessary for sloping tops, and this factor should be investigated before reaching a decision. On the other hand, when flat, locker tops are low enough to allow frequent dusting, a flat surface does provide a convenient place for books while the locker is being opened. The latching device for lockers should provide three-point latching at the top, bottom, and door handle. Rod guides at the top and bottom give proper security. Lockers that provide a recess at the door lock to keep the lock from projecting

into the aisle allow for easier passage.

When lockers are placed back to back, a 3"-4" forced air space should be left between the rear panels for adequate ventilation. The bottom of the locker should be attached to an 8"-16" base. This permits floor hosing and eliminates corrosion. (Figure 6-16)

Benches should be secured to the floor with non-corrosive equipment. A fiberglass, plastic, or hard wood seat 8 inches wide, with rounded edges and smooth surface, would be 16 inches from the floor. Space between lockers and benches should be planned for traffic control and dressing comfort. The recommended allowances are 30 inches from locker to bench with an allowance of 8 inches for bench width. Benches should extend the full length of each locker bank, with breaks at intervals of 12 feet.

A second arrangement is also very effective. A solid pedestal slab is placed over the locker base and extended out to form a bench on either side of the lockers. The aisles are unobstructed, cleaning is simplified, safety is improved, and the floor area is conserved. An alternative to this plan requires

Figure 6-16
Use of moveable benches in locker room at Student Rec. Center at Texas Tech University.

only one bench per aisle. Seldom does a locker room need more. The pedestal slab is used alternately between rows of lockers so that only one pedestal bench is available in each aisle. This represents a saving of one foot in each locker bank spacing. (Figure 6-17)

The pedestal locker system, however, has its drawbacks. Since the bench slab should be 16 inches high, the lockers will extend 8 inches higher than with the traditional 8-inch base. It is inconvenient for elementary school youngsters or short students to operate lock combinations on the top row of storage lockers. A 60-inch locker arrangement is recommended rather than 72 inches. If 72-inch lockers are selected, the effects of lighting dispersion and room ventilation should be analyzed.

SPECIAL FEATURES OF ELEMENTARY LOCKER ROOMS

Extended community use of elementary schools requires planning of locker facilities. In these buildings, lockers should allow pupils to change uniforms and shower. In these grades, teachers should control security. Baskets on dollies that can be moved to secure areas are

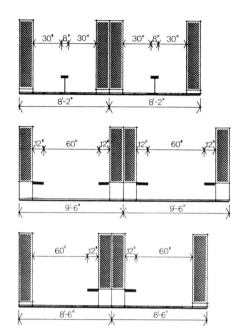

Figure 6-17
Dressing bench arrangements.

adequate. Another acceptable system is a series of shelves of box lockers secured by padlock doors. The teacher need only open several locker doors for each class, and the pupils have no need to operate locks. (Figures 18; 18A)

For the upper elementary students, wire mesh lockers of sufficient size to hold personal equipment should be available. If these lockers are purchased as a part of the system to include individual lockers, the large

lockers serve a dual use for after-school activities. Providing facilities of this nature enable school personnel to develop and plan a comprehensive program for the future.

The locker-shower complex should contain sufficient individual lockers to encourage faculty to assist with the school student activities and to be active to their own recreation.

Adult education and community groups should have lockers and space available for night classes. It is recommended that at least 600 square feet be designed to accommodate adult use. Serious consideration should be given to an area that can be used by athletic teams.

The height, size, and amount of service facilities as showers, urinals, and drinking fountains should reflect the school-community philosophy and provide suitable units for all age groups.

THE ATHLETIC TEAM LOCKER ROOM

The development of diverse athletic teams and the tremendous growth in numbers of participants mandate special attention for team locker rooms. For example, as a school increases its population, a varsity football program may

Figures 6-18, 18A
Combination of locker system with contrasting colors used in the HPER Building at the University of Arkansas.

Service Areas

expand to include separate junior varsity and freshman teams. At the same time, the fall sports program may be broadened to include soccer, cross-country, and other teams. The development of women's teams and intramurals may also contribute to this increase.

A well-developed master plan will permit orderly expansion. The following recommendations should be considered: (1) Locker rooms should be planned so at least one wall is an outside wall of the building, allowing for convenient addition in the future; and (2) The physical education locker arrangement can include team lockers interspersed throughout the room without undue interference.

There are advantages to providing separate outside athletic locker rooms for sports such as football, soccer, baseball, track, and lacrosse. The space under bleachers or in a separate building allows for excellent facilities. Planners should consider the following points:

- Cleaning costs are reduced because players do not go through the school building with soiled uniforms.
- Cleaning can be accomplished by hosing down.
- Construction does not need to be as elegant as the school building.
- The cost of utilities can be shared by the public facilities and the locker room facilities.
- Participants in after-school programs can continue to use school facilities without interference.
- Outside facilities such as public toilets, ticket booths, and refreshment stands can easily be made a part of the total complex.
- The locker room is easily accessible from the playing site.
- Visiting teams can use one

of the locker rooms.

The development of a total complex for the team should include offices for coaches and dressing; and locker, dressing, and toilet facilities for players, visiting teams, officials, and coaches. A training room, equipment issue room, meeting or lecture room, storage facilities, and adequate ventilation system for drying clothes are other needs for these team locker areas.

Locker doors should be of open construction to encourage air flow for drying. All team lockers should be from 60 to 72 inches in height and at least 12 inches in width. If football equipment is stored in lockers, the lockers should be 18 inches in width. Serious consideration should be given to eliminating clothes lockers and providing proper hanging space and a small security locker for valuables in the football area. Ventilation, controlled automatically, involves the total area and assures proper drying.

Provisions should be made to separate the dressing areas of the various teams for security purposes. To ensure flexibility, partitions can be constructed of heavy mesh screening.

The lecture room should be large enough to seat the members of a squad informally. It should include a bulletin board and chalkboard and be equipped for such audiovisual equipment as films, overhead projector, and videotape review.

Storage Rooms

Over a period of years, a suitable storage system has significant economic advantages because of increased security and because of the proper care and maintenance of supplies and equipment. Adequate storage space is imperative.

Planners of any kind of storage area must be familiar with fire laws. For example, certain state fire laws do not permit storage under stairways unless the total construction is concrete and

includes the installation of metal fire doors.

Several kinds of storage areas must be developed. Although in many cases it is possible to combine these areas, they are considered individually in the following sections.

Supply Issue Room

Central to the locker-dressing room area, there should be a storage room for issuing physical education clothing and instructional equipment. It can also serve for towel issue and retrieval. It should be fitted with shelving and a hanging system. A dutch door can facilitate the dispensing of equipment. This room should be secured with a sturdy lock. (Figure 6-19; 19A)

Out-of-Season Storage and Repair

An equipment storage space for extra supplies and out of season equipment is best located immediately adjacent to the issue room but separated by a solid wall with a door. A small area should be provided for equipment repair. This room should be organized for easy inventory and effective administration. Tilted shelves or noncorrosive bars are convenient for ball storage and other items. Installing these devices about an inch from the wall facilitates cleaning. Level shelves are needed to store most other items. Bins are convenient for gymnasium equipment, hockey sticks, and baseball bats. Proper ventilation and humidity control are absolutely necessary for this room to prevent deterioration of supplies.

Gymnasium Storage Room

This room should be located on the gymnasium level and be immediately adjacent to the teaching station. When partitions are used to divide the gymnasium into several stations, each station should have either a separate storage room or a separate opening to one large storage area.

Figures 6-19, 19A
Service center makes towel distribution easy at University of Arkansas' new HPER facility.

Double doors with flush sills and sufficient height will facilitate movement of apparatus and equipment such as ping-pong tables and tumbling mats. Invariably, these rooms are made smaller than necessary. Although a minimum area needed for storage of large equipment is recommended at 250 to 300 square feet, the specific needs of the school's program should be evaluated. The following procedure is recommended:

- Make a list of all equipment, including planned purchases, that need to be stored.
- On graph paper, draw to scale the storage space needs for each item and cut out templates.
- Arrange templates on scaled graph paper to indicate space needs.
- Present data to administrative personnel as verification of space needs.

In facilities that contain a separate gymnastics and tumbling room, apparatus can remain in that room when not used thus eliminating storage needs. Selected activities that do not require a full teaching station can use that room when gymnastics classes are not conducted.

Some school systems transport gymnastics equipment from school to school to save duplication of purchases. As a result, a school retains the apparatus only while it is being used, and only one school of the group requires space for gymnastics equipment storage.

Community Recreation Storage

The community recreational program requires storage space. The sharing of equipment and the misuse of equipment are frequent sources of contention between school and community groups. It is recommended that designated storage spaces be provided for the community program and adequate security measures be taken for both school and community equipment.

Audio-Visual Equipment Storage

Videotape and instant replay equipment are invaluable as teaching aids. To assure their effective use, they should be kept at the instruction site. Effective use of audio-visual equipment mandates that accessible, well-protected, and secure areas be located at the instruction site. In order to reduce damage due to mishandling, a small secure area should be available to store the equipment on a movable cart. The equipment can then be made

readily operational.

There also is need for one audio-visual equipment storage room accessible from the administrative areas. This can be used as a master storage area for audio-visual equipment and auxiliary supplies.

Outside Field Storage

If the main building is used for storage of outdoor equipment, the storage room should be located near the field exits. Such equipment would include archery targets, linemarkers, bases, football charging sleds, tools, and the like.

It is preferable to store these materials away from the main building and near the play areas to prevent dirt from being tracked into the school and to allow easy access to the equipment. A building designed as a separate athletic team locker room affords an excellent space. Small outside sheds are frequently used, but they are subject to vandalism unless they are well-constructed and have a good locking device.

Athletic Team Storage Room

Team equipment and uniforms will be stored, repaired, issued, inventoried and retrieved in this room. For purposes of control and accountability, storage rooms for athletic teams should be independent of other storage areas. They should be adjacent to the team locker room for orderly issue of equipment. Shelving that allows easy categorizing of sizes should be provided. Open-end cubicles facilitate the storage of bulky items and provide for free circulation of air.

Cedar-lined closets safeguard woolen goods. Tables are needed to fold clothes prior to distribution. A work area for the repair of equipment should be nearby. Controlled ventilation, temperature, and humidity are necessary to prevent deterioration of clothing, leather and rubber goods. Each team should have its own securable section of shelving. Storage space must have maximum security.

Custodial Areas

Custodial storage rooms should be located conveniently on each floor in each building. There should be at least one 6 foot by 8 foot custodial room for each 10,000 square feet of floor space, and there should be at least one on each floor. Each room should have a service sink with a pop-up drain and a mixer type faucet. Shelves and hanging boards should be constructed in each room for storage of supplies and tools. A small room about 6 feet by 8 feet should be provided near the service entrance of each building for storage of tools and supplies used in building maintenance within the building.

LAUNDRY

A healthful school environment may benefit by the operation of laundry facilities for physical education and athletic programs. Reduction of illnesses and skin infections, minimizing of odors, improved appearance of uniforms, and a general attitude toward cleanliness are all potential benefits of a laundry.

The decision to institute a laundry involves a complete feasibility study to determine if it is more satisfactory than relying on students to launder items at home and more economical than contracting with commercial companies. Renovation or conversion of existing space in old buildings for the installation of laundry equipment is often costly due to extensive work related to gas and/or electric utilities, venting, waste drainage, and environmental control equipment, to name a few factors. A cost analysis should include such items as personnel, equipment, building maintenance and use, utilities, supplies, and deliveries.

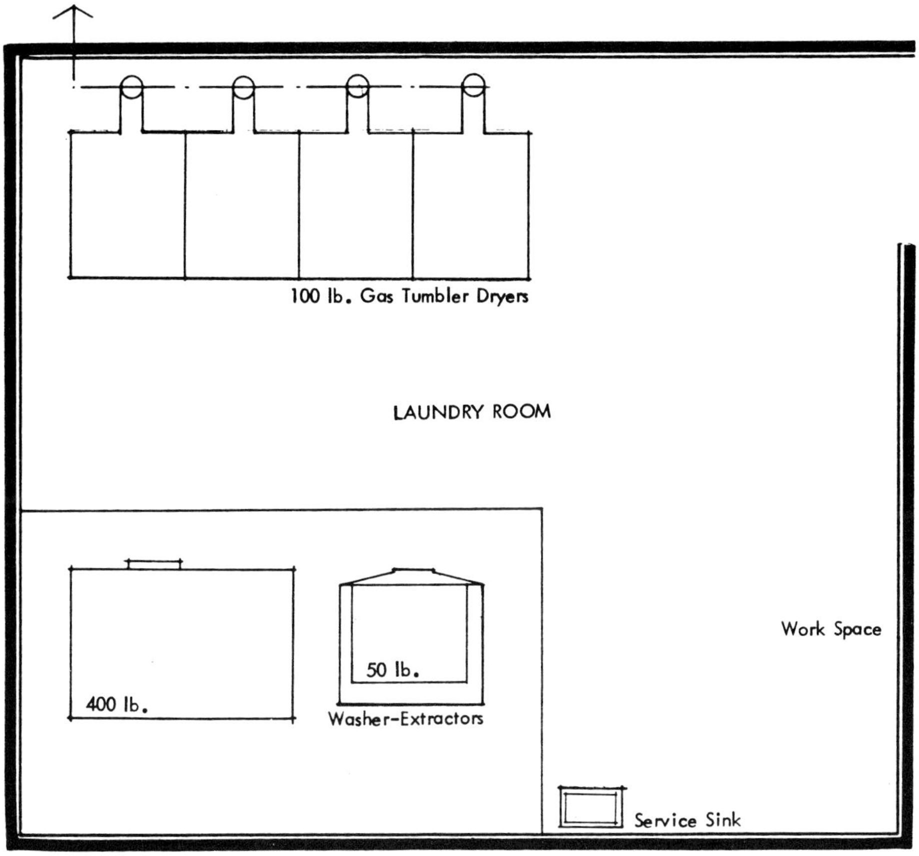

Location

The laundry room should relate directly to a corridor, preferably near the locker room area. Plumbing installation costs can be minimized if the laundry is situated near the shower and toilet facilities. The room should have direct access to a service roadway for transporting laundry to and from areas located away from the main site (if necessary). Ramps should be installed if laundry dollies are to be transported from different floor levels.

Often times it is cost effective in terms of space utilization and supervisory personnel to include the laundry facility as part of the total equipment issue room. Towels can be laundered at the site where they are distributed to students. (Figure 6-20)

Size

The total size of a laundry room is dependent primarily upon the quantity of laundry to be handled and the number and kind of machines to be installed. Other factors include storage shelves for clothes and supplies, space for laundry dollies, tables for folding and ironing, and a work space for issuing clothing and for general organizational purposes. Sufficient

100 lb. Gas Tumbler Dryers

LAUNDRY ROOM

Work Space

400 lb.

50 lb.

Washer-Extractors

Service Sink

Figure 6-20
Suggested laundry room layout.

space should be left around the machines to facilitate maintenance.

Equipment

Selection of equipment should precede architectural planning. Decisions relating to equipment purchase merit careful deliberation. Literature from the various manufacturers describes special features and should be compared closely.

The size of the machines depends upon the size of peak loads. It is often preferable to purchase several machines of different sizes instead of one large machine to wash all items. Delicate fabrics can usually be handled in the smaller machines, and at least one of the machines would be available to handle all of the work in the event that repairs must be made on others.

An investigation should be made concerning the purchase of the combination washer/extractor or separate machines. The combination has advantages for institutional use since it allows greater loads to be handled in a given period of time. It also requires less space, less employee time, and less capital outlay.

For most institutions, a series of dryers is preferable over one large dryer. Preference for gas, electric, or steam must be decided on a local basis according to the cost of equipment, energy medium, and personnel time. The same is true of the special features offered by various companies.

There should be at least a minimum ironing service available. Modern fabrics have eliminated the need to iron athletic uniforms, but on special occasions some ironing service will be necessary.

A sink should be installed for items requiring special care for stain removal or special rinsing.

Physical Features
Walls

The side walls should be soundproof to prevent the noise of the machines from disturbing nearby school activities. In addition, some of the walls should be clear of obstacles or windows to allow for well-organized shelving spaces. Space should be provided for storage of laundry room supplies as well as for systematic storage of clothing or uniforms by sizes.

Doorways must be sized to permit replacement of machinery. Swinging doors with protective guards attached at the bottom are recommended. Flush sills allow laundry trucks to move in and out freely.

Ceilings and Lights

Ceilings should be moisture-resistant because of the high humidity. Acoustic treatment will reduce noise transmission to upper floors. Beams should be of sufficient strength to assist movement of machinery with pulleys. Lights should furnish 50 footcandles of lumination throughout the room.

Floors

Floors should be sloped to drains. They should have a moisture-proof, non-skid surface that is resistant to detergents and bleaching materials. The floor should be durable enough to withstand considerable vibration and weight. Most machine manufacturers specify the construction of elevated, concrete bases for the installation of machines. In some instances shock-absorbing armatures are built into the machines which eliminate the need for bases.

Utilities

The heavy demands of laundry equipment require close conformity to manufacturers' recommendations on utilities. Laundry equipment should be selected prior to pipe installations.

Institutional machines use large amounts of hot and cold water. Steam may also be necessary. Machines must allow regulation of water temperature for various fabrics.

Provisions must be made for both 220 and 110 volt outlets. Manufacturers' specifications should be followed to prevent overloading. Sufficient outlets for auxiliary use should be spaced throughout the room.

Control of heat and humidity is always a problem unless adequate provision has been made to control climate. A location in the building that allows for good exhaust ventilation is an economical asset.

TRAINING ROOMS

There is a growing demand in our nation's schools for more thoroughly prepared and equipped athletic trainers. This demand should be recognized in planning the facilities which contribute so much to the health and safety of young athletes.

The training room will be used for the storage and distribution of medical supplies and for the administration of physical therapy. Its size will depend upon such factors as the number of individuals it must serve, availability of assistant trainers, and the treatment areas contemplated.

Some universities with large athletic departments have training rooms in as many as five or six buildings. A central training area will have offices for the sports medicine staff during the morning hours, and later, during athletic practice times, the staff is assigned to auxiliary training rooms in the other buildings. Many secondary schools have a designated athletic trainer, and this individual is on duty at practice sessions and all scheduled athletic events.

Location

Training rooms should be accessible to both men and women and located adjacent to their respective locker and shower rooms. There should be easy access to the area for ambulance services. In some universities and colleges the sports medicine staff also supervises rehabilitation of injured athletes and usually the rehabilitation area is adjacent to the main training facility and offices. In this way, constant supervision of this area can be maintained.

Physical Features

The floor of training rooms should be constructed of concrete and covered with vinyl tile or one of the suitable synthetic materials. These coverings facilitate easy cleaning. The training facility will be subjected to moisture, and therefore the floor construction should be of a non-slip type of surfacing.

The first five feet of wall space should be constructed of easily cleaned building material such as tile, vinyl coated wallboard, or epoxy painted concrete block. The remaining wall space can be painted with a moisture-proof paint.

The ceiling should be at least 10 feet high and constructed of acoustic tile or its equivalent. This height will allow athletes to stand on a table for strapping.

Lighting should consist of at least 50 footcandles at a height of 4 feet. Sufficient wall plugs of both 110 volts and 220 volts should be located at appropriate areas around the room, not more than 2 feet from the floor. Make sure that all switches and terminals are properly grounded. Ground fault interrupts (GFI) must be used on all outlets in hydrotherapy areas.

Proper ventilation is of importance to any area of a building but of particular importance to the training room. Steam and moisture from hydrotherapy areas and heat from other apparatus can make this room very uncomfortable without well-planned ventilation. The room should have its own thermostat because of the minimal clothing worn by the athletes.

Layout

Most modern main training rooms are organized with six areas in mind: 1) general first aid and taping area, 2) hydrotherapy area, 3) electrotherapy area, 4) rehabilitation area, 5) athletic trainer's office, 6) a good-sized storage room.

Traffic control is important for efficient use of these spaces. The frequently used areas should be located close to the entrance and placed as follows: First, the taping tables, second, the electrotherapy section, and third, the hydrotherapy section. The rehabilitation area may have another entrance. (Figures 6-21; 6-22)

Equipment

The equipment needed for each area of the training room will depend on the availability of space, the number of trainers employed, and the size of the athletic program. In the taping area of a large central training room, at least 6-8 taping tables approximately 42 inches high are needed. They should have foam padding and be covered with a tough vinyl-coated fabric. A small shelf can be constructed at one end of each table to accommodate storage of tape, gauze, etc. Ankle wrap rolls should be accessible to each table. Also, a freezer should be located in this section. A new trend for saving space allows for one long taping table that should

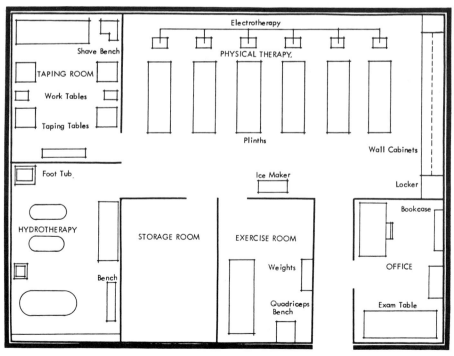

Figure 6-21
Suggested layout for primary athletic training room.

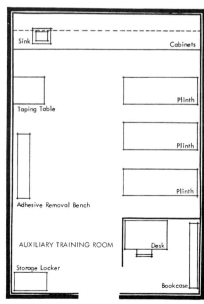

Figure 6-22
Auxiliary training room layout.

accommodate 8 to 10 athletes at one time.

The hydrotherapy section should be enclosed by a curb so that water which occasionally overflows from the equipment can be contained. The floor should be constructed of a non-skid tile and should slope toward the drain. Whirlpools which use both hot and cold water and the ice-making machines are kept in this enclosure. The proper electrical outlets and plumbing hook-ups must be provided.

The electrotherapy section should have treatment tables of similar construction to the taping table but with a minimum length of 6 feet to allow an individual to lie out full length. Electrical outlets should be planned for each table of sufficient voltage to accommodate electrotherapy equipment. Outlets should be 2 feet off the floor so that arms, legs, and backs will not accidentally come into contact with receptacles.

The rehabilitation section should have a synthetic floor because of the constant use of weights for conditioning. The type of equipment needed will depend on the size of the school's program and the academic training of the trainers.

Trainer Offices and the Physical Examining Room

The trainer offices should have partial glass walls for a view of the treatment areas. Other equipment would include a desk and chair, a bookcase, filing cabinets, and a bulletin board. Each office should have a phone.

The physician's examining room should be completely enclosed and include an adjustable examining table, secure medicine cabinet, and a small desk with chair. An adjustable surgical lamp may prove useful.

Storage Section

A storage area adjacent to the training room is needed. This room should be large enough to accommodate supplies that will be used during the year. The area should have climate control and a heavy locking door.

FACILITIES FOR FACULTY AND STAFF

Administrative Units

Properly programmed and effectively designed office suites and work rooms facilitate an efficient working relationship among the various divisions and enhance the success of the program. Staff members develop increased morale and motivation, which foster increased productivity, when office spaces and service areas provide a pleasant environment and a functional setting in which to work.

Planners can generalize about the relationship of the various spaces, but the unique problems of individual schools make it difficult to establish hard rules. Planners should consider the following guidelines in relation to the special needs of the individual institution.

Centralization of faculty offices normally improves communication among the various departments. Working as a unifying group develops a valuable esprit de corps among faculty members. In larger institutions, the trend has been for athletic coaches and administration to locate apart from physical education faculty. Since the athletic program is expensive, the separation allows for efficient athletic administration independent of physical education. However, over a period of time, with separate of personnel and subsequent changes in staff, a communication gap can develop and little interaction may take place between the two segments.

Planning committees need to weigh carefully the factors affecting administration prior to decentralizing a staff. At the same time, there are divisions that can function more efficiently if the staff is housed as a unit in a favorable location. It is recommended that staff members be grouped as working units according to their function but retain a close proximity to other departmental personnel. Normally, the following units might comprise efficient working units: Athletics, Intramurals, Professional Preparation, Basic Instructional Program, Recreation/Leisure Studies.

The trend is for basic instructional programs for men and women to merge into a single administrative unit. New and better coeducational programs are encouraged when the responsible individuals can discuss problems frequently. The location of facilities and congestion caused by large numbers of participating students bears heavily on the location of this area. Basic instructional programs involve the greatest number of staff and students and should be so located as not to interfere with other facets of administration.

Essential Administrative Facilities

Essential facilities related to administration include administrative and faculty offices, secretarial and clerical offices and workrooms, conference rooms, reception and waiting rooms, athletic offices (depending on size of institution), storage rooms, and faculty/staff shower and rest rooms.

Administrative Offices

Administrative offices should be centrally located with easy access from main entrances. A reception area, controlled by secretarial assistants, should be available for guests and for scheduled appointments.

The administrator's office should have a minimum of 200 square feet. A large facility may contain a suite of offices for several administrators. These offices should be located close to the secretarial area and should be provided with a private rest room area.

The decor should produce pleasant working conditions and present a favorable impression upon visitors and guests. Consideration should be given to acoustics, including the transmission of sound through the walls and the sounds resulting from heating and cooling units. Carpeting and drapes are assets in these offices for improved acoustics, aesthetics, and morale.

Faculty Offices

Faculty offices should allow the staff to work comfortably. Particularly at the college level, many staff hours are spent in the office on tasks associated with teaching. Writing, planning, counseling, and routine administrative work are important facets of the job.

Office spaces should be large enough to accommodate the following items: large work desk with lock, comfortable desk chair, filing cabinet, bookshelves, side chair, and compact storage cabinet.

This private office is recommended and should be a minimum of 100 square feet. If rooms are larger, a common practice is for a second person to be assigned to the office when additional staff is hired.

Air conditioning is recommended if a summer program is conducted.

Secretarial and Clerical Offices

Planning for secretarial and clerical offices should include a job analysis for each position. Normally, secretaries are expected to perform, in varying degrees, the following duties:

- Act as receptionists for students, faculty, visitors, salespersons, press representatives, and others.
- Take and transcribe dictation, and perform a variety of typing chores.
- Receive and redirect telephone calls.
- Receive and distribute mail and other communications.
- Answer written correspondence.
- Schedule appointments and keep track of faculty.
- Operate a variety of office machines, such as duplication, mimeograph machines, ditto machines, and computers.
- File department papers, correspondence, forms, and other materials.
- Perform such business operations as bookkeeping and accounting.
- Prepare copies of class tests and other teaching materials as needed in courses.
- Dispense tickets for spectator events.

In small schools requiring one or two secretaries, a single office usually suffices for all the tasks. At universities conducting extensive programs in physical education, recreation, and athletics, it is preferred that secretaries be dispersed to various areas according to their functions.

Secretaries should be located in accessible areas, but in such a position that individuals do not pass in the immediate vicinity of the area unless business is to be conducted. Socializing with students must be discouraged.

If the reception room/office arrangement is used, the reception responsibilities often make it impossible to carry out important tasks. Under this arrangement, if more than a single secretary is located in the office, it is best to use a system whereby a visual barrier will isolate those secretaries serving as receptionists.

For each secretary, an operating space of at least 120 square feet should be planned exclusive of the reception and storage areas. Filing cabinets, desks, storage cabinets, typewriter space, and a work counter are the requisites for the secretary.

With the advent of electronic mail and computer work stations, the secretarial work station will need to be reassessed in terms of space and support equipment.

The telephone system should be convenient for all. The main telephone, containing all extensions and intercoms, should be at the receptionist's desk.

Easily accessible individual mailboxes should be located in the office. It is important that messages be readily seen and formal security be established for the mail.

A work room for carrying out routine clerical duties must be available. It should contain copying machines with ample counter space to work efficiently. Metal shelving for paper and mimeograph supplies is required. Equipment for running and filing stencils should also be placed in this room. If work space for calculators and other office machines is not available in the main office, the work room should be used for this purpose. Rather than duplicate the purchase of costly machines, secretaries from various units, even though not located together, might use the same work room. The room should, therefore, be so located as to be accessible to the secretarial staff of a number of units.

Audio-Visual Storage

Audio-visual equipment represents a large capital outlay, and thus proper security of these items is essential. Videotape with instant playback, movie projectors, strip films, record players, and cameras are common equipment items. Additional supplies such as films, tapes, spare parts, and cords must be properly stored and inventoried.

It is recommended that secure storage areas be planned at the respective teaching stations for equipment normally used at the site. Such an arrangement encourages use of the teaching aids and reduces preparation time. However, in addition to these satellite areas, it is necessary to have a main audio-visual storage room with a good inventory and issue system and with one person responsible for security.

Schools expecting to use videotape and replay equipment need to establish several small areas in which staff and students may view and evaluate tapes or review tapes for preparation purposes. If normal classrooms are not available, a special room should allow several students to view tapes simultaneously. Methods teachers, student-teacher supervisors, and skill instructors have the most need for viewing films and should be consulted concerning needs.

Conference Room

A conference room should be included in the plans for a modern physical education plant to serve athletics, physical education, and recreation. There is frequent need for inter-departmental administrative and staff meetings. Student oral examinations and small group discussions are best carried out in a room designated for these purposes.

A large table with adequate seating situated in a well-ventilated, attractive room is recommended. A closet area is convenient for visitors and guests. Usually, a small table for refreshments is provided. Consideration should be given to a kitchenette. Depending upon the needs of the particular school, the room can serve such other purposes as staff lounge, reading room, film viewing area, and so on.

SELECTED REFERENCES

Arnheim, D.D. and C.E. Klafs. **Modern Principles of Athletic Training.** Fourth edition. St. Louis: The C.V. Mosby Company, 1977.

Bronzan, Robert T. **New Concepts in Planning and Funding Athletic, Physical Education and Recreation Facilities.** St. Paul, Minnesota: Phoenix Intermedia Inc., 1974.

Dressing Rooms and Related Service Facilities for Physical Education, Athletics, and Recreation. Washington, D.C.: Council on Facilities for Physical Education, Athletics, and Recreation. Council on Facilities Equipment and Supplies. American Association for Health, Physical Education, and Recreation, 1972.

Ezersky, Eugene and Theibert, Richard P. **Facilities in Sports and Physical Education.** St. Louis: The C.V. Mosby Company, 1976.

Flynn, Richard B. and Gonsoulin, Sid. "Preventive Measures Can Combat Vandalism." **Athletic Purchasing and Facilities** (June 1981): 12-26.

Frost, Reuben G. and Marshall, Stanley J. **Administration of Physical Education and Athletics: Concepts and Practices.** Dubuque, Iowa: Wm. C. Brown Company, 1977.

Penman, Kenneth A. **Planning Physical Education and Athletic Facilities in Schools.** New York: John Wiley & Sons, 1977.

(See other chapter references for related materials.)

CHAPTER VII
Facilities For Recreation, Parks and Open Spaces

THE PLANNING PROCESS FOR PARKS AND RECREATION

Recreation and leisure are experiencing a multitude of factors and trends which are impacting the planning and delivery by leisure service systems. Planning principles are not typically subject to change, but inputs to the process are undergoing substantial change.

The 1980's are characterized by a variety of trends:

- Changing attitudes toward recreation and leisure
- Changes in employment and in the workplace
- A changing population and household composition
- Marked advances in medical care
- Dramatic innovations in leisure equipment technology
- Changing housing patterns
- Usage of electronic games, cable TV, and computers
- Changes in world energy
- Changes in regional economies
- Unstable political environments
- Increased and continuing emphasis on doing more with less

Recreation is increasingly recognized and accepted as a significant factor in the maintenance of health. Physical and psycho-social benefits of recreation are regarded as essential elements within the human lifestyle. Recreation is much more than just a weekend of activity. Recreation and leisure lifestyles have incorporated leisure activity as a part of the daily American routine. Recreation is now viewed as a means to an end, and its place along with the work ethic is firmly established.

Facilities and open spaces must clearly be designed to accommodate the dramatic changes of the 1980's. The planning process will continue to need the involvement of the varied publics to be served.

A Master Plan Concept

(Figure 7-1) The planning process, regardless of the size of the community involved, typically occurs at three levels. First, there must be a master plan conceptualized at the policy-making level. Second, there

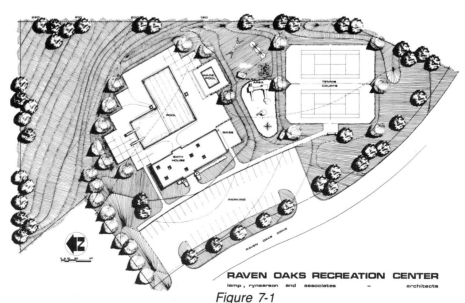

RAVEN OAKS RECREATION CENTER
lamp , rynearson and associates   -   architects

Figure 7-1
Raven Oaks Recreation Center is a neighborhood project located in an established area of suburban Northwest Omaha. Shown here is the master plan development.

is a concept plan which concerns physical matters in that it is site-specific and incorporates factors associated with landscaping, layout, facility mix, and construction. Third is the planning stage which has a focus on operation and maintenance for facilities, parks, and open spaces. All three levels are critical to sound planning; however, the master plan level is the most important since it is at the policy-making level where critical initial decisions are made which guide and control all future decisions at the second and third levels of planning.

Through the use of standards established for parks, recreation, open space, facilities, management, finance, etc., goals and objectives can be translated into specific achievements. The effective use of policies and standards readily facilitates the acquisition, development, and operation of park, recreation, and open space resources.

A master plan is the key to the facilitation of an orderly provision for goal and objective attainment whether it be for programs or for facilities and areas. The plan must be recognized, accepted, and approved by the group responsible for overall decision making (committee, board, council, commission, PTA, etc.). Regular review and updating of the master plan is a must. It is the one document that represents a continuous planning process and records the orderly evolution only for a specific unit of time.

The content of a master plan will be comprehensive and will reflect the expressed and established goals and objectives of the group/community concerned. It will define the role of each of the providers including public agencies, private membership organizations, and commercial business enterprises. There will be an inventory of expressed and documented needs and interests. Potential and available resources (human, physical, financial) will be

documented and analyzed. The overall inventory process may be achieved in many ways. It may be as simple as using pen and paper tabulations or as complex as computer simulation and/or remote sensing. Whatever the method, it should be appropriate to the needs and circumstances.

Contributions to the development of the master plan should come from a pool of professional disciplines and be representative of all persons within the group/community. Professionals who can be most helpful would include, to cite a few, leisure specialists, facility specialists, urban planners, landscape architects, lawyers, engineers, market analysts, ecologists, psychologists, economists, sociologists, bankers, university educators, and specialists from the media.

During the 1970's and continuing to the present, planning in America has shifted away from being primarily physical in nature and has become much more policy-oriented and socially responsive. Needs and demands for participatory planning/involvement, management of growth, and neighborhood/community preservation, along with the growth of new leisure patterns, have resulted in a shift from traditional, project-oriented planning to planning with a variety of interactive modes involving far more consideration of local citizen goals and policy issues.

Community Involvement

In developing plans for new recreation, park, and open spaces, and in proposing improvements to existing facilities and areas, all planning, as suggested within the master plan concept, must reflect the wants and needs of the community. Public cooperation and involvement in the initial planning stages will serve to strengthen community interest both actively and financially.

There are many ways to involve the public in the planning process.

One is the public meeting. Although time-consuming, a series of well-organized public meetings is an effective means of presenting proposed plans.

A survey of leisure behavior and attitudes can be useful in determining the needs and desires of the people within a planning area. Many users are found in the community at large, outside school populations. Thus, inter-agency agreements for shared use of facilities is on the increase. Also, cooperation between community agencies and organized groups facilitates planning, promotes financial considerations, and assures community involvement.

The field of industrial recreation is developing as a major area of progress in the recreation field. Management and employees are discovering the benefits of industrial fitness programs. Industries throughout the nation are expanding current facilities or establishing new recreational and fitness complexes. Programs such as these range from multi-million dollar facilities with special equipment and a medical and professional staff to programs offered in conjunction with local Y's or school systems.

Again, because industrial recreation/fitness programs encompass such a wide range of opportunities, public and private interests must cooperate to provide the best facilities and programs possible.

Planning Considerations for Urban Areas

As a result of population shifts to urban centers, open space is at a premium within the confines of the urban areas, and there has been a general decline in the environmental quality of these areas. This has led to a growing public concern about recreational facilities and services. Therefore, the following factors must be considered when planning recreational facilities within congested urban areas:
- Lack of open space and

often lack of economic resources make it mandatory that all government and public agencies cooperate in planning facilities for maximum use.

Recreational use of public housing facilities, social and health care programs in recreational centers, and swimming pools adjacent to or part of fire stations are just a few examples of ways in which the public can maximize facility use.

- Additional or secondary uses of all facilities, both public and private, must be considered. For example, the parking lot of a large industrial plant can be used for recreational purposes on weekends with little or no additional cost if properly planned.
- The mobility of people in dense urban areas is often restricted. Therefore, facilities must be easily accessible to the people.
- Plans should be revised for maximum use of existing facilities. Twenty-four hour use should be considered as a possibility in some areas.

Multiple Use

Planning facilities for multiple use is a major consideration in the establishment of playgrounds and other recreational properties. Multiple use facilities require space that can accommodate varied activities for all age groups during various times of the day, week, month, season, or year. Most activities are associated with specific times and/or seasons. Basketball and hockey are considered winter activities, baseball is played in the spring and the summer, and football is a sport for autumn. Thus, a facility that is planned to accommodate a single use becomes an expensive investment if allowed to stand idle much of the year. Changing recreational preferences requires that indoor and outdoor areas not be restricted with permanent spatial and architectural fixtures designed for specific activities in a set period of time. There must be a flexibility built into indoor and outdoor facilities comparable to the open classroom in the field of education.

The character and location of the population are constantly changing. The ethnic, socio-economic, and demographic features such as age and family size can vary within neighborhoods. With today's mobile population, a community facility that is planned on the basis of a static population soon has many obsolete features.

Eliminating Architectural Barriers

It is essential that all recreational facilities be designed to serve the handicapped. Therapeutic recreation services must involve the special members of the population in the planning process to ensure that activities and facilities will serve their needs. Guidelines for the elimination of architectural barriers are detailed in Chapter 8.

INDOOR COMMUNITY AREAS AND FACILITIES

Related aspects of the various types of planning units (neighborhood, community, city or school district, and county or region) were discussed in Chapters 1 and 3. Relations among planning units, however, are often changed by physiographic or demographic changes occurring in the planning entity. A new neighborhood might be formed by a significant change in housing or in nationality, or a community might be divided into two neighborhoods by a new expressway. These factors are taken into consideration when defining units.

Use of Planning Units

Population units form the basis for planning programs and activities.

The park and recreation agency, in order to plan and manage its services properly, establishes its activities and facilities on the demands of a known population with given economic and ethnic characteristics. The larger the planning and managing agency, the broader the population group with which it will be concerned. An undefined population unit results only in arbitrary allocations of services and provides no accountability or relevancy. Every effort should be made to provide for recreational programs and areas in the most effective and efficient manner.

General Recreational Buildings

Recreational buildings should be planned to meet the needs and interests of all people in the neighborhood or community, regardless of age, sex or ability. They should provide a safe, healthful, and attractive atmosphere in which every person in the community or neighborhood may enjoy his leisure by participating in activities of a social, inspirational, cultural, or physical nature.

Recreational buildings may range from the simple picnic shelter to the complex community recreational building with its variety of special service facilities. They may vary in design from the rustic to the contemporary.

Unlike many of the early structures, present-day buildings provide for adaptability and multiple user. This change from the simple to the complex has stimulated the development of a variety of recreational buildings. These are classified by function and then categorized by size. The size of recreational buildings is usually based on the population to be served and the program to be conducted.

The Neighborhood Center

The facility which is, perhaps, closest to the grass-roots service level is the neighborhood center. A neighborhood recreation center is designed to service an area of approximately 8,000 people.

Such a building encloses 15,000 to 25,000 square feet. The size will depend also on whether the building is a separate entity or part of a park-school complex where facilities are available in the school.

The neighborhood center usually includes the following facilities:
- Multi-purpose room or rooms
- Gymnasium (if not available in neighborhood school)
- Shower and locker rooms, when a gymnasium is provided
- Arts and crafts room
- Game room
- Kitchen
- Restrooms
- Lounge and lobby
- Office
- Large storage areas.

The Community Center

The community recreation center functions beyond the primary purpose of serving a neighborhood. It is designed to meet the complete recreational needs of all the people in the community.

The size of the building depends on (a) the number of people to be served, (b) the projected program plan, and (c) whether it is a part of a park-school site or a separate building. This building usually contains 20,000 to 40,000 square feet of space, and is usually located in a major recreational area such as a park-school site or community park.

The community center usually includes the following facilities:
- Multi-purpose rooms
- Gymnasium
- Shower and locker rooms
- Stage and auditorium (sometimes combined with gymnasium)

- Rooms for programs in the arts (art, dance, music, drama)
- Game room
- Kitchen
- Restrooms
- Lounge and lobby
- Office
- Large storage areas
- Clubs or classrooms
- Possible specialized areas as program dictates (racquet courts, gymnastics, weight and exercise room, photography workshop, and so on).

Multi-Purpose Room

The multi-purpose room should be designed to accommodate such activities as general meetings, social recreation, active table games, dancing, dramatics, music, concerts, banquets, and the like.

The area of this room should be approximately 2,000 to 3,000 square feet. It should be rectangular in shape, with a minimum width of 40 feet. The minimum ceiling height should be 16 feet.

Vinyl-asbestos flooring is recommended. The floor should have a nonskid surface to prevent many common accidents. It is recommended that the floor also be level to permit multiple use for meetings, dancing, dramatic presentations, and so on.

The entrance should contain double doors and should be at the end opposite the stage. Each door should have a minimum unobstructed opening of at least 32 inches, with a removable mullion.

Gymnasium

The structure should be at least 90 by 100 feet, with a minimum height of 24 feet. This size will permit a basketball court of 50 by 84 feet, with additional room for telescopic bleachers seating approximately 325 spectators on one side of the gymnasium.

Provision should be made for a

mechanical ventilating system with air-conditioning considered where climate dictates. It is preferable to have no windows in the gymnasium. However, if desired, windows should be placed at right angles to the sun at a height of 12 feet or more, and they should be equipped with protective guards. The wainscotting, or tile, in the gymnasium should provide clear, unobstructed wall space from the floor to a height of 12 feet.

Floors with synthetic surfaces have become predominant in recreational gymnasiums. Maple flooring continues to be selected as an alternative to a synthetic surface. If maple flooring is used, the cork spring clip or other type of expansion joint should be installed on all four sides. If suspended apparatus requiring wall attachments is used in the gymnasium, these attachments should be at least seven feet above floor level.

Recessed drinking fountains should be located where they will cause a minimum of interference. Fountains should be hand- or hand-and-foot operated, with up-front spouts and controls. Protective floor covering or drainage at the base of the fountain should be considered to avoid floor damage. More detailed information concerning gymnasium construction is found in Chapter 3.

Locker and Shower Rooms

Locker and shower rooms must be provided for physical activities, athletics, faculty, and the like. For further details concerning locker rooms and facilities refer to Chapter 6.

Stage and Auditorium

A stage and related facilities may be built in conjunction with the gymnasium or multi-purpose room. If space and funds allow, a separate unit is preferred.

The stage proper should be about 20 feet in depth and the proscenium opening should be at least two-thirds the width of the room. The approach to the stage from the floor of the main room should be by inclined ramp with a nonskid surface to facilitate the physically disabled and aging and to accommodate movement of equipment.

The room should be equipped with a modern public address system, permanently installed with matched speakers and outlets for additional microphones and phonographic equipment. Consideration should be given to a master control from the office of the building. All stage lighting should be modern and should be controlled from a dimmer-control cabinet equipped with a rheostat.

The base and wall of the room should be equipped with electrical outlets to accommodate floor and table lamps, motion picture equipment, floodlights, and other electrical apparatus. A heavy-voltage line may be necessary. Provision should also be made for installing television program equipment.

The entrance should contain double doors. Stage doors should be of sufficient width and height to facilitate the movement of scenery. It is desirable to have a door at the rear of the stage area to permit the handling of stage properties and scenery. Adequate exit doors should be provided and should be equipped with panic hardware. Door frames and thresholds should be flush.

Space should be provided for the storage of chairs, tables, and portable staging. This space can be under the stage or in an adjacent storage room provided with dollies having swivel ballbearing fiber or rubber-covered casters.

Acoustics are an important factor in an auditorium and should be kept in mind in the selection of materials for walls and ceilings. Rigid acoustic materials for ceilings are more economical and discourage vandalism better than suspended acoustical tile.

Arts and Crafts Room

A separate room for arts and crafts is desirable. However, if this is not possible, at least one club room should be equipped for crafts, with provision for gas, compressed air, and a modern sink with hot and cold water. The sink should have a clay trap.

Ample storage cabinets, closets, or lockers should be included for the safe storage of craft materials, unfinished projects, and exhibit materials. Base and wall plugs should be provided in all club rooms for the operation of electric irons, sewing machines, power tools, movie projectors, and other equipment. If a kiln is used, it should be equipped with a heavy-duty 220-volt electrical outlet. Bulletin boards and exhibit cases may be used to display completed projects.

Game Room

The game room, approximately 30 by 64 feet in size, is designed for a variety of games, including pool and table tennis. In planning this room, sufficient storage space should be provided for the various items of game equipment and supplies. (Figures 7-2; 7-3)

This room should be close to office supervision and should be acoustically treated. The choice of floor material should be carefully considered because of the heavy traffic anticipated in this room. Windows should be placed high in the walls to reduce glass breakage. A chair rail or wainscotting to prevent the marring of walls should be installed to a height of three feet above the floor. Whenever possible, noncontact (nonmarring) furniture should be used.

The game room should include tables for billiards, table tennis, and other popular table top games.

Kitchen

A kitchen is desirable for most community and neighborhood recreation buildings. If large dinners or banquets are to be served, provision should be made for a full-size kitchen that

conforms to local health regulations and has a free floor space at least 54 inches wide.

The kitchen should be located near the club rooms and the gymnasium so it can be used for small gatherings in the club rooms and for large banquets in the

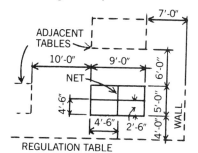

REGULATION TABLE

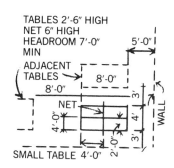

SMALL TABLE 4'-0"

Figure 7-2
Table Tennis

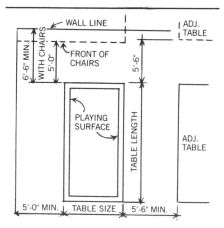

DIMENSIONS FOR BILLIARDS & POCKET BILLIARDS

TYPE OF TABLE	PLAYING SURFACE		TABLE SIZE	
	W.	L.	W.	L.
ENGLISH (SNOOKER)	6'-0"	12'-0"	6'-9"	12'-9"
STANDARD POOL OR BILL.	5'-0"	10'-0"	5'-9"	10'-9"
STANDARD POOL OR BILL.	4'-6"	9'-0"	5'-3"	9'-9"
STANDARD POOL OR BILL.	4'-0"	8'-0"	4'-9"	8'-9"
JUNIOR POOL	3'-6"	7'-0"	4'-3"	7'-9"
JUNIOR POOL	3'-0"	6'-0"	3'-9"	6'-9"
TABLE HEIGHT 2'-6" ±				

Figure 7-3
Billiards and Pocket Billiards (Pool).

gymnasium. The kitchen is often placed between two club rooms and made available to both rooms by the use of aluminum roll-up doors.

Adequate storage space, cabinet space, and electrical outlets for such appliances as the refrigerator, range, dishwasher, and can openers should be provided. Exhaust fans should also be installed.

Lounge and Lobby

The lobby is located just inside the entrance of the recreation building. The lounge should open off the lobby and, if possible, should be close to the central office and to the multi-purpose room and/or gymnasium. The lounge and lobby are often combined into one room.

This facility should be attractively lighted and should contain a wall-mounted, recessed drinking fountain, a lighted trophy case, and a bulletin board. Provision should be made for public telephones, and at least one telephone should be installed to accommodate a person in a wheelchair. Adequate space, preferably recessed, and electrical and water connections for automatic vending machines should be included.

Lobby entrance doors present a problem from the standpoints of aesthetics, safety, security, and vandalism. Solid-glass panels — from ceiling to floor — and solid-glass doors are quite popular and attractive, but can be easily broken. Good aluminum doors with a minimum of glass are preferable.

Carpet floor covering is desirable for the lounge and lobby area. However, terrazzo, quarry tile, and patio tile are preferred when cigarette damage is a possibility.

Office

The office area, containing approximately 120 square feet, should be located near the main entrance with adequate window space to provide maximum supervision. However, provision must be made to ensure privacy when dealing with disciplinary problems, small meetings, and the like. Secretarial and program offices should be adjacent to the director's office.

An adjoining shower/dressing unit with a floor surface area of not less than 100 square feet is recommended. A storage closet with burglar-resistant door for storing valuable supplies and equipment should adjoin the administrative offices.

Storage Areas

One of the most common errors in planning recreation buildings is lack of sufficient storage space for equipment, maintenance, and custodial purposes.

An area adjacent to the gymnasium should be provided for such storage. It should have a six-foot-wide opening with flush, louvered doors and a flush threshold to permit passage of the most bulky equipment.

The minimum size of the storage room should be approximately 250 square feet. Provision should be made for storage of inflated balls, bats, softballs, and other supplies, either in separate cabinets or a special closet. Appropriate bins, shelves, and racks are suggested. In addition, a recessed alcove for the storage of a piano is desirable.

The maintenance storage room varies in size, depending on the adjacent outdoor space and the size of the building. The room is ordinarily located on the ground level, adjacent to the outdoor areas. An outside entrance should be provided by means of a burglar-resistant door large enough to permit the passage of motorized maintenance equipment. Recessed wall shelving and cabinet storage should be provided for tools, supplies, and equipment. This space should contain hot and cold water, a slop sink, a lavatory, a water closet, and a clothes closet. The floor should be concrete and pitched to a central drain. The junction of the floor and wall should be coved.

A supply closet equipped with a slop sink and space for mops, pails, brooms, and cleaning supplies should be centrally located on each floor level.

Club or Classrooms

Experience indicates the desirability of providing a minimum of 500 square feet of floor space per club room. For community recreation buildings, at least three to five club rooms should be provided for multiple use. At least one large club room should be located adjoining the kitchen.

When windows in club rooms and lounges are placed high in a wall, they are not broken as often as low windows and they also allow more space for furniture, bulletin boards, pegboards, chalkboards, and exhibits. Since broken window glass is a major problem, a nonbreakable type of pane is preferred. Windows may be omitted and sky domes and vent domes used, thus eliminating the need for draperies, Venetian blinds, and curtains — all items subject to vandalism.

A chair rail or wainscotting to prevent the marring of walls should be installed to a height of three feet above the floor. Whenever possible, noncontact (nonmarring) furniture should be used. Floor-level radiant heat in rooms where programs for small children will be conducted should be considered.

Photography Room

A special room can be equipped as a darkroom. Ventilation should be provided through light-proof ventilators. Hot and cold running water, special light plugs (both wall and base), and photographic sinks for developing and washing prints should also be provided. A mixer is desirable to control the water temperatures accurately. A filter should also be provided if the water quality is not good. Doors must be light-proof.

Music Room

The size of the music room should be determined by the potential number in the choral or instrumental group using this facility at any given time. A guide commonly used is to allow 20 square feet for each participant. Provision should be made for the storage of music, instruments, band uniforms, and supplies. Shelves are commonly used for storage of music equipment.

Auxiliary Gymnasium

The auxiliary gymnasium is for such activities as wrestling, weight-lifting, tumbling, fencing, and apparatus work. Acoustic treatment for this room is desirable.

The size of the room and height of the ceiling will depend on the various activities for which this facility will be used. The floor should be treated with material that will withstand the use of such equipment as heavy weights.

At least one well-ventilated storage room will be needed for equipment and supplies used in the auxiliary gymnasium. If the apparatus is to be cleared from this room, an additional apparatus storage room should be provided.

Instructor's Office

If the recreation program is of considerable size, there should be an office for instructors and leaders. It should be approximately 120 square feet in size and should be adjacent to the gymnasium.

A dressing room opening into this office should be provided for the activity leaders. This facility should contain a shower, water closet, lavatory, and clothes closet. Proper ventilation should be provided for all rooms.

Checkroom

The size of the checkroom will depend on the magnitude of the program. This room should open into the lobby and be equipped with a Dutch door, shelves, and portable hanger racks.

Specialized Recreation Buildings

Many cities and communities provide recreation programs that require specialized facilities. While the construction of these facilities can be justified in the majority of cases, care must be taken to provide for maximum year-round use. The specialized centers should be centrally located to serve all the public.

Art Center

In recent years many cities have constructed a community art center to satisfy the public demand for programs in the arts. The size of the facility will be determined by the number of people to be served and type of art programs to be conducted. Generally, art centers will include work areas for ceramics, sculpture, painting, and sketching. Depending on the interests in the community, a center may also include facilities for woodworking, lapidary, stonecutting, and other arts and crafts. Some art centers include facilities for dance, music, and dramatic classes and programs as well.

Pre-School Center

Pre-school centers for day care, Head Start, and nursery school programs are being built in some communities with the aid of grants or federal funds. These buildings are smaller than neighborhood center buildings, and the design scale is geared to pre-school children. Generally the centers include a large multi-purpose room, small rooms for small-group activities, an office, possibly a kitchen and eating facilities, and ample storage space. Special care should be taken to ensure good acoustic treatment in the center.

Senior Citizen Centers

Senior citizen centers are similar in design to neighborhood recreation centers. However, more emphasis is placed on facilities for the arts, areas for discussion, and rooms for passive games than for large-scale physical activities. While a gymnasium is seldom found in a senior citizen area, a large multi-purpose room is needed for square dance, shuffleboard, and similar activities.

The senior citizen center should be a single-floor building, and special care should be taken to eliminate all hazards such as steps and protrusions on walls.

Swimming Pool (Natatorium)

Many neighborhoods and communities have a considerable interest in swimming and demand that a swimming pool be included as part of the recreation building. For maximum year-round use, the indoor-outdoor pool is recommended. The construction cost of this type of pool is greater, but the value of having a year-round rather than a seasonal activity is more important to the community or neighborhood. (See Chapter 4 for complete information on swimming pools.)

Teen Centers

While teen centers have been very popular and continue to be built, the trend today is to construct multi-use centers that will provide opportunities for teen programs along with other activities. For example, a teen office and lounge are provided in many community recreation centers.

When a separate teen center is desired it should include:

- multi-purpose meeting rooms
- gymnasium
- shower and locker rooms
- rooms for programs in the arts
- restrooms
- game room
- lounge and lobby
- office

Other Specialized Facilities

The planning of any specialized recreation building demands a precise and logical approach. Since a recreation building reflects the unique needs and interests of a neighborhood or community, the specific design will vary, but the preliminary considerations of planning objectives will be the same. (Figure 7-4)

The successful incorporation of accepted planning objectives will ensure maximum use of the building. The initial functional/spatial specification and the continuous reevaluation of the architectural specifications of the building prior to its construction should be considered in terms of the following:

A Check List for Indoor Recreation Facilities

1. Has the most effective use of the entire structure been determined? ☐

2. Does the preliminary sketch include all the essential facilities necessary to fulfill the program objectives? ☐

3. Does the layout provide for flexibility in use and for future expansion? ☐

4. Does the floor plan permit convenient access to, and facilitate circulation within the building? ☐

5. Does the floor plan provide for ease of supervision and administration of the building? ☐

6. Have individual rooms been located to encourage multiple use within safety limits? ☐

7. Has the building been designed to ensure opportunity for its use by all members of the community, including the aging and the disabled? ☐

8. Does the design encompass accepted aesthetic qualities that relate harmoniously to the surroundings? ☐

9. Is the building designed to ensure cooperative use with other public or private agencies? ☐

10. Is the building designed to permit economy in construction and subsequent maintenance? ☐

OUTDOOR FACILITIES AND OPEN SPACE

Growth projections for the next decade provide evidence that few, if any, metropolitan areas in the United States have sufficient open space to meet the demands of the future. Based on these projections, it is imperative that planning boards and commissions on all levels of government review previous planning philosophies with the intent of revision or, when necessary, the development of new master plans.

As open space becomes less and less available, greater consideration must be given to multiple use of these lands and every measure taken to use them most efficiently. Municipal and school authorities should acquire, plan, and develop areas for joint use. This process calls for professional guidance in the fields of planning, designing, and engineering, and for the advice and counsel of professionals in the fields of education and recreation.

The most efficient and successful planning is accomplished when everyone in the organization, particularly those who will be identified with the finished product, have an opportunity to participate in the planning. Those who are to be served also should have a voice in the planning through community meetings.

Standards

A variety of standards for the size, location, and number of educational and recreational areas and facilities have been proposed over the years by persons with a great deal of experience in the operation of such areas and facilities. These standards are sound when formulated to make possible a program to serve the basic needs of people for physical education and recreation. However, they are not valid in prescribing specific activities or facilities for every neighborhood. While they are a useful guide in

Figure 7-4
The Tenneco Employee Center has a training and health facility for use by all employees.

Facilities for Recreation, Parks and Open Spaces

the acquisition and construction of a property, standards can seldom, if ever, be applied completely or without modification because a typical or common situation is seldom found. Standards are formulated to indicate a basis for the intelligent development of local plans. Therefore, the standards for areas and facilities should be reviewed and appraised for each planning unit and modified whenever changing conditions warrant their revision.

Standards for areas and facilities developed by private planning firms, public agencies, and service organizations at the local, state, and national levels have been widely endorsed throughout the United States and have provided the basis for recommendations in scores of long-range plans for school, park, and recreation systems. The proposal that at least one acre of recreation and park space be set aside by urban areas for every 100 of the present and estimated future population has been more widely accepted than any other space standard. However, this standard does not relate to the demographic or physiographic character of particular locales and is becoming obsolete. Professional and governmental authorities, including the National Recreation and Park Association and the National Park Service, have pointed out the desirability of providing an even higher ratio of land to population in towns and small cities.

Modification of this general standard has been suggested for all planning entities based upon local requirements for populated cities. Some municipal planning officials believe the development of large outlying properties owned by the municipality will help meet the recognized deficiency in the inner municipality. However, this proposal should be considered as a practicable substitute indicative not just of necessity but also of feasibility.

Actual studies of recreational

behavior patterns verify that people tend to form neighborhood recreational groups with others of similar social backgrounds. The resulting patterns might follow or be divided by arteries, depending on whether transportation is provided.

Previous number standards related to the number of tennis courts or swimming pools per thousands of people and so forth. Such numbers do not take into consideration the land or people and the climatic and geographic locale of the planning entity. The specification and allocation of facilities per thousand are arbitrary. They neither reflect the requirements of the community or neighborhood nor are universally applicable. A planning process of interaction and participation by the public should determine the number of facilities from one end of town to the other.

Recreational acreage should be based on usage. Guidelines for acreage allocations for different park types are only illustrative. Every activity has a public demand. The demand for some activities is often met by the private or voluntary sector. Ski lodges, tennis centers, and other corporations all conduct market

studies to ascertain the leisure needs of and probable use by their clientele. Public agencies must conduct comparable studies to analyze demand. If the municipality can ascertain the probable use, turnover, capacity, and low/peak load for each activity, it can compute the number of activity stations and facilities for each activity group. This analysis is comparable to processes used to determine the indoor and outdoor space requirements for a school. The recreational acreage is then computed for actual facilities, for circulating paths and roads, for landscaping, and for other features. (Figure 7-5)

Park and Recreation Areas

The types of outdoor recreation areas described here represent a variety of service units which may be used in programs of athletics, sports, physical education and recreation. Local conditions will dictate to a large extent which types are to be used in any given locality. Hence, different combinations of areas and facilities will emerge as the solution to the problem of meeting the needs and interests of a

NOTES:
All measurements for court markings are to the outside of lines except for those involving the center service line, which is equally divided between right and left service court.

All court markings to be 2'' wide.

Fencing required — 12'0'' high with 16-gauge hexagonal, galvanized 1'' flat wire mesh fabric.

For net post details see manufacturers' literature.

Net height to be 3'1'' at posts and 2'10'' at center court.

ISOMETRIC SHOWING FENCE (TYPICAL WOOD CONSTRUCTION)

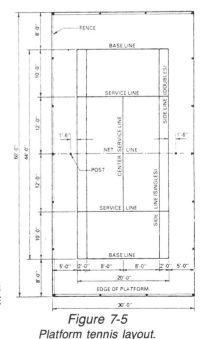

Figure 7-5
Platform tennis layout.

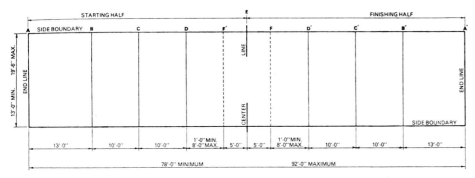

Figure 7-6
Layout of a Bocce court.

particular locality. (Figures 7-6; 6A)

There is some controversy over parkland aesthetics as measured by the terms active and passive recreation. Many individuals with inherent interest in recreational or leisure pursuits associated with nature denounce the intrusion into parklands by tennis buffs or ball players. Obviously, these two groups have different attitudes about the character of parklands. Parklands can be designed for active or passive use, or both, without destroying the aesthetic values. The use of parklands should reflect the greatest good for the greatest number and the

protection of the health, well-being, and safety of all.

If a community is split over use of parklands, a cost-benefit analysis should be made to ascertain the feasibility and costs of trade-offs. There is no sense in preserving a swamp that was created artificially and lacks any ecological value, but a natural swamp might be found elsewhere and preserved to meet specific needs and interests. There are alternatives in every planning process, and they should be considered. The aesthetic values of a parkland, whether oriented toward play apparatus or floral

displays, do not have to be sacrificed because they are termed passive or active.

Abandoned industrial sites, such as strip mines, waste disposal areas, and sand and gravel pits, offer tremendous possibilities for park and recreation development. In many cases, recreational use is not only the most beneficial, but the most economic use of such sites. The recreational planner must not overlook the possibility of obtaining these sites for public use. If possible, cooperative planning should be started while the site is still being used by industry so landscape features can be developed to make it more appealing for recreational use.

Playlot/Mini-Parks

Location, Size, and Features

A playlot/mini-park is a small recreational area designed for the safe play of pre-school children.

As an independent unit, the playlot/mini-park is most frequently developed in large housing projects or in other densely populated urban areas with high concentration of pre-school children. More often, it is incorporated as a feature of a larger recreation area. If a community is able to operate a neighborhood playground within a one-quarter mile zone of every home, playlots should be located at the playground sites. A location near a playground entrance, close to restrooms and away from active game areas, is best.

The playlot/mini-park should be enclosed with a low fence or solid planting to assist mothers or guardians in safeguarding their children. Thought should be given to placement of benches, with and without shade, for ease of supervision and comfort for parents and guardians. A drinking fountain with step for tots will serve both children and adults.

Play equipment geared to the pre-school child should combine attractive traditional play apparatus with creative, imaginative

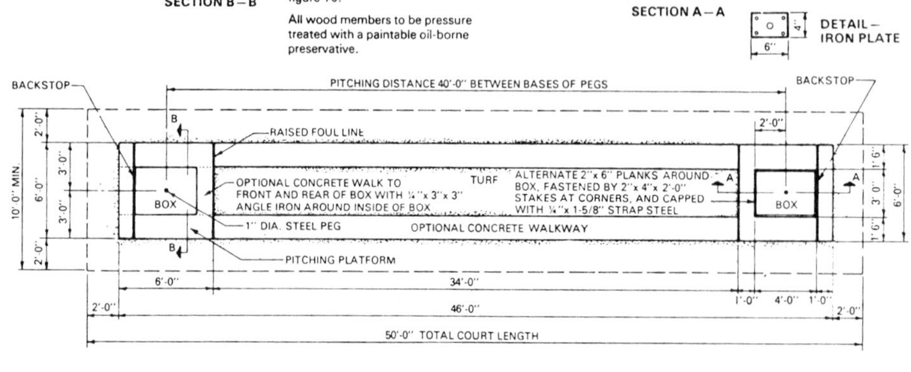

Figure 7-6A
Horseshoe pitching layout.

Facilities for Recreation, Parks and Open Spaces

equipment. Such proven favorites as chair, bucket, and glider swings; six-foot slide; and a small merry-go-round can be used safely. Hours of imaginative play will be enjoyed with such features as a simulated train, boat, or airplane; a playhouse; and fiberglass or concrete animals. A small climbing structure and facilities for sand play should be included.

Play Structures and Areas

The design of playground equipment and play areas can significantly affect children's psychomotor, affective and cognitive development. In order to meet psychomotor needs, equipment should stimulate locomotor, non-locomotor, and manipulative actions which stimulate the development of large muscles. Equipment should elicit repetitive responses as well as increasingly new complex responses. Some equipment should be permanent and stable in order to stimulate the child to move, but children should be able to move some pieces from place to place. The equipment should be child-sized, some designed specifically for younger children and some for older children. Modularized wooden structures are ideal for providing variable environments and arrangements and are readily modifiable by professional personnel. Many play equipment manufacturers carry a full line of modular equipment, both wood and metal.

Younger children need opportunities to create, build, and manipulate the environment. Older children need play settings which stimulate multiple responses — more than one way to move from one piece of equipment to another.

Cognitive needs of children may be met by providing equipment which is multi-purpose in design. Equipment should whet children's curiosity, stimulate exploration, and elicit a variety of responses. Children use a variety of bases of

support as well as different kinds of level, direction, and range of movement on different pieces of equipment. No one piece provides adequate variety for all children, so a variety of equipment is necessary.

Affective needs may be met by varying the shapes of pieces such as squares, circles, and rectangles. Varying spaces increases a variety of responses — some should be narrow, wide, large, small, high, and low. Some pieces should be thick (planks) while others should be thin (bars). Sculptured animals and natural objects such as tree trunks are widely used. Textures should vary from loose, soft, and smooth such as sand, bark, and wood chips to hard, shiny, dull, and rough such as metal, wood, plastic, fiberglass, and concrete.

Colors impregnated in plastic and cement prevent frequent painting. The color of the equipment should be in contrast to the ground covering in order for a child to see the support on which to place a foot. In contrast to adults, color does not affect children's choices of equipment significantly.

Some equipment should encourage socialization. Others should provide for quiet contemplation. Some play apparatus should sustain the

interest of individuals. Other pieces should appear unpredictable in the nature of responses available.

Equipment chosen for outdoor areas should be consistent with materials used indoors to illustrate a coordinated curricular philosophy of recreation interests. Equipment should be usable in physical education classes as well as at recess. (Figure 7-7)

Play equipment must be durable, safe, and sanitary. Some pieces should be resilient. All pieces requiring cement footings should be covered by dirt or a softer ground cover. Footings should be deep enough to maintain stability. Metal pieces may need shade to keep them cool. Paint on equipment prevents rust and makes the piece cleanable. Moving parts should be oiled regularly. Nuts and bolts should be tightened frequently. Equipment requiring low maintenance is advisable.

The surface treatment under apparatus equipment is very important. Various types of materials that have been used are sand, wood chips, tanbark, asphalt, and a variety of synthetic surfaces. The use of asphalt covered with a synthetic material has been gaining in popularity because of the safety and aesthetic aspects even though the

Figure 7-7
A typical elementary school playground.

initial cost is higher. A level surface is always maintained with this treatment, which is safer for the children at play. Water puddles do not appear under swings, and less maintenance is required for this surface.

Enclosing the area may be appropriate to prevent nuisance legal problems. If equipment cannot be played on safely without adult supervision, a fence with a lock is a necessity.

Although home-made equipment may be durable and cost less initially, legal concerns may warrant the purchase of commercial equipment. Comparative shopping may reduce the cost of commercially made pieces by as much as 50 percent.

The whole play area should be designed with the aid of educational consultants and/or commercial planners. Pieces of equipment should not only be placed by age groups, but, more importantly, they should also stimulate movement from one piece to another. Moving parts require spaces for a range of movements. Equipment needs to be placed for ease of supervision and safe traffic patterns. Modularized wooded structures and free-standing equipment should be changed frequently to provide children with new opportunities to explore the environment. Play areas throughout the community should reflect variety. Funds should be allocated to change locations of pieces of apparatus on each playground and between playgrounds.

Small Games Courts

The playlot/mini-park may also include courts and areas for such activities as hopscotch, marbles, and circle games. The entire small-games area can be used as multi-purpose space. These areas are located primarily in neighborhood and community park-schools and may be used for both class instruction and recreation programs.

The small-games area should be a minimum of 25 by 25 feet, adjacent to the crafts-and-apparatus area. It should be well-drained and surrounded by a fence or shrubbery barrier for maximum safety and control. The surface should be of sandy loam, asphalt, or concrete.

Hopscotch is popular with children. A special court may be marked off in one section of the small-games area. (Figure 7-8)

Kinds of Play Areas

One-Time User. Usually a commercial play area designed to sustain interest for a short time span.

Returning Client Play Area. Usually a school or public recreation area. Should be designed to stimulate multiple responses and some elements of unpredictability.

Adult. Currently commercial and educational planners are experimenting with equipment designed for adults. The designs are adult in size and in challenge.

Adventure. Play areas originally conceived in Europe. Children are involved in the planning, creating, and building of an area. A play leader will facilitate play and construction. Some parts are fixed while others are movable. Parts can be changed frequently (daily) or periodically (at the end of a season).

Creative. Play areas which stimulate children to elicit a variety of responses rather than a single response. Loose materials as well as fixed objects are part of the setting.

Junk. Constructed, usually by adults, from discarded materials. A variety of materials enhances the choices available and stimulates multiple sensory responses. Examples include tires, telephone cablespools, railroad ties, sand, wood, turf, rope.

Thematic. Usually built around a central idea. Some examples are pioneer, Treasure Island, Indian, seafaring, and circus traffic or transportation which may feature a combination of planes, cars, or boats. Variety is important in the settings as is the appropriateness with the local environment and safety of the objects. Glass and locks should be removed.

Traditional Play Areas. Generally feature metal equipment including swings, slides, see-saws, merry-go-rounds. They are single purpose in design and tend to move children rather than stimulate children to move.

Vestpocket Playgrounds. Originally created by Paul Friedberg in New York for high school students, they are within one lot between buildings, designed on an adult scale to be compact and indestructible.

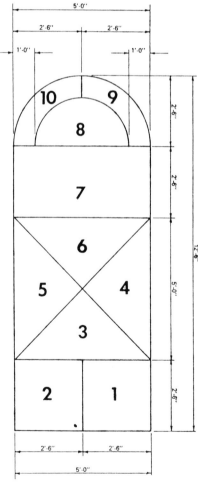

Figure 7-8
Hopscotch Court layout.

Facilities for Recreation, Parks and Open Spaces

Playgrounds and Play Areas

The neighborhood playground is the primary area in planning for recreation. It is established primarily to serve children under 14 but should have additional features to interest teen-agers and adults. The trend in recent years is for the neighborhood playground to become the center of activity for a wide variety of needs and interests expressed by all residents. The more diversified pursuits of today's recreation consumer challenge the facility planner to provide for a broader program, with more attention devoted to multiple use by different age groups.

The neighborhood playground serves the recreational needs and interests of the same population served by neighborhood elementary school. Its major service zone will seldom exceed one-half mile, with most of the attendance originating within a quarter-mile distance. It should be centrally located in the area to be served and away from heavily traveled streets and other barriers to easy and safe access.

The neighborhood playground normally requires a minimum of five acres. The particular facilities required will depend on the nature of the neighborhood, with space being allocated according to priorities, as follows:

	ACRES
Turf area for softball, touch football, soccer, speedball, and other field games	2-3
Hard-surface area for court games, such as netball, basketball, volleyball, and handball	0.50
Open space for informal play	0.50
Corner for senior citizens	0.30-0.50
Space for quiet games, story-telling and crafts	0.20
Playlot	0.20-0.50
Children's outdoor theater	0.15
Apparatus area for elementary age children	0.25-0.50
Service building for restrooms, storage, and equipment issue or a small clubhouse with some indoor activity space	0.15
Circulation, landscaping, and buffer zones	1-2
Undesignated space	0.75
TOTAL	5-10

Depending upon the relationship of the property to schools and to other recreational facilities in the neighborhood, such optional features as a recreation building, tennis courts, or swimming pool might be located at the neighborhood playground. If climatic conditions warrant, a spray or wading pool may be provided. The following space for optional features should be added to the standards listed above:

	ACRES
Recreation building	0.2
Landscape areas (if there is no neighborhood park)	2.0
Swimming pool	0.5
Tennis courts	0.4
TOTAL	3.1

The addition of optional features may require provisions for off-street parking.

The Neighborhood Park

The neighborhood park is land set aside primarily for both active and passive recreation. Ideally, it gives the impression of being rural, sylvan, or national in its character. It emphasizes horticultural features, with spacious turf areas bordered by trees, shrubs, and sometimes floral arrangements. It is essential in densely populated areas but not required where there is ample yard space at individual home sites.

A neighborhood park should be provided for each neighborhood. In many neighborhoods, it will be incorporated in the park-school site or neighborhood playground. A separate location is required if this combination is not feasible.

A separately located neighborhood park normally requires three to five acres. As a

Figure 7-9, 9A
Synthetic grid surface adds new life and color to old concrete play areas.

measure of expediency, however, an isolated area as small as one or two acres may be used. Sometimes the functions of a neighborhood park can be satisfactorily included in a community or city-wide park.

The neighborhood park plays an important role in setting standards for community aesthetics. Therefore, it should include open lawn areas, plantings, and walks. Sculpture forms, pools, and fountains should also be considered for ornamentation. Creative planning will employ contouring, contrasting surfaces, masonry, and other modern techniques to provide both eye appeal and utility. (Figures 7-9; 9A)

Community Parks and Playfields

This type of recreational area is required in a community where it is not feasible or possible to acquire and develop a community park-school. The community park and playfield, like the neighborhood playground, is designed primarily to provide facilities for a variety of types of organized recreation activities, but it should also have the characteristics of a landscaped park. It usually serves as the playground for the children living in the immediate neighborhood, but its primary service is to a much wider age group. Thus, it supplies a greater variety of facilities and more extensive service than can be justified at the neighborhood playground. The school child, teen-ager, young adult, hobbyist, senior citizen, and family group all find attractive facilities at the well-developed community park and playfield. Because there is no school building at this area, some type of indoor facility is needed. In many cases, a multi-purpose recreation building is provided to meet this need.

City-Wide or District Parks

The city-wide or district park serves a district of a large city or a total community of a small city. It

should serve a population of from 50,000 to 100,000 with a wide variety of activities.

The ideal location for this area is in combination with a high school as a park-school complex. Where this is not feasible, consideration should be given to placing the park as close as possible to the center of the population to be served. The land available will be a determining factor in site selection. While the service zone will vary according to population density, a normal use zone is two to four miles. The size may range from 50 to 100 acres.

Depending on available acreage, topography, and natural features, the city-wide or district park will contain a large number of different components. These would include, but not be limited to, the following:

- Field for baseball, football, soccer, and softball
- Tennis center
- Winter sports facilities
- Day-camp center
- Picnic areas (group and family)
- Cycling paths or tracks
- Swimming pool
- Water sports lake
- Pitch-and-putt golf course
- Recreation building
- Nature trails
- Skating rinks (ice and roller)
- Playlot and apparatus
- Parking areas
- Outdoor theater

The above facilities should be separated by large turf and landscaped areas. Natural areas and perimeter buffers should be provided.

Special-Use Areas and Facilities

Bicycle Facilities and Pathways

Most of the recommended bicycle programs and facilities will require considerable investments of time and money to bring them to fruition. The development of bicycle paths through urban, residential, and outdoor recreation areas will require costly investments that are not always available from public budgets.

An alternative program might be considered. This program would develop bicycle touring routes in and across the country, using rural and low volume vehicular routes. The only expenses involved in the creation of this system are for initial system planning, printing bikeway maps, and marking intersections. County and city governments together with schools and universities have implemented touring systems.

The steps in the development of bicycling facilities are:
- Appoint a committee from interested groups of individuals, including representatives of the school or university and the recreation department.
- Make a survey of county road maps and mark a conceptual bicycle system on a work map. One of the objectives is to create a roughly circular route. "Spoke" routes would radiate from the campus to the peripheral route. Select the safest possible routes. High volume roads and intersections should be avoided. After the road map is finished, the committee should find that it has the framework for an adequate bicycling touring system.
- The next step involves field reconnaissance of the roads marked on the working map. Alternate routes may be selected if the original roads are not appropriate for bicycling. Actual travel by bicycle is recommended for the reconnaissance.
- Following the completion of the field reconnaissance, the next step is the drafting of the final bikeway map. Titles and safety information are also placed on the map. The back of the map may be filled with a variety of information. The bikeway

Facilities for Recreation, Parks and Open Spaces

should be marked, especially the abrupt turns. Marking may be done by painting distinctive symbols and arrows on the pavement of the road. Standard highway marking paint may be used, and stencils for the symbols may be cut from heavy gauge linoleum.

Figure 10 offers a schematic of the bicycle facility planning process.

Bridle Paths and Rings

Horseback riding is popular with all age groups but is generally restricted to the larger park areas because of space requirements. Riding trails are usually a minimum of 10 feet wide to permit riders going in opposite directions to pass in safety. Except on very steep terrain, very little is required in the way of construction. Clearing, a small amount of leveling, removal of large rocks and boulders, and trimming or removal of low-hanging tree limbs constitute the major items. Most small streams can be forded, but an occasional bridge may be required as well as cross drainage on steep gradients. No special surfacing is required except that a gravel base may be needed in wet or boggy areas that cannot be avoided. Tanbark, cinders, and other materials are also used frequently on heavily used trails and in areas of concentrated use around hitching racks and in riding rings.

Stables and adjoining facilities, such as feed racks, holding corrals, riding rings, and hitching racks, should be located at least 500 feet from the nearest public-use area because of the fly and odor problem. The size of

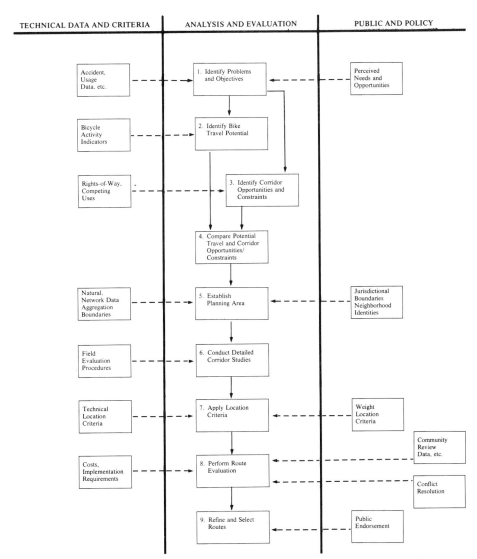

Figure 7-10
Bicycle facility planning process.

these facilities will depend on the number of horses. However, the stable will ordinarily contain a limited number of horse stalls, a feed-storage room, a tack room, a small office, and toilet facilities for men and women. A fenced enclosure, commonly called a holding corral or paddock, into which the horses can be turned at the end of the day, is required. A surfaced riding ring, sometimes encircled with a rail fence, is frequently provided for training novices in the fundamentals of riding.

Exercise Trail

The physical fitness boom of the 1970's and 1980's has inspired a unique total body conditioning program — exercise trails. Marketed commercially under a variety of names including Fitness Trail, Fit-Trail, Lifecourse, and Parcourse, the trail combines cardiovascular development, agility, flexibility, strength, and endurance.

The exercise trail consists of a number of exercise stations located at various lengths along a jogging course. A typical trail could have a 1.5 mile distance with 13 exercise stations. The running intervals and exercises are designed for flexibility, agility, strength, all the while developing the participant's cardiovascular system. (Figure 7-11)

Orienteering

Outdoor enthusiasts use compass directions to guide them in exploring new terrain. One of the ultimate uses for compass directions is in the fast-growing sport of competitive orienteering. The sport of competitive orienteering involves finding one's way with a map and compass along an unknown stretch of ground to one's pre-selected destination.

For whatever the reason — sport exercise, nature study, or just to enjoy the quiet beauty of the wilderness — orienteering provides the means by which one can navigate.

Alpine Slide

The Alpine Slide is one answer to the ski area operator's biggest problem — summer.

The Alpine Slide is popular and successful in both the United States and Canada. The slide provides an ideal means of using mountain areas, especially ski resorts with all their existing facilities, in a way that is designed to be compatible with the environment. (Figure 7-12)

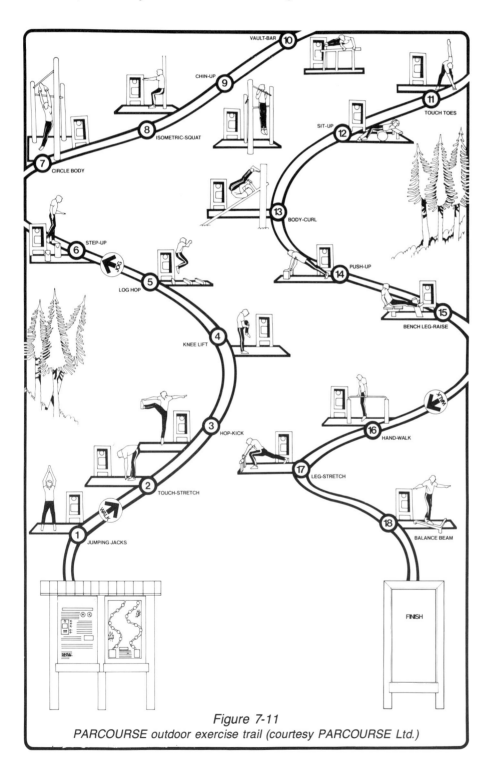

Figure 7-11
PARCOURSE outdoor exercise trail (courtesy PARCOURSE Ltd.)

Facilities for Recreation, Parks and Open Spaces

Figure 7-12
The big thrill — riding the Alpine Slide at Bromley, Vt. Riders can control their speeds as they travel the 4060-foot downhill run on plastic sleds through dual cement flumes.

Figure 7-13
Baylor University Marina is used for instruction during the day and is open for recreational use in the afternoon and evening.

Golf Courses

The design, construction, operation, and maintenance of golf courses is too vast a subject to be covered in detail in this publication. For general information and guidance, write the National Golf Foundation at 200 Castlewood Drive, North Palm Beach, FL 33408.

Assuming the land is suitable for construction of a golf course, the following space requirements must be taken into consideration:

- For a standard 18-hole course — 120 to 160 acres
- For a standard 9-hole course — 70 to 90 acres
- For a 9-hole par three course (including a couple of par four holes) — 45 to 60 acres

The planning should provide also for an administrative clubhouse, a practice putting green, and a practice driving range.

Marinas

America abounds in waterways. The myriad of inland lakes, the rivers and streams, the vast Great Lakes, and the thousands of miles of coastline serve to invite America's citizens to take advantage of this natural resource. Today, boating commands more of the recreational dollar than baseball, fishing, golf, or any other single activity. There is a need for efficient, realistic, and functional planning for facilities to accommodate the present needs and the future growth that this

recreational interest will precipitate. (Figure 7-13)

The launching, mooring, and storage of yachts and rowboats are the function of a marina that will serve the needs of the recreational-boat owner.

It is suggested that knowledgeable and experienced personnel be engaged to study the number, types, and sizes of existing boats in the area; the number and size of existing berthing facilities, and the condition of such existing facilities. The survey should also include the potential population growth in the community and surrounding area to determine the future boat ownership. An accurate and comprehensive evaluation of such a study is the first step in planning a marina.

Facilities for Recreation, Parks and Open Spaces

The study will determine the next important consideration in laying out a marina: choosing the correct number of slips of each size that will be required. Based on the needs of the community to be served, planners will determine the necessary number of slips to accommodate boats of various sizes.

Because marinas vary so greatly in their design, function, location, and capacity, it is virtually impossible to arrive at standard conclusions and judgments concerning a model marina. Each planner will be able to apply the general principles to his unique circumstances. From that point, however, he must adapt his marina to the peculiar needs and characteristics of his community.

Roller Skating

Roller skating may be permitted on a multi-purpose area or on sidewalks and streets under proper safety controls. If a rink is built, it is suggested that the area be 100 by 200 feet. A track for speed skating can encircle the figure or leisure skating area. The track should be banked at the curves, and the interior should be slightly pitched for drainage. Boundaries of the track should be defined with flags, wooden blocks, or pylons. Mark each turn with pylons, and indicate the starting and finishing lines. The rinks should be oriented so that skaters travel in a north-and-south direction.

The surface should be smooth wood (wide) or concrete sprinkled with rosin or a similar substance. If the areas for skating are speed rinks or multi-purpose areas, they should be fenced for safety and control.

Ice Skating

Ice-skating facilities are feeling the impact of modern technology in more and more communities each year. With the advent of mechanical freezing, the skating season has been extended from a

20- to 60-day average season to a 140-day season and, depending on climatic conditions, to as much as 240 days.

While natural ice rinks have not gone out of style, artificial rinks are replacing them as central or regional facilities. Natural ice rinks are continuing to serve as a supplemental neighborhood facility in many communities. A considerable number of skaters still prefer the rugged pleasure of an old-fashioned skating experience.

Ice Hockey

Ice rinks may have a sport function as well as providing a recreational service. If ice hockey is to be part of the rink's activity schedule, goals will be needed, and a four-foot high solid fence, called the dasher, will have to be installed to enclose an area as near 85 by 185 feet as possible. Dasher boards are heavily reinforced to stand the shock of players being pushed against them and are lined on the rink side with either wood or plastic. There is normally a chain link or clear plastic barrier another four to six feet on top of the dashers to enable spectators to view games safely. The dasher board enclosure should have round corners, because square corners present a hazard. A kick board, six to eight inches high, is fastened at the base of the dasher boards and is replaced as often as necessary.

Because dasher boards reflect sunlight and cause melting of the ice, they should be painted a dark color. However, it is difficult to follow the puck if the dasher boards are too dark, so a shade of grey is recommended. If the hockey rink is indoors, the dasher boards can be painted a light color without causing a melting problem.

Information describing the complete ice arena is included in Chapter 5.

Curling

Curling is an ice sport popular in Canada and the northern United States. Sponsored by clubs and

leagues, it is played with hand-propelled 42.5 pound stones, referred to as rocks. There are four members on a team, each shooting two rocks. The object is to slide one team's rocks nearest the center of a circle, called the house, at the far end of the rink.

The advent of artificial ice has broadened the popularity of curling and extended its geographical interest zone.

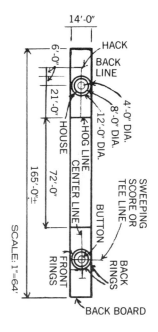

Figure 7-14
Curling

Performing Arts Areas

In the past few years there has been increased demand for suitable indoor and outdoor facilities for operas, plays, band and orchestral concerts, pageants, festivals, holiday programs, and civic celebrations. When performed outdoors, such activities usually require a stage or band shell with adjoining amphitheater capable of accommodating large numbers of spectators.

Selection of the proper site for an outdoor theater is of primary importance. It should have good acoustic properties and be located in a quiet place away from the noise of traffic or of groups at play. A natural bowl or depression on a hillside with a slope of 10 to 20 degrees, preferably bordered by slopes or densely wooded areas, provides a fine location.

At some theaters, people sit on the slope of the amphitheater. At others, permanent seats are installed. Terraces with a turf surface are not recommended because they are too difficult to maintain. Sufficient level space should be provided at the rear of the seating area for the circulation of spectators, and aisles should be wide enough to facilitate the seating of large numbers in a short period of time. Public comfort stations and refreshment facilities are usually provided near the entrance to the amphitheater. Provision for the nearby parking of automobiles is essential, but parking areas must be located where noises and car lights do not disturb the stage action.

The dimensions of the stage are determined by the proposed uses, but rarely should a stage be less than 50 feet in width or 30 feet in depth. The rear of the stage may be a wall or high hedge, or even a planting of trees, and the wings may be formed by natural plant materials. The band or music shell, however, is more satisfactory for projecting voices and sound free from echoes and interference. A vertical rear wall with inclined ceiling is not only the simplest and most economical to construct but affords excellent acoustic qualities.

The band shell usually contains dressing rooms, toilets, storage space, and control centers for amplifying and lighting equipment, although sometimes these facilities are provided in separate structures near the back of the stage. An orchestra pit is generally located between the auditorium and the stage.

Mobile storage units with self-contained lighting and acoustic systems are becoming very popular because they can be used in many parks instead of restricting programs to one permanent location. Equipped to serve as a band shell, stage,

puppet theater, or platform for other performing arts, these mobile units can bring productions to audiences never exposed to such activities. Excellent units can be obtained at a cost less than that required for a permanent band shell.

Archery Range (Recreational)

This sport appeals to a sizable group in most communities. Sufficient space is needed to ensure the safety and enjoyment of the participants.

The range should provide shooting distances of 100, 80, 60, 50, 40, and 30 yards. For junior use, target ranges can be from 10 to 50 yards. Targets are 48 inches wide and should be at least 15 feet apart. Generally, the target line is fixed and varying shooting lines are used. The side boundaries should extend 10 yards beyond each end of the range.

In the interest of safety, additional space should be provided beyond the target, free from stones and other substances that might cause the breakage of arrows falling wide of their mark. This space may be protected by an earth bunker or bales of hay and straw piled up to the top of the target.

An archery range should be fairly level. Orientation should be north and south so the archers will not be facing the sun. A fence enclosure is desirable, but not essential. The public should be controlled in some manner, however, so they do not walk through the range.

Storage sheds for butts and other equipment are sometimes a part of the archery range. Some storage rooms have been placed within the earth bunker behind the targets.

So the facility may be used by the disabled, it is desirable to design a four-foot wide, ground-level, hard-surface walk for wheelchair use along the shooting lines. Another walk could extend to the target line (preferably down the center) and perhaps another

walkway behind the targets to provide access for extracting arrows. Such walks reduce interference from inclement weather, increase the use of the range, and reduce maintenance costs.

Field archery is a simulation of actual shooting conditions in the field. Up to 28 targets are used on the field course. The site selected for such a course should be heavily wooded and have rolling terrain. It should be fairly well isolated or in an area that can be controlled so the general public will not intrude.

Targets should be mounted on built-up banks or on the side of a hill. Each target has various pins (shooting positions). The farthest target is 80 yards and the nearest is 30. The target should simulate either animals or concentric circles. The size is dependent upon the distance from the target. The scoring is similar to that for golf — the score is totaled for each target, the grand total giving the score for the complete round.

Clout shooting requires a variation in target size and arrangement. The target face is marked on the ground with white lines. The size of the target is enlarged so that one inch on a regular 48-inch target would equal 12 inches on the ground. The center of the bull's-eye must be indicated by a single-color flag. The range for men is 180 yards; for women and juniors, 120 yards.

The field dimensions for flight shooting are approximately 200 by 600 yards. The field should be roped off on all sides except that from which the archers shoot. A distance of not less than 10 yards behind the shooting line is reserved for the flight shooting space. Officially, the flight must be from a series of colored or numbered pegs set in the ground, usually about six feet apart.

Figure 15 depicts a sample outdoor archery range lay-out and target details. Additional information regarding archery is included in Chapters 2 and 3.

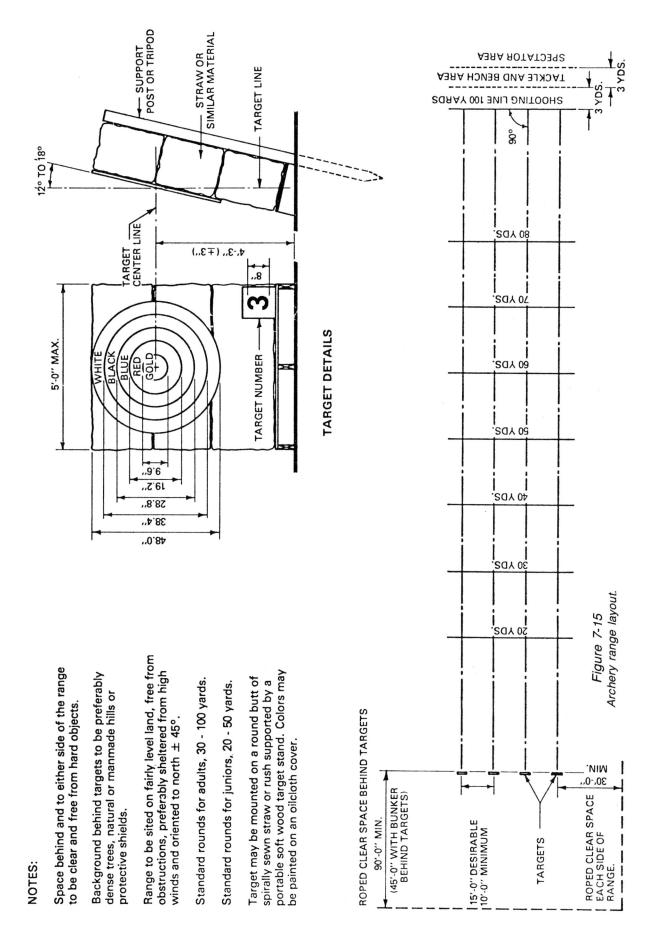

NOTES:

Space behind and to either side of the range to be clear and free from hard objects.

Background behind targets to be preferably dense trees, natural or manmade hills or protective shields.

Range to be sited on fairly level land, free from obstructions, preferably sheltered from high winds and oriented to north ± 45°.

Standard rounds for adults, 30 - 100 yards.

Standard rounds for juniors, 20 - 50 yards.

Target may be mounted on a round butt of spirally sewn straw or rush supported by a portable soft wood target stand. Colors may be painted on an oilcloth cover.

SUPPORT POST OR TRIPOD

STRAW OR SIMILAR MATERIAL

TARGET LINE

12° TO 18°

TARGET CENTER LINE

4'-3'' (±3'')

8''

WHITE
BLACK
BLUE
RED
GOLD

5'-0'' MAX.

9.6''
19.2''
28.8''
38.4''
48.0''

TARGET NUMBER

3

TARGET DETAILS

ROPED CLEAR SPACE BEHIND TARGETS

90'-0'' MIN.

(45'-0'' WITH BUNKER BEHIND TARGETS)

15'-0'' DESIRABLE
10'-0'' MINIMUM

TARGETS

30'-0'' MIN.

ROPED CLEAR SPACE EACH SIDE OF RANGE.

20 YDS.
30 YDS.
40 YDS.
50 YDS.
60 YDS.
70 YDS.
80 YDS.

90°

SHOOTING LINE 100 YARDS

3 YDS.

TACKLE AND BENCH AREA

3 YDS.

SPECTATOR AREA

*Figure 7-15
Archery range layout.*

Snow Sports

Ski Courses

Skiing has become very popular. If climatic conditions are suitable and desirable topographic features are available, a school or a park and recreation department might look into the possibility of developing the facilities needed to foster this sport. A variety of artificial surfaces simulating real snow has brought skiing instructional opportunities to all sections of the country independent of climate.

The provision of skiing in a school or public recreation system should be approached from an instructional standpoint, the theory being to give participants some basic instruction so they can enjoy it as a leisure-time activity in the resort areas that have more ideal facilities. If the park system contains ideal skiing hills with plenty of room, regular ski courses may be developed. Some of the basic facilities required for skiing instruction include proper topographical features; a headquarters building for rental of equipment, a refractory, and similar purposes; a ski tow; and various slopes for instructional purposes.

Normally, the series of classes is broken into three units — beginners, advanced, and expert. It is the opinion of ski instructors that the beginners' ski class is by far the most important for recreational skiing.

Basic instruction in skiing may be conducted in classes not exceeding 25 to 30 beginners. For this group, a gentle and short slope with a relatively large flat run-out area is desirable because it permits a beginner to have complete control of himself and allows him to gain confidence in the use of his skis. In the advanced group, classes are much smaller and in the expert group, instruction becomes almost individual. For each successive group, hills become longer and a little steeper.

The following criteria are recommended for the selection of facilities for beginners' classes:

- Flat-top hill area, 50 square feet per skier, 25 skiers per class
- Slope about 75 feet to 100 feet long, drop in grade of 15 feet, or 4:1 ratio
- Starting line at top of slope, 100 feet wide
- Run-out at bottom of slope either flat or uphill
- Slope facing east or northeast
- Instructional area free of stones, woods, and other impediments
- Protective cover, such as trees or brush, around the area

The following criteria are suggested for advanced classes:

- Top of hill about the same as for beginners
- Slope is most important: ratio about 3:1 and length 100 to 150 feet
- Width of hill or slope, minimum of 150 feet because of speed and space required for turning movements.

The following criteria are recommended for the selection of facilities for expert classes:

- Either the same hill as advanced classes or, preferably, a longer and steeper hill
- Enough downhill length to permit a minimum of three turning movements — for example, 250 feet on a 3:1 slope
- Greater width than that of slope for advanced classes.

Cross-Country Skiing

The cross-country skiing revival came in the mid-60's, and its popularity has increased dramatically. The rebirth of cross-country skiing, which has become known as ski touring, has attracted many people who cannot afford to keep up with "alpine" or "downhill" skiing price tags, or

standing in long lines at the lifts.

Ski touring deserves a place in physical education and recreation programs. One of the attractive features of ski touring is that a successful program can be developed with limited facilities. Unlike downhill skiing, it is not vital to have hilly terrain or several inches of snow base. Such areas as athletic fields, golf courses, parks, and nearby vacant land serve as ideal training courses.

Specially designed skis with rollers mounted on the bottom have made grass skiing possible and this activity is gaining in popularity as a summer activity in parts of Europe.

Coasting, Sleighing, Tobogganing

Often a community has a hill or hills suitable for coasting, which become meccas after every snowfall for children with sleds, toboggans, and other coasting devices. In the absence of a natural coasting hill, some park and public works departments have built such a facility. These hills are usually located in a park safely guarded from the hazards of street traffic.

In developing local sledding (coasting) areas, care should be taken to incorporate adequate safety features. Plenty of room should be provided between sled runs, and up traffic should be isolated from the down traffic. The area should be as free as possible from hazards, such as nearby trees, grills, benches, or other park paraphernalia.

Communities with an extensive response to sledding or skiing may want to counter adverse weather with the use of artificial-snow equipment or improve the activity with a ski lift.

Sleighing is a recreational activity that uses sleighs drawn by horses or oxen. It can take place on roads, trails, or paths.

Tobogganing is a thrilling sport requiring designed space. Occasionally, natural slopes are used if they are free from obstructions and have a long bottom run-off. The common practice is to choose a hillside with a reasonable steep and even grade. A chute is constructed using a wooden trough. It can be permanent or built in sections.

Snowmobiling

According to a recent survey, snowmobiling ranks as one of the fastest-growing sports in the United States. Assuming snowmobiling will continue to be popular, the predictions have it that approximately 10 million people will take to the sport by 1985. As with cross-country skiing, areas such as athletic fields, golf courses, parks, and vacant land can serve as ideal training courses for snowmobilers.

Many lake and park areas in the northern United States used previously during summer months have now proven to be a haven for snowmobile enthusiasts.

AREAS FOR OUTDOOR EDUCATION/RECREATION

Future historians will surely note the decades following World War II as a time when the outdoors came into prominence as a significant place for both education and recreation. The unprecedented growth of all types of outdoor activities necessitating land areas and facilities can be expected to continue. A growing awareness on the part of educational and recreational leaders that the present generation and those to come are far removed from the land and the rural life of their forebears has caused much interest and concern in the development of outdoor education programs. Because school-age children and many adults know little about the outdoors, programs and facilities must be designed to educate them in, about, and for the outdoors. An ecological approach to outdoor education has both recreational and educational implications. (Figure 7-16)

Outdoor education is a term

that refers to learning activities in and for the outdoors. Such activities can be provided in the curriculums of schools, colleges, and universities as well as in the programs of recreational, camping, and community agencies. Outdoor education has been broadly described as follows:

Outdoor education means learning in and for the outdoors. It is a means of curriculum extension and enrichment through outdoor experiences. It is not a separate discipline with prescribed objectives, like science and mathematics; it is simply a learning climate offering opportunities for direct laboratory experiences in identifying and resolving real-life problems, for acquiring skills with which to enjoy a lifetime of creative living, for building concepts and developing concern about man and his natural environment, and for getting us back in touch with those aspects of living where our roots were once firm and deep.

Outdoor education and outdoor recreation encompass a great variety of activities, many of which can be conducted on a single, large tract of land. With careful planning, facilities, some in or near an urban area and others in

more distant places, can be used. An outdoor-education complex on one piece of land or on several plots in close proximity has many advantages in the areas of administration, leadership, equipment, and transportation. Such a site lends itself to wide community use, with responsibilities for leadership and finances shared by several agencies. Obviously, the size and physical characteristics of an outdoor-education complex will depend on the geographic location and the topography of the land.

Some of the facilities and types of site treatment for a complex that would accommodate a broad program of outdoor education and outdoor recreation, and which would constitute an outdoor laboratory or field campus, are briefly described. It is assumed that there will be many areas and facilities, public and private, that can also be used in a comprehensive program. (Figures 7-17; 7-18; 7-19; 7-20)

Considerations in Selecting and Developing Sites
Size

The type of program planned should determine the size of the

Figure 7-16
Halfcourt tennis is being played in limited back yard space.

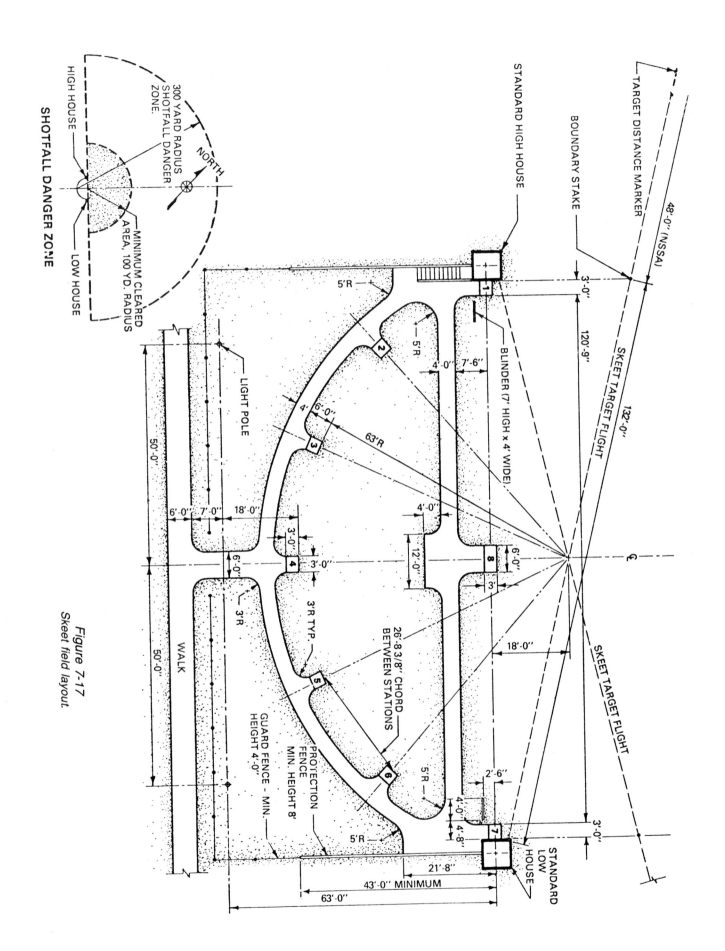

SHOTFALL DANGER ZONE

300 YARD RADIUS SHOTFALL DANGER ZONE.

HIGH HOUSE

LOW HOUSE

NORTH

MINIMUM CLEARED AREA, 100 YD. RADIUS

STANDARD HIGH HOUSE

BOUNDARY STAKE

TARGET DISTANCE MARKER

48'-0" (NSSA)

3'-0"

120'-9"

132'-0"

SKEET TARGET FLIGHT

BLINDER (7' HIGH × 4' WIDE)

5'R

5'R

4'-0"   7'-6"

4'   6'-0"

63'R

LIGHT POLE

50'-0"

6'-0"   7'-0"   18'-0"

3'-0"

3'-0"

6'-0"

3'R

4'-0"

12'-0"

6'-0"

3'

18'-0"

26'-8 3/8" CHORD BETWEEN STATIONS

3'R TYP.

5'R

GUARD FENCE - MIN. HEIGHT 4'-0"

PROTECTION FENCE MIN. HEIGHT 8'

50'-0"

WALK

5'R

5'R

2'-6"

4'-0"

4'-8"

STANDARD LOW HOUSE

3'-0"

SKEET TARGET FLIGHT

21'-8"

43'-0" MINIMUM

63'-0"

℄

Figure 7-17
Skeet field layout.

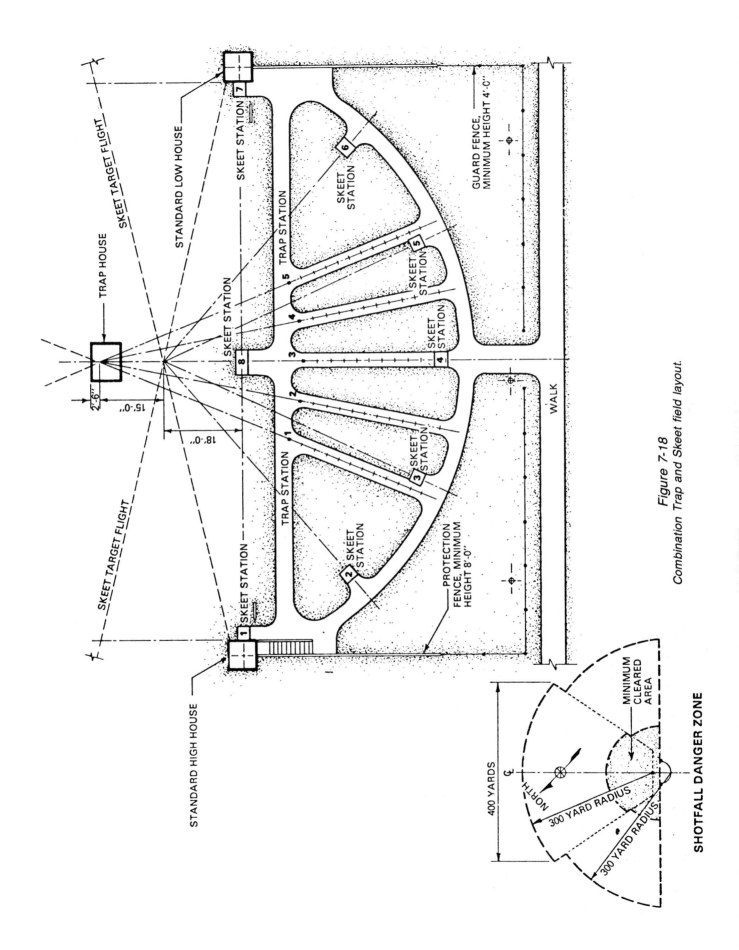

Figure 7-18
Combination Trap and Skeet field layout.

TRAP HOUSE

SKEET TARGET FLIGHT

STANDARD LOW HOUSE

SKEET STATION

SKEET STATION

TRAP STATION

SKEET STATION

SKEET STATION

SKEET STATION

SKEET STATION

TRAP STATION

SKEET STATION

SKEET TARGET FLIGHT

STANDARD HIGH HOUSE

GUARD FENCE, MINIMUM HEIGHT 4'-0"

WALK

PROTECTION FENCE, MINIMUM HEIGHT 8'-0"

2'-6"

15'-0"

18'-0"

400 YARDS

NORTH

300 YARD RADIUS

300 YARD RADIUS

MINIMUM CLEARED AREA

SHOTFALL DANGER ZONE

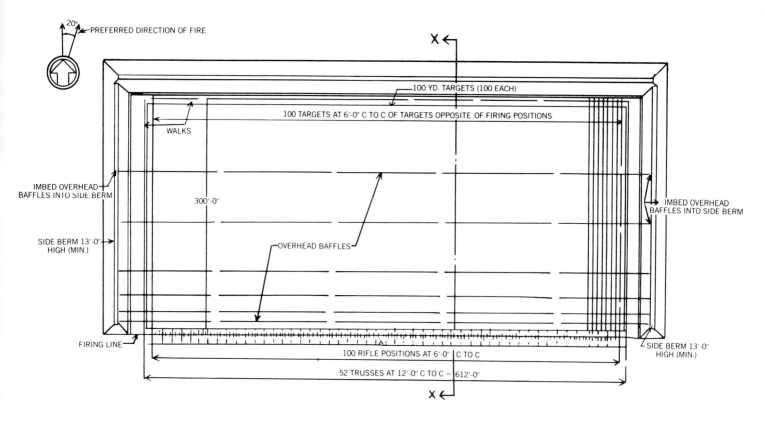

Figure 7-19
Small bore rifle and carbine range.

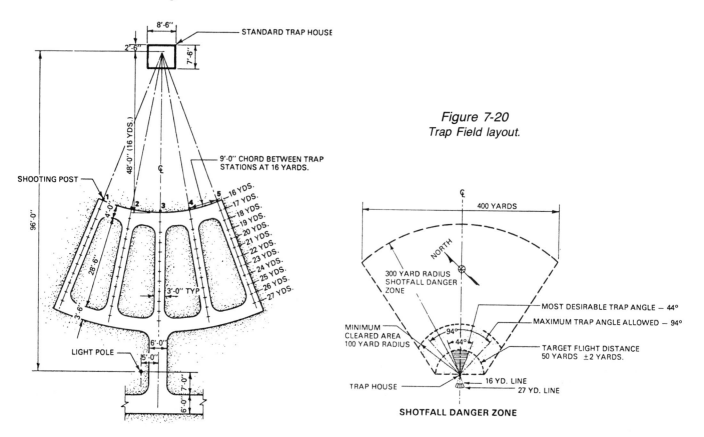

Figure 7-20
Trap Field layout.

site. Size alone does not necessarily mean much except that it does affect the numbers of certain species of wildlife that might live in the area. A large area does not necessarily have a diversity of physical features. It may just be level land, harboring only a few species of trees, with no particularly outstanding features. Nevertheless, such an area could be made interesting from an educational point of view, provided good leadership is available.

Many schools, recreation departments, and community agencies already have school sites, parks, and recreational areas that could be developed for outdoor programs. Schools, as well as other agencies, in some sections of the country also have forest lands that could be developed and used in a broad educational and recreational program.

Site Characteristics

The characteristics of the site are also determined by the type of program planned. If plans call for a resident camp, many more requirements must be met than if the site will be used only on a daily basis. If the land and facilities are to contribute to all aspects of the educational curriculum, or if there is to be special emphasis on science, conservation, and outdoor skills, many characteristics will need to be considered, such as the following:

- A location to give some privacy and solitude
- Year-round accessibility by road
- A minimum of natural and man-made hazards
- Interesting geologic features, such as rock outcroppings, open field, flat terrain, and a variety of soil types
- A variety of native vegetation, including woods
- Wildlife that can be

maintained with good management
- A pond, stream, seashore, or large body of water
- Demonstration areas for conservation practices
- Woods for practicing outdoor skills and use of native materials
- Sanitary facilities, including good drainage and good drinking water
- Simple shelters in the event of inclement weather
- Proximity to adequate medical and hospital services

Special Features

Many kinds of developments are found in various types of outdoor education areas. Some of these are appropriate for camps, some for outdoor laboratories or nature centers, and some for outdoor recreation and sport centers. An outdoor education and outdoor recreation complex would include many site plans and facilities not possible in more limited areas. The adaptability of the area to the proposed program, the cost of construction, maintenance problems, aesthetic considerations, and available leadership are all factors in determining what facilities might be developed in a particular land area or cluster of acreages.

Listed below are some of the special developments that might be included in appropriate sites. Some of the features listed are discussed elsewhere in this text and are merely mentioned here. Others, not mentioned in other places, are discussed in more detail.

- Grass, shrubs, and trees. They provide shade, prevent soil erosion, provide food and cover for wildlife, serve as windbreaks, mark the boundary of the property, act as a buffer zone to ensure privacy against an adjacent (presently or potentially) populated area,

demonstrate principles of plant growth, serve as a resource for ecological studies, and give practice in forest management. A school forest offers many popular activities.
- A vegetable garden or a bog garden.
- Soil-erosion demonstration areas. Such an area should be rich in vegetation, feature good conservation practices, be situated on inclined terrain, and be located next to a piece of land denuded of its vegetation and also located on an incline. Comparisons can then be made over a period of time to determine what happens to the quantity and quality of soil in both areas.
- Snake pit. A variety of reptiles found in the local area could be kept in a circular pit about 20 feet in diameter and constructed of concrete and stone. Concave walls and a water-filled moat surrounding an island will prevent the snakes from escaping.
- Wildlife sanctuary. Provide mixed plantings and construct birdhouses, feeders, and bird baths to attract a variety of birds.
- Weather station. This is for the study of meteorology and should be located in an area that can be fenced off and locked.
- Council ring. This facility provides a place for campfires, for conducting orientations before field trips, and for other special programs. The council ring should be located in a wooded area to ensure a feeling of isolation. Use logs for seats.
- Nature trails. Develop, if space permits, a variety of trails, each serving a different purpose. One

may be a geology trail, winding its way through an area rich in geologic features. Another trail may emphasize the study of erosion, while still another may lead to an historic spot.

- Pioneer living area. Social studies lessons are vividly illustrated in such an area. Dramatize the life of the pioneer, including such activities as making dyes from plants, cooking outdoors, constructing shelters, learning to identify edible plants, and learning other survival practices.
- Observation platform. This platform can be used for observing birds and for studying astronomy. It should be located on the highest point of the property.
- Outdoor zoo. Animals indigenous to the local area are featured. Be certain that arrangements can be made to care properly for the animals caught.
- Miniature gardens. Each garden features a particular grouping of native plants found in the typical setting in which they normally grow.
- Plant grafting. A demonstration area that provides interesting studies in genetics.
- Animal-baiting area. Put a salt lick and some meat in a cleared area. Spread loose dirt around the baited spot, press it down with the feet, and smooth it out. Animals attracted to the area will leave their footprints, which can then be observed and studied.
- Natural preserve. An area could be set aside in which no developments would be made. It would be given complete

protection and would provide a spot for the observation of ecological aspects.
- Orienteering courses. The development of several courses for map and compass use would stimulate educational and recreational use of the area.
- Greenhouse. A place for the propagation of plants, some of which may be used for area improvement, is important. A greenhouse would make possible an acquaintance with plants and would be a means of providing projects for study during the off season.
- Winter-sports area. Places for skating, skiing, and coasting would be desirable in those parts of the country that have sufficient snow and cold weather to make these sports feasible.
- Natural play area. An area set aside for children, containing such elements as climbing logs, ropes for swinging across low areas, sandbanks, and hide-and-seek areas, can provide play opportunities different from those found in the city.
- Turtle pit. An attractive pit with water and plantings would make possible the study and observation of turtles and other amphibians.
- Rifle and skeet ranges. Such an area will provide opportunities for instruction in gun safety as well as for participation in rifle and skeet shooting.
- Casting and angling area. Developments for casting and angling would serve both instructional and recreational uses.
- Amphitheater. For large-group programs, an

amphitheater would be important. It could be used for lectures, drama, music, and a variety of demonstrations.
- Astronomy area. A special area for astronomy may be developed on a large open area, waterfront, dock, or even a roof. Seating facilities are desirable, and sometimes a telescope is permanently mounted to facilitate observations.
- Bird feeding station.
- Historical markers. Sites of old farms, early settlers' homes, Indian trails and village sites, and pioneer roads are illustrations of the kinds of historical sites that might be used for student projects.
- Shelters. Adirondack or picnic shelters can serve day-camp and day-use groups during inclement weather.
- Tree stump. Locate a fairly well-preserved tree stump. Make a sloping cut, smooth the top by sanding, and treat it with clear waterproofing material, such as fiberglas resin. Much can be learned about tree growth from carefully studying a tree stump.
- Herb garden. This garden features food seasoning and medicinal plants and serves as a useful teaching aid for a home economics class.
- Photographic blind. Construct a blind near a bird-feeding station for taking pictures of wild birds.
- Evergreen tree nursery. Trees can later be transplanted to desired areas.
- Field archery. Targets are set up in wooded areas or fields, simulating actual hunting conditions.
- Natural areas. Such areas

are left relatively undisturbed, and man-made modifications . should be avoided as much as possible. These places serve as excellent resources for scientific studies of natural phenomena.

- Picnic site. It is desirable to locate the picnic site on the periphery of the property.
- Seashore areas. Communities adjacent to seashores may have areas set aside for study and observation. Developments might include ramps or walks to facilitate observation. Walkways through tidelands may be developed as nature trails. One of the national parks has an underwater nature trail.

Outdoor Laboratories

The term **outdoor laboratory** is used for a piece of land (including wetlands, lakes, and seashores) set aside by a school for learning experiences directly related to land and its resources. It may be located close to an individual school, or it may serve a group of schools. It may be a part of the school grounds or a section of a park-school development. It may consist of only a few acres nearby or of several hundred acres, nearby or many miles away. It may serve individual elementary schools, high schools or universities, or all of them jointly. Because outdoor laboratories are extremely varied in their site possibilities and their purposes, no rigid format for their development is possible.

The term **land for learning** has been applied to the school laboratory. It implies the opportunity of school groups to study, explore, and experiment with land and its resources. Outdoor study, field trips, and experiments with water, soil,

plants, and animals constitute its major functions.

Developments may range from nothing more than a few trails, with the area left natural, to nature trails, class and museum buildings, horticultural plots, developed ponds, forest plantations, gardens, and small-farm operations. The creativity of the teacher or outdoor education specialist, the potential of the available site, and funds available may be the only limiting factors in the development of program facilities.

If a laboratory is heavily used, water and toilet facilities might be essential. A storage building for tools and supplies might also be desirable.

Nature Centers

The term **nature center** is used to designate a particular type of development that will facilitate learning in the outdoors and the growth of recreational interests. The establishment of nature centers is being promoted extensively by several science and nature related organizations. Several hundred such centers have been developed in the United States in recent years. Children's museums may be considered a part of this development, although some of these museums lack adjacent lands for outdoor education.

Nature centers have been developed principally by three types of financing and management: schools, private associations, and public park and recreation departments.

The Site

Some of the suggestions for the school outdoor-education laboratory are applicable here. Nature trails, ponds, bogs, gardens, forest plantings, and the like may provide the variety essential for a rich outdoor education program.

The Building

The building should be designed so as to permit expansion as the program grows and as more funds become available. In its initial stage, the building should contain a minimum space of 2,500 square feet, which is large enough to contain one class adequately. The building should be designed according to the needs set by the program. The following general facilities are recommended:

- Office for staff
- Toilet facilities. Access should be provided to the outside as well as to the interior of the building.
- Large meeting room. The wall space can be utilized for exhibits. Low cabinets along the walls should be provided for storage of educational aids. A long counter providing work and display space should be constructed on top of the cabinets.
- Classrooms. Two classrooms should be provided so that a class may be broken up into smaller groups if necessary.
- Workroom. This room would be used for constructing displays and for arts and crafts.
- Science laboratory. A room should be equipped with microscopes, soil- and mineral-testing equipment, and other materials necessary for scientific studies.
- Library. The large meeting room can contain the library, which would occupy one section of the room. The library should contain reference material, field guides, magazines, and novels concerned with the outdoors.
- Storage room. Adequate space should be provided for storage of the many pieces of instructional and janitorial equipment that will accumulate over the

years.

It should be emphasized again that it is not essential for one center to have most of the facilities described here. Dynamic leadership is, to a large degree, more important, and not even the ultimate in good facilities can ever satisfactorily replace the need for effective leadership.

Interpretive Centers

Although the name **interpretive centers** might well be applied to the outdoor laboratories and the nature centers mentioned earlier, it has a specific use in describing certain facilities of public parks offered as a service to the general public and, in some cases, to school groups. The National Park Service has the most extensive development of such centers, although state and metropolitan parks have, in recent years, been expanding the number of their interpretive centers. The U.S. Forest Service is beginning to develop information centers that are essentially interpretive centers.

The primary purpose of interpretive centers is to help visitors understand and appreciate the natural, historical, or archeological features of the areas in which the centers are located. Inasmuch as the problems of interpretation of each area are different, facility developments are likewise varied.

Interpretive centers frequently contain a trailside museum or interpretive-center building. This may vary in size from 10 by 20 feet to a large, multi-roomed structure. The size depends on the groups to be accommodated, the interpretive materials available, and the types of programs to be presented. A large building may contain some or all of the following:

- Display rooms with habitat cases and other exhibits
- Office space for staff members
- A laboratory for research and the preparation of display materials

- Meeting rooms for lectures, slides, or movies
- Lavatories and toilets
- A counter for the sale of books and the distribution of pamphlets
- An outdoor amphitheater or campfire area for lectures and movies
- Trails to points of interest (often self-guiding nature trails)
- Parapets or other special observation points, often including mounted telescopes and pointers indicating places of interest
- Interpretive devices at points of interest, including bulletin boards, maps, diagrams, and displays
- Parking areas

School groups often visit interpretive centers, usually by school bus on a one-day basis. In some cases, picnic areas are provided for such groups. Work space, where children can work on projects at the center, is often a desirable feature.

School and Community Gardens, Farms, and Forests

Gardens, farms, and forests provide direct experiences with growing plants and, in some cases, with domestic animals. Schools, park and recreation agencies, and a few private agencies have been responsible for the development of facilities. Even when facilities are developed and operated by park and recreation departments or private agencies, some direct relationship with schools is often provided through an instructional program in which the school children are enrolled.

Display Gardens

Gardens of various kinds should be developed to provide for visual, cultural, and educational equipment.

A formal garden may be composed entirely of one type of

plant (such as roses), of various types of assorted plant materials, or of a series of individual gardens comprised of single types of plant units. Features such as a water fountain and statuary can be incorporated into the design.

Informal gardens should have long, sweeping lawn areas to serve as a setting for plants and flower beds. Plants may include large specimen trees, flowering trees, shrubs, and vines. The flower borders can be of varied plants.

All the plants should be of interest to the average homeowner and should be useful in helping him select plants for his own yard. Attempts should be made to keep abreast of the latest introductions and to display those types of plants that are hardy to the particular region in which the garden is located. This aspect of planting for the homeowner should be stressed in both formal and informal gardens, and demonstrations of plant cultural practice should be provided.

Naturalistic and native, or wildflower, gardens are established in a wilderness location, where the plants native to the region can be assembled in one area so they are easily accessible to the citizens. Developers will probably need an area of varied topography — lowlands, highlands, and prairies — and an area with varied soil conditions — from alkaline to acid — to accommodate the various types of plants.

Tract Gardens

In a tract garden, which is the most common type of school or community garden, a piece of property ranging in size from one to ten acres is divided into small tracts for the use of individuals. A typical plot size may be 10 by 20 feet, but adults and families can use larger gardens. A garden program with 25 plots can be set up on one-fourth acre of land, although more space is desirable. Four acres of land can hold 100 gardeners with plots of varied size and community crops. This size allows space for a service building and activity area. It should be on rich, well-drained soil with water available.

Garden programs may involve instruction, environmental projects, field trips, and science activities. Community projects may include novelty crops such as a pumpkin patch, gourds, Indian corn, and a Christmas tree farm. Gardening appeals to all ages and is an excellent program for families.

Some of the necessary or desirable features of the tract garden are the following:

- Garden building — either a small building for the storage of tools and equipment or a building large enough for class meetings and indoor activities during bad weather
- Toilet facilities adequate to care for the maximum number of participants expected on the garden plot at one time
- Greenhouse for plant propagation
- Ready access to water, with spigots and hoses available for limited irrigation
- Fencing for protection of the garden
- Pathways and walkways to provide easy access to all plots
- A demonstration home yard, with grass, flowers, and shrubs
- Good landscaping

Preferably, the tract garden should be located within walking distance of the homes of the participants. In many cases, gardens are developed on or adjacent to school grounds.

Tract gardens for adults and families have been established in some communities. They are usually intended for people living in crowded urban centers or apartments who would not otherwise be able to garden. In some communities, these gardens are located some distance from homes, and transportation is left up to the individuals concerned.

Farms

Community or school farms are becoming increasingly important, especially near metropolitan centers, and offer opportunities for a rich and varied program. Farm programs include animal care and training and traditional rural activities such as hay rides, picnics, and nature activities. Model farms are heavily used by families who just want to walk through to see and pet the animals.

Simple barns and pens contain horses, cows, pigs, chickens, sheep, and other domestic animals, which children can help care for and feed. In an urban setting it is essential that the facility be attractive and well-maintained. There must be water, feed storage, and adequate exercise space for the animals. An office, restrooms, drinking fountain, indoor and outdoor activity areas, and storage space are needed for the people.

In addition to the buildings that are generally found on a diversified farm, there are meeting places and exhibits that make it possible to carry on indoor instruction. Picnic areas, farm ponds, day-camp facilities, campfire circles, and hiking trails are often developed also.

Working farms are sometimes adapted for recreational purposes. This type of facility actually produces while city residents visit to learn, observe, take part in, and enjoy farming activities. Groups may use the farm on a day basis, and overnight accommodations can be provided. In either case, a large room and open outdoor space are needed for activity and instruction.

Farm camps offer opportunities for a farm-oriented camping experience. The farm camp is a farm not worked for production, but set up for resident programs in environmental education, farm activities, natural history, science, and other outdoor recreation. There may be a large farmhouse converted to a program building and farm buildings converted to cabins. Facilities needed are a kitchen, dining area, sleeping quarters, restrooms, large activity room, and ample storage space. Additionally, barns, farm equipment, and other facilities will be needed. These facilities and animals will be required dependent on program direction.

Forests

Numerous school and community forests can be found throughout the United States. Many of these were acquired from tax-delinquent land, through gifts, or through protection programs for community watersheds. Their use has followed diverse patterns. Some schools have carried on field trips, forest improvement projects, and other outdoor education activities. In general, however, schools have not made the maximum use of such areas.

Many of these forests could be developed as outdoor education laboratories. Some might be suitable sites for nature centers, day camps, or even resident camps.

School and community forests may serve valuable purposes even without extensive development. Water, trails, and toilets may be all the developments need to provide useful educational facilities. Such areas may serve their best functions as places in which to study the ecological changes taking place over a period of years.

Outdoor Skills and Sports Areas

Outdoor skills or sports areas should be included in the outdoor education-recreation complex, but it may be necessary to acquire special sites, depending on the topography of the land. These areas should provide opportunities to learn and practice skills, but they may also be used as outdoor laboratories.

The following are some of the specialized program facilities that might be included in the outdoor skills and sports area:

- Casting and angling — platforms and open, level spaces
- Outdoor shooting range
- Archery range — target field course, archery golf, and other games
- Campcraft skills area
- Overnight camping area
- Outpost camping — Adirondack shelters
- Facilities for water sports, including swimming, canoeing, boating, sailing, skin diving, and water skiing
- Area for crafts with native materials — carving, lapidary, weaving, and ceramics — with a simple structure to provide shelter in inclement weather and to house equipment
- Water sports — ski slopes and tow, ski shelter, tobogganing, and ice-skating rinks

Natural Areas

Natural areas are generally thought of as representative of the original, undisturbed plants and animals of a locale. They may encompass a variety of habitats, such as woodlands, deserts, swamps, bogs, shorelines, or sand dunes.

It is almost impossible today, even in the wilderness, to find undisturbed areas. Most places categorized as natural areas are protected lands that indicate the least disturbance and that, through protection, planting, and development, approximate the original characteristics.

It is characteristic of natural areas that they are protected from nonharmonious developments and activities. Simple access trails, protective fencing, and simple interpretive developments such as entrance bulletin boards are usually acceptable. In designated natural areas, the enjoyment and study of the natural features are encouraged, and uses that detract from the natural features are discouraged.

Schools, parks, and camps are often the agencies that develop, maintain, and protect natural areas. Such areas are valuable assets in environmental education.

Other Outdoor Areas

Information pertinent to other outdoor facilities is available in Chapter 2.

Camps and Camping

Historically, the word **camping** signified simple living outdoors and engaging in activities related primarily to the outdoors. Today the term has broadened tremendously and encompasses a wide spectrum of developments for families and children. **Resident center, day camps, group camps, family camps, and wilderness camps** are the common designations used for the various types of camps.

Camps have been developed by public agencies at all levels of government and by many voluntary youth-serving organizations. The rapidly increasing participation of children and adults in camping necessitates careful consideration of desirable areas and facilities.

Although most organized camping takes place on agency-owned or private property, public land is becoming increasingly involved. Public land is one of the major resources for school outdoor education programs, and many resident centers have been constructed on public property or by public funds. Schools use the facilities during the school year, and park and recreation agencies use them during the summer. The purposes of outdoor education, whether sponsored by park and recreation departments or by schools, are similar in many respects, and cooperative planning is not only necessary in order to get the most from the community dollar but imperative if suitable lands and sites are to be obtained. If adequate facilities are to be provided to meet the needs of both organized camping groups

Figure 7-21

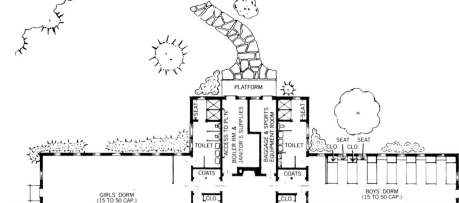

Floor plan of large overnight camp unit.

Facilities for Recreation, Parks and Open Spaces

and schools, the facilities must be designed for year-round use.

Program Facilities — What to Expect

Following are some of the facilities used for various camp programs. Specifications and construction details for most are found elsewhere in this book.

Water-related activities are among the most popular in summer camps. During the fall and spring, school groups and other groups may use developments for fishing, canoeing, and boating.

Lakes, ponds, streams, bays, and inlets offer many recreational opportunities. All should be studied in detail with regard to currents, eddies, depth, slope, shoreline, debris, and other factors.

Canoeing, boating, and sailing are activities that may be conducted on a lake, pond, river, reservoir, bay, or other body of water. The water area should have accessory facilities such as floats, docks, markers, or buoys. Various sizes of water bodies are required for different activities and events. For instance, canoe-racing courses are 100, 200, 440, and 880 yards as well as one mile. Sailing requires a wider body of water because the boats usually finish to windward. The different classes of sailboats, such as Sunfish and Sailfish, require different courses.

Casting is simulated rod-and-reel fishing. Practice casting on a playing field or in a gymnasium is possible the year round. If a pond or lake is nearby, a beach or dock affords an excellent facility for the casting program.

In order to teach all phases of the activity, an area 300 by 100 feet is desirable. A football, soccer, hockey, or lacrosse field is ideal for class instruction.

Casting targets, which are 30 inches in diameter, are easily constructed and can be an excellent project for any woodshop program. It is recommended that at least 10 targets be made.

Others can be added as the program expands. Targets for use on the water are also 30 inches in diameter and are made of hollow metal tubing. They float and can be easily anchored.

Other program facilities include campfire circles and council rings, for which most camps develop centers for meetings and evening programs, and craft centers, which can range from canvas-covered areas with provisions for storing tools to extensive and well-equipped craft shops.

Day Camps

A day camp is an area and facility intended to provide a program similar to that of the resident camp except that campers sleep at home. Many of the considerations of planning for resident camps apply to day camps. However, facility problems are simpler because day campers sleep at home and usually eat two of the day's meals at home. Provisions, however simple, must nonetheless be made for water, toilets, rainy-day shelters, eating and cooking, refrigeration, first-aid and health, and program supplies. The focus of this section is that of selecting an appropriate day camp facility.

Abundant land for programs is extremely desirable, particularly when the emphasis is on outdoor-related activities. Reasonable isolation and a varied topography with outdoor program possibilities are essential. Natural parks, park-school areas, and community forests often lend themselves to use as day-camp sites. Some communities have developed special day-camp areas; others make appropriate picnic areas available for this special use.

Buses are often used to transport campers to the day camp. If more than half an hour is consumed in daily travel each way, the effectiveness of the program is reduced.

Day-camp groups are divided into units or counselor groups

ranging from 8 to 20 campers. Most day camps provide simple facilities for each unit, including a fireplace for cooking, storage cabinets, and tables. Some day camps serve a daily meal in a central dining hall, reducing or eliminating the need for unit cooking facilities.

Storage is needed for equipment, food, and program supplies. Some day camps use trailers or trucks for storage, hauling them back and forth each day. Also, a well-equipped first-aid station and a rest-area facility are necessary.

Group Camps

Many public agencies today provide special campsites for small groups, such as scouts, church groups, and school classes. These sites generally accommodate from 10 to 40 persons. In most cases, the groups stay from one to five days. Small units in decentralized resident camps sometimes have facilities that can be used for group camping. Simple fireplaces for cooking, picnic shelters for use in bad weather, toilets, and safe drinking water are necessities.

The great increase in winter camping by small groups often necessitates special developments. Some winter campers live completely outdoors in the cold, even in snow. Usually, however, winterized buildings are used for cooking, sleeping, and evening activities.

Family Camps

At one time "family camping" meant the activity of families pitching tents in natural areas, living and cooking simply, and finding their own interests outdoors. Today the term may include sleeping in tents or living in expensive motor homes, stopping overnight or vacationing in completely equipped resorts with varieties of entertainment.

Overnight or transient camps are usually strategically located for travelers passing by or for those wishing to visit nearby points of interest. These camps need to offer very little, chiefly cleanliness and comfort for short stays. They generally do not provide natural areas and recreational facilities.

Family resident camps offer complete meal and living accommodations for families or just adults. The facilities may be similar to those of resident camps except that some of the sleeping

quarters may be adapted to families.

Most of the campgrounds in state or federal areas are destination camps. Campers generally stay more than one night and often for several weeks.

In recent years a great many resort camps have sprung up. These resorts, generally privately developed, are more or less

complete vacationlands in themselves, offering, frequently under leadership, a recreation program and facilities including swimming pools, recreation buildings, children's playgrounds, special game courts, marinas, horseback riding trails, and the like.

SELECTED REFERENCES

A Model Playground for the Multiply Handicapped. Urbana/Champaign: University of Illinois, William W. Fox Developmental Center, Office of Recreation and Park Resources, 1982.

American Alliance for Health, Physical Education, Recreation and Dance. "Adventure Programming Resource File." **JOPERD Journal** 49 (April 1978): 54-55.

Bammel, Gene and Burrus-Bammel, Lei Lane. **Leisure and Human Behavior.** Dubuque, Iowa: William C. Brown, 1982.

Bowers, Louis. "Tomorrow's Play." **JOPERD Journal** 54 (February 1983): 40, 41.

Bruya, Lawrence D. "Playing the American Dream." **JOPERD Journal** 54 (February 1983): 38.

Buchanan, Edsel. "Playground Safety for the Handicapped." Washington, D.C.: **ERIC Reports,** 1979.

_____. "Views From the Bridge: From Where We Are to What Play Is and Could Become." **JOPERD Journal** 54 (February 1983): 37.

Buchanan, Edsel and Crawford, Michael. "Playground Programming for Developmentally Retarded Adults." **TAHPERD Journal,** Texas Association for Health, Physical Education, Recreation, and Dance 50 (February 1982): 18-19, 55.

Camp Sites and Facilities. Boy Scouts of America, 1980.

Camping Standards. Martinsville, Indiana: American Camping Association, revised periodically.

Coppa and Avery Consultants. "Adaptation and Design of Parks and Recreational Facilities for the Handicapped." **Vance Bibliographies** (November 1980).

Dickey, Howard L. "Outdoor Adventure Training." **JOPERD Journal** 49 (April 1978): 34-35.

Doell, Charles E. and Twardzik, Louis F. **Elements of Park and Recreation Administration.** 4th edition. Minneapolis: Burgess, 1979.

Dustin, Daniel. "Shady Trails: A Therapeutic Camp for Communicatively Handicapped Youth." Ann Arbor: **University Innovator,** School of Education, University of Michigan, 1980.

Ellis, M.J. **Why People Play.** Englewood Cliffs, New Jersey: Prentice-Hall, 1973.

Fink, Ira and Body, David. "Developing a Sports and Recreation Master Plan." **Planning for Higher Education** 11 (Spring 1983), 1-17.

Fitness Systems by Landscape Structures, Incorporated: Healthbeat, Wheel Course, Vita Course, Fitcore. Delano, Minnesota: Landscape Structures, Inc., 1984.

Fitzgerald, Sharon E. "Will-A-Way: Georgia's Unique Facility for the Handicapped." **CEFP Journal** 21 (January/February 1983), 8-9.

Flynn, Richard B., ed. "Focus on Facilities for Community Recreation." **JOPERD Journal** 48 (November/December 1977): 45, 46.

_____. "Maximizing Use of Facilities." **JOPERD Journal** 49 (October 1978): 25-33.

Fulfilling Recreation and Open Space Requirements in Water Quality Management Planning. Washington, D.C.: Heritage Conservation and Recreation Service, 1980.

Glickman, Carl D. "Problem: Declining Achievement Scores; Solution: Let Them Play." **Kappan** 60 (February 1979): 454, 455.

Godbey, Goeffrey. **Leisure in Your Life: An Exploration.** Philadelphia: W.B. Saunders, 1980.

Gold, Seymour M. "Recreation Planning for Energy Conservation." **Parks and Recreation** 12 (September 1977): 61-63, 83-89.

Haering, Franklin C. "Recreation and Park Program Safety." **Urban Data Service Reports** 12 (March 1980), 1-11.

Hasegaqa, Sandra and Elliott, Steve. "Public Spaces by Private Enterprise." **Urban Land** 42 (May 1983), 12-15.

Hazard Analysis of Injuries Relating to Playground Equipment. Washington, D.C.: U.S. Educational Resources Information Center, ERIC Document ED. 120102, 1975.

Hogan, Paul. "Working for Play." **JOPERD Journal** 54 (February 1983): 39.

Jarrell, Temple R. "Bikeways Design — Construction — Programs." Arlington, Virginia: National Recreation and Park Association, 1974.

Jensen, Clayne R. **Outdoor Recreation in America.** 3rd edition. Minneapolis: Burgess, 1977.

Knudson, Douglas M. **Outdoor Recreation.**

Revised Edition. New York: Macmillan, 1984.

Kramer, Bruce M. and Mertes, James D. "The Pros and Cons of Mandatory Dedication." **Urban Land** 38 (April 1979), 3-12.

Lancaster, Roger A., ed. **Recreation, Park, and Open Space Standards and Guidelines.** Alexandria, Virginia: National Recreation and Park Association, 1983.

Lehew, Edward and Lehew, Shirley. "White Oak Village Offers Wide Variety of Recreational Facilities for the Handicapped." **CEFP Journal** 21 (January/February 1983), 9-11.

Levy, Joseph. **Play Behavior.** New York: John Wiley & Sons, 1978.

Lopez, Stephen. "Preserving Open Space Via Community Stewardship." **Parks and Recreation** 17 (January 1983), 66-69.

Maguire, Meg. "An Open Letter to Park and Recreation Advocates." **Parks and Recreation** 17 (November 1982), 44-52.

McAvoy, Leo. "Outdoor Leadership Training." **JOPERD Journal** 49 (April 1978): 42, 43.

Meier, Joel F. "Is the Risk Worth Taking?" **JOPERD Journal** 49 (April 1978): 31-33.

Mitchell, A. Viola and Meier, Joel F. **Camp Counseling: Leadership and Programming for the Organized Camp.** Sixth Edition. Philadelphia: W.B. Saunders, 1983.

National Urban Recreation Study: Technical Reports. Washington, D.C.: Heritage Conservation and Recreation Service, 1978.

Nationwide Recreation Survey (1982-83). Washington, D.C.: Bureau of the Census, Government Printing Office, 1984.

Nelson, Charles M. and Leroy, Lawrence. "County Parks — State of the Art Today." **Parks and Recreation** 17 (January 1983), 84-86.

Orr, James. "Urban Parks and Open Space." **Vance Bibliographies** (December 1978).

Recreation Innovations — Abroad. Washington, D.C.: Heritage Conservation and Recreation Service, Technical Notes, 1980.

Safety Requirements for Home Playground Equipment. PS 66-75. Washington, D.C.: National Bureau of Standards, July 1976.

Sandman, Peter M. "Green Acres in the 80's." New Jersey County and Municipal Government Study Commission, June 1983.

Shea, Thomas. **Camping for Special**

Children. St. Louis: C.V. Mosby, 1977.

Shedlock, Robert E. "Water-Play Parks on Public Land: A Revenue Source and a Public Benefit." **Parks and Recreation** 17 (March 1983), 38-40.

Staffo, Donald F. "Children's Play Area." **Journal of Physical Education and Recreation** 48 (November-December 1977): 39.

Sutton-Smith, Brian. **A History of Children's Play, New Zealand, 1940-1950.** Philadelphia: University of Pennsylvania Press, 1981.

U.S. Consumer Product Safety Commission. **A Handbook for Public Playground Safety: General Guidelines for New and Existing Playgrounds: Technical Guidelines for Equipment and Surfacing,** 1978.

U.S. Consumer Product Safety Commission. **A Look at the Playground Safety Education Materials: "Play Happy, Play Safely,"** 1978.

U.S. Consumer Product Safety Commission. **Consumer Deputy Final Report on Playground Surfaces,** 1980.

U.S. Consumer Product Safety Commission. **Playground Equipment,** April 1979.

U.S. Consumer Product Safety Commission. "Injuries Associated with Public Playground Equipment," 1979.

U.S. Department of Agriculture National Technical Information Service. "Open Space Reservation: Federal Tax Policies Encouraging Donation of Conservation Easements," 1978.

U.S. Department of Housing and Urban Development. **Private and Volunteer Sector Involvement in Urban Recreation: An Information Bulletin of the Community and Economic Development Task Force of the Urban Consortium,** 1980.

U.S. Department of Housing and Urban Development. **A Playground for All Children/City of New York,** 1978.

U.S. Department of the Interior. **Citizen's Action Manual: A Guide to Recycling Vacant Property in Your Neighborhood,** February 1979.

U.S. Department of the Interior. **Fees and Charges Handbook: Guidelines for Recreation & Heritage Conservation Agencies,** March 1979.

U.S. Department of the Interior: HCRS. **Land Conservation and Preservation Techniques,** March, 1979.

U.S. Department of the Interior: HCRS. **Private Sector Involvement Workbook.** Second Edition, October 1979.

U.S. Department of the Interior: HCRS. **Foundations . . . A Handbook,** October 1979.

U.S. Department of the Interior: HCRS. **Volunteer Handbook,** September 1978.

U.S. Department of the Interior: HCRS. **Urban Parks and Recreation: A Trends/Analysis Report,** August 1980.

Watkins, William. "Administrative Guidelines for Community Use of Physical Education and Recreation Facilities." **Journal of Physical Education and Recreation** 49 (October 1978): 32.

Weiskopf, Donald. **Recreation and Leisure: Improving the Quality of Life.** Second Edition. Rockleigh, New Jersey: Allyn and Bacon, 1982.

Wolfram, Gary. "The Sale of Development Rights and Zoning in the Preservation of Open Space." **Land Economics** 57 (August 1981), 398-413.

Zito, Anthony J. "Park Board Members: What Do They Want To Know?" **Parks and Recreation** 18 (July 1983), 54-55, 68.

CHAPTER VIII
Planning For The Handicapped

"Our society has an obligation to provide the handicapped with means to enjoy their basic civil rights: the right to vote, the right to equal educational opportunities, and freedom of movement." — *William O. Douglas, United States Supreme Court Justice.*

Recent federal, state, and local legislation, along with the development of new advocacy groups, have mandated providing services to individuals with disabilities. Responsibilities for providing these services have shifted to include both special service organizations and community recreation agencies. Increasingly, personnel in community recreation programs are being required to make facilities and activities more accessible to all persons in our society, including individuals with various disabilities.

Despite civil rights and laws about architectural accessibility, architectural barriers still deny millions of citizens with handicaps their rights to enjoy and participate in many activities which most of us take for granted.

Removal of these barriers in facilities used for athletics, physical education, and recreation must be accomplished. Yet, attitudinal barriers between leaders and participants, planners and users, therapists and patients also must be eliminated. To convey a positive attitude toward problems of access for all, the term accessibility rather than architectural barriers is recommended.

The importance of actively involving the handicapped persons themselves in all aspects of planning and evaluating facilities cannot be overemphasized. Unique need of individuals with different handicapping conditions can provide valuable input which may not be available from others involved in planning processes. This same consumer involvement needs to be incorporated in planning for programs which are to exist in given facilities.

Accessibility and Attitudes

Architectural barriers deny many members of society convenient access to indoor and outdoor facilities. Architectural accessibility is complex and requires a great deal of thought and cooperation among those involved. Accessibility implies meeting minimum standards of architectural design such as providing legally required curb-cuts to allow wheelchair users to travel from sidewalks into streets; or providing recessed or raised lettering on elevator buttons so that blind individuals can independently determine the correct buttons to push.

Accessibility, therefore, deals with architectural barriers that are fairly straightforward. A doorway either is, or is not measured easily. Also, the presence of raised or recessed lettering either exists or does not exist. Both are clear examples of measurable accessibility (The Illinois Dept. of Conservation, 1977).

While many facilities might satisfy requirements for architectural accessibility, many factors in environmental design are not presently taken into account in accessibility standards. For example, accessibility without usability exists when a restroom doorway meets the minimal requirement of the 36-inch width, but the modesty wall which prevents passers-by from seeing the restroom occupants is built directly in front of the restroom door, thereby providing too sharp and small an area for the wheelchair user to get beyond the doorway. This is accessibility without usability, in that it satisfies the minimum legal requirements of an architectural standard, yet does not allow a wheelchair user to utilize the facility. By building the modesty screen further back from the doorway, the so-called "accessible" doorway also becomes usable.

Many such examples exist, and although public agencies try to include all aspects in their standards, there are too many variables in architectural design to cover them all. Therefore, it is vital that accessibility planning stresses the usability factor to better accomplish the goal of providing opportunities for all citizens to engage in physical education, recreation, and sport activities (The Illinois Department of Conservation, 1977).

Architectural barriers not only affect individuals with permanent or obvious physical conditions but persons with temporary or hidden conditions as well. Individuals with baby strollers, persons who must temporarily use crutches, those wearing leg braces, or individuals with heart conditions are just a few affected by architectural barriers to accessibility and whose needs are often overlooked. Only 17% of physically impaired persons are born with such conditions. The other 83% acquire disabilities through disease, accident, war, or old age. Most people, at one time or another, are personally affected by architectural barriers. Even if an individual is not so affected, the need for all facilities to be accessible to everyone is imperative as basic human and civil rights.

Despite federal, state, and local legislation requiring that all facilities be accessible, many communities and states continue to isolate special populations in segregated facilities or in special classes in regular schools. Able-bodied persons still impose their wishes on special populations whether these approaches and procedures are appropriate or desired by those for whom such services are designed. Special projects, task force groups, advisory panels, planning committees, and countless other groups explore problems of facilities and equipment for special groups. Unfortunately, few of these planning groups ever invite input from those most directly involved — the impaired, disabled, and handicapped consumers and their families.

By obtaining input from consumers and providers of services, facilities can be made functional for programs, activities, populations, and leaders who are going to direct and guide activities in these facilities. Some of the most practical, functional, and inexpensive recreational facilities developed for the impaired, disabled, and handicapped have been planned by these people themselves.

HEW regulations for Section 504 require that handicapped individuals be consulted in developing accessibility plans. One useful approach is to include handicapped people on the planning team. Handicapped clients and employees are likely candidates for a consumer panel. Local organizations of handicapped people are also recommended as a source of knowledgeable assistance. A number of national consumer organizations have local chapters that may be able to provide assistance. Among them are:

American Coalition of Citizens
    with Disabilities
1346 Connecticut Avenue NW,
    Room 817
Washington, D.C. 20036
(chapters in states)

American Council of the Blind
1211 Connecticut Avenue NW,
    Suite 506
Washington, D.C. 20036
(state and local chapters)

Disabled American Veterans
3725 Alexandria Pike
Cold Spring, Kentucky 41076
(state and local units)

National Association of the Deaf
814 Thayer Avenue
Silver Spring, Maryland 20910
(local chapters)

National Association of the
    Physically Handicapped
76 Elm Street
London, Ohio 43140
(local chapters)

National Congress of
    Organizations of the Physically
    Handicapped
6106 N. 30th Street
Arlington, Virginia 22207

National Paraplegia Foundation
333 N. Michigan Avenue
Chicago, Illinois 60601
(state and local chapters)

Paralyzed Veterans of America
4330 East West Highway,
    Suite 300
Washington, D.C. 20014
(state and area chapters)

Additional assistance may come from your state Governor's Committee on Employment of the Handicapped or your state Department of Rehabilitation as well as from local affiliates of national voluntary health organizations such as:

Arthritis Foundation
1212 Avenue of the Americas
New York, New York 10036

Association for the Aid of Crippled
    Children
345 East 46th Street
New York, New York 10017

International Society for
    Rehabilitation of the Disabled
219 East 44th Street
New York, New York 10017

Muscular Dystrophy Association
    of America
1790 Broadway
New York, New York 10019

National Foundation for
    Neuromuscular Diseases
250 West 57th Street
New York, New York 10019

National Multiple Sclerosis Society
257 Park Avenue South
New York, New York 10010

National Easter Seal Society for
    Crippled Children and Adults
2023 West Ogden Avenue
Chicago, Illinois 60612

United Cerebral Palsy Association, Inc.
66 East 34th Street
New York, New York 10016

Litigation and Legal Liability

As in every other area of civil rights, litigation has played, and will continue to play, an important role in exploring, defining, demanding, and ensuring the fullest realization of equal opportunity in recreation and physical education services for the handicapped. Test cases have resulted in two major areas for designers and planners to be concerned: supervision and security.

Both supervision and security relate to legal liability and should be considered during the planning phase. The design of buildings should focus on central inspection points where traffic can be controlled with a minimum of personnel. Examples include entrances and exits, concession areas, equipment check-out points, and internal activity areas such as handball courts and rifle and archery ranges. The planner, familiar with the programs which the building will accommodate, must identify these points of effective supervision.

Negligence, that aspect of liability which is interpreted as an improper action or a lack of action on the part of a reasonably prudent person, is closely related to the supervision function. It is the primary allegation in most litigation brought against the professional. While litigation involves a supervisory authority, the faulty design and/or maintenance of a facility often is the unseen contributory cause of the incident that precipitated the legal action. Examples of faulty facility design might include: narrow stairwells, locker rooms and swimming pools on two separate levels requiring use of a stairway, obstacles blocking sight lines on playing fields, improper lighting in gymnasiums and swimming pools, misalignment of locker rows, poorly designed backstops, and improperly hung doors. These and the many other examples of faulty design must be anticipated and eliminated by the planner.

Security is a planning function, usually considered in two phases — design construction and implementation safety. The planning phase will include consideration of: a comprehensive master/submaster key system; traffic patterns; monitoring control points; number of emergency exits; location of entrances; the building's communication system; sectioning the building for specific use functions; type of lockers, fire doors, and windows; and outdoor building lighting and landscaping.

Building safety includes: proper distance between court markings and walls, padding of walls and posts, provision of hand and/or guard rails where necessary, accessibility to rescue and life support equipment, proper lighting, non-slip floor surfaces, traffic passageways free of obstructions, and proper drainage in shower areas and pool decks.

Security measures and safety procedures should be designed for simplicity of operation. The more complicated and time-consuming it is to secure a facility and its equipment, the less likely that it will be done properly. There is little doubt that within areas of physical activity it is impossible to eliminate every situation which could lead to an accidental injury. However, planners must make every effort to design a facility that will minimize the potential for unauthorized use, injury, and vandalism.

Legislative Foundation

A brief review of the significant federal legislative activity pertinent to the delivery of physical education, recreation, and sport activities is provided in Table One. Among these mandates, three key laws with which everyone responsible for and involved in planning, implementing, and evaluating building and renovation processes should be familiar are: The Architectural Barrier Act (Public Law 90-480), the Rehabilitation Act of 1973 (Public Law 93-112), and The Education for All Handicapped Children Act (Public Law 94-142) (Table 1)

Among the major points of P.L. 94-142 are (1) physical education has been included as a required program under the law and (2) recreation is included as a "related service." Related services are to be implemented as necessary to assist a handicapped child to benefit from special education. This is the first time the term "recreation" appears in print in educational legislation.

One of the essential points of Section 504 of the Rehabilitation Act of 1973 is that no recipient of or applicant for federal financial assistance is permitted to discriminate against qualified handicapped persons. What constitutes a qualified handicapped person?

In the Section 504 regulation, HEW identifies a handicapped person as anyone with a physical or mental disability that substantially limits one or more of such major life activities as walking, seeing, hearing, speaking, working, or learning. A history of such disability or the belief by others that a person has such a disability, whether accurate or not, is also recognized as a handicap by the regulation. Handicapping conditions include, but are not limited to:

Alcohol*
Cancer
Cerebral palsy
Deafness or hearing impairment
Diabetes
Drug addiction
Epilepsy
Heart disease
Mental or emotional illness
Mental retardation
Multiple sclerosis
Muscular dystrophy
Orthopedic, speech, or visual
 impairment
Perceptual handicaps such as

Planning For The Handicapped

**Figure 1: Legislation Affecting
Recreation for Handicapped Individuals
Considerations for Construction
of New Aquatic Facilities**

LAW	IMPACT
A. Vocational Rehabilitation Act, 1963	Training and Research funds for recreation for the ill and handicapped. The first recognition by a federal agency of the importance of recreation services.
B. PL 90-480 Architectural Barriers Act, 1968	Simply states "Any building or facility, constructed in whole or part by federal funds, must be accessible to and usable by the physically handicapped."
C. PL 88-29, Nationwide Outdoor Recreation Plan, 1963	Directed the formulation and maintenance of a comprehensive nationwide outdoor recreation plan. The plan was completed in 1973 and included emphasis on compliance with PL 90-480. Concerns for the handicapped have been listed as a priority area.
D. Rehabilitation Act of 1973, PL 93-112	A comprehensive revision of the 1963 Vocational Rehabilitation Act which included an emphasis on the "total" rehabilitation of the individual. Special provisions included: 1) personnel training, 2) Special projects and demonstrations for making recreational facilities accessible, 3) Powers to ensure accessibility compliance for parks and parklands, 4) States must develop a comprehensive plan which ensures that they comply under section 504 that individuals shall not be discriminated against solely by reason of their handicap.
E. Public Law 93-516 Rehabilitation Act Amendment of 1974	Authorized the planning and implementation of the White House Conference on Handicapped Individuals which was conceived in 1977. Recreation was cited as one of sixteen areas of concern.
F. Public Law 90-170 Education for Handicapped Children Act, 1967	Established the Unit of Physical Education and Recreation for Handicapped Children within the Bureau of Education for the Handicapped. Became the largest federal program for training, research, and special projects.
G. Public Law 94-142 Education of All Handicapped Children Act, 1975	Requires a free and appropriate education for all handicapped children. Physical Education is listed as a direct service and recreation as a related service.
H. PL 91-517 Developmental Disabilities Services and Facilities Construction Act, 1971	Developmentally Disabled persons are specifically defined and recreation is listed as a specific service to be included as a fundable service.
I. The Social Security Act	A compilation of law, including numerous amendments over the last several years related specifically to the elderly and disabled, including provisions for physical education and recreation through: 1) formal procedures for review of professional services, 2) establishing funds to states for self-support services for individuals, 3) grants to states for providing community based care.

dyslexia, minimal brain dysfunction, or developmental aphasia
*The U.S. Attorney General has ruled that alcoholism and drug addiction are physical or mental impairments that are handicapping conditions if they limit one or more of life's major activities.

Recipients are forbidden from (directly or indirectly) providing any aid, benefit, or service which is not equal to that afforded nonhandicapped persons or is not as effective as that afforded such persons. The concept of providing separate but equal services is specifically rejected, except as a measure of last resort. In other words, services must be provided in the most integrated setting appropriate to the handicapped person's need. Separate services are not permitted unless such action is necessary to provide qualified handicapped persons with aid, benefits, or services that are as effective as those provided to others.

Regarding program accessibility, the law reads that any facility or part of a facility constructed after the effective date of the regulations must be readily accessible to handicapped persons. In addition, any new construction which is performed on an existing facility or part of a facility which could affect the usability of the facility by the handicapped must, to the maximum extent feasible, be altered in such a way as to make the facility accessible to handicapped persons.

Each of the fifty states has adopted corresponding laws regarding the intentions of federal legislation P.L. 90-480, P.L. 93-112, and P.L. 94-142. Such state legislative information needs to be part of planning processes since state requirements must meet federal requirements and in some instances are more stringent than federal laws.

Design Guidelines

At the present time a variety of

resources deal with adapting facilities to make them free of architectural barriers. The American National Standards Institute (ANSI) Standards for Making Buildings and Facilities Accessible to and Usable by Individuals with Handicapping Conditions were issued in 1961 and reaffirmed in 1971. A project at the Syracuse University School of Architecture to adapt and extend these standards was completed in 1977.

Although standards for architectural accessibility may vary to some extent according to specific conditions and unique factors at state and local levels, most jurisdictions use directly or modify slightly basic ANSI standards. However, experience has shown that in some instances facilities meet standards but are not really functional or usable. For example, a small porch or stoop that is only three feet wide meets the standard but is functional only if the door opens outward. These inconsistencies emphasize the need for input from the consumers themselves. (Figure 8-1)

Although most standards pertain to basic accessibility of buildings and related structures, such barrier-free design features apply also to physical education and recreation area facilities. In fact, basic accessibility and availability are far more important factors to consider in these areas than specialized facilities per se. Basic factors to consider for accessibility of all facilities are:

- Avoiding making old facilities accessible through addition of new facilities without carefully analyzing how old facilities can be made usable to persons with handicapping conditions.
- Avoiding designs which provide accessibility for part of a facility and create extreme internal barrier problems in other parts of the facility.
- Minimum height factors for

mirrors, telephones, lavatories, faucets, elevator buttons, and switch controls should consider their locations as well as populations being served.
- Ramp gradients and turns need to consider all forms of wheelchairs — e.g., self-propelled, electric.
- Sufficiently large restrooms with grab bars and accessible sinks and mirrors.
- Low public telephones.
- Low and easily operated water fountains.
- Non-skid floors.
- Elevators, ramps, and/or special lifting devices rather than steps.
- Proper lighting.
- Doors at least 32 inches wide.
- Ramps with a slope not greater than one foot rise in twelve feet.
- Hand rails that are smooth, extend one foot beyond the top and bottom, and are placed on at least one side of ramps that are 32 inches high.
- Door thresholds flush with the floor.

- Curb-cuts.
- Special and extra large parking spaces for vans with sufficient space between cars when doors are open.
- Braille markers on elevators and in other key informational locations.
- Sound system for emergencies and other program uses.
- Visual warning system for emergencies.
- Pedestrian-operated traffic signals with standardized time-delay to allow deaf or blind persons enough time to cross streets safely.
- Meeting rooms designed so deaf persons can clearly see interpreters, visual display areas, and others in the meeting.
- See-through panels in doors, unless privacy is necessary, to allow deaf persons chances to see into rooms before entering.
- Anti-static carpets to avoid interference with hearing aids.
- Flashing light attachments on phones to indicate rings.

Figure 8-1
All facilities should be planned, designed, and constructed so that they are accessible to everyone.

Planning For The Handicapped

- Fire alarm and smoke detection systems attached to strobe lights to ensure that deaf persons are notified of dangers.
- Other emergency messages conveyed graphically, e.g., a sign in an elevator could flash that help is on the way should the cab become stuck.

Modifications and Adaptations

Modification of any existing building is predicated on the principle that needs of impaired, disabled, and handicapped people are exactly the same as those of able-bodied individuals. Where facilities are available to physically able persons, they should be designed to be accessible to and usable by physically impaired persons. Conversely, all facilities should be planned, designed, and constructed so that they are accessible to everyone, including the most severely, profoundly, and multiply impaired persons.

Many factors must be considered when establishing priorities for modifying facilities. However, it is difficult to recommend a set of priorities which apply to all building types. It is necessary to consider individuals with different handicapping conditions. So often the only considerations are given to individuals with mobility difficulties while the needs of those with sensory impairments are ignored.

Most necessary facility adaptations are included in American National Standards Institute standards — pitch of ramps, size of restrooms and adaptations of stalls, heights of drinking fountains and telephones, size and placement of parking spaces, type and pitch of walks, size of door jambs, placement of hardware — and only need to be applied to athletic, physical education, and recreation facilities. Common sense application can be made to certain aspects of these facilities, for example:

- Extend pitch of ramps for nature trails, walks, and other areas requiring locomotion.
- Make nature trails, walks, swimming pool decks, and similar passage areas a minimum width for two wheelchairs to pass.
- Lower basketball goals and reduce apparatus size for elementary school age youngsters because of their sizes, chronological ages, and functional levels, not because they are in wheelchairs.
- Use lights behind basketball backboards that are synchronized with the game clock and timer's horn to assist those with hearing problems.

These kinds of planning recommendations from participants are very important. Many of the most practical, functional, and realistic adaptations have been suggested by the consumers.

Although early legislation focused on accessibility requirements for new construction, emphasis is now shifting toward making existing buildings barrier-free. Some state and municipal building codes, such as those in Massachusetts and Chicago, stipulate, with certain exceptions, that any remodeling of public buildings must result in accessibility for everyone. North Carolina has made a two million dollar fund available for remodeling state facilities to make them accessible. Federal tax credits can be obtained by companies as incentives to remove architectural barriers.

Beyond the standard facility adaptations needed for buildings, there are a number of specialized facilities that have been developed in recent years which extend simple consideration of accessibility for the disabled to active program design and creative custom construction techniques. Programming areas

Figure 8-2
An adapted physical education laboratory designed to serve physical and orthopedic conditions.

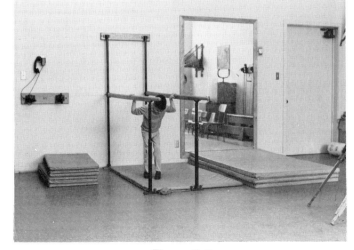

Figure 8-3
Wall-attached parallel walking bars are added to a gym for students with handicapping conditions to use.

included in this process are: physical education and recreation facilities, playgrounds, outdoor education and fitness trails, camp facilities, and swimming pools. A brief elaboration of each of these along with further resources will provide a clearer understanding of the extent to which program accessibility in combination with architectural accessibility has been pursued.

Physical Education Facilities

Many schools, elementary as well as secondary, make provisions for adapted physical education with special additions to existing facilities. Physical educators increasingly are asked to design special facilities for adapted physical education and to recommend equipment and supplies for outfitting these facilities. Therefore, physical educators should study and evaluate carefully the school population to determine conditions which are to be served through the adapted physical education program so facilities, equipment, and devices best suited to meet specific students' needs can be recommended. Not all special items of equipment and supplies have to be obtained at once, since the needs of the current population should influence decisions regarding immediate priorities. Additional items can be added in subsequent years as population needs change and different kinds of equipment and supplies are required. (Figure 8-2)

An example custom facility is:
Sports Complex for the
    Handicapped
The 52 Association
Ossining, New York 10562
Some of the specially constructed features include wheelchair ramps leading down to a lake which allow occupants to enter and exit the water totally unassisted; low built barbecue pits, also for use by wheelchair occupants; a concrete tandem bike path for the blind; paddle boats for paraplegics and amputees; and

paved wheelchair and volleyball courts. (Figures 8-3)

Recreation Facilities

By law recreational facilities must be accessible to all persons if they are owned or leased by the U.S. Government or if they are financed in whole or part by the U.S. Government. Numerous facilities do not comply with Public Law 90-480. However, there is plenty of information available for getting help in complying with it. Additionally, there are numerous examples of public recreation agencies that have assumed primary responsibility for programming for handicapped individuals by developing specialized accessible recreation facilities. One example is:

Recreation Center for the
    Handicapped
207 Skyline Boulevard
San Francisco, California 94132
Within this facility doors are color coded for easy identification. In the daycare areas, floors are heated for small children. All rooms throughout the building have floor to ceiling windows. A large pool is ramped for wheelchairs and gurneys. The pool design also includes a wading area and therapeutic water temperature of 90 degrees.

The Joseph H. Cole Recreation
    Center
31st and G Streets, S.E.
Washington, D.C. 20019
Steps have been eliminated from the building design as well as all curbs inside and out. Other design modifications include lowered sinks, electric switches, mirrors, drinking fountains, and other wall-mounted items, wrist action handles on drinking fountains, and oversized toilet stalls with grab bars. All public doors are color coded and braille-identified. Automatic door closers with delayed action timers are used to give wheelchair users ample time to pass through. The swimming pool can be reached by ramp.

Playgrounds

Children with special problems need specially designed playgrounds. The environment in which they play must respond to that part of them which is healthy and capable, with help, of growth and development. For these children the ordinary playground presents a series of dangerous and frightening conditions: bare expanses of hard pavement, treacherous seesaws and swings, and precariously high slides. Even what appear to be relatively neutral materials, such as sand or dirt, can be a source of discomfort. Some disabled children cannot play in sand because they wear prosthetic devices which can jam if sand gets into the joints. Sponge rubber and grass are two surfaces which can be substituted for sand or dirt. (Figure 8-4)

Therapeutic playgrounds are designed to help users develop specific skills, including physical, perceptual, emotional, social, and educational skills. Not all handicapped children need a therapeutic playground. Those who engage in play behavior readily with their peers and who have accessible play facilities need no intervention. However, children in

Figure 8-4
An example of a playground design accommodation so that individuals with various physical/orthopedic conditions can use the facility fully.

rehabilitation hospitals or who are severely mentally, physically, or emotionally handicapped may need the help of a special facility in learning to play.

Like any playground, the therapeutic playground must be equipped with stable and safe apparatus. Handholds, footholds, and resting places are essential for the handicapped child, providing support and allowing for rest when needed. It is also important that equipment not become a barrier to communications between children. Provisions for cooperative play are a must, especially when children with communication disorders (visual, auditory, or speech) are using the facility. Ideally, the therapeutic playground will:

- Allow children freedom of movement within a space that takes into consideration their physical abilities and limitations;
- Allow space for both solitary and cooperative play;
- Consist of various textures and shapes that stimulate the child's fantasy life;
- Challenge the child physically and perceptually to enhance development.

There are several model playgrounds across the nation that have been developed to accommodate wheelchair-bound and multi-disabled children. One is located at the William W. Fox Developmental Center in Dwight, Illinois. Its approach to design included the development and integration of several different play zones. The project included the construction of many unique equipment designs and accessibility features including:
  Wheelchair Whirl
  Wheelchair Maypole
  Wheelchair Swing
  Special Inclines and Connecting
      Arches
  Sand Tables
  Touch and Smell Areas
  Musical Bridge
  Water Wall
  Water Wheel
  Water Bed
  Echo Chamber
  Busy Box and Chime Wall
  Vestibular Rockers
  Obstacle Course
  Slide-on-a-Slope
One of the facility design by-products of the project is a checklist to aid others in the creation of unique outdoor playscapes for the disabled.

In Baton Rouge, Louisiana, a city park utilizing equipment designed for the disabled from three separate commercial manufacturers has been developed. In this park, picnic tables, water boxes, and sand boxes are at wheelchair level. Additionally, a wheelchair basketball court, bouncing bridge, hand propelled swings, and a special safety seat slide are featured.

Wheelchair users may also now participate in the benefits of outdoor fitness or "vita" trails, with stations and equipment designs now commercially manufactured to accommodate their needs. Many manufacturers offer marketing systems and several custom-made courses are also in existence.

Outdoor Recreation Facilities

The vast majority of outdoor recreation facilities in the United States are usable only by people who do not have serious sensory, mobility, or intellectual impairments. A workbook providing general guidelines and common sense design considerations is available from the Heritage Conservation and Recreation Service. Entitled **A Guide to Designing Accessible Outdoor Recreation Facilities,** this manual has design characteristics for:
  picnic grounds
  campsites
  pathways and trails
  amphitheaters
  beaches
  docks and piers
(Figure 8-5)

A particularly novel and helpful section within the manual is the section devoted to trails and trail surfaces. A model classification system is provided in which trails are rated Class 1 through 5 based on the criteria of width, slope, surface preparation, cross slope, and trail edge. Benefits to both users and providers of such a system include: (1) encouraging individual choice of a trail based on the degree of difficulty one can expect to encounter, (2) eliminating stigmatizing labels,

Figure 8-5
A wheelchair vita course station emphasizing flexibility and range of motion work.

e.g., senior citizens/handicapped trail, and (3) providing an easy framework for inventory of the total system of recreational trails offered.

Whenever possible a deliberate effort should be made to create recreational activities within existing parks which offer a range of accessibility. "Special parks" stigmatize the users and separate them from the rest of society. By providing for a spectrum of preferences and abilities, we encourage people to participate in recreational challenges which meet or exceed their needs. This "range of accessibility" notion for each type of outdoor recreation activity is fairly easy to implement in a cost-effective manner if overall accessibility problems are identified early in the design process. (Figure 8-6)

In designing outdoor recreation facilities that are accessible to and usable by all individuals, certain important considerations should not be overlooked. Most

modifications in design and construction of outdoor recreation facilities for persons with handicapping conditions are relatively minor and are also beneficial to all users. Many of these changes are practical in the administration of high-use recreation areas as well. For example, use of hard surface pathways and campsites helps protect the site itself. Some able-bodied persons prefer more challenging primitive wilderness areas, while others want campgrounds with all the comforts of home. Some individuals with handicapping conditions may want longer and more difficult trails than others with similar handicapping conditions. Large numbers of impaired, disabled, and handicapped persons are able to, and want to enjoy a wider range of experiences than many planners think they are capable of handling. Low expectations of, and paternalistic attitudes toward such individuals are often as great or

greater a barrier to accessibility than a flight of steps. (Figure 8-7)

Since only about ten percent of blind people read braille, and braille lettering is neither weather- nor vandal-resistant, information, instructions, and other material about outdoor recreation programs, activities, and exhibits can best be presented to visually impaired persons with audio-cassettes. This is also more effective for sighted users of the facility. When the federal government first began to respond to mobility needs of persons with handicapping conditions and to problems of architectural barriers, many recreational facilities were designed and labeled as being special braille trails, trails for the blind, or areas for the handicapped. Now, planners and park managers are learning that the majority of persons with handicapping conditions neither want nor need segregated facilities. The U.S. Forest Service now recommends using the

Figure 8-6
The design of cabins and other outdoor facilities should include a ramp so individuals in wheelchairs and on crutches can use the facilities.

Figure 8-7
A camping area which permits wheelchair users to take an active part in programming.

American National Standards Institute's Standards for Making Buildings and Facilities Accessible to and Usable by the Physically Handicapped for the development of all park and recreational facilities.

Additionally, the American Society of Landscape Architects for park and camping facilities recommends:

- Level ground around high use areas — shelters, lavatories, swimming areas, food preparation areas.
- Picnic tables resting on a hard surface at least three to four inches wider on each side than the table. So that a wheelchair can slide under the table, a minimum of twenty-nine inches of space should be allowed between the bottom edge of table and the ground.

- Fireplaces raised eighteen inches to twenty-four inches off the ground, which are easier to use from a seated position than are ground level fireplaces.
- Provision of some grills, because these are more convenient than fireplaces for cooking food over charcoal.

An example of such a facility within the National Park Service is:
Broken Bowl Picnic Ground
Willamette National Forest
USDA-Forest Service
210 East 11th Avenue
P.O. Box 1272
Eugene, Oregon 97401
Safety considerations necessitated handrails along trails built on banks and bumper curbs around the trail ramp near streams. Maintaining less than five percent grade on trails proved very difficult but was considered

essential. Other design adaptations included pedestal fireplaces and 32" hydra-fountains with a hard surface approach. In restrooms mirrors that tilt downward were installed for wheelchair users.

At Indiana University, Camp Riley at Bradford Woods represents a model camping facility for the physically disabled. The camp features completely accessible cabins, pool, boat dock, nature center, amphitheater, lodge, and an arts and crafts center. Additionally, the camp facilities are interconnected with specially designed, ramped, and graded trailways, including a multi-sensory leisure education interpretive trail for the sensory impaired.

There are several design standards manuals available for outdoor facilities, including one from the American Camping Association and one from the Department of the Interior.

Suggestions for Trail Construction

The following suggestions have been gathered from a variety of sources:

- Make the trail surface firm; materials such as soil cement, compacted trap rock dust, or asphalt are suitable for light or moderate traffic.
- Keep trail well manicured from poison ivy, fallen trees, low branches and other potential obstacles. Maintain vertical clearance of eight feet six inches from the pathway to tree canopy. (Figure 8-8)
- Be sure rest areas are adjacent to walkways with enough space for at least one wheelchair and one fence.
- Do not make nature trails too long — one-half mile should be about maximum — but consider that some users will want a longer, more challenging trail.

Figure 8-8
An example of a low-grade, hard-surface trail providing accessibility to all users.

- Make the width of a trail wide enough for two wheelchairs to pass — five feet six inches minimum; grades of less than five percent are most accessible.
- Make signs on the trail; for blind hikers, a photoplated upraised eighteen-point type print is preferable to braille; tactile maps might also be used for helping to orient the blind better.
- Recorded messages at stations are excellent but expensive. Brochures should be available. An interpreter is the best source of information in both communicating and getting others involved in the outdoor setting. Translate interpretive walks for the deaf by use of sign language and fingerspelling.
- Include in a trail program as much sensory involvement as possible — smell boxes, textures, shapes, sounds of running water, birds, opportunities to taste water from natural spring, etc.
- Incorporate innovative fun and learning ideas into stations or fun areas along a trail, motor and perceptual. Motor development for slow-learners and mentally retarded groups can be a part of station activities. Physical fitness stations can also be set up.
- Pay attention to the fragility of the interpretive resource — replacement of plants and other items to be touched.

A trail example is:
The Widener Trail
Schuylkill Valley Nature Center
Hagyps Mill Road
Philadelphia, Pennsylvania 19128

This nature trail, built through a grant from a private foundation, is a hard surface, gradual-grade trail.

It provides aquatic study equipment for use at the pond. A built-in radio broadcast system enables visitors to hear taped messages interpreting natural and social history of the area through receivers carried either by hand or on a neckcord. A telesonic unit with a two-frequency broadcast potential makes it possible to simultaneously broadcast two sets of messages; thus a parent and child can walk the trail together and each hear an interpretive talk addressed to his/her own level of understanding. The system works by broadcasting from a continuous loop tape machine in the building into antenna wires buried under the trail.

Aquatic Facilities

Swimming pools represent one of the most needed facilities for the disabled and have also been the subject of considerable design study. There are two basic types of pools to consider. One is a therapeutic pool, the other a multi-purpose pool which must accommodate wheelchair users.

Therapeutic Pools

Regarding the design and construction of therapeutic pools, there are a number of design types available including:

A unique set-up used by the *Veterans Administration Hospital in Miami, Florida.* The twenty-five by forty foot pool has a ramp four feet wide and twenty-one feet long sloping down at the shallow end. Handrails flank both sides of the ramp; a winch is mounted on a wall opposite the ramp and can be hooked to a wheelchair, permitting another person to lower or pull out someone who is unable to walk.

The *Longview, Washington, YMCA* program makes use of a monorail system in conjunction with a truck hoist and special chair. This is used because pool decks are too narrow to permit passage of a wheelchair along the edge of the pool from dressing rooms to the desired point of entry into the water. The participant is placed in the special chair at the dressing room door, secured with a safety belt, lifted approximately two inches above the floor by

Figure 8-9
A therapeutic pool design used exclusively for preschool handicapped and retarded children.

Planning For The Handicapped

means of the hoist, and pushed horizontally along the pool edge. At the desired point, an attendant in the pool manipulates the ropes or chains on the hoist and lowers the participant until the chair rests on the bottom of the pool. The safety belt is then unfastened and the occupant assisted from the chair. When leaving the pool, the sequence is reversed.

Another outstanding swimming/aquatic facility is the *CAR (Community Association for the Retarded) Swim Center in Palo Alto, California.* This indoor H-shaped pool is seventy-five feet long, forty feet wide at each end, and twenty feet in the center. Depth of the pool is three to nine feet with a wide bank of shallow steps providing even greater variations of depth. A wheelchair ramp, set of steps in the shallow end, and ladders in the deep end are provided. Water temperature is kept a constant eighty-six degrees.

Multi-Purpose Pools

Lack of a specially designed swimming pool area should not keep a group or agency from providing a swimming program for individuals with various handicapping conditions. When existing facilities are used, instructional and recreational swimming programs and aquatic activities must be adapted to the facility. Some problems most often mentioned when existing pools and aquatic facilities are used include:

- Difficulties in adequately increasing water temperature.
- Difficulties in gaining access to pools at reasonable times on a continuous basis due to already crowded schedule.
- Insufficient shallow water areas for small group and one-to-one instruction.
- Inability to use outdoor swimming pools because of extremely cold water and atmosphere.
- Difficulty in getting individuals in and out of the water.
- Architectural barriers that prevent use of locker room, showers, and rest rooms as well as getting in and out of the building itself.

Generally, existing facilities can be made more usable and functional for special populations by adding or altering equipment and reorienting pool operation to provide the best possible teaching and swimming environments for individuals with different handicapping conditions.

Accessibility to the pool basin for construction of new facilities represents a problem easily solved if attention is given to standard wheelchair design dimensions for hallways, doorways, showers, bathrooms, etc. Modification of existing facilities naturally poses more unique and challenging problems. Solutions to accessibility problems for existing structures have included the use of exterior elevator towers, ramps, and physical renovation of doorways and corridors.

How to facilitate a comfortable and dignified entry and exit remains an issue of considerable debate among designers, architects, and disabled consumers. One solution is to provide for a permanent concrete ramp at the shallow end, not only facilitating ease of entry and exit for the wheelchair user but for the elderly and small children as well. Other solutions include the use of a number of equipment options including:

- Bring an individual into the pool on a litter and let him/her float off to greater independence; give only the amount of assistance necessary regardless of the type or severity of a condition.
- Use a wide board so individuals can slide or gradually make their way down forward or backward into the pool where they are on their own to the degree each can handle.
- Take full advantage of wide steps; an individual can scoot his/her way into the pool.
- Use a conventional plastic

Figure 8-10
A multi-purpose pool is made accessible for the disabled by the addition of a ramp.

tumbling mat as a slide for entering a pool as well as for support once an individual is already in a pool.

- Take a wheelchair directly down a ramp or wide steps into the pool; the individual moves or is helped out of the chair and into the water.
- Carry a small child piggy-back into the pool.
- Adapt various one-, two-, three-, and four-person first aid carries so an individual can be physically lifted and carried in and out of the pool.
- Let an individual roll from the top of the ledge into the water and use as much control as necessary according to the capabilities of the individual.
- Build a temporary or portable ramp according to the types and severities of the conditions of the individuals.
- Build a platform near a side or wall of the pool so an individual can bring a wheelchair to it in such a way that he/she can move from the chair to the platform and then into the water.
- Adapt starting blocks so they can be used to assist individuals with entry into and exit from pools.
- Use gym scooters or similar devices which an individual can move on from the deck into the pool.
- Dig a ramp on one side of a pool; by going down to the end of the ramp, the seat of a wheelchair is even with the pool side which makes for easier transfer.
- Improvise sling seats with towels, canvas, and other materials to use in getting an individual in and out of

a pool.
- Install a commercial lift or hoist when absolutely necessary.
- Use combinations of suggested ways and improvise specific procedures and techniques according to need of individuals taking part in the program.

Adequate shallow water areas are important to the success of instructional swimming programs for handicapped individuals, especially the young, timid, and fearful. Some instructors have advocated lowering water levels for some programs to facilitate beginning instruction. However, in many pools lowering water levels incapacitates the filtering system. The system can be shut down for short periods of time, but it is not considered a wise practice. Lowering the water level one foot in a large pool represents many thousands of gallons of water and usually requires a shutdown of several hours to remove the water; refilling usually takes longer. Health authorities usually frown on lowering water levels in a pool. A wading pool or some device to raise the level of the bottom is considered a more satisfactory and effective practice for those purposes. Some manufacturers have developed an aluminum platform that can be easily and quickly assembled and disassembled as a means of raising the bottom of a pool for individuals who need shallow water. Portable, mobile, and plastic backyard pools of various sizes should not be overlooked for these purposes.

Recently, a pool with a movable bottom was introduced and made available in this country. With a false or second pool bottom operated hydraulically, water depths are controlled by the push of a button so that they range from a few inches to several feet. One of the first installations of this type in the United States was at the YMCA in Olean, New York.

Another unique approach has been installed at the University of New Mexico in Albuquerque. Hydraulically controlled walls make it possible to section off a portion of the regular pool for special uses. The temperature of water in this section can be raised independently of water in the rest of the pool. In this way individuals needing special water conditions can receive this attention without affecting the rest of the pool. Walls retract through switch control so the entire pool can be used for instructional, recreational, or competitive swimming.

Additional considerations for adapting and/or using existing swimming pools or aquatic facilities for special populations include:

- Special chairs should be light weight and corrosion-resistant. A chair, particularly a folding type with tubular aluminum or magnesium tubing framework with rope or fabric back and seat, is satisfactory.
- Power associated with devices to aid entry into and exit from pools should be *mechanical* rather than electrical because of the simplicity of operation and the hazards associated wtih operating electrical equipment in water or highly humid air.
- When a pool is used for programs including both able-bodied and disabled populations, it is imperative that all aids to pool entry be capable of being dismantled and stored when not being used by impaired, disabled, or handicapped persons. This reduces the attractive nuisance features of the apparatus to youngsters.
- Exercise bars and extra handrails are simple but effective additions to a pool to add to its

accessibility and functional use by individuals having various degrees of ambulation.

Considerations for Construction of New Aquatic Facilities

Often common-sense, easily implemented, and inexpensive approaches can be used in building a swimming pool or aquatic facility for use by individuals with various handicapping conditions. Important to the health and safety of these participants and to the success of their programs is warm water and correspondingly warm air. Ideally, water should be 80-90 degrees with air temperature five degrees above water temperature. Often when pools are used for therapeutic purposes or for individuals having severe physical limitations or multiple conditions, water temperature may be several degrees higher than the generally recommended range.

Some popular shapes providing multi-purpose areas are L-shaped, T-shaped, H-shaped, and Z-shaped pools. The multi-purpose pool should be designed so areas can be roped off for special programs. Some pools have been designed so that a movable bulkhead allows water temperature in the bulkhead area to be raised independently of the rest of the pool. Specially designed units of this type are quite expensive. Often the same purpose can be realized by a separate pool or spa unit with return lines from the heater. This arrangement can give better, more rapid control of water temperature at a lower cost.

A variety of design treatments of deck level pools is available. Likewise, there are a number of innovations in recessed gutter type pools. In both of these types, the size, shape, and location of the overflow is of great importance to the operation of the complete recirculating system. Architects designing these pools are urged to consult with competent hydraulic engineers or swimming pool consultants in the choice of the recirculating system. Other modifications which have been used for easy entry and exit are ramps going down into the water or underwater steps with a handrail for support also going into the water.

A widespread misconception exists concerning water depth for impaired swimmers whose needs can supposedly be met in a learning pool where depth may range from two-and-a-half to three-and-a-half feet. Without the assistance of normal lower limbs, an impaired swimmer relies on the body's center of gravity being below pool water level to maintain buoyancy. To achieve this, an adult of average height requires a water depth of about three and three quarters to four feet. Usually only water depths in general pools meet these needs. Certainly a small impaired child and those who are especially timid or fearful of the water can find satisfactory conditions in learning pools.

Financial Considerations

An often-used rationalization for not making existing facilities barrier-free and accessible has been cost. Some preliminary estimates for acceptable renovation projects have been as high as forty to one hundred percent of projected costs. Removal of barriers has actually been accomplished in many of these same projects for as little as three or four percent above costs of the renovations without the special considerations. When plans to make buildings barrier-free and accessible are included from the beginning, increase in costs has been found to be in the range of one-tenth of one percent to one percent above total project costs without these factors being considered. Other comparisons include one cent additional per square foot to make a building accessible and thirteen cents per square foot to keep floors in this same building clean!

The concept of creating a barrier-free environment is more readily accepted than the cost of making facilities accessible. Lack of research into cost-benefits as well as actual costs of barrier-free construction are two factors that allow fear of exorbitant costs to continue.

It is difficult to make a direct comparison between original construction costs and costs for renovating a building years later. Modifications to existing buildings usually cost more than new construction because often something must be removed or changed drastically before making changes to ensure that the facility is barrier-free and accessible.

Despite possibilities of increased costs, existing facilities must be made accessible as soon as possible. The cost of removing barriers must be included in established maintenance budgets as well as those used for capital improvements.

Another argument dismissing the cost myth is evidence that such buildings have fewer hazards that result in accidents and liability claims. With safer conditions, rate reductions may be obtained on liability insurance. A study by the American Mutual Insurance Alliance noted the following advantages of accessible facilities:

- Fewer accidents in public buildings reduce losses and rates under health insurance policies.
- Since buildings with aids for individuals with handicapping conditions have fewer hazards that result in accident and liability claims, insurance rate reductions may be obtained on public liability policies when architectural barriers are removed.
- Elimination of barriers also reduces chances of work-connected accidents so that employers benefit through reduction in compensation insurance premiums.

Guidelines for Community Action

Communities must make sure that appropriate barrier-free provisions are incorporated into locally applicable building codes while at the same time ensuring compliance with federal and state laws already on the books. The following are considerations for initiating community action:

- Ensure the best possible results with respect to removing and eliminating architectural barriers by imposing on architects, engineers, and contractors even more rigorous requirements than those found in current building codes and popular standards.
- Form an architectural barriers task force to inform decision-makers about problems of architectural accessibility, focusing on both practical and social aspects of accessibility.
- Develop a standing committee on architectural barriers to encourage local interest in eliminating barriers, serve as basis for continuing community education, organize and oversee such projects, be an advocate for rights of those with special needs.
- Approve all architectural designs for new and reconstructed facilities, and be involved in all dimensions of the decision-making process relative to facility design as it affects accessibility and usability for individuals with special needs.
- Inform newspapers, television, radio, newsletters, and local periodicals of this important message.
- Develop a guidelines position paper to use in recruiting influential individuals to join this

effort. This document could be developed by the standing committee previously mentioned or a general advisory committee. It should include essential features such as:
  — a general philosophical position on accessibility and usability by those participating in the facility as well as by those employed or visiting the facility;
  — a clarification of the meanings of terms such as impaired, disabled, handicapped, special populations, individuals with special needs;
  — a statement on provisions for appropriate access and traffic elements, restrooms and equipment, building equipment and furnishings, environmental controls, gradients and textures, communication and orientation methods; and
  — a statement as to legal materials and other resources which are to be used to ensure that the architectural design truly meets the needs of special populations.
- Provide all architects engaged in designing the facility with copies of the guidelines position paper and legal resources identified in the document.
- Conduct a survey to determine accessibility of community buildings.
- Prepare a guide on accessibility of community facilities.
- Set up a watchdog program for continuous contact and follow-up with building owners, architects, and builders to ensure that new and renovated

buildings are accessible to and usable by all individuals.
- Include representative numbers of impaired, disabled, and handicapped persons in all aspects of planning, implementing, and evaluating all such projects and activities, especially at decision-making levels.
- Develop an information resource center containing essential information relative to barrier-free design and construction and related laws and legislation. Essential information identified in the guidelines position paper could be communicated to architects, engineers, and contractors retained to design the facility and to those persons responsible for finally approving any facility design as it affects persons with handicapping conditions.

Figure 8-11
At Indiana University Camp Bradford Woods, all users can take advantage of all areas.

Planning For The Handicapped

**Questions and suggested
standards for outdoor
recreational facilities.**

Parking
   a. Is an offstreet parking area
      available adjacent to the
      building? ☐
   b. Is the parking lot surface
      hard and smooth? ☐
   c. Are there parking spaces
      wide enough to allow a car
      door to be opened to full
      extension (approx. 12'
      wide)? ☐
   d. Are there specifically
      identified parking spaces
      for the handicapped? ☐
   e. Are there curbs, wheel
      stops, or parking barriers
      within the parking area? ☐
   f. Has a curb-cut, ramp, or
      passageway been provided
      to eliminate these
      barriers? ☐

Building Access
   a. Are walkways at least five
      feet wide with smooth hard
      surfaces (no sand or
      gravel), free of deep
      cracks, ruts or sudden
      changes in level? ☐
   b. Is the most accessible
      entrance to the building
      one which avoids unsafe
      traffic crossings from the
      parking area to the
      building entrance? ☐
   c. Is the approach to the
      entrance door on ground
      level? ☐
   d. Are there steps in the
      approach to or at the
      entrance door, and if so
      how many are there? ☐
   e. If there are steps, is there
      a sturdy handrail in the
      center or either side of the
      stairs? ☐
   f. If there are steps, has a
      ramp been provided to
      eliminate the barrier? ☐
   g. Are the ramps constructed
      in such a way that the
      grade does not exceed a
      1:12 ratio, that is, for every
      foot in length it gains no
      more than 1'' in height? ☐

Building Entrance
   a. Is the doorway at least 30''
      wide? ☐
   b. Are thresholds and door
      saddles flush with floor or
      no higher than ½''? ☐
   c. Is the door automatic? ☐
   d. Are there steps or interior
      level changes? ☐
   e. If there are steps or
      interior level changes,
      have ramps been provided
      to eliminate these
      barriers? ☐

Visually Impaired
   a. Have braille markers or
      relief graphics been used
      to communicate important
      information to the visually
      impaired? ☐
   b. Have textured paint or a
      change in surface texture
      been used to alert the
      visually impaired to
      curb-cuts, sudden level
      changes, or other vital
      information important to
      the independent use of the
      area by the visually
      impaired? ☐
   c. Have any other
      adaptations for the visually
      impaired been provided? If
      so, please indicate. ☐

Elevator or Lift
   a. Is the building
      multi-story? ☐
   b. Is there a passenger
      elevator or lift? ☐
   c. Does the elevator or lift
      provide access to all
      essential areas? ☐
   d. Are there any steps, or
      interior level changes
      between essential areas,
      which are not served by an
      elevator? ☐
   e. Have ramps been provided
      to eliminate these
      barriers? ☐

Rest Rooms
   a. Would one need to go up
      or down steps to reach the
      rest room? ☐
   b. If yes, have ramps been
      provided to make these

      areas accessible? ☐
   c. If there are steps, does
      each flight of stairs have a
      sturdy handrail in the
      center or on either side? ☐
   d. Is the width of the toilet
      room entrance doorway at
      least 30'' wide? ☐
   e. Are thresholds and door
      saddles flush or no higher
      than ½'' to the floor? ☐
   f. Is there enough space
      within the rest room to
      allow a wheelchair to turn
      around (approx. a 5'
      diameter)? ☐
   g. Is the width of the toilet
      stall door opening at least
      30''? ☐
   h. Are toilet stalls and urinals
      equipped with grab
      bars? ☐
   i. Does the stall door open
      outward? ☐
   j. Has the door been
      replaced with a privacy
      curtain to eliminate
      doors? ☐
   k. Are sinks and mirrors low
      enough for use by children
      or a person in a
      wheelchair (bottom of
      mirrors no higher than
      40'')? ☐

Telephone
   a. Is the public phone
      mounted low enough to be
      used by children and
      person in wheelchair (the
      coin slot or receiver arm
      50'' or less from the
      floor)? ☐
   b. If located in phone booth,
      is the opening into the
      booth at least 30'' wide? ☐
   c. Would one have to go up
      or down steps to use the
      telephone? ☐
   d. If yes, have ramps been
      provided to make the
      telephone area
      accessible? ☐

Wall Mounted Controls
   a. Are all vital wall controls
      (light switches, door knobs,
      elevator controls, etc.)
      located within reach of

child or person in wheelchair approximately 48'' from the floor? ☐

b. Are all emergency equipment (fire alarms, instruction panels, fire extinguishers, etc.) located within the reach of handicapped individuals and children (approx. 48'' or less from floor)? ☐

Water Fountains

a. Are water fountains low enough to be used by children and persons in wheelchairs (bubblers approx. 33'' from floor)? ☐

b. Are there any barriers, such as steps, around or leading to the water fountain? ☐

c. If so, have ramps been provided to eliminate these barriers? ☐

The Accessibility Survey Checklist was compiled by a special HCRS Northwest Regional Office Accessibility Advisory Committee on the Disabled, using American National Institute Standards (ANSI) and Washington State Rules and Regulations for Barrier Free Design as required by Washington State Uniform Building Code. (Laws of 1974, as amended 1975.)

Participating agencies in the Seattle-Everett-Tacoma Metropolitan Area used these checklists to survey each of their public outdoor recreation areas and related buildings. Checklist returns were then recorded in a computer data bank, and the evaluative criteria applied from which the "Good, Fair/Poor, Poor" formula was derived.

Accessibility categories used in the checklists are listed below, together with the ANSI standards which the committee considered mandatory to access for persons with varied types of disabilities. In addition, those marked with a # sign are recommended, but non-compliance did not detract from the "Good" rating where

size, terrain, and circumstances may make some variation acceptable. Minor measurement differences do not always make a facility unusable. Or omission of a # standard may indicate "not needed here." For example, some areas for day use only would never require night lighting.

Ratings are also influenced by the stage of development of each area, and components therein. An undeveloped site would probably rate "Poor" in all categories. To avoid disappointment, the prospective visitor is advised to select another destination. The user is urged to decide for himself what meets personal needs and interests.

Public Transportation

"Yes" indicated bus stops at or near a specified recreation area. For service information to Seattle and King County destinations (route, proximity, frequency, and type of bus), call Metro Transit (625-2583).

Off-Street Parking

Good: 12'6'' wide, load, unload area near primary entrance, no parking allowed. Access symbol and/or posted signage. 12'6'' parking spaces, level, firm, non-slip. Level walking or curb-cut ramps. #Lighting. #Travel route directional signs.

Fair/P: If any of the above not specifically excepted, do not meet standards.

Poor: No provision for access; parking too remote; surface not level or non-skid.

Curb-cuts (not associated with parking)

Good: 1:12 max. center slope. 36'' min. center width. Firm, stable, non-slip surface.

Fair/P: Slope more than maximum and width less than minimum.

Poor: If curb-cuts needed and not provided.

Walks — Paved

Good: Firm, stable, non-slip. 48'' min. width; 1:12 max. slope; 1:50

cross slope. No steps. Vertical changes no more than ½''. Signage. #Lighting. #4' benches in unobstructed 4'x3' area.

Fair/P: If first six items above not met.

Paths — Trails — Unpaved

Good: Firm, stable surface. 48'' min. width; 1:20 max. slope. 1:50 cross slope. No steps. Vertical changes no more than ½''. #Lighting. #Signage, particularly directionals.

Fair/P: If any of above, not specifically excepted, have not been met.

Ramps (Same specifications for outdoor and indoor ramps)

Good: If needed and one ramp meets specifications. 1:12 max. slope. Stable, firm, non-slip surface. Handrails (if more than 1:20 slope), 32''-36'' high; oval 1¼''-2'' diameter; 1½'' wall clearance; extend 18'' beyond ramp end. Level platform 6' bottom of ramp, 5' x 5' top of ramp, 30' intervals or where ramp turns. #Lighting.

Fair/P: If slope and handrails do not meet specifications.

Poor: If no ramps where needed or specifications not met.

Rest rooms (Same specifications for outdoor and indoor areas)

Good: 32'' min. clear door opening. 5' diameter turnaround floor area. Vestibule 3'6'' wide, 6'6'' length. 1 stall each restroom for wheelchair with 32'' min. outswing door, clear opening. Each stall min. 3' wide x 5' depth; 2 grab bars, 32'' above floor. Toilet seat, 16''-18'' high. 1 each wall dispenser and towel rack, 40'' high max. Lighted. #Toilet 18'' from near wall. #19'' max. urinal rim. #29'' lavatory clearance under rim. #Lavatory drains insulated and guarded. #40'' high max. bottom mirror or shelf.

Fair/P: If any one of the above criteria, not specifically excepted, have not been met.

Poor: If restrooms do not have one designated stall in each men's and women's facilities or if none of the specifications, not specifically excepted, have been met.

Water Fountains
Good: Hand-operated front spout. If wall mounted, 34" high max. with 48" x 32" accessible space. If floor fountain exceeds 34", a second lower fountain needed.

Fair/P: Not hand-operated and spout not in front, fails to meet height or 48" x 32" access space.

Poor: If none of specifications met.

Public Telephones
Good: Coin slots 48" max. height. Space 48" x 32".

Fair/P: If phone available, but does not meet both specifications.

Miscellaneous Items — See comments, right column each page.

RELATED BUILDINGS

Entrances/Exits/Doors
Good: If one entrance and exit and/or door meets all specifications — 32" wide, clear opening; 6'6" vestibule; ½" min. threshold height change; 5' level both sides opening with 12" wall clearance outgoing side. No elevators needed in most park buildings, but if one exists, primary access should accommodate disabled.

Fair/P: None of the specifications met.

Corridors
Good: 48" min. width.
Fair/P: Less than 48" width.

Ramps — Indoor
Specifications same for indoor, outdoor. See previous statement.

Stairs
Good: 7" high risers. No abrupt nosings or risers; 11" min. tread depth. Handrails both sides, 1¼"-2" diameter, 18" extension top and bottom of steps, 1½" wall clearance.

Fair/P: Accessibility depends on degree and type of disability of individual, but steps must meet most of above specifications.

Poor: Steps that lack handrails must meet most of above specifications.

Floors
Good: Non-slippery surface. Level, or properly ramped.

Poor: Specifications above are safety features needed by everyone.

Rest rooms
Same specifications as listed for outdoor areas.

Water Fountains
Same as listed for outdoor areas.

Public Telephones
Same as listed for outdoor areas.

SELECTED REFERENCES

Section A
Resources Bibliography: Design

Accessibility Modifications by Ronald L. Mace, available from the Special Office for the Handicapped, North Carolina State Department of Insurance, P.O. Box 26387, Raleigh, North Carolina 27611, 1973.

Barrier Free Site Design, by the American Society of Landscape Architects Foundation. Available from U.S. Government Printing Office, Washington, D.C. 20402 (Stock No. 023-000-00291-4), 1979.

Design Criteria: New Public Buildings Accessibility, Available from General Services Administration Business Service Center, 7th and D Streets, Washington, D.C. 20407, 1978.

Ersing, Walter F. "Guidelines for Designing Barrier-Free Facilities." **Journal of Physical Education and Recreation** 49 (October 1978): 65-67.

Specifications for Making Buildings and Facilities Accessible to, and Usable by, the Physically Handicapped, available from American National Standards Institute, Inc. (ANSI), 1430 Broadway, New York, New York 11018, 1971.

Several states have published excellent illustrated guides to design requirements for accessibility. Among them are:

Accessibility Assistance: A Directory of Consultants on Environments for Handicapped People, 1978, from National Center for a Barrier Free Environment, Seventh and Florida NE, Washington, D.C. 20002.

Access for All: An Illustrated Handbook of Barrier Free Design for Ohio available from the Governor's Committee on Employment of the Handicapped, 4656 Heaton Road, Columbus, Ohio 43229, 1976.

Barrier-Free Design: A Selected Bibliography. Paralyzed Veterans of America, Suite 301 W. 7315 Wisconsin Avenue N.W., Washington, D.C. 20014 (Peter L. Lassen), 1981.

Barrier-Free Environment Resources (Update #20), American Alliance for Health, Physical Education and Recreation (Information and Research Utilization Center, 1201 16th Street N.W., Washington, D.C. 20036), October, 1978.

Barrier-Free Environments, Dowden, Hut- chinson & Rose, P.O. Box 699, 523 Sarah Street, Stroudsburg, Pennsylvania 18360; 1977, 278 pp, Michael J. Bednar, ed.

Barrier-Free School Facilities for Handicapped Students, Educational Research Service, 1800 N. Kent Street, Arlington, Virginia 22209 (1977).

Barrier-Free Site Design, U.S. Department of Housing & Urban Development, Washington, D.C. 20402, 1980.

Barrier-Free Site Design, American Society of Landscape Architects Foundation, Supt. of Documents, U.S. Govt. Printing Office, Washington, D.C. (1974).

Opening Doors: Handbook on Making Facilities Accessible to Handicapped People, National Center for a Barrier-Free Environment, 7th Street and Florida Avenue, N.E., Washington, D.C. 20002, 1978, 31 pp.

Building Needs for the Handicapped, Bureau of Elementary and Secondary Education (Dept. of Health, Education and Welfare — Office of Education, Washington, D.C.) 57 pp, 1975 (ED 140 535).

Illustrated Handbook of Handicapped Sections of North Carolina State Building Code, available from North Carolina Department of Insurance, Special Office for the Handicapped, P.O. Box 26387, Raleigh, North Carolina 27611, 1979.

One out of Ten: School Planning for the Handicapped, National Facilities Laboratories, 850 Third Avenue, New York, 1974, 27 pp (IRUC Order #1158).

Removing Architectural Barriers: An Illustrated Handbook of the New Mexico Uniform Building Code, Available from Division of Vocational Rehabilitation, New Mexico Department of Education, P.O. Box 1830, Santa Fe, New Mexico 87503, 1978.

Rules and Regulations of the Architectural Barriers Board, Commonwealth of Massachusetts Department of Public Safety, available from the Architectural Barriers Board, Room 1319, 1 Ashburton Place, Boston, Massachusetts 02108, 1977.

Urban Wheelchair Use: A Human Factors Analysis (Wachter, Lorenc & Lai), Access Chicago Rehabilitation Institute of Chicago, 345 East Superior Street, Chicago 60611 (1976).

Section B
Resources Bibliography: Outdoor Recreation Facilities

Access National Parks: A Guide for Handicapped Visitors. Washington, D.C.: U.S. Government Printing Office, 1979.

American Foundation for the Blind. **Policy Statement on Nature Trails, Braille Trails, Footpaths, Fragrance Gardens, and Touch Museums for the Blind.** New York: The Foundation, 1972.

Beechel, Jacque. **Interpretation for Handicapped Persons: A Handbook for Outdoor Recreation Personnel.** Seattle, Washington: National Park Service, Pacific Northwest Region Cooperative Studies Unit, College of Forest Resources, AR-10, University of Washington (98195), July, 1975.

Bureau of Outdoor Recreation and National Recreation and Park Association. **Outdoor Recreation Planning for the Handicapped.** Washington, D.C.: U.S. Government Printing Office, 1967.

Camp Facilities for the Physically Handicapped. North Brunswick, New Jersey: Camping and Engineering Service, Program Services Division, Boy Scouts of America (08902), 1976.

Carroll, Arthur J. "Efforts to Adapt National Forest Recreation Areas for Use by the Handicapped." **Therapeutic Recreation Journal** 7 (1973): 41-44.

The Easter Seal Directory of Resident Camps for Persons with Special Health Needs. Chicago: National Easter Seal Society for Crippled Children and Adults, 1973.

Knorr, John. **A United States Guide to Nature Centers and Trails for the Visually Handicapped.** Madison, Wisconsin: Center for Environmental Communications and Environmental Studies, 1973.

Masek, Marshall. "Trails, Playgrounds, and Activities for the Handicapped," in **Expanding Horizons in Therapeutic Recreation III.** Edited by Gary Robb and Gerald Hitzhuzen. Columbia, Missouri: University of Missouri, 1975.

Nielsen, Ruth M. "Forest Service Facilities for Wheelchair and Nature Lovers." **Paraplegia News** 25 (July 1975): 8-9.

Goodwin, Virginia and Uloth, Ray. **Outward Bound and the Physically Disabled.** Wayzata, Minnesota: The Project Center, Minnesota Outward Bound School, 1979.

Robb, Gary M. "Camping for the Physically Handicapped — A Rationale and Approach." **Rehabilitation Literature** 34 (1973): 130-133.

Section C
Resources Bibliography: Aquatic Facilities

Kaiser, Dave. "City Equips Swimming Pools for Accessibility." **Data and Reference Annual.** Fort Lauderdale, Florida: Hoffman Publications Inc., 1971.

Lyttle, Robert M. "Integrating Families of Handicapped Individuals into the Public Swimming Facility." **Therapeutic Recreation Journal** 10 (1976): 55-60.

McKee, James I. "Wheelchair Transfer to Swimming Pool." **Physical Therapy** 54 (December 1974): 1308.

National Hearing on Recreation for Handicapped Persons: Statement submitted by Craig Huber on behalf of ACPA Inc. to Architectural and Transportation Barriers Compliance Board, 1976. 20 pp (IRUC Order #545) American Alliance for Health, Physical Education and Recreation, 1201 16th St. N.W., Washington, D.C.

"Pool for the Blind." **Swimming Pool Review** (United Kingdom) 16 (September 1975): 102. Available from the National Documentation Center for Sport, Physical Education and Recreation, The University of Birmingham, Birmingham B15 2TT, England.

Resources for Planning Accessible and Barrier-Free Recreation, Play, Swimming and Related Facilities for Use by Impaired and Disabled Persons. Information & Research Utilization Center, American Alliance for Health, Physical Education and Recreation, 1201 16th St. N.W., Washington, D.C. 20036, 1979.

Sports Centers and Swimming Pools: A Study of their Designs with Particular Reference to the Needs of the Physically Disabled (Felix Walter). Disabled Living Foundation, 346 Kensington High St., London W. 14, England 1971.

Sport for All: Low-Cost Swimming Pools. Cultural & Scientific Affairs, Council of Europe, Strasbourg, France 1970.

Stein, Julian. "Pool Facilities for Impaired and Disabled Persons." **Pools: A Guide to Their Planning, Design and Operation.** Third edition. Edited by M. Alexander Garielsen. Fort Lauderdale, Florida: Hoffman Publications, Inc., 1975.

Section D
Resources Bibliography: Playground

An Adaptive Playground for Physically Disabled Children with Perceptual Deficits: The Magruder Environmental Therapy Complex. Orlando, Florida: Orange County Board of Public Instruction, Forest Park School, 1982.

An Instructional Playground for the Handicapped Using Tires as Inexpensive Playground Equipment: Activity Construction Manual. Albany, New York: The University of the State of New York, the State Education Department, Division for Handicapped Children, Special Education Instructional Materials Center, n.d.

Austin, Richard L. **Playgrounds and Playspaces for the Handicapped.** Austin, Texas: Theraplan, Inc., 1974.

Etkes, Asher B. "Planning Playgrounds for the Handicapped." **Journal of Psychiatric Nursing and Mental Health Services** 6 (1968): 339-343.

Gordon, Ronnie. **The Design of a Pre-School Therapeutic Playground: An Outdoor Learning Laboratory:** Rehabilitation Monograph 47. New York: Institute of Rehabilitation Medicine, New York University Medical Center, n.d.

Kidder, Worden. "A Rebuilt Playground." **Journal of Physical Education and Recreation** 47 (September 1976): 16-18.

Morris, Robert. "Evaluation of a Play Environment for Blind Children." **Therapeutic Recreation Journal** 8 (1974): 151-155.

Smiley, Charles W. "Playground for the Mentally Retarded." **American Journal of Occupational Therapy** 28 (September 1974): 474-477.

Section E
Resources Bibliography: Physical Education and Recreation

Assorted Articles on Teaching Shooting Sports to the Handicapped. Washington, D.C.: National Rifle Association, 1978.

Kenney, Alice P. "Museums from a Wheelchair." **Museum News** 53 (December 1974): 14-17.

McAvaddy, Jim. **Facility Consideration for Handicapped Intramural Participants.** Edison, New Jersey: Middlesex County College, 1973.

National Recreational Boating for the Physically Handicapped. The U.S. Coast Guard Office of Boating Safety and the Human Resources Center, 1978. Available from Human Resources Center, I.U. Willets Road, Albertson, New York, 11507.

Recreation and Handicapped People. Proceedings of a National Forum on Meeting the Recreation and Park Needs of Handicapped People, August 1974. President's Committee on Employment of the Handicapped. (IRUC Order #106 for hardcover Xerox copy.)

The Wheelabout Garden: An Easter Seal Society Exhibit. Chicago, Illinois: The National Easter Seal Society for Crippled Children and Adults, 1977.

Tole, Dove. "Should Museums Serve the Visually Handicapped?" **The New Outlook for the Blind** 69 (December 1975): 461-66.

Walter, Felix. **Sports Centers and Swimming Pools: A Study of Their Design with Particular Reference to the Needs of the Physically Disabled.** Thistle Foundation, 1971. Available from the Disabled Living Foundation, 346 Kensington High Street, London, W. 14, England.

"A Zoo Made Accessible." **Paraplegia News** 29 (November 1976): 11.

Photos provided as courtesy of the National Park Service.

CHAPTER IX
Trends in Facility Design

The 1980's is an era of exercise and sports emphasis. The number of joggers, bicyclers, and aerobic exercise participants has increased by millions in the U.S. in the past decade. Eighty million Americans now participate in sports and exercise and, from a health standpoint, this desirable trend continues to grow. Americans of all ages are participating — from the infant in "tots" swim to the senior citizen in biking and social dancing. Programs for the handicapped abound with children now mainstreamed into regular physical education classes in the schools and post-coronary patients participating in cardiac rehabilitation exercise prescription programs. In summary, exercise is becoming a way of life for many Americans, and facilities are needed to accommodate this lifestyle.

Providing facilities for the varied groups of sports and other activities challenges both the building designer and the financial provider. The ever-changing interests, "crazes," and popularity of particular sports, as well as the invention of new sports and equipment, also require that facilities be flexible enough to meet the needs of those new activities. For example, the great boom in the number of racquetball courts constructed in the late 1970's, which came from the "craze" of that sport has, in some cases, resulted in courts available for considerable periods of time because of the wane of the sport. Walleyball and basketball backboard facilities are now being installed in some of those courts. Pickleball is adaptable to badminton courts and has become popular in schools and senior citizen centers. Numerous indoor single purpose tennis facilities were forced to close down in the early 1980's due to a state of over-building and/or to the desire of the American public to belong to clubs offering a variety of recreation opportunities. Some indoor tennis centers have found it to be economically advantageous to convert a few courts to multi-purpose fitness areas to attract a larger membership. Others, especially in the North and Midwest, have converted in part or entirely to indoor soccer, taking advantage of the growing popularity in soccer, the limitation of outdoor fields, and the problems associated with scheduling dependent on the weather. Facility planners and building designers must thus be alert to changing interests and popularity. Multi-purpose design protects both the planner and owner from the embarrassment and financial disaster associated with non-use. (Figure 9-1)

Participation in sports and physical activity is no longer a youth phenomenon. Fitness programs for the aging are being recommended by medical authorities and demanded by senior citizens. Business and corporate employers, concerned for their employees' health, are promoting fitness programs and providing facilities for these activities. The expansion potential of these fitness programs is immense and must affect future commercial building planning and senior citizen centers.

Participants are demanding facilities and, where these are not provided by the public sector, private sports clubs and private industry have constructed facilities for participants willing to pay a fee. The number of fitness/sports clubs, especially multi-purpose (tennis, squash, jogging track, racquetball, and swimming), is increasing. Membership in private multi-purpose clubs usually includes all ages with activities for the entire family. The demand is not only for additional court space and swimming; physical fitness aspirants and sports innovators are asking for fitness trails, weight training and aerobics facilities, and softball parks. The demand at present outweighs the ability of public agencies to provide these spaces, and a new industry in sports and health facilities is growing.

Financing and operation of sports and fitness facilities have also changed considerably in the past ten years — from mostly public recreation and educational agencies to private businesses and employee/employer related programs. Facilities furnished by the employer within the corporation/company plant is a fast-growing trend. Private sports and fitness clubs, weight training gymnasiums, aerobic dance and exercise studios, and business-related water slides and swimming pools with wave making machines are springing up throughout the country. The operation of a sport or fitness club is big business. "Pay for play" in public recreation is becoming routine practice as the public demands more and varied programs, and the use of school and playground facilities for such activities as aerobics, swimming, or league play is common. Cost recovery fees for increased maintenance and personnel require funds in addition to those taxes can support, because of the heavier uses and increased number of participants.

Rental fees for the use of a facility are increasingly used to help defray the cost of construction, operation, and maintenance. Some public agencies operate facilities on a lease-back arrangement. A private party constructs the facility and the public agency operates it on a lease arrangement over a period of years. Or, the facility is constructed with public funds and operated by a private company. Rental of school or college facilities to non-school or off-campus groups, e.g., a college hockey rink being rented to a youth hockey league, enables the school to recover some of the costs of construction and operation, gives greater utilization of the facility, and usually gains community support because of the reduction in overall school costs.

Private clubs and businesses charge membership fees and/or use fees on an hourly basis to cover operation, maintenance, construction, and profit. Judging from the growth in the number of private clubs and the substantial membership fees, individuals are willing to pay if they can be assured of a place to participate in the sport of their choice. Planners of these facilities may need to plan to accommodate rental groups with additional space, service facilities, traffic patterns, and security provisions.

Economic factors again will be a major factor in the treatment of new and remodeled facilities. State and federal governments and even private enterprise at present are unwilling to spend enormous amounts to build a Superdome, a Montreal Olympic stadium, or a palatial college sports complex. The practice of the recent past is toward the moderate size and priced facility with the cost of construction and operation a primary consideration. Older buildings and stadiums are being remodeled with considerable success in meeting the demands of new programs.

(Figure 9-2) In schools, the trend having the most impact in recent years is the closing of many schools and a reduction in new school construction due to a decreasing student enrollment.

Figures 9-1, 1A

Three indoor tennis courts were converted at Westroads Raquet Club in Omaha, Nebraska to a nautilus area, a jogging track, a dance floor, and a basketball/volleyball area resulting in a dramatic increase in new members.

Trends in Facility Design

However, demographics indicate a greater birth rate in the late 1980's, which will result in increased enrollment in the elementary grades (Figure 9-3); as these enrollments grow so will the needs for new schools or remodeled older facilities. High school and college enrollments will probably remain level for a number of years with the result that the trend will be towards the replacement or remodeling of older facilities.

In many high schools and colleges the number of students involved in intramurals, sports clubs, varsity, and general recreational activities overcrowds existing facilities. The demand by women for equal use of facilities and equal programs, and by the handicapped to be involved in recreational programs challenges program directors to provide sufficient and suitable facilities for each program. Additional activities requested to be included as programs include rugby, soccer, lacrosse, team handball, and aerobics. Accommodations of enlarged programs may require that facilities be available from early morning to late evening and that outdoor facilities be usable in the evening and during inclement weather. An illustration of the demand for play space is the ice hockey community where some rinks are open around-the-clock to accommodate all the groups that want ice time.

A health-related trend is the development of cardiac rehabilitation centers being set up either as part of a hospital or medical complex or as an individual unit with an agency such as a YMCA. Facilities for exercising and monitoring the cardiac patient require activity areas and service facilities in addition to the usual medical facility. Sports medicine and exercise physiology are fast-growing professions that work with both the healthy athlete and the handicapped and require specific facilities and exercise

Figure 9-2, 2A
Available rooftop space can support activities such as tennis.

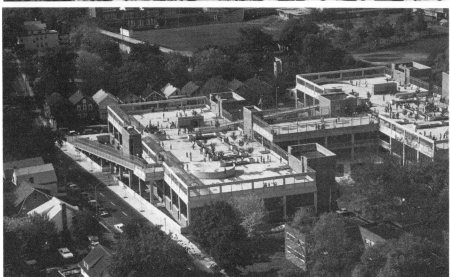

Figure 9-3
East Orange (N.J.) Middle School makes effective use of roof.

Trends in Facility Design

areas for training. Building designers should be aware of these types of activities and their related needs.

Sports and athletics, while always popular, have been given great impetus with the growth of the Olympic movement in the U.S. The Olympic Training Center at Colorado Springs is but one example. Training centers are being developed in different locations for various sports to support research, training, and sports medicine practices. The concentration of athletes and research in one sport at one site portends changes in practices, needs, and facilities for that sport. For example, the Olympic sponsorship of bicycling in a velordome predictably will call for the construction of like facilities throughout the United States. With the U.S. serving as host country for the 1984 Summer Olympics, public interest to Olympic related sports has recently blossomed.

Legal Requirements and Educational Legislation

Trends in facility construction and remodeling will be influenced by the legal requirements of several federal laws in addition to those safety codes and construction regulations already applicable. The Occupational Safety and Health Act (OSHA), enacted in 1970, requires safety in construction, maintenance, and equipment installation. An example of the type of regulatory concern in this act relates to noise level. Under the act, workers shall not be exposed to as many as 90 decibels for more than an 8-hour day. Many states and municipalities have similar safety and health ordinances as well as environmental pollution legislation that requires all construction to meet the safety and heatlh requirements of their codes. Facility planners must review the requirements of statutes to meet standards for a particular facility.

Title IX of the Educational Amendment Act of 1972 is designed to end sex discrimination in American education. The act requires that educational institutions receiving federal funds take measures to equalize their programs and facilities. Institutions must provide equal intercollegiate, club, recreational, instructional, and intramural athletic opportunities to members of both sexes. Among other criteria, equal opportunity in athletics is assessed by determining whether appropriate equipment and supplies are provided; games and practice times are fairly scheduled; locker rooms, practice and competitive facilities are equitable; and medical and training facilities are equally provided. Separate restrooms, change and locker rooms, showers, baths, and toilet facilities, permitted by Title IX on the basis of sex, must be comparable in convenience and quality.

Although recent interpretation of Title IX rulings would suggest an easing of requirements, practical and moral responsibilities associated with equal opportunities should influence the planning, remodeling, and/or building of school facilities for athletics, physical education, and recreation.

The Women's Educational Equity Act of 1974 (WEEA) was enacted as Section 408 of the Educational Amendment Act of 1974 (Public Law 93-380). The purpose of the law is to provide educational equity for women. Among the provisions of this act are the expansion and improvement of educational programs and activities for women in vocational education, career education, physical education and educational administration. This act also has implications for administrators in planning, remodeling, or construction of physical education facilities for women's programs.

The regulations of the Education for All Handicapped Children Act, Public Law 94-142 and Section 504 of the Rehabilitation Act of 1973 which became effective in October of 1977, are designed to assure that all handicapped children have available to them a free appropriate public education and that they are educated to the optimal degree possible with their non-handicapped peers in the least restrictive environments. Physical education is the only curricular area included in the definition of special education; recreation is specified as one of the related services that can be provided handicapped children. Mainstreaming the handicapped person may require adaptations of facilities and equipment. Additional information related to the handicapped is provided in Chapter 8.

The "Amateur Sports Act of 1978" provided a one-time supplemental appropriation for amateur sports in the United States. The federal government's involvement in the amateur sport movement will have long-term effects on both athletic programs and facilities. The recent establishment of national training centers as mentioned earlier will influence the design and type of future athletic, physical education, and recreation facilities. Other countries throughout the world are well ahead of the United States in providing national facilities for amateur sport.

Curricular Trends and Activity

Another major factor which needs serious consideration in school facility planing is the rapid expansion of the physical education activity and scientific curricula. Classes in recreation-oriented activities now include hiking, camping, canoeing, sailing, rock climbing, survival activities, surfing, wind surfing, fishing, downhill skiing, cross-country skiing, self-defense activities, ice hockey, ice skating, and bicycling. These activities along with the traditional individual, dual, and team sports, aquatics, and dance-rhythmic activities, need special facilities, some on campus, others off campus.

New buildings should also be designed for the student's increased awareness and need for physical fitness, and his increased participation in dual and individual sports. The trend in colleges is toward greater participation in intramural sports with shared facilities and integrated programs for students, staff, and faculty. Women's competitive sports continue to expand. New facilities need to be designed differently than the traditional gymnasium and field house. The scientific curriculum in exercise physiology, health-related exercise programs, biomechanics, and motor learning require the accommodation of special equipment in special environments. The facilities should support the new curriculum and accommodate viable activities. Buildings must also be planned for new methods of teaching, the greater use of newer and more sophisticated audiovisual teaching aids, and the new technology for testing, scoring, and recording activity data. (Figure 9-4)

Environmental, Economic, and Aesthetic Factors

While it is now possible to design almost any type of structure, there are economic and environmental factors that influence the facilities built. The emphasis on environmental protection requires planners to consider the impact of construction and design on the environment, the site, the traffic created because of the new building, and changes the facility will bring to the surrounding area. An impact study is usually required prior to construction and may result in changes in the final plans. Energy costs affect building design and operation. Natural gas, oil, and electric power to provide heat and electricity will be costly and in short supply. The possible alternative sources of energy and heating and lighting equipment need to be studied to take advantage of the new technologies available, such as solar heat.

Use of the Aquifer

One of the most recent innovative trends in facilities heating and cooling is the use of the aquifer. An aquifer is an underground layer of sand or gravel which contains water. An aquifer can be likened to a rock sponge which retains water existing between non-porous rock layers. There are enormous amounts of underground water available in the United States which would be adequate for aquifer cooling.

The concept for cooling with an aquifer system is relatively simple. During cool winter weather, the water in the aquifer is pumped up to a cooling tower where its temperature is reduced to a desirable temperature and then returned to the aquifer. During air conditioning months, the cool water is pumped from the aquifer and passed through an air handling system. An air handling system simply delivers the air which is blown across cooling coils containing the cool water and distributed as needed to cool and air condition a facility. The water, now at a higher temperature after being used to cool a facility, is pumped back into the aquifer to be stored and recooled again the next winter, completing the cycle. Aquifer water temperature is normally the same as the average annual ambient temperature. A number of wells tap the aquifer and the water is drawn up during winter months and cooled to approximately 30-50 degrees depending on the existing winter temperature in that geographic area. The water is then filtered to prevent contamination, piped into adjacent wells, and replaced in the aquifer, a distance away from the "warm" water. As more and more water is chilled and pumped back into the ground, it displaces the existing "warm" water, and a larger and larger area of the water in the aquifer becomes 30-50 degrees.

During hot weather the cool water from the aquifer is pumped through the air handling system and is used for air conditioning. This system works just as if water were chilled in a conventional system. After the cool water has passed through the cooling coils once, it is returned to the aquifer

Figure 9-4
The Kline Life/Sports Learning Center at Dickinson College in Carlisle, Pa. uses a hyperbolic paraboloid roof system with 130 foot clear-span interior. Waste energy reclamation and utilization are the key to a unique earth sink system which interferes with rooftop solar collectors.

at approximately 50-60 degrees. The net results are that the temperature of the water in the system is reduced with each annual cooling cycle and consequently the system becomes more and more efficient.

Economic savings of an aquifer system are site specific and theoretical. It does appear as indicated by the present body of research that aquifer utilization for heating and cooling may be predicted to accrue a substantial saving at existing energy cost levels. An aquifer system can produce the same cooling and heating of a conventional system for approximately 50 percent reduction in cost.

In addition, a conventional air conditioning system has a life expectancy of approximately 10 years at which point a completely new system is required. With an aquifer system, the replacement costs are only in replacing well and chill tower pumps. Utilizing specific geographic increases in kilowatt hour rates around the country, the savings should increase and the number of years for recovery of the aquifer cost should be reduced significantly.

An aquifer system also can be used to heat a facility utilizing the same basic approach as is used with the cooling operation. Water would be heated by utilizing the ambient air temperature which exists in summer or by a variety of heating means. Solar collectors could be one method which may be used to assist in raising the water temperature to an acceptable storage temperature. Once the water reached an appropriate storage temperature, it could be injected back into an aquifer to remain until needed in the colder months. Hot water during winter would then be drawn up, passed through an air handling system, releasing heat to a facility's atmosphere.

Other Natural Resources

Many areas in the United States and abroad may be able to utilize subsurface deposits of natural resources. Areas where geothermal activity may produce energy in the form of steam for hot water and heating may, and should, be considered for incorporating into existing or future building.

In addition, there are areas of the country which have coal, gas and oil available. Facilities do exist which utilize methane gas to fire boilers for hot water as well as heating. Geographic areas which produce coal may be probable candidates for methane gas consideration. Also, facilities should utilize any waste heat produced either at the facility site or which is produced by adjacent facilities which could be used to supplement heating requirements. (Figure 9-5)

Construction Trends and Variables for Conservation

When possible, facilities should have a long axis east-west orientation. Such a simple idea

Figure 9-5, 5A
Oaklawn Elementary School in Monticello, Indiana was renovated in 1983 to incorporate solar technology in order to reduce energy costs.

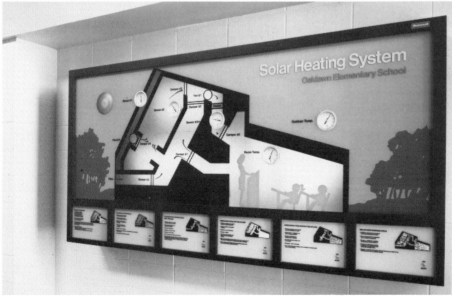

Trends in Facility Design

as this allows for a greater period of time for the sun to pass over and to the south of a facility than if the building had a north-south orientation. Such an alignment allows for considerable use of passive solar heat in winter months.

Solar sensitive dual pane glass should be considered for windows having southern exposures. This type of glass could be installed along the entire length of the southern side of a facility with consideration given to avoid glare on activity areas. Solar sensitive glass has the capacity to darken during bright summer light and become lighter in color during less sun-intensed days. The ability of sun sensor glass to change colors allows for reflection of bright summer sun, not needed in hot weather, and the entry of winter sun when passive solar heat is needed in colder weather.

The construction of a large eyebrow may be considered over the south side of a facility. The eyebrow would prevent the summer sun's ray from shining directly into windows and/or on wall surfaces by providing shade. The eyebrow, because of the winter sun's low horizon orientation would not interfere with the warming rays of the winter sun. Another trend for energy conservation is to simply place rows of deciduous trees along the southern side of a facility. In summer, such trees will provide shade to the facility and consequently reduce air conditioning costs. In winter the leaves fall from the trees and allow the winter sun, now needed, to shine unabated either into windows or onto walls assisting in heating the facility.

An economizer system may be considered to be cost effective in energy conservation. The Economizer is analogous to a whole house attic fan. This form of cooling is a very old method of energy saving now being revitalized and pressed into service. A simple thermostat and

sensor determine the interior temperature of a facility and also the exterior ambient temperature. At any point in which the exterior ambient temperature drops to approximately 60 degrees or less and the interior temperature of the facility demands cooling, the economizer becomes automatically operational. This system shuts down the facility's normal air conditioning system and at this point the fans of the economizer draw cool exterior air into the building, pass that air through existing air handlers, dehumidify it, and cool the facility.

It is difficult to accurately assess the economic impact of the trends and innovations discussed because all are site specific. It should be noted that all of these systems utilize existing and dependable technology and materials which have the capacity to reduce energy cost.

Aesthetics and Flexibility

There has been a growing emphasis on innovative ideas which enhance the aesthetic design, flexibility, and function of the building and provide needed areas less expensively. Costs of conventional structures are consistently rising. The challenge is to update existing facilities and provide more usability of the available space in an attractive, economical, and efficient manner.

Reassigning space for future programs by providing large areas that can be subdivided and/or changed as needed can prove quite functional. The concept of providing portable indoor recreational facilities might not be too far-fetched. Consider a mobile structure fitted with locker, shower, and changing facilities and attached by a breezeway to an air-supported structure. This self-contained locker and showering facility, with an air structure, could be moved from one part of the community to another and from one community to another as the need arose. The portable service areas could also

serve alternate activity areas such as a stadium.

The aesthetic quality, outside and inside, of a sport, physical education, and recreation facility must be considered throughout the planning stages. The vast size of such structures requires that they blend with the surroundings. Aesthetic appeal can be achieved inside the facility through the selection of appropriate colors, textures, and materials for floors, walls, and ceilings. The use of color, murals, and design art can enhance the aesthetics of indoor areas and should be incorporated where appropriate.

Technological Advances and Equipment

The designs now possible in facility construction due to improved technology seem astounding and are presently being incorporated into new buildings. Some innovative concepts which may affect future facility design in physical education-athletic complexes include rotating permanent seating; pool surfing; climbing walls; electric carpeting; paper structures; air roofs and walls; use of synthetics, fabrics, and membranes; new lighting and acoustical treatments; and electronic security and energy management systems. Examples of these innovations are described below.

Surfing is a popular sport which previously could only be offered at schools in close proximity to an ocean. Now, through use of mechanization, surfing pools can be built. Electrical carpeting installation in classrooms and in audio-visual centers and laboratories makes conventional sockets and extension cords unnecessary. The total floor is an electric circuit. Beneath the floor covering is a grid of electricity. The equipment cord can be pushed into any spot on the floor to obtain electricity.

More and more demand for usable space may bring about the

use of elevated platforms for activity areas in high ceiling gymnasiums. The platforms may be controlled by air pressure or hydraulics and consist of whole teaching stations such as a gymnastic area or weight area. The platforms would be suspended at varying heights and be completely movable when high ceilings are necessary. Wasted space would not be a problem; the new problem may be how to employ all available space.

New security systems are being employed in high risk areas to protect equipment and facilities. The use of internal electronic security systems can detect any attempt to enter a protected area and relay the break-in to a central control panel in the school's security area. The exact area of entry is visible on a central control board within a second after entry. Entire buildilngs can be totally equipped with this internal system.

Electronics also may be employed in energy control. Electronic computer systems limit peak electric demands, control temperature, program motors, lock doors, and operate lights. The system can control doors in case of fire to seal off the fire area. Other electronic usage can be found in scoreboards, lasers, and daily computerized schedule boards in locker rooms.

Many other new products are adaptable for physical education-athletic facilities and designers of future complexes should investigate their uses. Many times it is difficult to convince architects and planners to try out new concepts, but the physical education specialist should be persistent in urging the investigation. This is a major challenge above and beyond the challenge of facility design itself. Specialists should keep abreast of new trends and have resource materials available to convince planners of the validity of these innovative ideas. It must be understood, however, that any new facility concept which is adopted

may encounter problems that cannot be foreseen until the concept takes its physical form. The solution is usually found and the concept perfected for future planners.

Computers

Computers are a fact of life in modern building maintenance and may be used to reduce operational costs. Computers are used to control and monitor building temperatures, water supplies, lighting, ventilation, and swimming pool circulation and filtration systems. Controls can be extended to include building security and other aspects of operation to save work hours and reduce energy costs.

Ideas for Planning Facilities

Following are some ideas for renovating existing buildings or for planning new construction that take into account current trends in education and technology:

- School districts and municipalities forced to close elementary schools because of falling enrollment should consider converting the buildings to sports and recreational

community centers.
- Facilities for learning outdoor recreation skills could be incorporated in urban facilities, i.e., climbing walls in the gymnasium or outer walls of the school building.
- An ice arena not used in the summer could be planned for multi-use, such as an exhibition hall, convention center, riding ring, or rodeo arena. Synthetic ice on the rink could provide year-round skating.
- Public recreation planners could consider including a restaurant, bar, and/or babysitting facilities in recreation centers. The practice is popular in Europe and private clubs and may help in cost recovery.
- Mini physical fitness corners in classrooms and corridors could be planned in elementary schools so activity is not confined to the gymnasium alone.
- Creative, adventure, and/or junk playgrounds could be installed for children's playgrounds in addition to

Figure 9-6
Carpeted floors and walls are used in gymnasium at Geneva Elementary School in Bellingham, Washington.

Trends in Facility Design

the traditional playground equipment.

- School districts or municipalities might consider stacking facilities — placing a complete sports facility in a few locations and minimal facilities in the remainder of the district to reduce costs while providing all facilities in the district.
- Adoption of the metric system should be incorporated in any new, remodeled, or converted facility to accommodate official game requirements.
- Carpets of the new long-wearing fabrics could be installed in all areas where the rug surface is compatible with use. The carpet is less expensive in overall cost than floor tile. Carpet on both walls and floors in an elementary gymnasium has become a reality. (Figure 9-6)

Listed below are 40 of the latest developments expected to affect facility planning recently cited by Bellemare:

1. **Synthetic Ice** — Many companies are now producing synthetic or "plastic" ice. It has not been widely used in traditional skating and hockey facilities. (Figure 9-7)

2. **Snowless Ski Hills** — Dendix Perma-Snow has produced snowless ski hills since 1961. The ski mat consists of brush-like strips of PVC filaments held together by stainless steel wire and braces.

3. **Climbing Walls** — Common in Europe, climbing walls are now being incorporated into the design of new facilities. Indoor and outdoor climbing walls have been developed to simulate many of the conditions encountered in rock climbing. (Figure 9-8)

4. **Air Roof** — Continuous jets of air meet to form a ceiling/roof to keep out the elements. The need for covered or domed stadia would be greatly reduced.

5. **Turntable Seating** — Spectator seating can now be constructed on a turntable platform to be rotated to various directions for viewing a variety of different activities.

6. **Swinging or Convertible Changing Facilities** — Locker rooms and team rooms are now being designed for interchangeable use by males and females. These same rooms can also be expanded into large change areas by removing temporary walls.

7. **Automated Facility Entry** — In Europe a participant can enter a facility by inserting money into a vending type of machine; the revolving gate is unlocked to allow one person to enter. The participant receives a disc which becomes the implement that

unlocks a private locker. A locker key is retained by the individual during activity. After activity the key opens the lock, the disc is returned, and it must be inserted into disc-operated machine to allow participant to exit facility.

8. **Facility Entry with Identification Card** — Doors can be unlocked through the use of an identification card system containing metal chips. Card reading sensors can be programmed to change entry codes at regular intervals in the day to permit entry at only specified times by specific user groups or staff.

9. **Elevated Platforms for Specific Activities** — A series of platforms can now be raised to provide activity space with various ceiling height requirements. This enables ceiling of large facility to be used more effectively.

10. **Convertible Facilities** — Through modern technology facilities can now be converted very quickly. Pool floors can now be raised out of the water and a dance activity can take place. Most modern stadia or arenas can convert very quickly through mechanical means without the necessity of employing large numbers of workers.

11. **Convertible Roofs** — In France a campaign was developed to create new pools throughout the country. Two award-winning convertible pool designs became

Figure 9-7
All-time hockey great Phil Esposito shares his expert stickmanship with some youngsters during a synthetic ice demonstration at Madison Square Garden.

Figure 9-8
Small games room with a climbing wall.

the prototype for pools throughout the country. In all cases the facility roof was convertible to allow the indoor pool to become an outdoor pool.

12. **Portable, Removable Floors** — Modern stadia and arenas are now equipped with removable wooden sport floors, rolls of synthetic grass, or removable sport carpeting to increase flexibility of use of floor.

13. **Roof Top Facilities** — Since the first tennis court was placed on a roof, great strides have been made in the development of roof top sport and recreation facilities. Parks and recreation spaces are now being planned for the roof tops of complete city blocks.

14. **Community Under the Bubble** — With the development of large clear span, air-inflated facilities, plans are now under way to cover complete communities, including shopping centers, sports facilities, and parking lots under one roof.

15. **Mobile Locker Rooms** — At various intervals locker space requirements can vary. By providing mobile locker rooms the need for additional changing areas can be met.

16. **Movable Bleachers Moved on Air** — Movable folding bleachers which can double as divider walls can now be easily moved by one person. Through the use of a machine attached with an air-hose the bleachers are lifted and moved on a film of air.

17. **Illuminated Game Lines** — Selecting appropriate game lines in the maze of floor markings can now easily be done. By flipping a switch game lines are illuminated and activated to aid participants and officials.

18. **Folding Racquet Courts** — Squash, handball, and racquetball can now be played in a large open gymnasium. The court walls can unfold to form a regulation court or they can be folded away against a wall.

19. **Coin-Operated Racquet Facilities** — A regulation size

court can be operated without staff employing "coin-operated vending machine" principle.

20. **Complete Glass Racquet Facilities** — Three- and four-sided glass racquet facilities are now available on the market. The employment of multi-wall glass has greatly assisted squash and racquetball to become popular spectator sports.

21. **Tissue Paper Game Lines** — Ice arena lines can now be created without the need for the messy process of painting lines. Tissue paper lines and other markings are fixed in place on the ice and coated with water. Line colors are sharp and rich in appearance.

22. **Jet Ice** — Great savings in energy costs can now be made through the use of a new process titled "Jet Ice." Demineralized hot water is used to create ice in an energy-efficient manner.

23. **Expandable Ice Surfaces** — Ice surfaces can now be expanded from the standard NHL size to international hockey standards. In addition, it is not unusual to see double, triple and even quadruple ice surfaces under one roof.

24. **Quick Make and Break Ice** — A process to remove ice quickly and to replace it in a shorter period of time is now being used in many major arenas.

25. **Ice Mats** — A system of flexible mats embedded with tubes, joined to a compressor, can create a portable or removable ice surface. Size of the ice surface is determined by number of mats employed. This system allows for temporary ice surfaces and is removable.

26. **Movable Pool Floors** — Different people require water at different depths in pools. Movable pool floors have been developed to create variable pool depths for various user groups and for different activities.

27. **Bubble Machine** — Air filled, bubbly water can now be created to assist the novice diver to land safely in the water.

Through use of an air compressor, air bubbles are released through the pool floor to create a form of water-air cushion.

28. **Changing Water Density** — Although the process has not been perfected scientists are altering water density to allow people to be more buoyant in the water.

29. **Hydraulic Diving Towers** — Diving board heights can now be changed through use of hydraulic diving towers.

30. **Movable Bulkheads** — One or more movable bulkheads have been constructed in pools to create a multi-pool concept in a single tank. Bulkheads can be stored against an end wall or lifted out of the water by mechanical means to create an official distance 50 meter racing pool.

31. **Spectacular Water Slides** — High, long and imaginative slides have been developed to create a total aquatic playground. In many areas the revenue potential has encouraged their development in new as well as existing centers.

32. **Wave Pools** — The beach is now simulated in a pool. Outdoor and indoor wave pools have been perfected to allow people hours of enjoyment in an imaginative aquatic setting.

33. **Underwater Floor and Ceiling Pacing Lights** — Pacing lights for competitive swimmers are being used in training sessions at the Sporthochschule in Cologne, West Germany.

34. **Surface-Mounted Diving Tanks** — Large European Leisure Centers are constructing diving tanks with viewing windows mounted on the deck of the pool. This eliminates need for deep excavation and it creates a tiered effect in today's pools.

35. **Pool Covers** — In both outdoor and indoor pools, covers are being employed to cut down evaporation and heat loss.

36. **Changeable Turnboards** — The State University of New York at Binghamton now allows swimmers the option of a visible wall above water in the deck level

pool. A movable turnboard panel allows swimmer the option even in the middle of a relay.

37. **Demand Control Systems in Sport Facilities** — An energy-saving device can now be installed to redirect energy requirements in a facility by turning off specific high energy equipment. This prevents all high energy items from coming on at the same time, thus reducing peak energy demand.

38. **Energy-Efficient Lighting** — Incandescent and fluorescent lights are now being replaced by High Intensity Discharge lights. Many older facilities have now been retrofitted with these more energy-efficient lights.

39. **Spa Equipment** — Many sport facilities now incorporate solariums, saunas, hot tubs, and swirl pools. These have been used extensively in hotels and health clubs and are now being incorporated into new municipal and university sport facilities.

40. **Movable, Collapsible Equipment and Apparatus** — With the advent of new air-inflatable facilities and other large clear span structures, equipment and apparatus have undergone many changes. Hydraulic basketball backboards, free standing gymnastics equipment and surface mounted badminton standards are some examples of the trend towards the flexible design of sport facilities.

Trends in planning facilities for athletics, physical education, and recreation are influenced by the participants and programs, by legal requirements and legislation, by technical innovations, and by social and economic factors within the agency. Facility planners should carefully assess the current trends in order to provide functional facilities for present as well as future use.

SELECTED REFERENCES

Bellemare, H.K. "A Look at What's Ahead in Sports Facilities and Components." **Athletic Purchasing and Facilities** 7 (October 1983): 20, 22-24.

Bonfils, R., Adnot, J., and Iris, P. "Solar Heating and Seasonal Heat Storage in Aquifers." **Proceedings in the Subsurface Heat Storage — in Theory and Practice Conference** (June 1983): 730-736. Stockholm, Sweden: Spangbergs Trychkerier AB. (ISBN 91-540-3907-X).

Boycheff, Kooman. "Trends in Planning of Rec-Sports Facilities." **NIRSA** 1 (1977).

Broom, Eric F. and Olenick, Norman F. **A Report — Study Tour of Sports and Recreation Facilities in Europe.** Victoria, B.C.: K.M. McDonald, Queens Printer, August 1974.

Crompton, John L. "Formulating New Directions with Strategic Marketing Planning." **Parks and Recreation** 18 (July 1983): 56-63, 66.

Davis, Bob A. "Partners in Progress: A Responsible Approach." **Council of Educational Facility Planners Journal** 21 (January-February 1983): 19-20.

Ebeling, L., Tostengard, S., Reddell, D.L., Harris, W.B., and Davidson, R.R. "The Effects of System Size on the Practicality of Aquifer Storage." **Proceedings in the International Solar Energy Society** (1979): 441. Newark, DE: American Section of the International Solar Energy Society Publishing Office.

Ezersky, Eugene M. and Theibert, P. Richard. **Facilities in Sports and Physical Education.** St. Louis: The C.V. Mosby Co., 1976.

Fitness Trails. Ottawa: The Minister of National Health and Welfare, Fitness and Amateur Sport Branch, 1975.

Flynn, Richard B., ed. "Focus on Community-Recreation Facilities," a series of articles in **Journal of Physical Education and Recreation** 48 (October 1977): 33-46.

Flynn, Richard B., ed. "Maximizing Use of Facilities." **JOPERD Journal** 49 (October 1978): 25-33.

Flynn, Richard B., ed. "Planning Facilities." **JOPERD Journal** 54 (June 1983): 19-38.

Flynn, Richard B., ed. "Timely Topics in Facility Planning." **Journal of Physical Education and Recreation** 51 (June 1980): 25-37.

Flynn, Richard B., ed. "What's Happening in Facilities," a series of articles in **Journal of Physical Education and Recreation** 49 (June 1978): 33-48.

Hammitt, Sally A. and Hammitt, William E. "Campus Recreation Users: Their Preferences and Administrative Priorities." **Journal of Physical Education and Recreation** 51 (April 1980): 38-39.

"Metal Building Systems Fit to be Tied," **Nation's Schools** (July 1974).

Michelson, J.L. "Solar Heating and Nature Cooling of Residences." **Proceedings in the International Solar Energy Society** (May 1979): 343. Newark, DE: American Section of the International Solar Energy Society Publishing Office.

Minor, J.E. "Seasonal Thermal Energy Storage Program." **Transactions of the American Nuclear Society** 34 (June 1980): 13-16.

Morofsky, E., and Mirza, C. "Overview of Canadian Aquifer Thermal Energy Storage Field Trials." **Proceedings in the Subsurface Heat Storage — in Theory and Practice Conference** (June 1983): 221-230. Stockholm, Sweden: Spangbergs, Trychkerier AB. (ISBN 91-540-3907-X).

Penman, Kenneth. **Planning Physical Education and Athletic Facilities in Schools.** New York: John Wiley and Sons, 1977.

Pettine, Alvin M. and Nettleton, John D. "No Money for New Construction." **Journal of Physical Education and Recreation** 51 (June 1980): 26-27.

"Planning the Educational Environment," (Dr. James Croackarell's report on suggestions for educational planners: "Seventeen Ways to Build in an Energy-Scarce Future." Candell, Bullock and Lawyer.) **Nation's Schools** (July 1974).

Schaetzle, W.J., Brett, C.E., and Grubbs, D.M. "Annual Thermal Energy Storage in Groundwater Aquifers." **Proceedings in the Solar Energy Storage Options Conference** (March 1979): 183-192. San Antonio, TX: National Technical Information Service, U.S. Department of Commerce, Springfield, VA 22161 (CONF-790328-Pl).

Schaetzle, W.J., Brett, C.E., and Richey, L.H. "Experience with Two 'Free Cooling' Systems Using Aquifer Thermal Energy Storage." **Proceedings in the Subsurface Heat Storage — in Theory and Practice Conference** (June 1983): 823-825. Stockholm, Sweden: Spangbergs, Trychkerier AB. (ISBN 91-540-3907-X).

Smith, G.C., Wiles, C.E., and Loscutoff. **Numerical Analysis of Temperature and Flow Effects in a Dry One-Dimensional Aquifer Used for Compressed Air Storage.** Richland, WA: U.S. Department of Energy, Pacific Northwest Laboratory. (E 1.28: PNL-2546).

Appendix A

State Requirements for School Construction 1981

COMMITTEE ON ARCHITECTURE FOR EDUCATION

State Requirements Survey — FOR NEW CONSTRUCTION K–12

SCHOOL FUNDING (per cent) | EARLY PLANNING REQ.'S | SIZE & RATIO REQUIREMENTS

State	LOCAL	STATE	FEDERAL	OTHER	STATE PRE-PLANNING AGENCIES	MANDATED COMMUNITY INVOLVEMENT	STATE PLANNING REVIEW	SITE ind	SITE ELEM	SITE JR.HIGH/MIDDLE	SITE HIGH SCHOOL	BLDG ind	BLDG ELEM	BLDG JR.HIGH/MIDDLE	BLDG HIGH SCHOOL	ROOM ind	ROOM ELEM	ROOM JR.HIGH/MIDDLE	ROOM HIGH SCHOOL	SCIENCE CLRM	SPECIAL ED. CLRM	INDUSTRIAL SHOPS	HOME ARTS CLRM	MUSIC ROOM	MULTI-USE ROOM	THEATER	CAFETERIA
ALABAMA	67	30	3	0	No	No	Yes	Rec	5b	10b	15b	Yes	30a/37a	28a/30a	27a/30a	Yes	900/1100	850/900	800/900	1000/1250	Based upon Number of Students →						
ALASKA	50	49	1	0	Yes	No	Yes	Rec	--- Not Given ---			Yes	100	150	150	none											
ARIZONA	94	3	3	0	No	No	No	none				none				none											
ARKANSAS	100	0	0	0	No	No	No	Rec	10b	20b	30b	none				none											
CALIFORNIA	0	90	5	5	Yes	No	Yes	Rec	---- varies ----			Yes	55	75	95+	Yes	900/960										
COLORADO	100	0	0	0	No	No	Yes	Rec	-- Not Given --			none				none											
CONNECTICUT		40/85			Yes	No	Yes	Rec	10b	15b	20b	Yes	90/96	113/131	136/147	Yes	25a/30a	25a/30a	25a/30a	35a/43a	75a/90a	120a/144a	55a/64a	25a	---- Code ----		
DELAWARE		60			Yes	No	Yes	Rec	10b	20b	30b					Yes	840	700	700								
FLORIDA	44	49	4	2	Yes	No	Yes	Req	5a	6a	7a	none				Yes	900/1020	840/960	750/870	1150/1300	750/1100	900/1170	1800/1980	Varies by Schedule →			
GEORGIA		74			Yes	No	Yes	Req	5b	12b	20b	none				Yes	750	660	600				1800/3600	Formulation by Population			
HAWAII	0	100	0	0	Yes	Yes	Yes	Rec	5b/8b	7b/12b	20b/30b	none				Yes	918	900	1600/2124	330/2260	1820/5534	1600/1895	1770/4857				3255/11153
IDAHO	100	0	0	0	No	No	Yes	Rec	5b	5b	30b	none				Rec	850	850	800	1400							
ILLINOIS	30/80	30/70	0	0	Yes	Yes	Yes	Rec	5b	20b	30b	Yes	76	120	140	none											
INDIANA	100	0	0	0	No		Yes	Req	-- Not Given --			Yes	30a	30a	30a	Yes	900	900	800	1200	900	1500	1200	1200	1800		10a/12a
IOWA	100	0	0	0	No		Yes	Rec	10b	30b	30b	none				none	---- Recommended Guidelines Publication ----										
KANSAS	90	0	0	10	No	No	Yes	none				none				Yes	20a	20a	20a	50a	20a	50a	50a	15a	15a	7a	15a
KENTUCKY	20	70	9.5	0.5	Yes	Yes	Yes	Req	5b	10b	10b	none				Yes	720	625	625	---- Recommended Guidelines ----							
LOUISIANA		No Response																									
MAINE	97				Yes	Yes	Yes	Rec	5b	10b	20b	Yes	70/90	90/110	110/130	Yes	800		625	1200	50a	3500	1400		800/1800	7200	7a
MARYLAND	3	97	0		Yes	No	Yes	Rec	10b	20b	30b	Yes	90/100	115	130	none											
MASSACHUSETTS		50/75			Yes	Yes	Yes	Rec	-- Not Given --			Yes	Max 115	Max 135	Max 155	Yes	---- None Given ----										
MICHIGAN	100	0	0	0	Yes	No	Yes	Rec	10b	20b	30b	Yes	91/128	173/208	170/210	Yes	900	900	900	1200	1000	3600	2000	1400/3000	2400	6800/10700	2400/7500
MINNESOTA	45	3	2	50	Yes	Yes	Yes	Rec	12/15	25/30	30/60	none				Yes	---- State Guide for Area ----										
MISSISSIPPI	50	50	0	0	Yes	No	Yes	Req	5b	15b	15b	Rec				Rec	600	600	600	800						8a	10a
MISSOURI	100	0	0	0	No	No	No	Rec	10c	20c	30c	none				none											

ABBREVIATIONS
LOC – LOCAL
REC – RECOMMENDED
REQ – REQUIRED
VAR – VARIES

NOTES
(1) SITE SIZE IN ACRES
 a. plus one acre for each 100 students over 300
 b. plus one acre for each 100 students
 c. plus two acres for each 100 students

(2) TOTAL BUILDING AREA BASED UPON STUDENT COUNT X SQUARE FEET ALLOWANCE
 a. for teaching station – student count x square feet allowance
 note: two figures represent minimum and maximum allowable

PREPARED BY: Committee on Architecture for Education. DISTRIBUTED BY: Council on Educational Facility Planners, International

(Elem.)	ELEMENTARY	JR. HIGH/MIDDLE	HIGH SCHOOL	DIFFERENTIATION BETWEEN URBAN & SUBURBAN SITES	REVIEW OF CONSTRUCTION DOCUMENTS (4)	STANDARD BUILDING CODE	UNIFORM BUILDING CODE	NATIONAL BUILDING CODE	BOCA	SOUTHERN BUILDING CODE	STATE CODE	LOCAL CODE	LIFE SAFETY, NFPA, ANSI, ETC.	(Spec. Req.)	ENVIRONMENTAL	HANDICAPPED	ENERGY	FIRE SAFETY	SEISMIC	WIND	SNOW	FLOOD	OTHER	STATE REQUIRED FIELD INSPECTION	(Testing)	CONCRETE	STEEL	FOUNDATIONS	PLUMBING	SOILS	OTHER	STATE FINAL CONSTRUCTION APPROVAL
Yes	24/28	30	30	No	Yes									Yes			O							No	none							Loc
				No										Yes				O						No	none							No
				No	Yes									none										LOC								
Yes	25	30	30	No	Yes		O				O	O	O	Yes		O	O	O						No	none			O				No
Yes	25(k)			Yes	Yes						O			Yes	O	O	O	O				O	O	Yes	none							Yes
Yes	20/29	160 per day	160 per day	No	Yes						O			Yes	O	O	O	O						Yes	Yes	O	O	O	O	O	O	Yes
none				Yes	Yes						O			Yes	O	O	O	O		O	O	O		No								No
Yes	26	33	35	No	Yes						O		O	Yes	O	O	O	O		O	O			No	none							Yes
Yes	30	30	30	No	Yes						O		O	Yes		O	O	O						No	none							No
Yes	25	25	25	No	Yes						O	O		Yes	O	O	O	O			O			Yes	Yes	O	O	O	O	O	O	Yes
Yes	26	37	37	No	Yes			O				O	O	Yes				O						No	none							Yes
Yes	25	25	25	No	Var	O					O	O	O	Yes		O		O	O	O				Yes	Yes	O		O			O	Loc
none				No	Yes						O													No	none							
Yes	23/30	35	35	No	Yes	O								Yes		O	O	O						Yes	none							Yes
none				No	Yes		O				O		O	Yes	O	O		O						No	none	---Per UBC criteria---						Loc
Yes	25/28	30	35	No	Yes			O					O	Yes	O	O	O	O						Yes		---Per code criteria---						Yes
Yes	varies with subject			No	Yes a						O			Yes		O		O						No	none							No
Yes	24 K-3			No	Yes	O					O		O	Yes		O	O	O	O					No		---Per UBC criteria---						No
Yes	varies with subject			No	Yes			O			O		O	Yes	O	O	O	O			O			No	none							Yes
Yes	21	varies		No	Yes						O			Yes		O		O						No	none							No
				No	Yes		O				O			Yes	O			O	O	O	O	O	O	No	none	----As required by A/E-------						Loc
Yes	---not given---			No	Yes						O			Yes		O		O						No	Yes					O		Yes
none				No	Yes						O	O	O	Yes	O	O	O	O		O	O	O		Yes	Yes					O		No
none				No	Yes	O					O			Yes		O	O	O						No	none							Yes

(3) ROOM SIZE BASED UPON ALLOWABLE LIMITS
    a. square feet allowance x student count

    note: two figures represent minimum and maximum allowable

(4) STATE CONSTRUCTION DOCUMENTS REVIEW
    a. barriers only

State Requirements Survey

FOR NEW CONSTRUCTION K - 12

SIZE & RATIO REQUIREMENTS

State	SCHOOL FUNDING (per cent)				EARLY PLANNING REQ.'S			SITE SIZE REQ.'S (1)				BUILDING AREA REQ.'S (2)				ROOM SIZE REQUIREMENTS (3)											
	LOCAL	STATE	FEDERAL	OTHER	STATE PRE-PLANNING AGENCIES	MANDATED COMMUNITY INVOLVEMENT	STATE PLANNING REVIEW		ELEMENTARY	JR. HIGH / MIDDLE	HIGH SCHOOL		ELEMENTARY	JR. HIGH / MIDDLE	HIGH SCHOOL		ELEMENTARY	JR. HIGH / MIDDLE	HIGH SCHOOL	SCIENCE CLRM.	SPECIAL ED. CLRM.	INDUSTRIAL SHOPS	HOME ARTS CLRM.	MUSIC ROOM	MULTI-USE ROOM	THEATER	CAFETERIA
MONTANA	95	0	5	0	No	No	Yes	Req	5a		10a	Yes	15a	15a	15a	none											
NEBRASKA	100	0	0	0	No	No	Yes	Rec	10b	20b	30b	none				none											
NEVADA	100	0	0	0	No	No	No	Rec	--Not Given---			none				Yes	----------Requirements Not Given-------										
NEW HAMPSHIRE	40/70	30/55	0	0	No	No	Yes	Req	5b	10b	15b	Yes				Yes	30a	30a	30a	50a	30a	75a	50a	35a	100a		10a/12a
NEW JERSEY	80	20	0	0	Yes	Yes	Yes	Rec	10b	20b	30b	Rec	85	125	155	Yes	28a/36a	28a	26a	50a/58a	53a/100a	117a/142a	83a	302/352	40a/125a	9a	12a
NEW MEXICO					Yes	No	Yes	Rec	5b	20b	30b	Yes	30a	30a	30a	Yes	900	30a	30a	35a		100a	30a	16a/20a		7a	
NEW YORK	40	40	0	20	Yes	Yes	Yes	Req	3b	10b	10b	Yes				Yes	770	770	770	1000/1200	900	2000	1200	770			
NORTH CAROLINA	70	30	0	0			Yes	Rec	10b	20b	30b	none				none											
NORTH DAKOTA	80	20	0	0	No		Yes	Rec	5b	5b	10b	Rec	25a/30a	22a/27a	15a/30a	Rec	750/900	660/810	450/900	750/1200	450/750	1000/1600	900/1500	750/1600			10a/12a
OHIO	95	5	0	0	Yes	Yes	Yes	Rec	10b	15b	25b	Yes	27a	29a	32a	Yes	27a	29a	32a	40a	27a/32a	150a	75a	15a/20a	75a	12a/13a	12a/13a
OKLAHOMA	90	0	0	5	No	No	Yes	none				none				none											
OREGON	100	0	0	0	No	No	No	none				none				none											
PENNSYLVANIA								NO RESPONSE																			
RHODE ISLAND	70	30	0	0	Yes	Yes	Yes	Rec	10b	20b	30b	none				Yes	25a/30a	25a/30a	25a/30a	30a/40a		60a/75a	30a/40a	30a/40a	30a/40a		
SOUTH CAROLINA	78	20	2	0	No	No	Yes	Req	10b	20b	30b	Yes	--Not Given---			Yes	----------Not Given-------										
SOUTH DAKOTA	100	0	0	0	No	Yes	Yes	Req	5b	7b	12b	Yes	30a			Yes	750										
TENNESSEE	100	0	0	0	No	No	Yes	Req	4b	4b	8b	No	25a	25a	22a	Yes	748	748	660			100a	2080/1600	20a		8a	
TEXAS	99	0	1	0	No	No	Yes	Rec	10b	20b	30b	none				none											
UTAH	87	12	1	0	Yes	No	Yes	Rec	10b	20b	30b	Yes	72/76	115/125	140/164	none											
VERMONT	70	30	0	0	Yes	Yes	Yes	Rec	10b	20b	30b	Yes	30a	30a	30a	Yes	30a	30a	30a	50a	30a	50a	50a	30a	30a	7a	15a
VIRGINIA	100	0	0	0	No	No	Yes	Req	4b	10b	10b	none				Yes	735/975	630	630								
WASHINGTON	20/90	20/90	10	0	Yes		No	Rec	5b	10b	10b	Yes	80	110	120												
WEST VIRGINIA	42	44	14	0	Yes	Yes	Yes	Rec	10b/15b	25b/35b	40b/52b	none				none											
WISCONSIN					No	No	Yes	Rec	10b	20b	30b					Yes	20a	20a	20a	30a	35a	50a	30a	10a/20a	10a	6a	10a
WYOMING	90	10	0	0	No	No	Yes	Rec	10b	15b	25b	none				none											

ABBREVIATIONS
LOC - LOCAL
REC - RECOMMENDED
REQ - REQUIRED
VAR - VARIES

NOTES

(1) SITE SIZE IN ACRES
a. plus one acre for each 100 students over 300
b. plus one acre for each 100 students
c. plus two acres for each 100 students

(2) TOTAL BUILDING AREA BASED UPON STUDENT COUNT X SQUARE FEET ALLOWANCE
a. for teaching station - student count x square feet allowance
note: two figures represent minimum and maximum allowable

BUILDING DESIGN REQUIREMENTS   CONSTRUCTION REQUIREMENTS

Footnote keys: (3) ROOM SIZE BASED UPON ALLOWABLE LIMITS   (4) STATE CONSTRUCTION DOCUMENTS REVIEW

Ratio(y/n)	Elementary	Jr.High/Middle	High School	Differentiation Urban/Suburban	Review of Constr. Docs (4)	Standard Bldg Code	Uniform Bldg Code	National Bldg Code	BOCA	Southern Bldg Code	State Code	Local Code	Life Safety NFPA/ANSI	(Spec.Req.)	Environmental	Handicapped	Energy	Fire Safety	Seismic	Wind	Snow	Flood	Other	State Req'd Field Inspection	(Testing)	Concrete	Steel	Foundations	Plumbing	Soils	Other	State Final Constr. Approval
Yes	30	30	30	No	Yes	○		○					○	Yes	○		○	○						Yes	Yes	○		○	○	○		Yes
none				No	Yes		○						○	Yes	○	○	○	○			○	○		Yes	Yes	○	○	○	○	○		Yes
none				No	No					○				Yes		○		○						No	none	— Local Option —						
none				No	Yes			○						Yes		○		○						No	Yes					○		No
none				No	Yes		○							Yes	○	○	○	○	○	○	○	○		Yes	Yes	○	○	○		○		Yes
none				No	Yes									Yes	○	○		○		○	○	○		No	Yes	— Via Public Safety —						No
none				No	Yes			○		○			○	Yes	○	○	○	○		○	○			No	Yes	○	○	○	○	○		No
none				No	Yes						○	○	○	Yes		○	○	○						Yes								Loc
none				No	Yes			○		○			○	Yes	○	○	○	○		○		○		Yes	Yes	○	○	○	○	○		Yes
Yes	20	25	25	Yes	Yes			○	○	○			○	Yes	○	○	○	○				○		Yes	none							No
Yes	26	26	26	No	Yes		○				○	○	○	Yes	○	○	○	○	○	○			○	Yes	Yes	○		○		○	○	Yes
none				Rec	Yes		○				○		○	Yes		○		○	○	○	○	○		Yes	none							Loc
none				Yes	Yes			○						Yes	○	○	○	○	○				○	Yes	Yes	○	○	○	○	○		Yes
none				Yes	Yes		○				○			Yes	○	○	○	○		○				Yes								Yes
none				No	Yes						○			Yes		○	○	○		○	○			No	none	— Local Option —						Loc
none				No	Yes		○						○	Yes		○		○	○	○	○			No	none							
Yes	30	30	30	No	Yes						○													Yes	Yes	— Per State Code —						
none				No	Yes			○		○			○	Yes	○	○	○	○						Yes	Yes	○			○	○		Yes
none				No	Yes						○		○	Yes	○	○	○	○						Loc	none	— Local Option —						Loc
none				No	Yes			○			○		○	Yes	○	○	○	○						Loc	none	— Local Option —						Yes
none				No	Yes						○			Yes	○	○		○						Yes	Yes				○	○	○	Yes
Yes	30	160 per day	160 per day	No	Yes		○						○	Yes	○	○	○	○	○	○	○	○	○	Yes	Yes	○	○	○	○	○	○	Yes
Yes	27	150 per day	150 per day	No	Yes					○	○	○		Yes	○	○	○	○	○	○	○			Yes	Yes	○	○	○	○	○		Yes
none				No	No									none										No	none							No

(3) ROOM SIZE BASED UPON ALLOWABLE LIMITS
    a. square feet allowance x student count
    note: two figures represent minimum and maximum allowable

(4) STATE CONSTRUCTION DOCUMENTS REVIEW
    a. barriers only

Appendix B

A BUILDING SERVICE CHECKLIST
Developed by David Griner
Dept. of University Recreation and Intramural Sports, Ohio State University

Programmed custodial and maintenance services are extremely important to the smooth, economical, and efficient operation of a facility for athletics, physical education, and recreation. The following list is a reference point for developing your own plan. Items may be added or deleted where necessary. Each facility manager must select the frequency of services for his facility based on several factors such as size, type of activity, number of participants and spectators, surface materials, hours of operation, etc.

Based on your needs, plan the frequency rate on the blank provided.

Twice Daily	Monthly
Daily	Bi-Monthly
Three Times a Week	Quarterly
Two Times a Week	Semi-Annually
Weekly	Annually
Bi-Weekly	As Required

GYMNASIUMS, MULTI-PURPOSE AND CONDITIONING ROOMS

_____ Dry mop, sweep all gymnasiums and all activity areas and their adjacent rooms, corridors, lobbies, stairways and courts

_____ Apply cedar san type sealer to all wood floors after each mopping. Remove all scuff marks

Synthetic Gym Floors

_____ Dust mop
_____ Wet mop
_____ Scrub
_____ Strip and re-coat (2 coats)

Wood Gym Floors and Handball Courts

_____ Dust mop
_____ Damp mop
_____ Strip and re-coat (2 coats)

Conditioning Rooms

_____ Vacuum carpet
_____ Dust mop tile floor
_____ Damp mop tile floor
_____ Strip and refinish tile floor
_____ Clean bleacher areas completely, including washing seats, cleaning floors, sealing floors
_____ Mats — Damp mop and disinfect

POOLS

_____ Clean and sanitize pool deck, showers, steam room, and corridors between these areas

Pool Decks

_____ Scrub with tergiquat solution (2 oz. per gallon)
_____ Pick up with wet/dry vacuum
_____ Rinse with clear water
_____ Pick up with wet/dry vacuum
_____ Clean out drains

Pool Bottom

_____ Sweep

RESTROOMS, SHOWER ROOMS, LOCKER ROOMS

_____ Clean, sanitize, service and restock restrooms, using an approved germicidal cleaner to disinfect lavatories, commodes, urinals, partitions, fixtures, mirrors, towel and soap dispensers

_____ Damp mop floors using clean water and a germicidal disinfectant

_____ Damp mop restroom floors
_____ Fill drain traps with water
_____ Sanitize urinals
_____ Sanitize restroom partitions
_____ Sanitize commodes
_____ Provide tissue paper as needed
_____ Sanitize sinks
_____ Provide hand soap and paper towels
_____ Clean and buff tile floors

OFFICES, CLASSROOMS, CONFERENCE ROOMS

_____ Do general housecleaning, including cleaning under and behind furniture and dust walls

_____ Vacuum carpeted areas. Spot clean spills as soon as possible
_____ Clean
_____ Inspect upholstered furniture. Vacuum fabric on upholstered furniture
_____ Spot wash vinyl and shampoo fabric as needed
_____ Damp mop vinyl furniture
_____ Clean classroom chairs and tables
_____ Damp mop all classroom/lab floors
_____ Clean and polish office desks and wood furniture
_____ A thorough and complete vertical and horizontal dusting of the following areas: furniture, file cabinets, desks, ledges, and sills, railings, partitions, picture frames, etc.
_____ Clean paneling
_____ Clean tables and chairs in conference rooms
_____ Damp mop lobby and first floor corridors per request of building coordinator
_____ Water and sponge clean all lab/classroom/conference room chalkboards and trays
_____ Vacuum and clean erasers. Restock chalk trays with chalk and erasers
_____ All chalkboards with DO NOT ERASE leave until cleaning is requested

GENERAL

_____ Empty and damp wipe all ashtrays
_____ Custodial employees shall not admit anyone into the building except properly identified recreation or department of safety personnel
_____ Check all entrances prior to leaving to see that building is secure. This includes closing and securing windows and interior doors
_____ Alert University Police by telephone of illegal entry, flood, found items, or emergency
_____ Immediately report all fires by telephone
_____ Interior doors may be unlocked only in the areas of active work performance
_____ Do not unlock all interior doors at the beginning of a shift
_____ Empty waste and sanitary receptacles. Remove soft and hard trash to assigned areas
_____ Custodial personnel will be responsible for policing the area around the dumpster
_____ Plastic liners for waste receptacles will be replaced as needed
_____ Soap and water clean all waste receptacles in the building
_____ Report any items requiring repair, i.e., lights, latches, doors, windows, etc.
_____ Note safety items
_____ Wash interior glass and sills of exterior windows
_____ All lights must be turned off except in the areas of active work performance
_____ Do not turn on large areas of lights at the beginning of a shift or during a shift
_____ Turn off lights except night lights after completing services
_____ Spot wash walls, interior doors and frames
_____ Dust mop/sweep concrete floors
_____ Damp mop concrete floors
_____ Seal concrete floors
_____ Dust coat racks, radiators, window ledges, doors, furniture, and lockers
_____ Clean supply and exhaust vents and grills
_____ Damp mop floor areas in all stairwells
_____ Wash all handrails and dust risers
_____ Thoroughly clean stairways (including dust mopping steps, landings, dusting rails, risers, and removing spillage with damp mop)
_____ Dust mop non-athletic wood floors. Strip and rewax.
_____ Clean and sanitize water fountain. Polish stainless steel.
_____ Exterminate (particularly pool filter) rooms, locker rooms.
_____ Clean all light fixtures, vents, grills (both supply and exhaust), ceilings, and walls.
_____ Dust mop resilient tile and terrazzo floor surfaces. Spray buff.
_____ Vacuum tracks and remove prints and smudges from doors and wall areas in elevators. Dust mop and spot mop.
_____ Sweep and/or dust mop all unoccupied areas.

Security and Safety Planning Checklist
David H. Griner

This topical checklist is intended as a program planning aid for athletic administrators.
It is a telescoping checklist for security/safety from day-to-day operation of athletic/recreation
facilities up to major athletic events.

1. General Information
   Day
   Date
   Time
   Facility
   Anticipated number of spectators
   Spectator profile
   Associated events
   Other scheduled events within same time frame
   Event history

2. Traffic Patterns (Auto, Bus, Pedestrian)
   Geographic service area
   Parking lot
   Wrecker lot
   Entry channeling

3. Personnel Protection
   VIP's
   Athletes
   Game officials
   Teams/athletes from foreign countries
   Seating, routes, vehicle requirements

4. Crowd control
   On field/court intrusion
   Altercations in spectator areas
   Intoxicated persons
   Emergency evacuation of spectator areas
   Demonstrators and pickets
   Sportsmanship programs

5. Facility Security
   Access to facility
   Facility integrity
   Key control
   Unauthorized entry into facility
   Identification procedures
   Closing security at end of event
   Gate/door (entrance/exit) security
   Seating assignments (Ohio's new Public
       Assembly Law)
   Power outages
   Perimeter versus interior security

6. Information
   Lost and found
   Facility information
   Travelers' aid and information
   PA announcements and procedures
   Lost persons

7. Fire Safety
   Reporting
   Alarm systems
   Liaison to servicing to fire agencies
   On-site equipment
   Mutual aid systems
   Bomb threat searches and evacuation
   Hazardous material
   Smoking restrictions/enforcement
   Exit routes/signage

8. Emergency Medical Services
   First aid training
   First aid treatment
   First aid stations
   Coordination with area hospitals
   Medical evaluation
   Reporting procedures
   Evaluation of accidents
   Preventions of accidents
   Special accidents; situations

9. Communication
   Command post
   On-site coordination
   Intra-agency coordination
   Communication to key personnel
   Personnel notification/recall
   Media relations
   Written plan, "panic" file

10. Inclement Weather
   Tornado warning or watch procedures
   Thunderstorm warning or watch procedures
   Winter storm warning or watch procedures
   Travelers' advisory procedures

11. Crime Resistance
   High visibility
   Adequate signage
   Violations of site, local, and state regulations
   Vandalism
   Personal property
   Facility property
   Dressing/shower areas
   Women's areas
   Training programs

12. Special Security
   Hostage situations
   Terrorist group activity
   Financial transactions
   Liaison between agencies
   Videotape systems
   Concessions
   Ticket sales
   Novelty sales
   Ticket scalpers
   Illegal vendors
   Response to specific threats

13. Facility Inspection
   Facility and equipment repair
   Preventive maintenance requirements
   Potential accident situations
   Safety standards/regulations

Prepared by David H. Griner, Department of University Recreation and Intramural Sports, Ohio State University

From JOPERD — June 1983

Appendix D   Water Polo: Field of Play

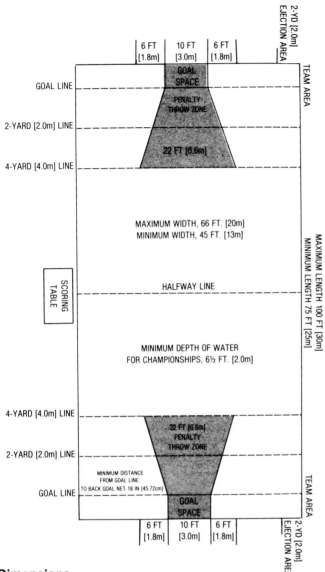

Dimensions

SECTION 1. The uniform distance between the goal lines must not exceed 100 feet (30m) nor be less than 75 feet (25m); the uniform width must not exceed 66 feet (20m) nor be less than 45 feet (13m). The minimum depth of the water shall be 6½ feet (2.0m).

While pools built prior to 1976 are exceptions to the foregoing standards, championship events should be conducted in only those facilities that meet the maximum standards.

It is the responsibility of the host institution to provide a field of play that meets as closely as possible the maximum measurements for length and width and the minimum depth given in the above standards.

Pool Markings

SECTION 2. There must be distinctive markers on both sides of hte field of play to denote the goal line, two-yard (2.0m) line, four-yard (4.0m) line, half distance between the goal lines and the ejection area on the goal line or ends of the field of play two yards (2.0m) from the corner of the field of

play on the side of the pool opposite the scoring table. Measurements for the two-yard (2.0m) line and four-yard (4.0m) line are to be taken from the front edge of the goal line, including the marker. It is recommended that all raised markers be flush with the edge of the pool. As uniform colors, the following are recommended for these markings: goal lines and half distance line — white; two-yard (2.0m) line — red; four-yard (4.0m) line — yellow; ejection area — red.

Penalty Throw Zone (Strike Zone)

SECTION 3. The boundaries of the penalty throw (strike) zone extend along the four-yard (4.0m) line a distance of 22 feet (6.6m), 11 feet (3.3m) in each direction from its midpoint, and thence in a diagonal line from each end of the 22-foot (6.6m) boundary to each goal post. There shall be penalty throw zone markers six feet (1.8m) from each side of the pool (22 feet [6.6m] apart) to denote the outside limits of the penalty throw zone at the four-yard (4.0m) line. (See Fig. 1-1.) It is recommended that yellow be used for these markers.

Space For Officials

SECTION 4. Sufficient space must be provided to enable the referees to have free way from end to end of the field of play. Space must also be provided at the goal lines for the goal judges.

GOALS

Dimensions

SECTION 5. The goal posts and crossbar shall have a flat surface three inches (.075m) wide and be of rigid material, such as wood or metal, with the face of the goal frame painted traffic yellow, orange or white. The goal frame must be fixed rigid and perpendicular to the surface of the water on the goal line, an even distance from each side of the field of play.

The goal posts must be 10 feet (3.0m) apart, and the crossbar must be three feet (.90m) above the water when the water is five feet (1.5m) or more in depth. When the water is less than five feet (1.5m) deep, the crossbar must be eight feet (2.4m) from the floor of the playing space, all measurements taken from the inside edges of the goal frame.

For floating goals, the goal lines should be attached one ball width from the front of the goal.

Artificial Standing Place

SECTION 6. Should any artificial standing or resting place exist (other than the floor of the pool) for the goalkeeper, it must be removed, or the goal posts moved to prevent its use.

Backing

SECTION 7. Canvas backing must be loosely attached to the goal fixtures to enclose the back and sides of the goal space in front of all supports. Floating posts shall have net backing attached.

The goal space must be a minimum of 18 inches (45.72cm) deep without any obstruction.

NCAA Approved Water Polo Layout
(from 1984 NCAA Water Polo Rules Book)

Status of Athletic Related Facilities at NCAA Member Institutions

	1961-62—536 Institutions		1966-67—577 Institutions		1971-72—663 Institutions		1976-77—722 Institutions		1981-82—753 Institutions		1981-82	
	Number Institutions	Number Units	Number Institutions	Number Units	Number Institutions	Number Units	Number Institutions	Number Units	Number Institutions	Number Units	Under Construction	Approved for Construction
INDOOR												
Archery Ranges	118	204	164	378	138	178	149	281	145	199	3	2
Basketball Courts	526	1,525	573	1,835	575	1,928	642	2,964	677	2,855	126	64
Bowling Lanes	209	1,358	232	1,723	218	1,595	201	1,564	212	1,670		
Golf Driving Ranges	290	493	172	311	139	184	113	207	97	181	22	2
Gymnasiums-Field Houses	459	826	573	1,045	542	790	589	965	604	1,022	34	102
Handball Courts	268	965	269	1,457	372	1,485	374	1,473	442	2,760	204	109
Ice Rinks	45	46	43	43	72	83	85	110	97	109	3	2
Rifle Ranges	216	259	209	232	185	218	153	193	187	192	2	2
Roller Rinks	5	5	12	12	5	5	12	12	16	14		2
Running Tracks	237	261	227	258	208	208	234	266	321	370	19	7
Swimming Pools	306	367	383	480	444	561	477	632	572	753	24	5
Tennis Courts	303	1,212	242	1,376	201	601	233	889	271	1,131	55	15
Wrestling Rooms	325	390	394	429	440	442	433	466	451	468	19	9
OUTDOOR												
Archery Ranges	264	475	298	551	272	389	235	410	204	250	3	2
Baseball Diamonds	497	696	482	634	295	943	561	689	580	663	17	12
Basketball Courts	174	435	253	755	529	653	326	1,160	311	1,169	9	7
Camping Areas	59	71	80	104	68	73	79	122	57	93		
Football Practice Fields	410	902	432	942	459	1,072	470	1,079	542	1,262	16	3
Football Stadiums	389	389	361	366	412	412	419	422	473	473	5	5
Golf Courses	118	130	102	116	117	120	121	128	131	150		
Golf Driving Ranges	98	127	143	197	143	151	134	141	133	136	3	2
Golf Greens	63	220	92	315	116	599	108	588	109	687	10	
Ice Rinks	59	61	52	54	50	63	37	41	17	48		
Lakes	82	98	100	186	86	100	99	167	97	145		
Play Areas	464	1,271	247	782	208	690	233	741	250	960	2	7
Ski Slides	32	37	29	30	40	44	69	79	38	54		
Soccer Fields	322	560	406	597	465	744	517	789	589	1,119	35	14
Softball Diamonds	451	1,849	452	1,912	428	1,867	471	2,001	523	1,824	19	21
Swimming Pools	87	122	139	214	118	142	133	224	164	250		2
Tennis Courts	510	4,845	508	4,682	583	5,737	640	7,799	677	7,974	83	88
Tracks	386	417	390	411	474	474	466	507	532	584	31	5
Trapshooting	4	4	16	16	19	19	30	30	19	26		

FROM: The Sports & Recreational Programs of the Natioanl Universities & Colleges
The National Collegiate Ahletic Association. Report No. Six

Appendix F

Use of NCAA Member Institution
Athletic Related Facilities by Outside Groups

	Permit Use		Number of
	Yes	No	Participants
Class A	164	16	410,026
Class B	15	4	6,210
Class C	54	14	66,590
Class D	90	22	103,210
Class E	140	30	90,194
Class F	61	15	44,732
Class G	84	24	80,766
Totals	608	125	801,728

Outside Agencies Using College Facilities Include:
- Alumni Groups
- Amateur Athletic Union
- American Legion
- American Red Cross
- Armed Forces
- Boy Scouts
- Boys Clubs
- Boys State
- Businessmen's Groups
- Chamber of Commerce
- Church Groups
- Community Recreation Associations
- Community Service Clubs
- 4-H Clubs
- Future Farmers Associations
- Girls State
- Handicapped Children's Programs
- High School Athletics
- Junior Chamber of Commerce (Jaycees)
- Junior Colleges
- Government Employees Groups
- Government Welfare Programs
- Police Associations
- Private Recreation Clubs
- Trade Unions
- Veterans of Foreign Wars
- Women's Clubs
- YMCA, YWCA

Types of Activities Conducted Include:
- Badminton
- Baseball
- Basketball
- Clinics (all sports)
- Cross Country
- Dancing
- Football
- Free Play
- Ice Hockey
- Ice Skating
- Golf
- Judo-Karate
- Lacrosse
- Physical Fitness
- Relays
- Rodeo
- Roller Skating
- Soccer
- Softball
- Swimming
- Tennis
- Track
- Volleyball
- Wrestling

FROM: The Sports & Recreational Programs of the National Universities & Colleges
The National Collegiate Athletic Association. Report No. Six

228

Appendix F

Appendix G

Valuation of Athletic Related Facilities at NCAA Member Institutions

The following valuation of facilities includes sports buildings, stadiums, tracks, fields, fixed equipment and the real estate upon which facilities have been constructed.

	Indoor	Outdoor	Total
Class A (187 institutions)	$1,499,172,313	$1,205,113,625	$2,704,285,938
Class B (21 institutions)	72,824,230	19,862,885	92,687,115
Class C (68 institutions)	202,129,900	65,695,876	267,825,776
Class D (114 institutions)	280,172,736	52,399,772	332,572,508
Class E (175 institutions)	550,763,162	115,955,739	666,718,901
Class F (78 institutions)	270,421,257	76,998,956	347,420,213
Class G (110 institutions)	234,635,319	53,976,829	288,612,148
	$3,110,118,917	$1,590,003,682	$4,700,122,599

FROM: The Sports & Recreational Programs of the National Universities & Colleges
The National Collegiate Athletic Association. Report No. Six

Appendix H

METRIC CONVERSION TABLES

These tables are extracted from the Standard Edition of METRIC CONVERSION TABLES, courtesy of Arena Publications Ltd., 325 Streatham High Rd., London, SW16 3NS, England. For complete distance conversion tables in quarter-inch increments to a distance of 350 feet, please refer to the original publication.

TABLE V—DISTANCE EQUIVALENTS. IMPERIAL - METRIC.

YARDS	METRES	MILES	METRES
50	45·72	1 mile (1,760)	1,609·34
54·68	50	2,000 yards	1,828·80
55	50·29	1 mile 427·23	2,000
60	54·86	1 mile 1,520·84	3,000
65·62	60	2 miles (3,520)	3,218·69
70	64·01	2 miles 854·45	4,000
75	68·58	3 miles (5,280)	4,828·03
76·55	70	3 miles 188·07	5,000
80	73·15	3 miles 1,281·68	6,000
87·49	80	4 miles (7,040)	6,437·38
90	82·30	4 miles 615·29	7,000
98·42	90	4 miles 1,708·91	8,000
100	91·44	5 miles (8,800)	8,046·72
109·36	100	5 miles 1,042·52	9,000
110	100·58	6 miles (10,560)	9,656·06
120	109·73	6 miles 376·13	10,000
120·30	110	6 miles 1,469·75	11,000
150	137·16	7 miles (12,320)	11,265·41
164·04	150	7 miles 803·36	12,000
180	164·60	8 miles (14,080)	12,874·75
200	182·88	8 miles 136·97	13,000
218·72	200	8 miles 1,230·59	14,000
220	201·17	9 miles (15,840)	14,484·10
250	228·60	9 miles 564·20	15,000
300	274·32	9 miles 1,657·81	16,000
328·08	300	10 miles (17,600)	16,093·44
330	301·75	10 miles 991·43	17,000
350	320·04	11 miles 325·04	18,000
437·44	400	11 miles 1,418·65	19,000
440 (¼ mile)	402·34	12 miles 752·27	20,000
500	457·20	13 miles 85·88	21,000
546·81	500	13 miles 1,179·49	22,000
550	502·92	14 miles 513·11	23,000
600	548·64	14 miles 1,606·72	24,000
656·17	600	15 miles (26,400)	24,140·16
660	603·50	15 miles 940·33	25,000
765·53	700	18 miles 1,128·40	30,000
770	704·09	20 miles (35,200)	32,186·88
874·89	800	24 miles 1,504·53	40,000
880 (½ mile)	804·67	25 miles (44,000)	40,233·60
984·25	900	Marathon*	42,194·99
990	905·26	30 miles (52,800)	48,280·32
1,000	914·40	31 miles 120·66	50,000
1,093·61	1,000	35 miles (61,600)	56,327·04
1,202·97	1,100	40 miles (70,400)	64,373·76
1,312·34	1,200	45 miles (79,200)	72,420·48
1,320 (¾ mile)	1,207·01	50 miles (88,000)	80,467·20
1,421·70	1,300	62 miles 241·33	100,000
1,531·06	1,400	75 miles (132,000)	120,700·80
1,640·42	1,500	100 miles (176,000)	160,934·40

TABLE IV—TIME CONVERSIONS FOR RUNNING EVENTS.

100yds./100 Mts. Add 0·8 to 1·0 sec.	220 yds./200 Mts. Subtract 0·1 sec.	440 yds./400 Mts. Subtract 0·3 to 0·4 sec	880 yds./800 Mts. Subtract 0·7 to 1·0 s.

The above additions and subtractions are those officially used by statistical organisations in converting times. As far as 120 yards and 110 metres (hurdles) records are concerned, metric times will also include a record at yards. The table below shows approximate conversions of middle distance events.

1 Mile	1,500M	2 Miles	3,000M	3 Miles	5,000M	6 Miles	10,000M
3:47	3:30	8:00	7:25	12:30	12:57	26:00	26:56
48	30·9	04	29	35	13:02	10	27:06
49·2	32	05	30	40	07	20	16
50	32·7	10	34	45	12	30	27
51·4	34	15	39	50	17	40	37
52	34·6	16	40	55	23	50	47
53·5	36	20	43	13:00	28	27:00	58
54	36·4	25	48	05	33	10	28:08
55·7	38	27	50	10	38	20	18
56	38·3	30	52	15	43	30	29
57·8	40	35	57	20	48	40	39
58	40·1	38	8:00	25	54	50	49
4:00	42	40	02	30	59	28:00	29:00
02	43·9	45	07	35	14:04	10	10
02·2	44	49	10	40	09	20	21
04	45·7	50	11	45	14	30	31
04·3	46	55	16	50	20	40	41
06	47·6	59	20	55	25	50	52
06·5	48	9:00	21	14:00	30	29:00	30:02
08	49·4	05	25	05	35	10	12
08·6	50	10	30	10	40	20	23
10	51·3	15	35	15	45	30	33
10·8	52	20	39	20	51	40	43
12	53·1	25	44	25	56	50	54
13	54	30	49	30	15:01	30:00	31:04
14	55	35	53	35	06	10	14
15·1	56	37	55	40	11	20	25
16	56·8	40	58	45	17	30	35
17·3	58	45	9:03	50	22	40	46
19·5	4:00	50	07	55	27	50	56
20	00·5	55	12	15:00	32	31:00	32:06
25	05·1	40	58	05	37	10	17
30·3	10	50	9:07	10	42	20	27
35	14·4	10:00	17	15	48	30	37
41·1	20	10	26	20	53	40	48
45	23·6	20	35	25	58	50	58
51·9	30	30	44	30	16:03	32:00	33:08
55	32·9	40	53	35	08	10	19
5:02·7	40	50	10:03	40	13	20	29
05	42·1	11:00	12	45	19	30	39
13·5	50	10	21	50	24	40	50
15	51·4	20	31	55	29	50	34:00
24·3	5:00	30	40	16:00	16:34	33:00	11

Note: Figures shown in brackets after miles in bold lettering, indicate the equivalent distance in yards; Continuation figures after miles in italics are yards, i.e. 11 miles 1,418·65 = 11 miles 1,418·65 yards.

* Marathon: The distance in mileage = 26 miles 385 yards.

Appendix I

Supplementary Photographs and Figures

Photos Courtesy of:
    Mott Mobley, McGowen & Griffin, P.A.; Architects
    IBC International
    Aquatic Consultants, Inc.
    The Eggers Group, P.C.
    Fanning/Howey Assoc. Inc.
    Duragrid, Inc.
    Holabird & Root
    CSHQA, Architects/Planners
    Skidmore, Owings & Merrill
    Daniel F. Tully Assoc., Inc.
    Astro Ice, Skate USA

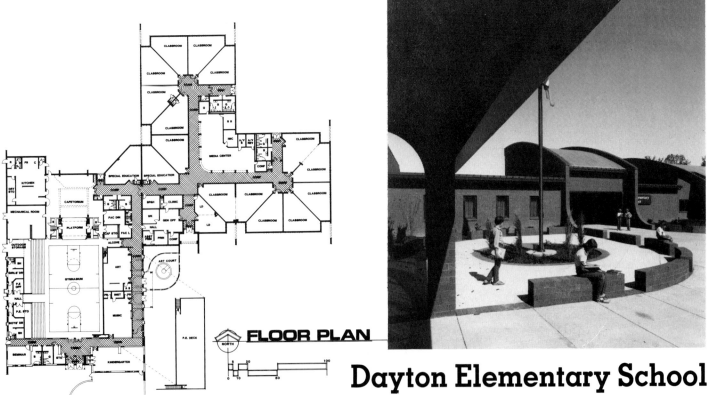

FLOOR PLAN

Dayton Elementary School
Dayton, Indiana

Square Footage: 39,305 (new)
                           17,937 (altered)
Cost: $3,926,508
Primary Architect: Fanning/Howey Associates, Inc.
                                Celina, Ohio
Date of Completion: 1983

Appendix I

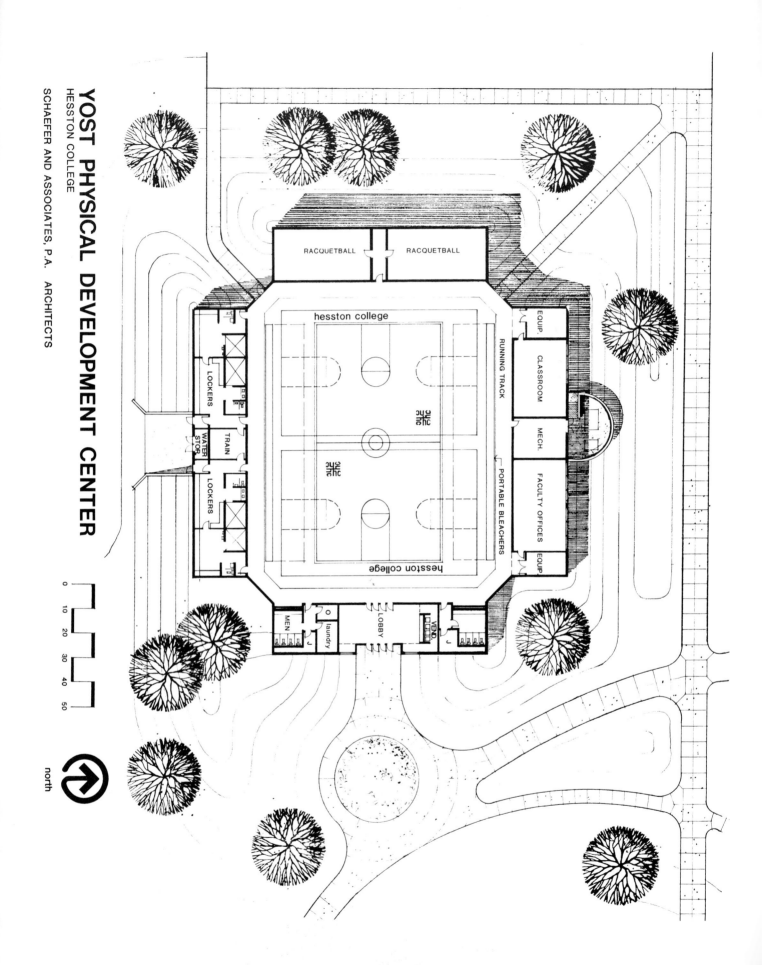

YOST PHYSICAL DEVELOPMENT CENTER

HESSTON COLLEGE

SCHAEFER AND ASSOCIATES, P.A.   ARCHITECTS

0
10
20
30
40
50

north

RACQUETBALL   RACQUETBALL

hesston college

hesston college

LOCKERS

WATER STOR.

TRAIN

LOCKERS

RUNNING TRACK

PORTABLE BLEACHERS

EQUIP.

CLASSROOM

MECH.

FACULTY OFFICES

EQUIP.

MEN

laundry

LOBBY

VEND.

Appendix I

Yost Physical Development Center
Hesston College
Hesston, Kansas

Square Footage: 23,000
Cost: $1,000,000.
Primary Architect: Schaeffer and Associates, P.A.
Completion Date: 1982

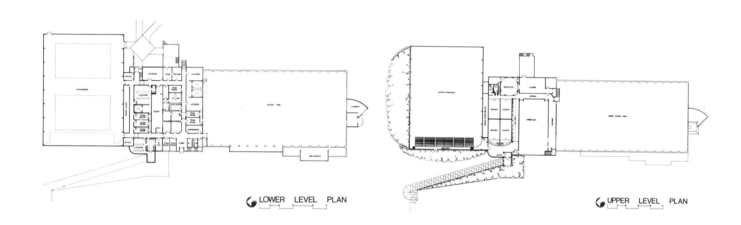

LOWER LEVEL PLAN   UPPER LEVEL PLAN

Cruikshank Athletic Center
The Taft School
Watertown, Connecticut

Square Footage: 32,000 (project was an addition to an existing structure which houses an ice hockey rink, a wrestling room, and locker & support facilities.

Cost: $1.6 million

Primary Architect: Herbert S. Newman Associates AIA P.C.
New Haven, Connecticut

Completion Date: 1981

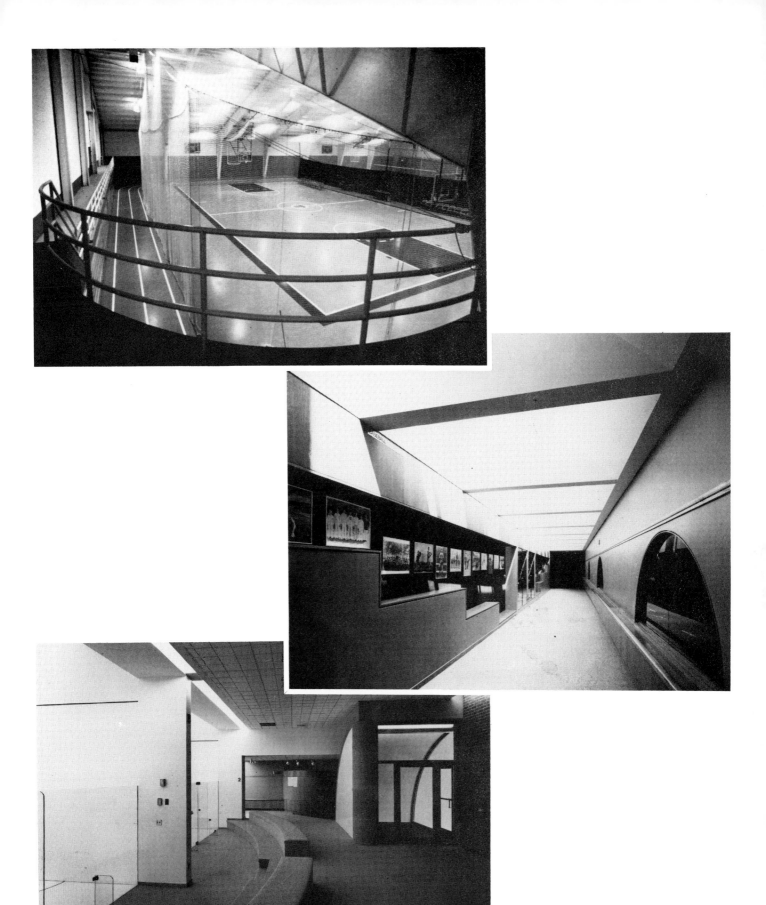

Appendix I

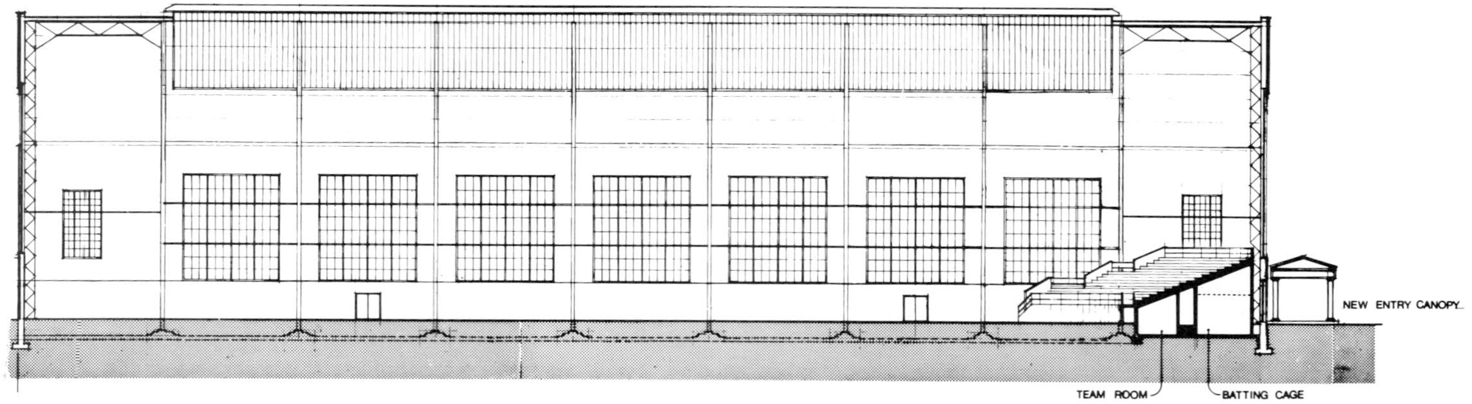

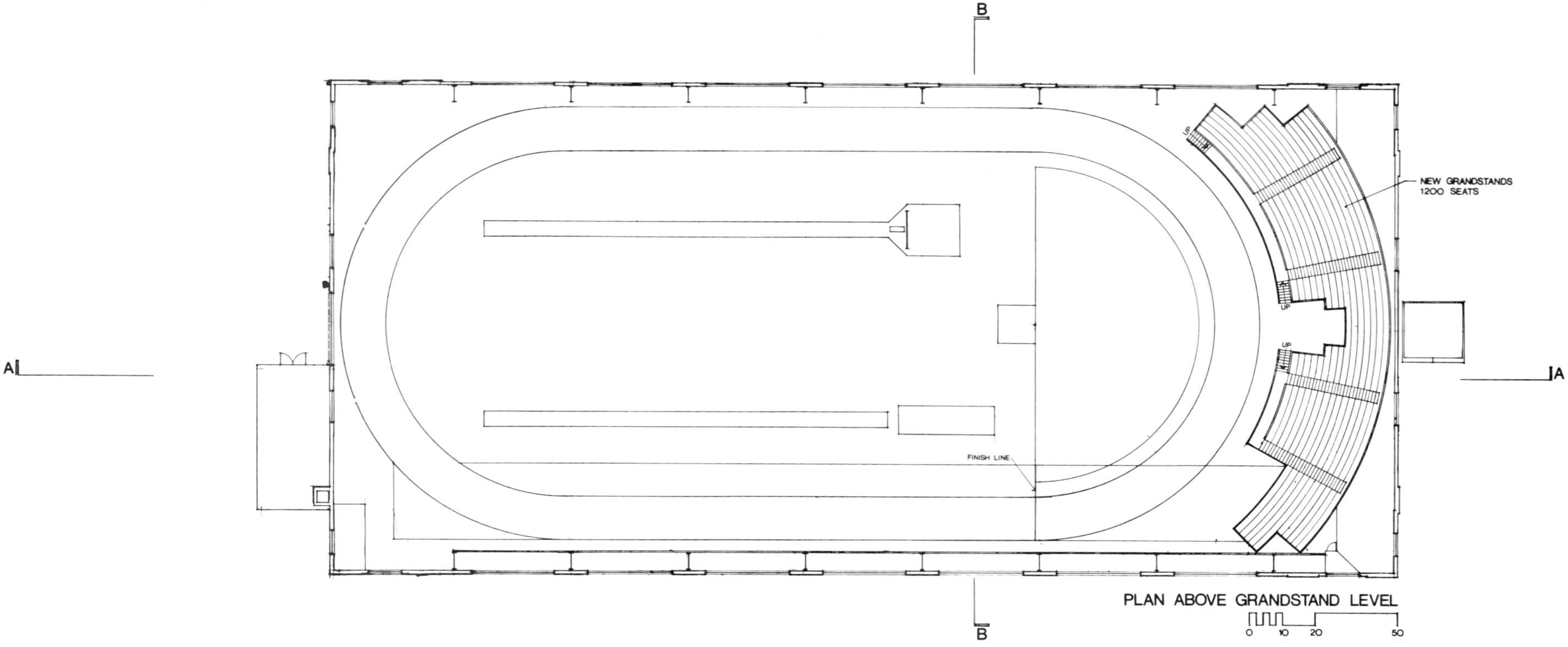

PLAN ABOVE GRANDSTAND LEVEL

0 10 20 50

FINISH LINE

NEW GRANDSTANDS
1200 SEATS

UP

A

AI

B

B

B

LONGITUDINAL SECTION A-A

TEAM ROOM

BATTING CAGE

NEW ENTRY CANOPY

COXE CAGE
YALE ATHLETIC FACILITIES STUDY
DEC.79   H.S.N. ASSOC. A.I.A. P.C.

PROJECT 2

Appendix I

Coxe Cage (Renovation)
Yale University
New Haven, Connecticut

Square Footage: 8000 (new)
          72,000 (altered)
Cost: $1,300,000.
Primary Architect: Herbert S. Newman Associates AIA P.C.
          New Haven, Connecticut
Completed: 1981

Appendix I

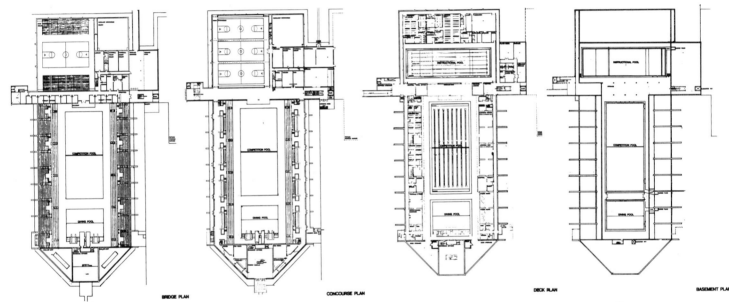

BRIDGE PLAN   CONCOURSE PLAN   DECK PLAN   BASEMENT PLAN

Indiana University School of Physical Education Natatorium Bldg.
Indiana University-Purdue University at Indianapolis (IUPUI)
Indianapolis, Indiana

Square Footage: 220,000
Cost: $21.5 million
Primary Architect: Browning, Day, Mullins,
                        Dierdorf, Inc.
                        Indianapolis, Indiana
Completion Date: 1982

Appendix I

Appendix I

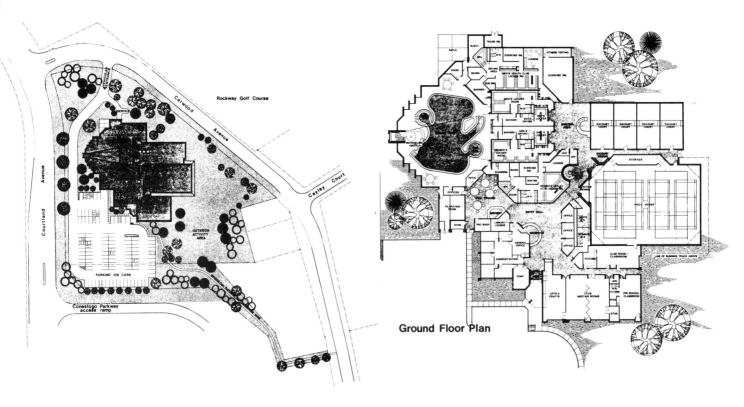

Ground Floor Plan

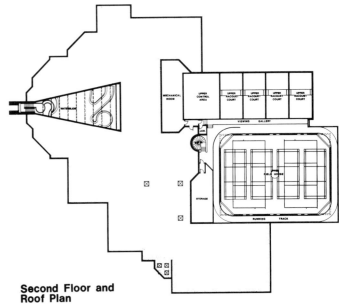

Second Floor and
Roof Plan

A.R. Kaufman Family
Y.M.C.A.
Kitchener, Ontario

Square Footage: 48,000
Cost: $3.3 million
Primary Architect: Horton & Ball (Architects)
        Walter, Fedy, McCargar, Hachborn (Engineers)
        Canadian Swimming Pool Design Assoc. Ltd. (Pool Engineers)

Appendix I

Appendix I

George W. Woodruff Physical Education Center
Emory University, Atlanta, Georgia

Square Footage: 185,000 interior; 65,000 roof tennis
Cost: $20,000,000. (construction $17,500,000.)
Primary Architect: John Portman and Associates
                   Atlanta, Georgia
Completion Date: 1984

Appendix I

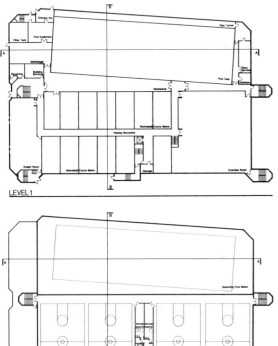

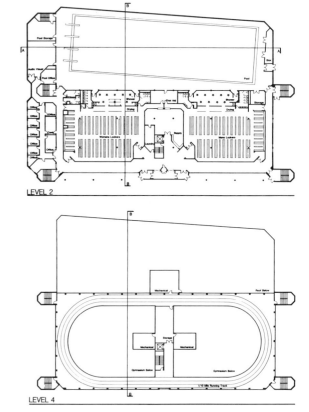

Southeast Regional Facility
University of Wisconsin — Madison
Madison, Wisconsin

Square Footage: 116,000
Cost: $7,500,000.
Primary Architect: Pfaller Herbst Associates, Inc.
Milwaukee, Wisconsin
Completion Date: 1983

Appendix I

Appendix I

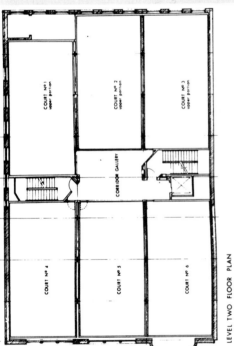

LEVEL TWO FLOOR PLAN

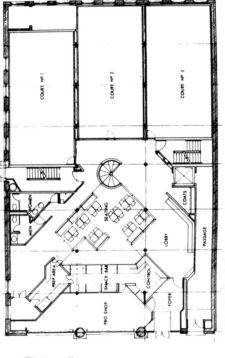

LEVEL ONE FLOOR PLAN

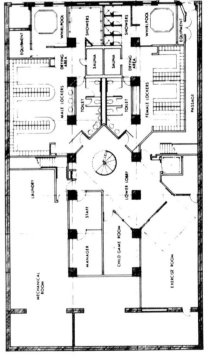

BASEMENT FLOOR PLAN

Back Bay Raquet Club
Boston, Massachusetts

Square Footage: 28,000 (alterations area)
Cost: $1.2 million
Primary Architects: Payette Associates Inc.
Graham/Meus Inc.
Boston, Massachusetts

Appendix I

Appendix I

Boise State University
Multi-Purpose Pavilion
Boise, Idaho

Square Footage: 270,970
Cost: $16,662,829.
Primary Architect: CSHQA Architects/Planners
                     Boise, Idaho
Completion Date: 1982

Southside Community Recreation Center & Educational Facility City School District of the City of Elmira, NY

Square Footage: 237,581
Building Cost: $12,621,998.
Primary Architect: Kaminsky & Shiffer, New York, N.Y.
                         Fanning/Howey Associates, Inc., Celina, Ohio
Completed: 1980

Appendix I

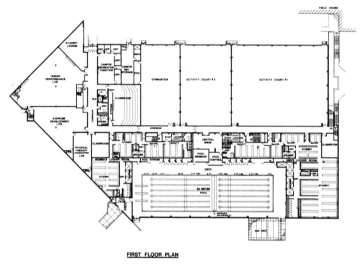

FIRST FLOOR PLAN

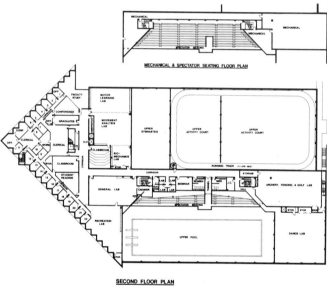

SECOND FLOOR PLAN

Health, Physical Education & Recreation Building University of Nebraska-Omaha, Omaha, Nebraska

BASEMENT FLOOR PLAN   OBSERVATION FLOOR PLAN

Square Footage: 155,000
Cost: $6.9 million (construction cost $5.75 million)
Primary Architect: Kirkham, Michael and Associates
                   Omaha, Nebraska
Completion Date: 1980

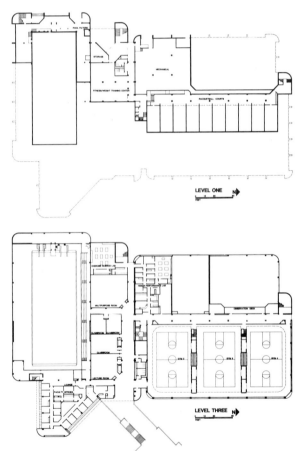

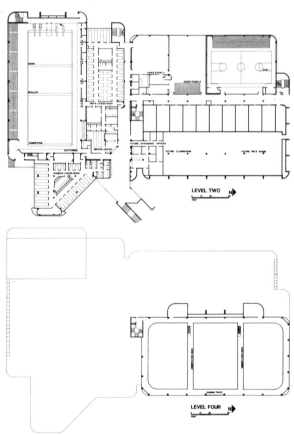

Health, Physical Education, Recreation Facility University of Arkansas Fayetteville, Arkansas

Completed: 1984
Total Cost: (construction cost
$12.5 million)
Square Footage:
Primary Architect: Mott Mobley
McGowan &
Griffin, P.A.
Fort Smith, Ark.

Appendix I

Appendix I